Advance Praise for Andrew Dornenburg and Karen Page's

Dining Out

James Beard Award-winning authors of *Becoming a Chef* and *Culinary Artistry*

"As far as I'm concerned, cheese doesn't come from cows or goats or sheep, but from Max McCalman at Picholine. McCalman's cheese guide in this book is an informative survey of all the things I've wanted to ask him but didn't have the time because I'm in love with an Irish Cheddar he's just put on my plate. This wonderful book finally lets us all take Max and his cheese cart home!"
—WENDY WASSERSTEIN, Pulitzer Prize-winning playwright

"A delicious look at the taste makers themselves. DINING OUT shows us that the love of food leads some people to the kitchen and others to the pen and that ultimately chefs and critics alike are all found on the same page—under 'P' for 'passion.'"
—MARY SUE MILLIKEN and SUSAN FENIGER, owners, Border Grill (Los Angeles) and hosts of "Too Hot Tamales" on the Television Food Network

"A must read! DINING OUT is an intelligent and courageous exploration of the restaurant review process. Understanding the minds of some of America's most powerful restaurant critics will no doubt improve the quality, performance, and design of restaurants and give diners a good understanding of how restaurants strive for excellence. Michael Donnelly's photographs capture brilliantly the people and the moments that make restaurants special."
—ADAM D. TIHANY, designer and restaurateur

"Leave it to Andrew Dornenburg and Karen Page to write the first scholarly treatise on restaurant critism! This book will enrich and enlighten anyone with an interest in dining out."
—PATRICK O'CONNELL, chef-proprietor, The Inn at Little Washington, Virginia

"The Guinness Book of World Records will now be forced to be the second most hotly-debated book in the nation's bars and cafés — at least the ones habituated by the world's foodies. I want to thank Andrew and Karen for lifting the velvet rope and letting us all mix it up a little."
—NORMAN VAN AKEN, cookbook author, consultant and chef-owner, Norman's (Coral Gables, FL)

"Chef Andrew Dornenburg and author Karen Page have done it again! Wonderfully and intelligently written, it takes away the fear, misunderstanding, and mystery of being reviewed and makes us see that restaurant critics are also people with heart. I enjoyed the book immensely."
—DIETER G. SCHORNER, Chairman of Pastry Arts, The French Culinary Institute (NYC)

"If you enjoy dining out, you're invariably influenced by reviews. Finally, here's a perfect look at how they're created. This book is a gem."
—RONN OWENS, radio host, KGO/San Francisco and KABC/Los Angeles

Dining Out

Dining Out

Secrets

from

America's

Leading

Critics,

Chefs,

and

Restaurateurs

Andrew Dornenburg and **Karen Page**
James Beard Award-winning authors of *Becoming a Chef* and *Culinary Artistry*

Photography by
Michael Donnelly

Art Director for Photography
Fiona Donnelly

John Wiley & Sons, Inc.
New York • Chichester • Weiheim • Brisbane • Singapore • Toronto

Published by John Wiley & Sons, Inc.

All rights reserved. Published simultaneously in Canada.

Library of Congress Cataloging-in-Publication Data:
Dornenburg, Andrew.
   Dining out: Secrets from America's leading critics, chefs, and restaurateurs / Andrew Dornenburg, Karen Page; photographs by Michael Donnelly.
      p.   cm.
   Includes index.
   ISBN 0-471-29277-X (pbk. : alk. paper)
   1. Food service. 2. Food writer—United States—Interviews.
3. Restaurants—United States. I. Page, Karen. II. Title.
TX943.D67   1998   98-16705
647.95—dc21   CIP

Printed in the United States of America

10 9 8 7 6 5 4 3 2 1

*"An animal swallows its food; a man eats it—
but only a man of intelligence knows how to dine."*

—Jean-Anthelme Brillat-Savarin (1755–1826)

*This book is dedicated to the chefs, cooks and staffs of the restaurants where
we enjoyed our most memorable meals in 1997-98 while researching and writing
this book, which sustained us body, mind, and spirit—and to the restaurant critics
whose reviews helped us find these treasures in the first place:*

Al Forno *(Providence)*
Bern's Steak House *(Tampa, Florida)*
Biba *(Boston)*
Blue Ribbon Bakery *(New York City)*
Bolo *(New York City)*
Bouley Bakery *(New York City)*
Campanile *(Los Angeles)*
Daniel *(New York City)*
East Coast Grill *(Cambridge, Massachusetts)*
Fleur de Lys *(San Francisco)*
Frontera Grill/Topolobampo *(Chicago)*
Jardiniere *(San Francisco)*
Jean Georges *(New York City)*
Le Cirque 2000 *(New York City)*
Lobster Club *(New York City)*
Lulu's *(Evanston, Illinois)*
Mo Better Meatty Meat *(Los Angeles)*
New York Noodle Town *(New York City)*
One Market *(San Francisco)*
Patisserie Cafe Didier *(Washington, DC)*
Payard Patisserie & Bistro *(New York City)*
Pearl Oyster Bar *(New York City)*
Picholine *(New York City)*
Provence *(Washington, DC)*
Red Sage *(Washington, DC)*
Solera *(New York City)*
Sushi-Ko *(Washington, DC)*
Union Pacific *(New York City)*
Zinfandel *(Chicago)*

With special note of the incredible desserts at:

Campanile *(Los Angeles)*
Farallon *(San Francisco)*
Susanna Foo *(Philadelphia)*

Contents

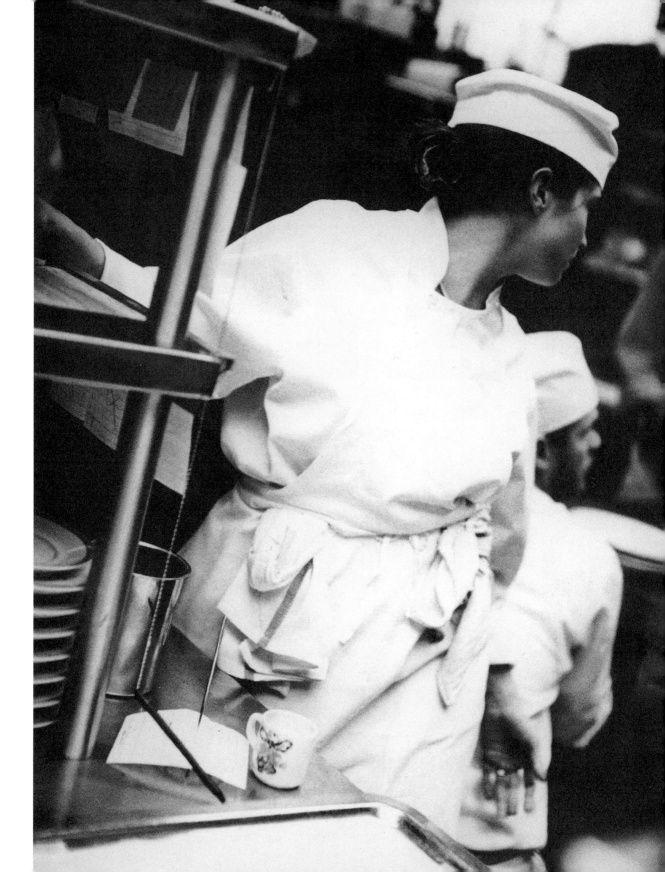

Preface

As any chef or restaurateur can tell you, there are few more stressful moments in the restaurant business than when a critic walks through the door:

Waiting on a Critic

My first interaction with a restaurant reviewer is as a waiter. Somehow, the restaurant is tipped off that he is coming in, and the *maitre d'* reserves the best table for his party, which happens to be in my section. The reviewer arrives with two women, wearing a light blue suit with a bright striped tie just this side of loud. He breaks the unwritten "restaurant critics' code" by managing to be neither anonymous nor inconspicuous.

After being seated, he asks my name. I never introduce myself to customers, but I tell him, and then go on to describe the specials and a few signature dishes on the menu. I know the chef is especially proud of his prime rib, which is aged and marinated and a bit unusual for such a contemporary restaurant. Despite my detailed and enthusiastic description of the prime rib, he orders a plain sirloin along with appetizers and entrees for the entire table. I drop off the order in the kitchen, and the chef's face reddens. "No prime rib?!" he asks, incredulous.

When serving a critic, I discover first-hand that night, waiters must try their best not to be driven crazy. You must keep reminding yourself that you know how to handle chefs, pour wine, set down plates, and replenish bread. You learn to discreetly eavesdrop when you're at the table and to offer word-by-word replays to chefs and owners on demand. You try to grin and bear the evening's dull tenseness: 'dull' because you are only assigned one table for the evening, so you don't have an opportunity to get into the dining room's usual rhythm; and 'tense' is evidenced by your churning stomach, because that this single table's happiness is so crucial to the restaurant's business success.

The critic finally leaves. The entire staff lets out a collective sigh. At the end of the night, none of us drinks anything weaker than a margarita before leaving for home.

About two weeks later, the review comes out. Curiously, the prime rib, which the critic never ordered, is described almost word-for-word as I'd depicted it. The review is positive overall, which is good because he had visited the restaurant only once. And for all my stress, I am referred to not by name but as "the service is proficient."

The Stakes Get Higher

I next encounter a critic as a young cook at the East Coast Grill in Cambridge, Massachusetts. Chef-owner Chris Schlesinger recognizes him immediately. I am still quite wet behind the ears as far as cooking for a critic is concerned—and am especially nervous when Chris asks me to make an order of hush puppies for the table.

Chris is very excited about this new dish. Not only are the hush puppies delicious, but Chris jokes that if Southerners knew we were getting $5 for a few hush puppies in Boston, they'd all laugh their heads off and move to town immediately.

But as much as I like the dish, there is one problem: when deep-frying food, getting it golden on the outside yet cooked in the middle can be a little dicey. This makes hush puppies about the last thing I am confident I will be able cook perfectly, especially for a V.I.P. To my great relief, however, there is not a single mention of an "undercooked hush puppies scandal at the East Coast Grill" in any of the following weeks' food pages. I soon return to normal sleep patterns.

New York, New York

New York City is home now, and my experiences here have a new intensity: Arcadia's host comes through the swinging doors to the kitchen to announce, "Andy Birsh is on table 8." After only a short time here, I find myself cooking for *Gourmet* magazine's critic! Chef-owner Anne Rosenzweig, who has been down this road many times before, is cool and calm. But for the rest of the cooks, the clock is ticking. We wait for his order, each of us wondering whether he will order any of the dishes we prepare.

After what seems like an eternity, the order comes in: Salmon. My station. I go through all my pieces of salmon, choosing not one but two. When cooking for a critic, I've learned, you should leave nothing to chance. It's best to have two of everything to choose from so you can select the better of the two or have a backup in case the first is accidentally dropped or spilled. I put the salmon on the grill to cook, turning the pieces 90 degrees to make cross-hatch marks. While the fish cooks, I choose the plates, double-checking for tiny marks or chips—even though I haven't seen a chipped plate in weeks.

Time to send out the food. I choose the more attractive of the two pieces of salmon, and present it to Anne so she can check its firmness. She also tastes the other ingredients before they make it onto the plate. One last inspection of the finished plate, and up into the window it goes to be picked up by the waiter. The line cooks heave sighs of relief as the palpable tension shifts down to the dessert station. Still, the pressure is not off—like all good cooks, we wait for the plates to come back to see how much Birsh has eaten.

Just Say Yes

A couple years later, at Judson Grill in Manhattan where I am one of the opening sous chefs, the kitchen receives a special request for French fries for a kid. They are not on the menu that night, but as a new restaurant eager to please, we comply. Later, the *maitre d'* comes back to the kitchen and says, "By the way, it turns out those French fries were for [*New York Times* critic] Ruth Reichl's table." The silence caused by our hearts stopping simultaneously is deafening, offset only by the clank of our jaws dropping open. We pull her table's ticket, but her entire order has already gone out. There is nothing we can do.

The restaurant gets a nice write-up in the *Times'* "Diner's Journal" column. Reichl's visit tips us off that we are on her radar screen and will likely be reviewed soon. With 180 seats to fill, we all know that much is riding on this review.

Cooking for Ruth Reichl

"Ruth Reichl is in the house," announces the chef soon afterward. An entire row of cooks' shoulders tighten. It is already the middle of a busy lunch, and suddenly the air gets a little thinner. Everyone tries hard to stay loose and to think like basketball players shooting free throws in the playoffs. The only difference is that there is only one person in the stands watching, and we don't know which team she's rooting for.

Reichl had already been in the restaurant two other times that we knew of, the last time accompanied by *New York Times Magazine* columnist Molly O'Neill. We guess that this might be Reichl's last visit. From our open kitchen, we spot her table in the corner. We all strain our necks trying to catch a glimpse of her face.

The order comes in for my station: soup, and then pasta. I ladle out two bowls of soup, and top each with three croutons. Chef Ed Brown is everywhere at once, tasting and choosing ingredients for the other dishes from her order. He is laughing, getting into the rush of the moment, yet his eyes are as sharp as an eagle's. He shaves truffles onto a salad, chooses the bowl of soup on the left, and gets ready to put them both into the pick-up window for the waiter. All eyes in the kitchen inspect the dishes one last time before the waiter whisks the plates away to Reichl's table.

Adrenaline takes over, and we return to cooking our orders for other tables and rush to catch up on a lost minute or two. Yet, in the backs of our minds, we are all waiting for those plates to come back.

Waiting for the Review

A few weeks later, a photographer from *The New York Times* is in to shoot the dining room for the review photo, and we are told that Reichl's review will run in Friday's paper. Tension in the kitchen mounts. We know that Friday's paper will be available on Thursday night by 10 P.M. at *The New York Times'* offices in Times Square. That night, the hours crawl by.

Finally, someone arrives at the restaurant, waving copies of Friday's paper. Everyone asks at once, "How many stars?" The restaurant receives a two-star review. We lean over the papers, reading each sentence by Reichl describing her verdicts on our dishes. Cooking is personal, so naturally every word that isn't one of praise makes us wince. It isn't until my third or fourth read-through that it registers that she actually likes many dishes.

We finish cleaning the kitchen, then head to the bar. Champagne is being poured. The next morning, we trade haggard grunts as each of us arrives an hour early. It will be a long, busy day. We just got reviewed.

• • •

As these dramas were unfolding in the restaurants, I couldn't help but wonder what was happening at the critics' tables. How had these individuals been deemed worthy of pronouncing judgments on fledgling restaurants? What were the distinctions being made during their visits? And how would diners' perceptions of our restaurant change after their verdicts were made public?

Up to that point, I only knew part of the story. I didn't happen to know any critics personally, nor anyone who had dined with them. Was my perception of their carefree lives of eating truffled salads and having only to decide whether or not they liked a particular pasta dish correct? I had no idea how the whole system really worked.

I came to realize that if, as a so-called restaurant "insider," not even I was clear how the entire process worked, then what about restaurant patrons? Could they be counted on to realize that a review represents only one side of the story— and only one person's opinion of it, at that? I sincerely doubted it, having witnessed the overnight rise and fall of restaurants after a single review.

Where Is Creativity?

In taking a closer look at restaurants, we drew on the framework of renowned University of Chicago professor Mihaly Csikszentmihalyi. In his book *Creativity*, he refers to the three considerations that are central in any examination of realms where creativity plays a role: 1) the **individual person or talent**; 2) the **domain or discipline** in which that individual is working; and 3) the surrounding **field** that renders judgments about the quality of the individuals and products. All three are mutually dependent. However, it is the field that selects which new works deserve to be recognized, preserved, and remembered, according to Csikszentmihalyi.

Using this paradigm to examine the culinary profession, our first book, *Becoming a Chef*, covers 1) **chefs**—who the leading professional chefs in America are, and how they got to be where they are today. *Culinary Artistry* examines 2) the realm of America's finest **restaurant cuisine**, through an exploration of the creative process of culinary composition. In these two books, chefs and food lovers alike are given a window into the creative process, but not the mysterious process of critique, which has previously been shrouded in secrecy, with many of its practitioners working incognito. The third book in our trilogy, *Dining Out*, explores 3) **the culinary field** which judges the quality of professional chefs' cuisines and restaurants, how it makes its evaluations, and the resultant impact.

The Food Intelligentsia

While many tastemakers' opinions carry great weight in this profession behind the scenes, including such author-educators as Julia Child and Madeleine Kamman, this book takes you inside the heads of some of America's most powerful restaurant critics, whose opinions are most directly shaping where and how Americans eat today, and will eat tomorrow. We look at the criteria upon which restaurants are rewarded, and the role played by such factors as style of cuisine, service and ambiance. The biases reflected by any food writer, but particularly a reviewer, help to determine what we as a nation value in dining out. What is rewarded is encouraged. What is damned is discouraged. And what is ignored or not seen at all isn't allowed to blossom or flourish.

This book also introduces some of America's leading chefs and restaurateurs, who are themselves a critical part of the food intelligentsia. The potentially crippling power of a review has contributed in part to their learning to use the media to their own advantage, circumventing the critics' power and resulting in an explosion of celebrity chef cookbooks, television shows and appearances.

These recent developments, which bring chefs and restaurateurs into the public's homes, underscore how much the restaurant experience has changed. The 1970s and 1980s saw the publication of a number of books that (perhaps tongue-in-cheek, perhaps not) aimed to educate restaurant patrons about the "restaurant game"—how to out-snob snobbish *maitres d'* and sommeliers, for example—which basically repositioned dining as a kind of combat zone, instead of an opportunity for hospitality. The era of greasing palms for a good table set up expectations in consumers' minds that the relationship between a restaurant and a customer was unavoidably adversarial.

The 1990s have seen a change in all that, so that now diners themselves are curious how things work in these days of the democracy of service. How, then, do I ensure myself of a great restaurant experience, they ask, in an age when bribing a *maitre d'* might be ineffective or, worse, seen as vulgar?

And service isn't all that's different. The food, which was still in a classic model as recently as ten or twenty years ago, has changed dramatically. While classic French cuisine might still have been seen as the standard-bearer of the 1980s, in the 1990s "anything goes." Today, you can find three-star Latin American, Mexican, and Thai restaurants. The advent of *nouvelle cuisine* opened the doors for chefs to experiment with a new larder of ingredients from all over the world, as well as for an expansion of food termed everything from "eclectic" to "fusion." How are these new creations to be evaluated?

What is the definition of a great dining experience in America today, and how can critics, chefs, restaurateurs and even diners achieve one? In the pages that follow, members of the food intelligentsia address this question. As food takes center stage both in our society and in our individual lives, we hope that growing numbers of people will care enough to listen, contribute to the debate, and thereby join their ranks.

Acknowledgments

As any author knows, a book is not solely the work of those whose names appear on its cover. Rather, many people played a role in inspiring, collaborating on, and publishing this book and bringing about our vision. It is our great pleasure to acknowledge some of them here.

- The chefs and restaurateurs who have shared both the joys and the challenges of their profession with us — both on and off the record. We are privileged to be able to share in this book the knowledge, passion, and deep concern that so many of them bring to their work and to creating a better experience for everyone lucky enough to cross their thresholds.

- All the restaurant critics who put anonymity aside and invited us to join them on reviews over lunch or dinner or drinks to interview them for this book. It inspired us to see the level of passion and thought that the best critics are bringing to their work in this industry. Special thanks to Ruth Reichl of *The New York Times* for her good humor in posing incognito for the book's cover.

- Pulitzer Prize-winning critics Tim Page of *The Washington Post,* Allan Temko of *The San Francisco Chronicle,* and David Shaw of *The Los Angeles Times* for sharing their insights on the critical process.

- Those who showed such tremendous support during the writing of this book, who often let us pass briefly through their homes or lives on our way to our next interview: Scott Hancock, Kelley and Scott Olson, Karen Springen and Mark Kerber, Barry Salzman, Trey Wilson; or were willing to show up for a photo shoot on a moment's notice: Pam Chirls, Laury Epstein, Lane Jantzen, Rikki Klieman, Loren Lortscher, Nancy Painter, Cynthia and Jeff Penney, Barry Salzman, Jeri Slavin, Linda Thompson, Steve Wilson, and Trey Wilson.

- Our inimitable literary agent Doe Coover for her passionate support and invaluable advice every step of the way, and for that amazing dinner at Topolobampo.

- Scott Olson, for his incredible generosity with his time in addressing the question of what makes good criticism. Ball State University is lucky to land you!

- Michael Batterberry, founder and editor of *Food Arts* Magazine, for being a deeply knowledgeable resource on the history and context of American restaurants and criticism.

- Lee Stern, for sharing his opinions.

- Our hard-working interns Rama Katkar, Carleste Hughes, and Michael Rose for their invaluable contributions.

- Our friends and colleagues who read through the early drafts of the manuscript and shared their thoughtful comments with us: Melissa Balmain, Bunny Ellerin and Geoff Vincent, Laury Epstein, and Jeri Slavin. Thank you for being so critical of our work! A special gold medal goes to Cynthia Penney for reading the earliest drafts. (We also want to thank Cynthia and Jeff Penney for nearly dragging us out for barbecue, beers, and Broadway, despite our protests of deadlines. Thanks—we needed that!)

- The beautiful photography in this book is the result of the extraordinary talent of photographer Michael Donnelly and artistic director Fiona Donnelly. We're awed that Mike's work could actually bring our words to a new level of life. Mike [and his able assistant Karen Stead] scoured Manhattan for the most stunning shots it had to offer, while Fiona brought her matchless eye and sense of style to the shoots—and found that perfect hat for the cover! We can't properly express our deep appreciation to Mike and Fiona for sharing their talent, friendship, and wonderful family (including Samantha, Sean, and William!) with us.

- The restaurants and other businesses that allowed our photographers to work on their premises, including Caffe Bondi, Chanterelle, Daniel, Gramercy Tavern, Hangawi, Jean Georges, Kitchen Arts & Letters, Le Cirque 2000, Lespinasse, Picholine, Union Square Cafe, the Union Square Greenmarket, and Vatan.

- This book marks a reunion with our first book *Becoming a Chef*'s acquiring editor Pam Chirls, in whose talented company we were delighted to work again, as we were with *marketer extraordinaire* Lane Jantzen and the world's best book designer Mike Suh. Special heartfelt thanks to Pam, Lane, and Mike for their truly extraordinary support both over the course of this project and over the years. (Thanks, too, to acquiring editor Justin Schwartz for getting things kicked off!) Many thanks to the entire team at John Wiley & Sons for all their enthusiastic efforts on behalf of this book, including P.J. Campbell, Edith Covington, Diana Cisek, Meg Hudak-Day, Rob Garber, Stacey Guttman, Andrea Johnson, Stephen Kippur, Lauri Sayde, Margie Schustack, and others.

- And finally, we thank each other, for dotting each other's i's and crossing each other's t's with the best of intentions.

Andrew Dornenburg & Karen Page

Photographers' Acknowledgments

Our photography for *Dining Out* had its inspiration in a lifelong delight in the pleasures of food, family, and friends. That several of the latter participated in this project made it all the more fun. The extraordinarily talented and dedicated group of professionals—chefs, writers, critics, restaurateurs, sommeliers, and others—who allowed us to photograph them at work presented us with an unrivaled creative opportunity. We hope the results bear testimony to their generosity. We will never look at a plate of food quite the same way ever again.

We are indebted most particularly to the authors, Karen Page and Andrew Dornenburg, whose passion for their subject knows no bounds and whose encouragement of and enthusiasm for our work was at all times an inspiration. Their generosity, in every sense, was unprecedented.

To the chefs and restaurateurs who allowed us to roam unfettered through their kitchens and dining rooms, thank you: Daniel Boulud and Jean-Luc Le Dû of Restaurant Daniel; Sirio Maccioni, Sottha Khunn and Jacques Torres of Le Cirque 2000; Gray Kunz of Lespinasse; Karen and David Waltuck of Chanterelle; Terrance Brennan and Max McCalman of Picholine; Danny Meyer and Michael Romano of Union Square Cafe and Gramercy Tavern; Jean-Georges Vongerichten and Phil Suarez of Jean Georges; and Antonio Settepani of Caffe Bondi. For also allowing us into their places of work, we thank Arthur Schwartz of WOR Radio; Nach and Maron Waxman of the venerable Kitchen Arts & Letters; and the owners and staffs of Hangawi and Vatan restaurants.

No lesser thanks to the courteous and professional assistants, managers and public relations staff who opened the doors to all the kitchens: Fern Berman (Le Cirque 2000), Geralyn Delaney (Jean Georges), Jamie Esparza (Lespinasse), Georgette Farkas (Restaurant Daniel), David Merves (Picholine), Alain Michel, Hilary Tollman (Restaurant Daniel), and Bridget Watkins (Gramercy Tavern).

We gratefully acknowledge Stefano Antoniazzi for his beautiful hair and make-up and Marina Killery for the glorious hat which allowed us to both disguise and celebrate *New York Times* restaurant critic Ruth Reichl, who appears on the book's cover as photographed at Jean Georges in New York City; Robert Clergerie for the shoes; and Ruth Reichl—as well as everyone at Jean Georges (especially Phil Suarez)—for their good-natured collaboration.

Our heartfelt thanks to our loyal crew, family and friends who, some of the time, fit all three categories; our erstwhile photo assistant Karen Stead, for whom no kitchen ever gets too hot; our sons Sean Donnelly and William Donnelly, whose support of their parents' endeavors is unflagging; our daughter Samantha Donnelly and pastry chef Bill Yosses, both of Bouley Bakery; Jane Burd and Ursula Wallis, who can be relied on to dress up and eat at the drop of a hat; Ann O'Malley, Phillip Odom, and Jack Gerson, who ate with gusto; and, for their tireless enthusiasm and encouragement, Cynthia and Jeff Penney. Our contribution to this book is dedicated to all of you.

Michael and Fiona Donnelly

Dining Out

One
I Eat—Therefore, I Am

"The pleasures of the table

belong to all times and all

ages, to every country and

every day; they go hand in

hand with all our other

pleasures, outlast them,

and remain to console us

for their loss."

—Jean-Anthelme Brillat-Savarin,
The Physiology of Taste

Phyllis Richman, *The Washington Post*'s restaurant critic for more than twenty years, has been cited as one of the 100 most influential people in the United States' capital city. *Newsweek* dubbed her "the most feared woman in Washington."

Richman certainly has reason to be among the most *fearful* as well. Over the years, she and her restaurant critic colleagues across the country have commonly been harassed and subjected to everything from disturbing phone calls to hate mail, rocks through the windows of their homes, brandished knives, even death threats—"perquisites" not regularly endured by other professional critics of the arts, even after a particularly harsh pan.

What makes it all worth their while?

"I have the most wonderful job in the world," Richman enthuses. And there probably isn't a single restaurant lover alive who would doubt her.

America's Obsession with Food and Restaurants

As long as restaurants have been in existence, Americans have been debating their merits with increasing passion. While food was once

simply one of the necessities of life, like shelter, clothing, or oxygen, it has moved from the realm of sustenance into a more complex component. Food has become our national obsession.

In this era of limited attention spans, food commands our senses and holds us rapt. We've become more fascinated than ever by how food is prepared, how it is presented, and the names of the chefs and restaurants behind its creation. Our increase in restaurant dining has led our palates to seek new stimulation through unusual ethnic cuisines, as well as innovative flavor combinations, techniques, and presentations. America's leading chefs strive to entice our patronage through ceaseless innovation.

Our increasing fascination with food, coupled with the advent of chefs as owners and therefore promoters of their own restaurants, have given rise to the celebrity chef phenomenon. Chefs have taken to publishing glossy, expensive books promoting their restaurants and cuisines, and come into our living rooms to show us how they prepare their signature dishes. Celebrity chefs have been the driving force behind the Television Food Network, which began in 1993 and has become the third fastest-growing cable network in the country. With semi-regular cooking segments, such mainstream talk shows as *Today*, *Good Morning America*, *Regis and Kathie Lee*, and *The Rosie O'Donnell Show* have also contributed to the phenomenon. Even the high-brow Charlie Rose has hosted chef-restaurateurs Mark Miller and Anne Rosenzweig, and edgier late-night hosts Jay Leno, David Letterman, Conan O'Brien, and Tom Snyder have occasionally featured top chefs like Daniel Boulud, Emeril Lagasse, and Jean-Louis Palladin on their shows.

The era of the chef as celebrity has produced an interest in chefs that borders on cultish. In a characteristic sign of the times, chef-restaurateurs Mary Sue Milliken and Susan Feniger, the Television Food Network's *Too Hot Tamales*, were featured in *People* magazine's 1996 "Best and Worst Dressed" issue, and *Entertainment Weekly* now considers it its purview to publish a list of "The 10 Most Important Names in American Dining."

Under continuous pressure to be innovative, to accommodate the changing tastes of the public, and to put forward their own personal, aesthetic statements of what food can be, chefs are increasingly finding themselves walking a fine line between art and profit, taste and health. Who is to judge the success of their efforts?

Restaurant Dining and Reviewing in America

With the proliferation of new restaurants, Americans have grown increasingly dependent on restaurant criticism to help them make more informed choices. Many restaurant lovers, especially in urban areas, follow restaurant critics almost as a sport, turning first to the

> *"Eating out is as much fun as you can have with your clothing on. And, after a meal, you usually don't have to apologize."*
> —Merrill Shindler,
>   Los Angeles *Zagat Survey*

restaurant reviews when they open a newspaper or magazine. Reviews become the topic of the day, with "How 'bout those Bulls?" being replaced by "Did you read Ruth's review of Le Cirque?" as a common conversation starter. In cities with the luxury of multiple opinions, diners find "their" critics, whose opinions they come to rely on. Some restaurant critics are revered or reviled so passionately that reading their critiques transcends utility. The pleasure of reading their columns is an end to itself for readers who may have no intention of visiting the restaurants serving as the critics' muses that week.

Looking at some of the restaurants, chefs, media, and critics that have influenced the American dining scene over the past two centuries helps to provide a sense of where America has been and where it is heading. Whereas, in earlier days, many American chef-restaurateurs simply adopted the French model as the gold standard, these points in history trace a country struggling to define, for itself, what great food is and what constitutes a great restaurant in terms that are distinctly American.

Various voices have challenged popular thinking on these questions—from writers Calvin Trillin and Jane and Michael Stern, who made Americans look anew at the pleasures of down-home regional cooking; to the "flower culture," who promoted freshness and purity in food through the health-food movement; to America's melting-pot population, which has embraced an ever-widening variety of ethnic restaurants. It has become clear that certain restaurant critics, too,

have played some of the most vital roles in shaping Americans' sensibility about food—from Craig Claiborne, who established restaurants as a subject worthy of serious critique; to Gael Greene, who awakened diners to their sensual possibilities; to Ruth Reichl, whose writing from the perspective of both gastronomy and sociology encourages people to look more deeply into the restaurant experience.

1700s–1900s
Late ... Early

The first restaurant, as we know it today with regular hours and featuring a menu listing available dishes served at private tables, is established in Paris.

The first restaurant opens its doors in Paris, selling restorative broths.

Various incarnations of **Delmonico's**, considered America's first great restaurant, feed New York City diners.

| 1765 | 1782 | 1800s | 1803 |

The Almanach des Gourmands, the first restaurant guide, is published in France. Restaurants have caught on, and now number 500 in Paris.

Late 1700s–Early 1900s

Antoine's opens in New Orleans, beginning a tradition of distinguished restaurants outside New York City.

The first *Michelin Guide* to French restaurants is published, and is a precursor to other restaurant guides and critical standards that follow.

"The original Michelin Guides came out specifically for wealthy people who had chauffeured cars, and one of the rubrics to get a third star or to be considered a fine restaurant, according to Michelin, was that you had to have service for the clients' dogs. Literally, there were chefs—like Vincent Guerithault [and Jean-Georges Vongerichten]—who did that. The dogs were to be given better food than the chauffeurs, I was told—sometimes right in the restaurant. The French don't like children in restaurants, but they do like dogs, for some reason."
—John Mariani, *Esquire*

| 1840 | 1900 1902 | 1920–1933 |

Escoffier publishes *Le Guide Culinaire*, codifying much of the cuisine served by the French for the next sixty years.

Prohibition in the United States causes a long separation of great food from fine wines.

Sunset magazine begins to introduce West Coast readers to a variety of then-exotic ingredients, such as cilantro, and techniques, such as wok cooking.

Henri Soulé's **Le Pavillon** opens in New York City and is said to be the equal of the five best restaurants of Paris—meaning, in the world.

Gourmet magazine makes its debut.

The *Michelin Guide* begins its influential star rating system.

1926   1930s   1936   1941   1946

Traveling salesman Duncan Hines publishes the first edition of his restaurant guide *Adventures in Good Eating,* which goes on to sell 100,000 copies a year.

Brennan's opens in New Orleans, establishing breakfast as a meal worthy of the same respect as dinner.

1950s

Craig Claiborne is appointed the first male food editor of *The New York Times* and declares the city "a culinary wasteland." The *Times* institutes the policy that the reviewer's visit is anonymous, paid for by the paper, with a candid appraisal.

"[Restaurant criticism] basically involves two things, the ability to write and conversance with food. I believe that the ability to write well and that 'taste' as it applies to dining are instinctive. I think that you are born with a seed for making a sentence that reads well, as well as one for learning to be discriminating where food is concerned."
—Craig Claiborne,
   The New York Times

Bon Appetit gets its start as a promotional booklet distributed free in liquor stores.

| 1955 | 1957 | 1959 |

"Clementine Paddleford was writing about restaurants for The New York Herald-Tribune *before me. Food was considered women's work. But in the first reviews I wrote, there is no way you'd know if I was a man or a woman. I did that deliberately. People wrote to me, 'Dear Mr. Greene.' Craig Claiborne, who broke a barrier in becoming the first male food editor of* The New York Times, *and James Beard were the ones who changed that notion. And now no one even thinks about it."*
—Gael Greene,
   New York

The Four Seasons restaurant opens in New York City at a cost of $4.5 million—said to be the most ever spent to open a restaurant anywhere in the world. In *The New York Times*, Craig Claiborne declares, "Both in decor and in menu, it is spectacular, modern, and audacious. It is expensive and opulent, and it is perhaps the most exciting restaurant to open in New York within the last two decades."

1960s

The first *Mobil Travel Guide* is published, rating restaurants in all 50 states from one to five stars.

Craig Claiborne begins *The New York Times'* tradition of weekly restaurant reviews.

Henri Soulé of Le Pavillon dies of a heart attack at age 62. In *The New York Times*, Craig Claiborne calls him "the Michelangelo, the Mozart, and the Leonardo da Vinci" of French restaurants in America.

1960   **1963**   **1966**

"The two most important restaurants to be reviewed in my first years of serious restaurant criticism were La Caravelle in November 1960 and Lutèce in March 1961."
—Craig Claiborne,
  The New York Times

"In Lutèce's first review, Craig Claiborne gave us one star. And a week later, he gave Chock Full O' Nuts one star, too."
—André Soltner,
  formerly of Lutèce

1960s

Gael Greene becomes *New York* magazine's "Insatiable Critic."

"In the early days, there were only the Soulé-style grand French restaurants; Lutèce and maybe one or two others were the only exceptions. The Chinese restaurants were better then. There were very few American restaurants that had any meaning, other than The Coach House and the Four Seasons."
—Gael Greene,
  New York

1968   **1969**

The first eponymous *Gault-Millau* restaurant guide is published by Henri Gault and Christian Millau.

I grew up with a hunger, based on not having enough good food in my childhood. And I went to France at seventeen and lived there for a year. My former husband was very interested in food, and his family ate out a lot. So we saved our money to go to great restaurants together—following the recommendations of, of course, Craig Claiborne [of *The New York Times*] and Clementine Paddleford, who was the restaurant critic of *The New York Herald-Tribune*. I cut out all of those reviews, and when we went to Europe or any place we'd follow in their footsteps. I also took some cooking lessons: I was interested in good eating and great dining.

I was a reporter for the [*New York*] *Post*, and I freelanced for magazines like *Cosmopolitan* and *Ladies Home Journal*—innocuous pieces that could have been written by anybody. I did fifty pieces for Helen Gurley Brown [at *Cosmopolitan*]—how not to get dumped by your husband on his way up, which I think I wrote anonymously, profiles of Clint Eastwood and Burt Reynolds, and lots of how-to stories. People called me to do anything. I did some pieces on "How America Lives" for *Ladies Home Journal*, and "How the Great Beauties Stay Beautiful" in *McCall's*. I was a utility writer.

Nobody thought of me in terms of writing about food. I didn't think of myself in terms of writing about food. The food stuff was just to try to find a way to get someone else to pay the expenses or be able to deduct all this eating from income taxes. I was really a newspaper reporter.

But I didn't like going to work at 10 o'clock every day and doing small things until there was a breaking news story—when you'd go out to the Bronx and interview the mother of the person who just got shot, and bring back a picture. That was the big thing, but there was a lot of in-between time. There's an author who wrote that the reason he became a writer was because his dream was to sleep until noon. I liked the fact that, as a freelance writer, you could make your own hours.

Then I did a piece on the reopening of La Côte Basque when Soulé had to take it over because the person he sold it to went bankrupt. It was for *New York* magazine when it was distributed in the *Herald-Tribune*. Clay Felker was the editor, and he got it in his head that I was a food writer. So, shortly after *New York* magazine started, he called and asked me to be the restaurant critic.

People would call me after I started writing for *New York* magazine and say, "Well, why don't you write for us like that?" And I would say, "Well, you never let me write like that. I had to write in the *Cosmo* style" or "I had to write in the *Ladies Home Journal* style." But suddenly they saw another way to express things—in the voice of a writer, rather than in their own voice.

That was a totally a result of Tom Wolfe and [Jimmy] Breslin and Gay Talese and Peter Maas, people who were writing in *New York* magazine. Perhaps most of all, it was the result of Tom Wolfe, who wrote in a speaking style. I found myself totally unleashed by that. If you look at *Tangerine Flake Baby*, it starts out with the sound of the 'rrrrr' of the car, and it's about the way people talk. Given that I'd been writing in the most conventional way and to suit whatever the demand was, now I thought that I could write in my own voice.

No one ever talked about anything I did in most of the other magazines that I appeared in. *New York* at that point was a very exciting magazine; everyone was talking about it. It was "the" magazine that everyone in media read. And everyone was imitating it all over the country.

The first time I did a piece on French restaurants, I wrote about La Pyramide [in France], and I imagined that most of the people who read it weren't going to get there. But I wanted them to know what it felt like because the sense memories of that experience were so strong: the smell, and the heat of excitement of eating and drinking too much. They were very vivid, and I thought that I would try to convey that. That became a mark of my writing—that I would put you there, in the scene, whether or not you could ever afford to go. I wanted to write something that would be interesting to read even if you didn't like food, so you would learn something about the sociology of New York.

I think that's where the style of "How does it feel?" and "How does it smell?" came from. Does your throat ache because it's so noisy and you're screaming, or do you have a headache when you walk out? Do you smell butter when you walk in the door? Or is the feel of the tablecloth uniquely silky because it's some custom rich cloth and not something from a linen supply store? I found myself being aware of, and writing about, all those things because I thought that was part of putting you in the scene.

1970s

Calvin Trillin writes in *Playboy*, "The best restaurants in the world are, of course, in Kansas City [his home town]," launching an ongoing debate about the meaning of "the greatest restaurant in the world."

"The other distinctive voice coming out of the 1970s was *Calvin Trillin*. He was considered a notable food writer when he would be the last to describe himself as such. His only interest in food was in what it said about the culture that produced it."
—John Mariani,
    Esquire

Alice Waters opens **Chez Panisse** in Berkeley, California.

"*La nouvelle cuisine* is nothing more than good taste. It is to prepare dishes to preserve their natural flavors."
—Fredy Girardet,
    Restaurant Girardet (Switzerland)

1971	1972	1973

Le Pavillon in New York City closes.

The term *nouvelle cuisine* is coined by *Gault-Millau*, the French food and travel magazine.

> *"I think it got very overblown in the late '60s and the '70s with the excitement about [Michelin] three-star chefs and nouvelle cuisine and all of that. It really put emphasis on the very fancy decor and extravagant plates and all that goes with it—and everybody having that as their signature: the pattern on the plate just as much as what was on top of the pattern."*
> —Alice Waters,
>   Chez Panisse

Le Cirque opens in New York City under the ownership of former Colony chef Jean Vergnes and *maitre d'* **Sirio Maccioni.**

Craig Claiborne and Pierre Franey dine at Chez Denis in Paris, tasting thirty-one dishes and nine wines—for a total $4,000 tab [picked up by American Express]. It is promoted as "the most expensive dinner in the world."

1975

THE 10 COMMANDMENTS OF NOUVELLE CUISINE, ACCORDING TO GAULT-MILLAU

1. Avoid unnecessary complications.
2. Shorten cooking times.
3. Shop regularly at the market.
4. Shorten the menu.
5. Don't hang or marinate game.
6. Avoid too-rich sauces.
7. Return to regional cooking.
8. Investigate the latest techniques.
9. Consider diet and health.
10. Invent constantly.

In the 1975 *Guide to San Francisco Restaurants* by Arthur Bloomfield, eight restaurants receive three stars, the highest rating. Three are Italian, two Chinese, one Japanese, one French, and the last is Trader Vic's.

1970s

Jane and Michael Stern publish their classic book *Roadfood*, a guide to mostly unheralded restaurants "serving great, inexpensive regional food."

Michael and Ariane Batterberry found *Food & Wine* magazine.

1977   **1978**

RESTAURANT CRITICISM: PROTECTOR OF THE FIRST AMENDMENT?

Noted architecture critic Allan Temko and *The San Francisco Chronicle* were slapped with a $2 million lawsuit in the late 1970s after Temko criticized San Francisco's Pier 39 in two articles that its architect claimed to be defamatory. "In the first article, I warned the city that it was going to be a disaster," says Temko. "The next one was a post-mortem that appeared in 1978. It started out, 'Corn. Kitsch. Schlock. Honky-Tonk. Dreck. Schmaltz. *Merde*,' and went on from there.

"Most of the precedents invoked by our lawyers were in culinary criticism," remembers Temko, winner of the 1990 Pulitzer Prize for distinguished criticism. "The decision [exonerating Temko and the *Chronicle*] was hilarious because it said architecture criticism is nothing compared to culinary criticism. There were funny excerpts from *The New York Times* and other newspapers which had really good phrases like 'Trout *à la* Green Death' and 'Chicken Bubonic Plague' or something like that, the inference being that no one takes this literally, but that it's free comment."

WILLIAM RICE OF *THE CHICAGO TRIBUNE* ON FOOD IN THE LAST 20 YEARS

The Critics

The pioneer critics have more or less been sword-fighters in the consumers' interest who would go in and examine the menu, essentially, and grade it, usually coming from a bias toward classic French cuisine. When I first got involved in this in the 1960s and early 1970s, it was almost totally predictable that 'the best' ten restaurants in any city, according to *Holiday* magazine or whomever was compiling the list, would be seven French restaurants, maybe one ethnic of some kind—in those days, most likely Eastern European or Asian—and maybe two serving "Continental" cuisine. The last were generally cooks who'd jumped ship from a cruise line.

The Standard-Bearers

At that time, America's take on grand dining came to some extent from Paris, but also to a large extent from hotels and cruise ships, where the pomp and formality was there, and behind it was a combination of cuisines. It isn't so surprising when you think of the amalgamation of nationalities that contributed cooks and waiters. French was still in the foreground because the French wrote the rules. But the practitioners weren't always French.

Chefs Come Out from Behind Their Stoves

It's funny. In this past week both Paul Bocuse and Alain Ducasse have been in Chicago, and Joël Robuchon is coming in a week or so. Twenty years ago, you could have gone through a lifetime before you'd ever see a live French chef in the middle of America!

Freedom in America

More than one European chef has said to me, "Your great advantage in America is you're not bound by generations of tradition." American chefs have the self-confidence now that they didn't have a few years ago. I trace it back to the American winemakers who were winning tastings in Paris and being looked on as world-class artisans. It brought a lot of wine people from around the world to the U.S., which meant they were also eating our food, from Lutèce to Chez Panisse.

The Melting Pot

America's become "the research pool" because of our physical situation, which is halfway to Asia, and this freedom and the fact that the right elements are within the society. We can go a mile or so from here and find a store that's selling Asian ingredients, whereas in Paris you'd have to go quite a way.

Chefs' Collective Voices

Chefs' acceptance and eagerness have convinced journalists that they ought to pay attention to these changes. One result is that now the *Zagat Survey*, for example, differentiates the highest score for food from the most popular. It is a tremendous breakthrough.

"When I started reviewing restaurants [in 1979], there were no other critics [in California]. I consider myself perhaps the first serious restaurant critic out here. Before that time, reviewing was done through private restaurant guides. I read Jack Shelton's guide religiously. Shelton was a good critic; he wrote well, and gave personal opinions. He was tough, but constructive. He was a great model for a critic, and used to go on in great depth. He had freedom to really turn out good work, and it was a hugely popular newsletter in San Francisco. Everyone got it."
—Patricia Unterman,
The San Francisco Examiner

1980s

"What Americans call haute cuisine is expensive, old-fashioned, decadent, and academic. There are only two kinds of cooking: cuisine bourgeoise and inventive cooking."
—Christian Millau, Gault-Millau

Gault-Millau publishes its first restaurant guide books in the English language.

Media across the country report the story of restaurateur Michael O'Keefe ejecting restaurant critic Mimi Sheraton of *The New York Times* from his restaurant, The Water Club, in New York City. Sheraton said it was the first time a restaurant had refused to serve her. O'Keefe recognized Sheraton even though she was wearing a wig.

1982   1983

Tim and Nina Zagat begin self-publishing and distributing their *Zagat Survey* of restaurants.

1983   Mr. Chow restaurant in New York City wins a $20,005 libel judgment in a jury trial in federal district court against the *Gault-Millau*, which gave the restaurant a negative review in its 1982 edition. Restaurant critics, as well as reviewers of everything from books to stereos, criticized the decision, arguing that reviews "are traditionally considered absolutely privileged under the First Amendment" and that the Mr. Chow review, "employing obviously figurative or hyperbolic statements, must also be considered to be opinion fully subject to constitutional protection."

1985   The above verdict is unanimously overturned after it is judged that "expressions of opinion are constitutionally protected." The appeals court decision, written by Judge Thomas Meskill with the concurrence of Judges Amalya Kearse and Richard Cardamone, determines that "reviews, although they may be unkind, are not normally a breeding ground for successful libel actions," and notes that Mr. Chow didn't cite "a single case that has found a restaurant review libelous....Perhaps Mr. Chow could prove that the reviewer's personal tastes are bizarre and his opinions unreasonable, but that does not destroy their entitlement to constitutional protection....The natural function of the review is to convey the critic's opinion of the restaurant reviewed. The author [of the review] obviously believed that the service was bad, the pork was too doughy, the peppers were too cold, the rice was too oily, and the pancakes were too thick. The average reader would understand the author's statements to be attempts to express his opinion through the use of metaphors and hyperbole....Because the average reader would understand the statements involved to be opinion, the statements are entitled to the same constitutional protection as a straightforward expression of opinion would receive."

1985

1986

Tim and Nina Zagat are featured on the cover of *New York* magazine, leading to an explosion of popularity of their New York *Survey*. Within a month, more than 75,000 copies of the guides are sold.

The James Beard Foundation is established, with the goal of rewarding and fostering excellence in the culinary field.

"I think what brought restaurants to the forefront in the 1980s was the demographic that moved through the culture with disposable income—the young people who chose food to be 'cool' with."

—Chris Schlesinger,
   East Coast Grill

1990s

The first James Beard Awards are given to "recognize culinary professionals for excellence and achievement in their field." This reflects one of the first important steps by the culinary industry to define its own excellence.

The Television Food Network begins broadcasting.

Two major food magazines see their debut: *Fine Cooking* and *Saveur*.

1991	1993	1994

Cook's Illustrated magazine launches.

"I don't like being in the [Dining In/Dining Out] section. I hate it! I liked being in 'Weekend' much better. I was told, 'You won't lose a single reader.' And I said, 'Wrong!' I feel that I've been ghetto-ized. It puts restaurants in a different category, and it makes a statement about what the paper thinks of restaurants. I'm very unhappy about it—but nobody asked me. I think one of the main reasons they did it was because the movie advertising takes up so much space, and they cannot physically make the 'Weekend' section larger than the front section."

—Ruth Reichl,
The New York Times

Even *Consumer Reports* now reviews
restaurants. After surveying its readers
on their impressions of restaurant
chains (on the basis of "Value, Food,
Mood and Service"), the magazine
reports Bob Evans, Cracker Barrel, Eat
'N Park, Houston's, Romano's
Macaroni Grill, and Ruth's Chris
Steak House as America's top-rated
family restaurant chains and dinner
houses.

Widely publicized incidents of
bacterial contamination in
foods ranging from ground beef
to processed fruit cause out-
breaks of illness and, in a few
instances, death, and generate
increasing public concern
about food safety.

The splashy debuts of two
New York restaurants, **Jean
Georges** and **Le Cirque
2000**, are trumpeted in
publications ranging from
Newsweek to *USA Today*,
becoming national events.

1996–1997   **1996**   **1997**

The New York Times'
September redesign moves the
weekly restaurant review from
the Friday "Weekend" section
to the new Wednesday "Dining
In/Dining Out" section.

Entertainment Weekly announces its list of "The Ten
Most Important Names in American Dining" for 1997:
1) Sottha Khunn, Le Cirque 2000 (New York City);
2) Jean-Georges Vongerichten, Jean Georges (New
York City); 3) Rick Bayless, Frontera Grill and
Topolobampo (Chicago); 4) Robert Del Grande, Cafe
Annie (Houston); 5) Allen Susser, Chef Allen's
(Miami); 6) Joachim Splichal, Patina (Los Angeles);
7) Charles Palmer, Aureole (New York City);
8) Mary Sue Milliken and Susan Feniger, Border Grill
(Los Angeles); 9) Tommy Tang, Tommy Tang's (Los
Angeles); 10) Emeril Lagasse, Emeril's (New Orleans)

1990s

Texas cattle ranchers take wildly popular television host **Oprah Winfrey** to court, accusing her of slandering American beef during an April 1996 show on mad cow disease, during which she told her audience that her concerns would prevent her from ever eating another hamburger. The trial represents the first legal test of "food disparagement" laws in place in thirteen states. If these laws are upheld, they could squash public debate on other food safety and handling concerns.

1998

The women's health magazine *Self* features an article on the twenty-five most influential people in the world of food—among them cookbook author Sheila Lukins; Culinary Institute of America President Ferdinand Metz; actor Paul Newman, founder, Newman's Own; talk show host Rosie O'Donnell; restaurant critic Ruth Reichl; chef-restaurateur Jean-Georges Vongerichten; author and PBS star Andrew Weil; and talk show host Oprah Winfrey.

JOHN MARIANI ON INFLUENTIAL AMERICAN RESTAURANTS

Certain restaurants have disproportionately influenced others. I'd be very catholic and say **Hard Rock Cafe**, **Spago** (1982), and the **Four Seasons** (1959). But **Jojo** (1991) leaps to mind. Jojo gave everyone the green light that you can actually run a bistro that doesn't have to serve steak frites, that you can have exciting food and not charge very much and have a four-star chef. **Le Bernardin** revolutionized seafood cookery. **Smith & Wollensky** upped the ante for New York steakhouses by having a great wine list. Obviously **Chez Panisse** (1971) was crucial to the development of fine dining. **The Quilted Giraffe** (1979), although it's long defunct, was one place that ushered in *nouvelle cuisine* at any price and was emblematic of a time when Americans became food-crazy. Depending on how far back you want to go, **Howard Johnson's** for franchising and, of course, the ubiquitous **McDonald's**. Much of it happens in New York, although it used to happen in California. California kind of owned the 1980s in certain respects, with **Chez Panisse** and **Spago** and **Campanile** (1989). There were all these places that were exciting new concepts. Things like fusion cuisine were mostly happening in Los Angeles, whereas in San Francisco, there was much more serious food, and more dedication to products and excellence at places like **Chez Panisse** and **Stars** (1984).

A HISTORY OF RESTAURANT CRITICS AT *THE NEW YORK TIMES*

Dates	Critic
1957–1972	**Craig Claiborne** was born in Missouri in 1920. He graduated from the University of Missouri with a degree in journalism. After a stint in the Navy, he attended *L'Ecole Professionnelle de la Societé Suisse des Hoteliers*. In 1963, he began writing 100-word weekly restaurant reviews for *The New York Times*, and in 1964, published *The New York Times' Guide to Dining Out in New York*. He left to start *The Craig Claiborne Journal*, a restaurant newsletter. Claiborne authored numerous cookbooks and a 1982 memoir, *A Feast Made for Laughter*.
1972–1974	**Raymond Sokolov** is a former reporter and book critic for *Newsweek*, who wrote *Great Recipes from The New York Times* during his tenure at the newspaper.
1973–1974 (9 months)	**John Hess** spent nine years in Paris as a reporter for *The New York Times*. He is the author of several books, including *The Taste of America*, written with his wife, food historian Karen Hess.
1974–1975	**John Canaday**, who had been the *Times* art critic, tried his hand at reviewing restaurants. Canaday (1907–1985) was an expert on nineteenth-century art who covered a wide range of art topics for *The New York Times* between 1959 and 1977.
1975–1983	**Mimi Sheraton** was an editor at *Good Housekeeping*, *House Beautiful*, and *Seventeen*. She has also been the food critic at *Time* and *Condé Nast Traveler*. She has written four New York City restaurant guides as well as several cookbooks.
1984–1993	**Bryan Miller** is a former reporter at *The Journal-Inquirer* (CT) and *The Hartford Courant*. He is the author of nine books, including *The New York Times Guide to Restaurants* and *Cooking for Dummies*.
1993–	**Ruth Reichl** was the restaurant critic at *The Los Angeles Times* for ten years. Before that, she reviewed restaurants for *New West* and was a chef-owner at the Swallow Restaurant in Berkeley, California. She has written for numerous publications, including *Vanity Fair*, *Family Circle*, *Metropolitan Home*, and *Food and Wine*. She is the author of *Tender at the Bone*, *Mmmm: A Feastiary*, and *The Contest Book*.

FOOD ON FILM

Especially in recent years, many movie makers have been captivated by the inspiration that food, chefs, and the restaurant setting can provide:

Movie	Description
Tom Jones (1963)	Won an Academy Award for Best Picture, and is considered one of the funniest and bawdiest food-loving comedies ever made
9 1/2 Weeks (1985)	Kim Basinger and Mickey Rourke, virtual strangers, explore food's erotic element
Babette's Feast (1987)	Based on the short story by Isak Dinesen, of a woman's creation of an extraordinary meal
Moonstruck (1987)	Cher falls in love with Nicholas Cage, a one-handed bread baker
Tampopo (1987)	An obsessive quest for the perfect Japanese noodle restaurant
Mystic Pizza (1988)	Julia Roberts, Lili Taylor, and Annabeth Gish all wonder: what is the secret ingredient?
The Cook, The Thief, His Wife, and Her Lover (1990)	A restaurant is the setting for a tale of love, sex, food, power, murder, decadence, and revenge
The Freshman (1990)	An odd banquet serves as a climactic scene in this Marlon Brando and Matthew Broderick film
Frankie & Johnnie (1991)	Michelle Pfeiffer plays waitress to Al Pacino's short-order cook
Fried Green Tomatoes (1992)	Adventures at The Whistle Stop Cafe, whose specialty dish serves as the movie's title
Like Water for Chocolate (1992)	Passion comes to a rolling boil through food during the Mexican revolution
Under Siege (1992)	Steven Seagal plays a Navy Seal-turned-shipboard cook: Can he save the day?
Eat Drink Man Woman (1994)	An Asian family bound by food and love
A Walk in the Clouds (1995)	Keanu Reeves falls for a Napa Valley winemaker's daughter
Big Night (1996)	Two brothers create a spectacular dinner, in the hope of getting press to save their restaurant
A Chef in Love (1997)	*Haute cuisine* takes on political oppression in pre-revolutionary Georgia
Addicted to Love (1997)	Matthew Broderick stalks his ex-fiancée, who has fallen for a New York City chef
My Best Friend's Wedding (1997)	Julia Roberts plays a food critic
Soul Food (1997)	Food as one of the ties that bind an African-American family

Even before celebrities became restaurateurs (and chefs became celebrities), there were celebrated food lovers among the famous, most notably the late Danny Kaye, who endowed a teaching theater at The Culinary Institute of America, and cookbook author Vincent Price. Celebrities' increasing involvement in food-related pursuits—whether writing cookbooks (e.g. Dom DeLuise, Jane Fonda, Barbara and Frank Sinatra), seeing their private chefs write cookbooks (e.g. Oprah Winfrey), marketing food products (e.g. Paul Newman), making beer (e.g. Clint Eastwood) and wine (e.g. Francis Ford Coppola, Fess Parker, and the Smothers Brothers), or opening restaurants (see below)—also stimulates public interest.

Restaurant	Celebrities Involved	Restaurant	Celebrities Involved
All-Star Cafe New York, NY	Andre Agassi, Wayne Gretzky, Ken Griffey, Jr., Joe Montana, Shaquille O'Neal, Monica Seles	Nobu New York, NY	Robert DeNiro
B.B. King's Blues Club and Restaurant Memphis, TN	B.B. King	onesixtyblue Chicago, IL	Michael Jordan
Dive! Los Angeles, CA	Steven Spielberg	Planet Hollywood (various locations)	Demi Moore, Arnold Schwarzenegger, Steven Seagal, Sylvester Stallone, Bruce Willis
Domingo New York, NY	Placido Domingo	Pondicherry New York, NY	Ismail Merchant
Fashion Cafe New York, NY	Naomi Campbell, Elle MacPherson, Claudia Schiffer, Christy Turlington	Rubicon San Francisco, CA	Francis Ford Coppola, Robert DeNiro, Robin Williams
Ici New York, NY	Eric Clapton	Savannah Miami Beach, FL	Diana Ross
Michael Jordan's Chicago, IL	Michael Jordan	Schotzi on Main Los Angeles, CA	Arnold Schwarzenegger
Mission Ranch Carmel, CA	Clint Eastwood	72 Market Street Los Angeles, CA	Dudley Moore
Mulberry Street Cafe Los Angeles, CA	Cathy Moriarty	Tribeca Grill New York, NY	Robert DeNiro

TWO
Who Is That Masked (Wo)Man?

"A maitre d' walked up to me

in a restaurant once and said,

'I know you! How are you,

Mimi?'"

—Gael Greene,
  New York

The identities of restaurant critics for major media are often shrouded in mystery since many of them attempt to guard their anonymity closely. Sharing too many details about themselves only makes it easier for them to be spotted. (While we researched this book, restaurant critics requested that we not describe their appearances, and more than one also specifically asked that we not mention the genders or ages of their children, with whom they occasionally dine.) For these reasons, misperceptions are rampant about how restaurant criticism really works and what critics are really like.

"Somebody told me, 'Oh, I saw *My Best Friend's Wedding* [a 1997 movie in which Julia Roberts's character is a restaurant critic]! Is that what it's really like?'" laughs Penelope Corcoran, restaurant critic for *The Arizona Republic*. "While I haven't seen the movie, I understand that she sits down and is recognized by the entire restaurant staff, who swoons over her. She tastes one bite and announces her opinion. And she's beautiful!"

Is there anyone who hasn't, at one time or another, fantasized about being a restaurant critic? Who are the people who actually have had this fantasy come true? And is the reality of their jobs as wonderful as our illusions?

"When I go into a restaurant, they don't swoon over me," admits Corcoran. "I don't get special treatment. And it takes me more than one second to come up with my opinion. In story after story, I consistently mention, 'on my third visit,' or 'after three visits.' At every opportunity, I will make it clear to people that I work incognito. And yet, the message just doesn't sink in to either readers or less sophisticated restaurateurs. Little mom-and-pop places still call me up and say, 'Come on in, we'll pay for your dinner!' And I have to say, 'Well, no, you don't understand how I do my job. But thank you, send me a menu....'"

What It Takes to Be a Restaurant Critic

Relatively few serious restaurant reviewing positions exist in America. The media putting the most earnest effort into restaurant reviews include major newspapers, city and travel magazines, and, increasingly, such Internet sites as Microsoft's *Sidewalk*, online city magazines featuring weekly restaurant reviews and searchable restaurant databases. This is also such a new occupation that people have usually fallen into it rather than pursued it as an intended career. But with the advent of the *Zagat Survey* and the Internet, through which millions can access restaurant reviews posted by individuals on both sponsored and unsponsored sites, now almost everyone's a critic—or can be.

What does it take to step into the role of a restaurant critic, according to those who have held this position? Craig Claiborne, who first reviewed restaurants for *The New York Times*, developed a clear opinion of what the position requires through nearly twenty years on the job. "Although an intimate reading knowledge of food and cooking is essential to the making of a good food critic and/or restaurant critic, there is nothing to equal a direct acquaintanceship with the taste of food and wine," according to Claiborne. "This is best achieved by learning the techniques of cooking and sampling the food under the guidance of a professional chef, either in a restaurant kitchen or a professional cooking school. The next best thing is an adventure in travel and eating....Finally, I would amass the greatest collection of fine books on food and cooking, starting with the French and branching off into international foods."

In addition, the physical demands of the job should not be underestimated. "Endurance and a strong stomach are, without doubt, extremely important," says William Rice, food and wine columnist for *The Chicago Tribune*. "This isn't an easy job. Everybody loves it the first couple of times until they realize what they've got to taste, and that they've got to keep thinking about it, and that they can't go back to that one terrific restaurant because they've got to move on to the next one. It's demanding, difficult work, and the glamour of it ebbs very fast when you consider how few really good restaurants there are."

Tom Sietsema, restaurant producer for *Washington Sidewalk* (at washington.sidewalk.com), points out that a restaurant reviewer should also know how to write. "I would rather get someone who is a fine writer and can be coached on the food aspects, than someone who is a good home cook or caterer who likes eating out at restaurants but can't write," he says. "I hired someone from a city newspaper here to be my associate, and I am grooming him. We go out to nicer restaurants that he hasn't been able to afford in the past, like Phyllis [Richman of *The Washington Post*] did with me. And I am helping him to raise the bar a little bit, and to understand that just because it is fancy and expensive doesn't necessarily mean that it's good."

For some of the major restaurant critics, their work also requires a willingness to be an object of great public curiosity. *The New York*

"I probably get food poisoning more than anybody in Los Angeles. Every month they have a list in the paper of all the restaurants that have been closed by the health department. Typically, I've eaten at two-thirds of them."
—Jonathan Gold,
  L.A. Weekly and
  Los Angeles

Observer once published an extensive article titled "Bring Me the Head of Ruth Reichl," about the lengths to which restaurants sometimes go to spot *The New York Times'* critic. "I knew that they were doing an article, and that morning while transferring buses I bought *The Observer* to see if it was in. I flipped through it quickly, but I didn't see it," Reichl recalls. "So I was skimming it again on the bus and when I [found it in] the second section, I literally jumped with a [little shriek], 'Aaaah!' And then the woman next to me tapped me on the shoulder and said, 'She lives in my building!' It was one of those situations where I thought, 'What do I say to her?' So I said, 'Oh, where do you live?'—and it *was* my building!"

Reichl has found her new "celebrity" status unnerving. "When I was at *The Los Angeles Times,* nobody cared. But when I took this job [at *The New York Times*], all these papers wanted to interview me," she says. "I was a restaurant critic for sixteen years before I came to New York, so I wasn't prepared for that reaction. I kept saying, 'I'm not a story. I'm just a journalist,' and turned everything down. Finally, the PR person at the paper called me and said, 'Of course, it's totally up to you, but....' And I suddenly realized that they spend a lot of money on this position, and they expect to get a certain amount of bang for their buck! It *is* part of this particular job. And I'd be lying if I said it wasn't fun; it *is* fun. But it's strange, because I never expected to be a public person."

Routes to Restaurant Criticism

Most restaurant critics were simply journalists who eventually combined their loves of writing and food. When William Rice, currently a food and wine columnist for *The Chicago Tribune*, re-routed his career from hard news into food journalism, his decision was considered so ground-breaking that it was featured in *The New York Times*. The other most popular, albeit circuitous, "routes" into restaurant criticism include earlier pursuits related to music, sociology, travel, and even restaurant work.

America's leading restaurant critics, while a diverse group, show some clusters of commonality. Many are Jewish, and grew up in either New York City (as did Ruth Reichl, Arthur Schwartz, Mimi Sheraton, and Merrill Shindler) or the Midwest (as did Michiganders Gael Greene, Robert Sietsema, and Patty Stearns, and Minnesotan Tom Sietsema). The other professional fields representing critics' most frequent prior education and/or activity outside journalism include music, sociology, and travel:

The Music World
- **Caroline Bates**, *Gourmet*—Studied music and English in college, and worked briefly for the jazz magazine *Downbeat*
- **Penelope Corcoran**, *The Arizona Republic*—Former music critic
- **Jonathan Gold**, *L.A. Weekly* and *Los Angeles*—Currently splits his time writing about music and restaurants
- **Marcellus Hudalla**, publisher, *Marcellino's Restaurant Report*—Former musician
- **Bryan Miller**, former *New York Times* restaurant critic—Former member of a zydeco band called the Pinballs
- **Merrill Shindler**, Los Angeles *Zagat Survey*—Head writer for Casey Kasem's *American Top 40* radio show
- **Robert Sietsema**, *The Village Voice*—A rock musician for fourteen years, he was a member of the group Mofungo

Sociology
- **Ruth Reichl**, *The New York Times* (B.A. in sociology, University of Michigan)
- **Phyllis Richman**, *The Washington Post* (graduate work in sociology, University of Pennsylvania and Purdue University)
- **Dennis Ray Wheaton**, *Chicago* magazine (Ph.D. in sociology, University of Chicago)

Road Warriors
- **Caroline Bates**, *Gourmet*, spent a year living "on the road" in the late 1950s
- **John Mariani**, *Esquire*, drove cross-country with his wife over the course of eleven weeks in 1977
- **S. Irene Virbila**, *The Los Angeles Times*, started writing to support her travel and photography

The idea of pursuing food journalism as a career is a relatively recent phenomenon. Only two critics we interviewed, Arthur Schwartz of WOR Radio (New York) and Tom Sietsema have been lifelong food writers. "There was no such career as 'food writing' when I graduated from college," explains Schwartz. "Craig Claiborne was the food editor of *The New York Times,* and I learned later that there was another male food editor in one of the Carolinas. But it was in 1966 or 1967 that Bill Rice left his job as a reporter—I think it was for *The Washington Post*—and went to France to learn about French food because he decided that he wanted to become a food writer. Craig Claiborne wrote a story about Bill in the *Times* because this was such a phenomenon, and that was the first time I had any idea that that was a possibility in life.

"My hobby, since I had been a child, was cooking. And certainly in college, I blossomed into a maniac cook, working my way through Julia Child's *Mastering the Art of French Cooking*," says Schwartz.

"So, one Sunday, instead of looking through *The New York Times'* classified section under 'J' for journalism, 'E' for editor, or 'R' for reporter, I looked under 'F' for food—and there was a job that said 'Assistant Food Editor, Large Suburban Daily, Up to $10,000.' I figured, 'What do I have to lose?' So I wrote a very flip, immodest, and funny letter, following the instructions of my college professor who told me to basically get in the door with something very attention-getting. I got a call the next day—from *Newsday*, and spent the first nine years of my career there."

Musical Taste

Jonathan Gold, restaurant critic for *L.A. Weekly*, mentioned that he had come to restaurant criticism in "a very peculiar way"—before we shared with him how many other restaurant critics we'd discovered who had once been, or were currently, involved in music. Gold explains, "I was the classical music critic at the *L.A. Weekly*, and I wrote some service pieces, including one on health insurance, of all things. The owner of the paper really liked it, and he asked if I'd like to edit the restaurant issue. Food had always been a hobby of mine. I was always the person who had been to every ethnic restaurant that anybody had ever heard of, and the one who was going to weird neighborhoods to check out new ones. But I didn't have any formal background at all."

Nor did Robert Sietsema, restaurant critic for *The Village Voice*, previously a rock musician for fourteen years in the band Mofungo. "As a musician, I didn't have a lot of money, but I had an incredible amount of time between the 5 P.M. sound check and the midnight, or later, set. So, there was nothing better to do than to go around to New York's ethnic restaurants and sit for hours and eat things to amuse myself," he laughs.

"I got a computer one Christmas, so I started doing a newsletter for friends, rock and jazz musicians and other people that I knew to be avid eaters, about the eating experiences that we'd had at ethnic restaurants. I think it was the very first food fanzine," says Sietsema. "It was modeled on the rock fanzines, which were published by fans of various rock bands. The idea was to be a fan of food in the same way. It became a kind of pornography, the idea that you can have the experience by reading rather than by just eating. And it also publicized restaurants that usually didn't have any constituency except the natives of that country. The idea was to try to popularize places, so that anyone would feel comfortable eating there. So, from there, it kind of grew, and eventually someone at *The Village Voice* saw it."

Social Relations

A number of restaurant critics came to the field after studying sociology. A Southerner and currently the chief dining critic for *Chicago* magazine, Dennis Ray Wheaton was a graduate student pursuing a doctorate in biology when he realized that he hated working in laboratories. He concluded that he'd rather do almost anything else, and virtually did, working as a cab driver, a laborer, and on the quality control staff at Fleischmann's Yeast. But after returning to school to pursue graduate study in sociology, his lifelong love of food eventually became his destiny.

"My mother was a terrific cook, and I grew up watching her in the kitchen. She was an incredible pastry cook," says Wheaton. "When I was older, I went to restaurants and asked, 'What's a profiterole?' When I tasted it, I said, 'Oh, Mom's cream puffs!'

"As an undergraduate, I traveled around the world, spending two months each living in Japan, India, France, and Poland," he recalls. "Finding myself suddenly immersed in a Japanese family and being fed breakfast, which was a little fish lying upside-down in your soup. I thought, 'It looks like something out of a minnow bucket from when I was a kid—but it doesn't taste bad!'

"When I came to Chicago, I found that the ethnic restaurants in this city were outstanding. [As a student] I couldn't afford the finer restaurants, so for years, we'd just go out to eat at Mexican and Eastern European and Asian restaurants. It was always just a passion of mine, which is why a friend of mine who was working at the AIWF [American Institute of Wine and Food] at the time said, 'Why don't you write a feature for us?' And a year or so later, I got a call from someone at *The New York Times*, who said, 'We're starting something called *At the Nation's Table*. Would you write about things from the Midwest?' I said, 'Sure!' If you're going to be a journalist, it's a good place to start, I guess!

"Later I got a call from *Chicago* magazine, asking if I'd be interested in trying my hand at reviewing. *Chicago* had a crew of four or five who wrote for the dining guide in the back. I thought it sounded like fun, so they told me to go to these three restaurants, write them up, and they'd pay for it," says Wheaton. "After I did it, I got a call from the secretary to the editor asking if I could come in for a meeting. I thought, 'I don't have time for this....' But I went, and he offered me the job to replace the Kelsons [*Chicago*'s founders] as chief dining critic."

Phyllis Richman earned an undergraduate degree in American studies before pursuing graduate work in city planning and sociology. "I was finishing my master's thesis in sociology when I fell into a part-time restaurant critic job for a small weekly paper in Baltimore, which was something I'd always fantasized about. My first national article for *Esquire* was 'The Watergate Gourmet.' It all reminded me how much I loved writing," she says. "I never finished the thesis, but four years later [in 1976], I was *The Washington Post*'s restaurant critic." Richman has held this position for more than twenty years.

On the Road

Jane and Michael Stern, who write a restaurant column for *Gourmet* on noteworthy restaurants throughout all parts of America, frequently relate the story of how they wrote their classic restaurant guide *Roadfood* in 1976 after spending two years on the road researching a book about truck drivers—and suffering through more than their share of ghastly meals. A similar sense of adventure, and hunger, led other restaurant critics to discover restaurants.

The travels of Caroline Bates, California restaurant critic for *Gourmet*, pre-date even the Sterns'. "I traveled around the country [in the late 1950s] in a tent with my husband," she recalls. "We went for a year-long camping trip, just to sort of discover the country, and we supported ourselves *en route* by writing travel articles for such magazines as *Redbook*, *Woman's Day*, and *Family Circle*."

Los Angeles restaurant critic Merrill Shindler possesses a similar sense of wanderlust. He recalls working in film distribution in New

York and packing his belongings and moving to Alaska in the early 1970s. "I did so for no particular reason except it was the early 1970s," he admits. "And later, I moved down to San Francisco on a lark and got a job with the *Bay Guardian* where I started reviewing restaurants."

Former Restaurateurs

A few restaurant critics once worked in restaurants themselves. In fact, S. Irene Virbila, restaurant critic for *The Los Angeles Times*, and Ruth Reichl once worked together at a cooperative restaurant in Berkeley, California, called The Swallow. And one critic, Patricia Unterman, of the Hayes Street Grill in San Francisco, is perhaps the only critic in the country to review restaurants while working as a restaurateur. Unterman reviewed San Francisco restaurants for both the *San Francisco Chronicle* and the *San Francisco Examiner*, and is the author of *Patricia Unterman's Food Lover's Guide to San Francisco*.

Ruth Reichl remembers her time in the early 1970s at The Swallow, a collective in which everyone had a hand in cooking, washing dishes, and mopping floors. "This was about a year after Alice [Waters] started Chez Panisse [in Berkeley]. We all cared passionately about making great food, so we made everything from scratch. We made quiche, and in those days people would come in and ask, 'What's a kwish?' We made really good salads with real oil and vinegar, and baked our own breads. It was more expensive for us to bake our own bread, and it was a big issue about whether we would bake our own bread or buy the bread. But cost was never a concern. We had a very good rent deal, and we really wanted to serve good food. I know I lost money, because I brought stuff—like saffron—in from home. But I loved working there."

"[Having a restaurant critic who is also a restaurateur] would only happen in San Francisco. New York would never stand for it. Patty [Unterman] said she could never review Stars because it was within one mile of her restaurant."
—Jeremiah Tower,
Stars

Reichl was cooking at The Swallow and writing freelance articles about food when she was approached about restaurant reviewing. "One of my editors from *New West* magazine, who often came in for dinner, asked me if I'd ever thought about doing restaurant reviews. My first review was fairly straightforward," Reichl recalls. "But for the second review, I took a group of friends out. We didn't have any money, so it was a huge thrill for us all to go out to eat. And everyone was trying to be helpful, and critical, so everyone was noticing things.

"For some reason, I fantasized that we were a hit gang from another restaurant who'd been sent out to find fault with this place," laughs Reichl. "And I wrote it that way, giving everybody fake names. So I handed it in, and I said to my editor, 'I don't know—this might be too off-the-wall, but see what you think.' And he said, 'This is great! Just stretch the form as far as you can.' And I did, for the next six years. Some [pieces] were set in the future; some were even love stories. The mentions of food were always factual, but I just wove stories around them.

"I've always thought that most restaurant reviews were boring," she says. "Some people assume that because the subject is interesting, it is innately interesting to read a review. But I've never bought that. The writing has to be interesting.

"Then, I was hired by *The Los Angeles Times* [in 1984], and after I wrote my first review, I showed it to a friend who was a reporter there. And he said, 'You know, a newspaper is not a magazine. You can't do this!' And I realized that I was going to have to modify my style," says Reichl.

Patricia Unterman explains how she combined running a restaurant and writing reviews. After she received her master's degree in journalism from the University of California–Berkeley, she says, "Instead of working for whatever newspaper some cub reporter would end up working on, I wanted to open a restaurant because that was really my passion. So we opened a little restaurant in Berkeley in 1972 called the Beggar's Banquet. It had eight tables. We rented it, walked in, and started cooking, sort of with one of Julia Child's cookbooks opened on the side next to the stove. We served three dishes every day."

At the same time, a college friend of Unterman's was dating an editor of *New West*, so when the magazine was looking for a restaurant critic, Unterman received a call. "In journalism school I had been interested in criticism in general—food, books, dance, movies. I've always been an analytical and highly critical person who had strong opinions, and was eager to offer them. That kind of writing and sensibility really interested me," she says. Unterman got the job.

"So, right from the beginning, I was in this odd position of running a little restaurant and cooking in the kitchen and writing the Underground Gourmet column for *New West* magazine," Unterman says. History went on to repeat itself. "After I did that for a number of years, in 1979, a group of us at the Beggar's Banquet decided to open a restaurant [Hayes Street Grill] near the Opera House and the new Symphony Hall, which wasn't quite built. And then at exactly the same time *The San Francisco Chronicle* called me and said they needed a restaurant critic for the Sunday section, so I started doing those two things concurrently.

"We discussed it very carefully and the thought was that if there was ever any question of conflict of interest, I wouldn't do it; I would avoid the restaurant," she says. "So I didn't do any fish restaurants, and I didn't do any restaurants within the geographical neighborhood [of the Hayes Street Grill]. If I personally felt a conflict, I would withdraw. And that's exactly how it worked."

Critics on Anonymity

While everyone knows which nights the theater critic is attending a play, maintaining anonymity is a big part of the job for many of America's leading restaurant critics.

"It is so desirable to be anonymous," says Gael Greene, restaurant critic for *New York* magazine. "I have had many French critics and restaurateurs tell me that it doesn't mean a thing, because there's nothing a restaurant can do to change the way they are and what's coming out of the kitchen. But that is totally untrue. If you are not known, you are likely to sit at a table that is much less attended. The least desirable tables are always with the least desirable waiters—the person who's training.

"There are many other ways it can be different, when a critic is recognized. You can have the kitchen be extremely careful. The chef can actually go behind the line, to make sure every dish is cooked right.

"Anonymity is important for reception and service. But what can they do to the cooking? If they're bad cooks with bad produce, there's not much they can do about it. You can tell pretty quickly."
—Henri Gault,
*   Gault-Millau*

For the last twenty-five years, the breadth and depth of knowledge that many food professionals have brought to their work have often gone far beyond spending time in a dining room or in front of a stove. In fact, this is one reason why American dining has been able to come so far so fast, overshadowing even French dining in being widely trumpeted as "world-class."

"One of the great advantages we've had in this country is that the good American chefs have made a career choice," says William Rice, food and wine columnist for *The Chicago Tribune*. "The kids in France were brought in by the ear by their fathers and turned over to the chefs at the age of thirteen. But many of our successful American chefs have done, or could do, something in another line of work with great success. So they've got antennae, and they go outside their kitchens."

Jonathan Gold, restaurant critic for *L.A. Weekly*, has observed the same phenomenon. "The generation of chefs who are in their forties now are generally well-educated and have interests outside of food," he says.

This is a far cry from the days when cooking was seen as a blue-collar profession, and food writing as something that "anyone" could do. The public's perception of food professionals is changing, however. "There is a still a sense in which food writing is devalued," says Alison Cook, restaurant critic for *Houston Sidewalk*. "I once wrote an article on the ten best and worst legislators for *Texas Monthly*, and one of the ten worst dismissed it, saying, 'Oh, she's just a food writer, anyway.'"

But food writers have found satisfaction in this line of work. "I've found that this work is deep and important to me in ways I didn't realize when I was younger," says Cook.

Phyllis Richman, restaurant critic for *The Washington Post*, shares this view. She muses about her educational background in sociology and urban planning. "I could have been a government demographer. Just think what fun that would have been!" she laughs. "No, this has really been the most fun I could imagine a job being—even though in some ways it's also been as difficult a job as I could imagine."

Name	School/Position
Rick Bayless	University of Michigan (linguistics) chef-owner, Frontera Grill and Topolobampo, Chicago
Alison Cook	Rice University (English literature) restaurant critic, *Houston Sidewalk*
Penelope Corcoran	Smith College (government); Syracuse University M.B.A.; Arizona State University M.F.A. restaurant critic, *The Arizona Republic*
Greg Cox	Duke University restaurant critic, *The Raleigh News & Observer*
Robert Del Grande	University of California, Riverside (Ph.D. in biochemistry) chef-owner, Café Annie, Houston
C. Dun Gifford	Harvard Law School president, Oldways Preservation and Exchange Trust, Boston
Jonathan Gold	UCLA (musical composition) restaurant critic, *L.A. Weekly* and *Los Angeles*
Joyce Goldstein	Yale University (fine arts) former chef-owner, Square One, San Francisco
Corby Kummer	Yale University (English) restaurant critic, *Boston* magazine
Elliott Mackle	Emory University (Ph.D. in American studies) restaurant critic, *Creative Loafing*
John Mariani	Columbia University (Ph.D. in English literature) restaurant critic, *Esquire*

Name	School/Position
Mark Miller	University of CA–Berkeley (anthropology) chef-owner, Red Sage, Washington, DC; Coyote Café, Santa Fe
Robert Parker	University of Maryland Law School wine writer
Ruth Reichl	University of Michigan (B.A. in sociology, M.A. in art history) restaurant critic, *The New York Times*
William Rice	Columbia University (M.S. in journalism) restaurant critic, *The Chicago Tribune*
Phyllis Richman	Brandeis University; attended graduate school in sociology and urban planning at University of Pennsylvania and Purdue University restaurant critic, *The Washington Post*
David Rosengarten	Cornell University (Ph.D. in dramatic literature) restaurant critic, *Gourmet*
Anne Rosenzweig	Columbia University (anthropology) chef-owner, Arcadia and the Lobster Club, New York City
Bill St. John	University of Chicago (M.A.s in economics and philosophy; Ph.D. in theology) restaurant producer, *Denver Sidewalk*
Arun Sampanthavivat	University of Chicago (M.A. in political science) chef-owner, Arun's, Chicago
Tom Sietsema	Georgetown University (foreign service) restaurant producer, *Washington Sidewalk*
Jeffrey Steingarten	Harvard Law School food writer, *Vogue*
Jane and Michael Stern	Jane: Yale University (M.F.A.), Michael: Columbia University (M.F.A.) restaurant critics, *Gourmet*
Jeremiah Tower	Harvard College (architecture) chef-owner, Stars, San Francisco
Barbara Tropp	Princeton University (Chinese poetics) former chef-owner, China Moon Cafe, San Francisco
Patricia Unterman	Stanford University (English); University of CA–Berkeley (graduate journalism) restaurateur and restaurant critic, *The San Francisco Examiner*
S. Irene Virbila	University of CA–Berkeley (textiles) restaurant critic, *The Los Angeles Times*
Alice Waters	University of CA–Berkeley (French cultural studies) chef-owner, Chez Panisse, Berkeley, California
Dennis Ray Wheaton	University of Chicago (Ph.D.s in sociology and biology) restaurant critic, *Chicago* magazine
Tim and Nina Zagat	Yale Law School founders and editors, *Zagat Survey*

Even if he only has so much talent, he can make sure it's going out the way it should," Greene says.

Dennis Ray Wheaton's anonymity has been so well-protected throughout his tenure that he has even gotten away with eating at the kitchen tables of two leading Chicago restaurants without being spotted. "I've laughed about the fact that I got in and out of Charlie Trotter's," says Wheaton. He adds that the chefs at Trio restaurant in Evanston, Illinois, at the time even got a kick out of the fact that Wheaton managed this. "The magazine got a letter from [former Trio chefs] Gale Gand and Rick Tramonto saying, 'We just laughed and laughed over this, because [Wheaton] talked to us all evening before reviewing us—and we can't even remember who he was!'"

Techniques for Staying Anonymous

Many serious restaurants post photographs of restaurant critics in their kitchens, which underscores the importance many critics feel in maintaining their anonymity.

"I work completely incognito, and I've managed to remain anonymous for eight years," says Penelope Corcoran. How has she accomplished this? "Well, you don't schmooze with chefs," says Corcoran. "And you don't walk around at conferences with your name badge on. I think it makes a difference. I get to see how they treat the average person walking in there, who isn't the doctor they know well, or a celebrity. And sometimes I become a regular and get to see how they treat regulars."

Gael Greene agrees. "When I go to a restaurant, I make a huge effort to get a reservation without using my name," she says. "Once in a great while, I've had to use my name, which I would do in a great restaurant that I love, that I know. If I had to get a reservation at the last minute at the Gotham, maybe I would use my name. For Le Cirque 2000, I had a hard time. I've been trying to get in for three days, trying to find somebody who would be willing to make a reservation in their name and let me go. Nobody would do it. They didn't want to upset Sirio [Maccioni, the owner] or possibly jeopardize their relationship with him.

"In addition, I like to have my guests get there first, so that they are seated before I arrive," she says, "and I have credit cards in various names. Mostly, my boyfriend pays with his credit card, but I think that his name is known now, too. So the reservation is always made in the guest's name. If the guest is known as a friend of mine, I make up a name."

"Today, a lot of restaurants have lists of the names and phone numbers critics use when they reserve. So I have to make up different phone numbers and different names," says Greene. "And then I have to remember the reservation name. But all that helps. Even if they recognize me the moment I walk through the door, the chef might not be there or they might be short a cook in the kitchen. Sometimes I hear about that afterwards."

Dennis Ray Wheaton asked of us, "Don't tell anybody, anywhere, what I look like! Because, so far, I've been fairly lucky. I don't talk about the food in a way that lets the waiter get suspicious about what I'm doing there. And I don't take notes. I use a tape recorder and transcribe it myself, so I spend a lot of time talking into my tie."

"At one point, on one of my many credit cards, I used the name 'Max Weber' [the German sociologist and author of many books, including *The Protestant Ethic and the Spirit of Capitalism,* who died in 1920]. Once a waiter looked at it and said excitedly, 'Hey, I think I've read your book!'

"Another thing I do to try not to be recognized is to bring other people who know an awful lot about food and wine and let them do the talking to the chefs," says Wheaton. "I just sit back and listen. The chef will come out, or the sommelier will come out, and within a few minutes it's like I'm not even there. They'll be focused on this guy because he really knows his business."

S. Irene Virbila maintains her anonymity by doing "the obvious: I never reserve under my own name, and I have different credit cards. I often have a man choose the wine and pay because they're look-

"I go to the full range of restaurants, from diners and ethnic joints to fancy places. But really only the top-level restaurants recognize the restaurant critic."
—Arthur Schwartz,
  WOR Radio

"If I were ever picked up by the police, I would have a lot of trouble, given all the different names on my credit cards."
—Dennis Ray Wheaton,
  Chicago

ing for a woman. And I try to watch my body language, so I'm not pointing at others at my table saying, 'And *you* will have....' But who knows how successful that is?

"Sometimes it's really obvious that I'm getting my food before the tables that came at the same time. Or there are just too many waiters. I'm very aware when the chef might know I'm out there and be con-cerned that I'm not eating everything, because it makes me eat more," she says.

Alison Arnett, restaurant critic for *The Boston Globe*, tries not to draw attention to herself in any way possible. "I don't order the wine, I don't ask for substitutions, and I don't make complaints," she says. "But it's not that I don't look for stories. When you need something to write about, it's always great to have something bad happen!"

Not "Looking Like A Critic"

Some critics believe they've had an edge in maintaining their anonymi-ty because of their appearances. "I don't look like what people expect Penelope Corcoran to look like," says Corcoran. "I think they expect me to look like a middle-aged, broad-shouldered, kind of plump, really authoritarian woman. Maybe not too snappily dressed. Solid shoes. And I just don't look like that, so they never think it's me."

Dennis Ray Wheaton admits, "When I was first hired, they said, 'One of the things we like about you is that you don't look like what people think a restaurant critic at a major magazine looks like.' I can even look very different just by getting my hair cut short."

Jonathan Gold also feels that he has gotten a great deal of mileage out of not looking like a restaurant critic. "I've looked like a slob for so long that I could go into places like Spago or Chasen's, and no one ever suspected me of being a restaurant critic," Gold jokes. "Now, I get recognized. But it was sometimes better for the story when I got crappy treatment."

When a Critic's Cover Is Blown

What happens when a restaurant critic is recognized? Gael Greene points out that restaurants can't really send out for good food. But, she remembers, with a laugh, "Whenever I walked into any of David Keh's restaurants [in New York City], shortly thereafter, many Chinese men in long overcoats would come into the restaurant and walk directly back to the kitchen. It's as if he would send them from his other restaurants to back up whomever was in the kitchen. It was so funny!"

Other times, Greene says, the reactions to her presence have run the gamut, "from total rudeness and being difficult, to suddenly everything you ask is yours—and then having little extra dishes come out to the table."

Tom Sietsema can also recall instances of stark contrast during evenings when his cover was blown while working in Seattle. "One night I walked into a very hot restaurant called Flying Fish, and I said, 'I was just strolling by and wondered if I might have dinner here this evening.' There was a sea of empty tables behind the host, but he pointed to his book and said, 'We're booked tonight, so I couldn't possibly seat you. If you want to eat with us tonight, you'll have to eat at the bar.' So I went to take a seat at the bar, passing two waiters whom I recognized as having worked at other good restaurants in town. Two minutes later, the same guy who had had no time for me came over and said, 'Oh, we have a lovely table by the window for you.' A table for four, for one person? Something by the window? And I just said, 'This is fine.' So, meanwhile, the bartender who had only been paying attention to the pretty girls around me, and not giving me the time of day, was tipped off, too."

Penelope Corcoran believes she has been recognized only twice. "In my first year at *New Times*, I went to Christopher's [in Phoenix]. I was asking a lot of questions, taking notes not surreptitiously, and they were on the lookout! In this town, among publicity-aware, chef-owned restaurants, they're really looking for you," she says. "That brings the 'girl from U.N.C.L.E.' aspect in. When the manager asked if I was from the *New Times*, I had to lie and say no. But then I had to go back. So I went out and bought a huge red wig, and instead of wearing glasses, I wore contacts and dressed completely differently. And they didn't recognize me.

"The King of Spain is waiting in the bar, but your table is ready."
—Sirio Maccioni, owner of Le Cirque, to *New York Times* restaurant critic Ruth Reichl

"'Look at this,' says my dining companion, unearthing a small fortune in truffles. 'See how generous they are?' I refrain from saying that the restaurant would quickly go bankrupt if they were that generous with everyone."
—Ruth Reichl's review of Judson Grill, *The New York Times*

"I used to steal menus by slipping them into my cowboy boots, but now I carry big bags."
—Alison Cook,
   Houston Sidewalk

"The other time might have been in Tucson, where I stole a menu. I had pulled the menu out of this big, grandiose leather-bound cover, and then I saw the waiter getting ready to give the same menus to another table and finding one empty. He looked right at me," laughs Corcoran.

Patty LaNoue Stearns, feature writer and former restaurant critic for *The Detroit Free Press*, says, "If it's a place where I think I might be known, I wear a wig. I have one wig, but it can be worn different ways. And I have a pair of really ugly glasses, and some hats."

Dennis Ray Wheaton has been recognized twice. "And that's because I'd met with the chefs before I became a critic. Once by Jean Joho at Everest, whom I had interviewed for *The New York Times*. The first time I walked into his restaurant after it was announced I got the job, he walked out of the kitchen, looked at me, and walked right back in the kitchen! And [Chicago restaurateur] Gordon Sinclair knows what I look like. He'll go out and talk to everyone in the restaurant but my table! He's really cool about it. Joho's that way, too. And as far as I can tell, they haven't told other people.

"Carla Kelson [Wheaton's predecessor] knows that it's not ever a good idea for a restaurateur to tell waiters that a critic's there because a lot of them will start screwing up. She tells the story of once going into a Chicago fish house that no longer exists with her husband, Allan, and being recognized. She says the waiter dropped a platter of food as they were being served. She looked at him and asked, 'You recognize who I am, don't you?' and the mortified waiter replied, 'Yes. In twenty years in this job, I have never done that before!'"

"You might say that for me it's impossible for me to ever get the real situation because people always recognize me from TV," says David Rosengarten, New York restaurant critic for *Gourmet*, who also hosts a daily show on the Television Food Network. "Of course, the magazine was a little concerned about that when they gave me the job. Critics always say if they don't know you're coming in advance they can't do anything. I know that theoretically they could stand there and make sure nothing goes wrong, and yet there have been times when I've thought, 'Could they possibly know who I am, considering the way they've screwed this up?' Even when I know the service is all over me, I'm still getting meat that's three stages past what I ordered."

When a Critic Isn't Recognized

At restaurants that are not looking to make a name for themselves, few people are on the lookout for a critic. We met Jonathan Gold for lunch at Yazmin, a Malaysian restaurant in Los Angeles where we had to walk by a huge, framed review with his byline on it before passing through the dining room. "This place is one of my favorites," Gold told us. "I've written about it a lot, and I have at least one piece in the window, maybe two. They don't have any idea who I am, do they?" (They clearly didn't.)

"But I don't think I should be treated differently, and I don't like it when it happens," Gold says. "One time, I decided to go to [a top-rated Los Angeles restaurant] on the spur of the moment, and they didn't know who we were. They seated us at a crummy table by the bar, and the food was several steps lower than it was when we'd had 'V.I.P.' written on our ticket. That's never a good sign."

Recognition can affect all aspects of the dining experience, according to S. Irene Virbila. "One of the reasons that a foodie's opinion of a restaurant would differ from mine so dramatically is that they don't make any effort to be anonymous, and they don't need to.

PHYLLIS RICHMAN OF *THE WASHINGTON POST* ON BEING RECOGNIZED

- I hate when the restaurant staff is sycophantic. At an Asian restaurant last night, they changed our rice three times.

- At a Thai restaurant I visited where the owner recognized me, we were overwhelmed with useless service. But what he didn't do was to give the real service we needed, which was to translate his Thai menu for us, or to steer us toward the dishes he was serving that other restaurants aren't offering.

- I think restaurants think that critics are looking for kowtowing, or that all critics want is to be treated royally. They don't realize that what restaurant critics want is to do their job well. They should be steering us toward the restaurant's specialties and making sure what we get is what other people will generally get, and not larger portions or whatever. Because if a restaurant critic orders, say, caviar, and is given what's obviously an enormous portion of caviar and writes about it, then everyone will expect the same thing.

- I would prefer to have my privacy. I'm not there to converse with the restaurateur; I'm there to do my own job, and to bring my own companions along. I don't need another one.

They're a great customer of the chef, or pals with the chef, so when they go there and he cooks for them, they have a very different experience," says Virbila. "The point is not to go there and be ushered to the best table in the room and get the best waiter—it's to go and see if they offer you the *worst* table the minute you walk in."

Is "Incognito" Inconsequential?

Anonymity is not as important as Phyllis Richman once thought it was. "I've discovered that when I'm recognized in restaurants, the food doesn't get better. The service is slower because God knows what they're doing in the kitchen. The food may be in larger portions or more elaborately garnished. And if they know something is bad, they'll probably say they're out of it. Generally, they're serving whatever food they know how to serve. It just astonishes me how much obviously bad food I get when I'm recognized in restaurants. I get 'more service'—not necessarily *better* service, but *more*.

"I don't wear wigs or other disguises. I tried that, and it's too silly or embarrassing, and it doesn't really work," she reports. "I was able to be anonymous for at least the first five years. There were hardly any women reviewing restaurants then [in the 1970s], and restaurants didn't notice women. They registered whether they were beautiful or stylish or whatever, but other than that they didn't really look. It was fairly easy, until some years into it, *Washingtonian* magazine published my picture. I was furious, and I tried to head it off. Once I began to be recognized, however, then I was recognized a lot more, because waiters move around and managed to spot me.

"Now, I would say, I'm probably recognized about half the time," says Richman. "A lot of the places I'm going are hole-in-the-wall Thai restaurants where they wouldn't recognize President Clinton if he walked through the door."

"I don't, frankly, think that it's critical to be anonymous," says Elaine Tait, restaurant critic for *The Philadelphia Inquirer*. "The theater critic goes on a day when everybody knows that he's going to be there, so I don't know that it's so essential. I abide by it, however, and I don't make reservations under my own name. But often, I've found, when you are recognized, they sort of shoot themselves in the foot because they try too hard."

Merrill Shindler admits, "I used to try hard to maintain anonymity, but finally realized, 'This is ridiculous!' It's not as though restaurants have a glass box in the kitchen that says 'Break glass in case of critic,' where they have a perfect 'emergency meal.' They do the best they can. Now, over at Spago, Tom Cruise will get a better table than me. But Tom Cruise and I are going to get the same pizza. No one in the kitchen is saying, 'Make a better pizza for Tom Cruise than for Merrill Shindler or for Joe Blow.' A kitchen does what a kitchen does."

Critiquing on the Spot

No one likes going to a restaurant hungry and being served bad food. However, the average diner who receives an undercooked steak can easily ask to have it cooked a little more, or can send back an over-cooked steak. But one of the drawbacks of being a critic is that most say they never complain to prevent drawing unnecessary attention to themselves.

Penelope Corcoran is an exception: "In a way, I think I'm generous. If I can help people correct things while I'm in the restaurant, playing 'the nice diner,' I'll try. I might pull someone aside and say, 'You know, you really shouldn't serve these yellowed arugula greens. What do you think?' I'm not looking for a comp. I just really want to show the chef what's come out of the kitchen that shouldn't have.

"In the real-life case of the arugula, I showed it

to the waitress, who came back from the kitchen and announced, 'The chef says this is yellow arugula, and it's supposed to be that way.' And that made me see red! Just to double-check, I called every well-informed produce person in town, and was told emphatically that there's no such thing as 'yellow arugula.' And similar things have happened a lot. Some restaurants do lie to the diner. They should just say, 'I'm sorry. That shouldn't have made it onto the plate.' That's all I'm looking for."

Corcoran recalls her frustration over another incident in which the restaurant could not admit its mistake. "Several years ago, I went to a fine dining restaurant in a local retirement community here, one that was really praised highly. I ordered French onion soup, and it came out with a hair in it. So I motioned to the waiter to come over and, *sotto voce*, whispered, 'I just wanted to show you that this soup has a hair in it, Could you please remove it?' After he took it away, he came back and loudly announced, 'Well, we went through it with a fine-tooth comb, and *we* couldn't find a hair in it!' First of all, why would I make it up? Secondly, I was trying to save *them* face!"

Corcoran admits, "I don't have to take quite as much action in the restaurant as I would if I were a regular customer. I know I have the last word. It is truly a luxury and is what makes this job wonderful."

Critics also "grin and bear" unbearable service, finding it all part of the job. S. Irene Virbila remembers, "At one very respected French restaurant [in Los Angeles], we arrived five minutes before our reservation. Our table wasn't ready and, since there was no place to wait, we sat outside on a planter. I think the hostess came outside once to say they were working on it, but never in nearly 50 minutes did they come out to offer us anything—a glass of wine, a glass of water, anything. That I find hard to understand. It's not very smart on the part of the restaurateur. Another customer would have gone ballistic, but I can't go ballistic!"

What happens when a restaurant experience is awful? "If something happened a couple of times at a restaurant, I might see what they're going to do about it. Or if they come up and say, 'Is everything all right?' when I'm not eating something, I might tell them if it was a little overcooked or whatever," says Virbila. "But I've been in restaurants where there's a tremendous amount of food on the table—not just mine, but everybody's tables—and they never ask a thing. You've taken three bites, and it's horrendous, and they're not asking. They don't want to know!"

A Week in the Life of a Restaurant Critic

A restaurant critic's work is never done, or so it seems. Ruth Reichl might have as many as twenty restaurants in her critical loop at any one point in time. "It's a lot," she admits. "But I go out for ten to twelve meals a week. I work weekends; I work all the time! And sometimes at the last minute I'll get a babysitter or my husband will volunteer, and I'll go out on a night I hadn't planned to."

Reichl also airs daily restaurant reviews on WQXR Radio. "I record them once a week, so I'm constantly eating everywhere for that," she explains. "But with twenty restaurants in the loop, I have a lot I can draw on for those, the *Diners Journal* columns, and the restaurant reviews."

After 30 years on the job at *New York*, it's no surprise that Gael Greene would want to cut back. "Now, I'm working only six months a year—three months 'on' and three months 'off'," says Greene. "I'm trying to finish a novel, and I'm writing a children's book. So when I'm [in New Yrok City], I have to eat out almost seven nights a week and normally two lunches. As the deadline approaches for 'Ask Gael Where to Eat [in *New York*'s year-end issue],' I will have to make more lunches.

"Monday is deadline day. The piece is due at 10 A.M., and the little 'Ask Gael' for the back of the magazine is due. So I usually get in at 6 A.M. and do the finished copy. I try to finish the research on Saturday, and clean up the desk. Then I write the first draft on Sunday. We spend a lot of time on the phone arranging reservations, cancelling, changing dates, calling people, putting in new people. The food magazines have sextupled—I think there was only *Gourmet* when we started. Now even *The New Yorker* has restaurant reviews! Have they no shame?" she jests. "I normally have my assistant send me a package every week of everyone's reviews—*New York* magazine, *The New Yorker*, *Nation's Restaurant News*, *Crain's*, *The Observer*, *Food Arts*, *Time Out*.

"I also read the mail, the press releases. I have a file called 'Alpha'—everything that's just opened or about to open or says they're

"This has the perception of a glamor job. People say, 'Oh, you get to go to all the glamorous places!' And I tell them that I get to go to all the crappy ones, too—three times."
—Penelope Corcoran,
   The Arizona Republic

going to open or everyone who has a plan. We have to call them all the time to see if they actually opened, and whether they're open for lunch, because the minute you get *Zagat*, it's out of date.

"Monday we edit, and Tuesday we finish editing. Wednesday and Thursday are totally lost, cleaning up from what didn't get done on Monday and Tuesday," sighs Greene. "On Friday, I have a standing date with my boyfriend for the first movie of the day at the Sony Theater, whatever opened that he wants to see.

"Then there's Citymeals on Wheels [a not-for-profit organization that delivers meals to elderly shut-ins, which Greene heads]. The most consuming time is October and November when we're doing the Power Lunch [an annual fundraiser held at the Rainbow Room]. And our solicitation letter that raises about one million dollars every year is sent out every Thanksgiving."

Occupational Challenges

Being a restaurant critic is not just a job—it's a lifestyle. "In many ways, it's a very wearing, difficult, invasive job because it's something you devote your whole body to," says Phyllis Richman. "You have to eat *what* you have to eat *when* you have to eat it. In the summer, when I'm working hard on my dining guide, I'm writing about food for the fall. So while all anyone in Washington wants to eat is a small dish of sorbet, I'm eating two major meals a day. It also means you're out night after night. And you eat a lot of bad food—probably more bad food than anybody who cares about food would choose to eat!"

The sheer logistics of coordinating so many meals under so many fake names, phone numbers, and credit cards can also be daunting. "The biggest part of being a restaurant reviewer is the 'social director' aspect of it: marshalling armies of people to go in every direction at various times," says Robert Sietsema. "It requires a lot of phone work, a lot of advance planning. And the earlier you do it before the date that you dine, the harder it is!"

Ruth Reichl agrees. "My best friend said to me, 'It's a good thing you're as social as you are.' I spend thirty hours a week at a table! I think almost the biggest requirement for a job like this is that you have to really want to spend a lot of time with people. And if you don't want to, you have no business being in this position. Because it's not just food and passing plates around. It's figuring out who you're going to spend every lunch and every dinner with."

Because they eat out so frequently in groups, restaurant critics can learn a lot about diners' prejudices. "People are very emotional about what they like," says S. Irene Virbila. "I take out a lot of different people, and not all of them are close friends because I need eaters every night. I find that I'm always kind of shocked at how I'll take out people who are fairly sophisticated in many levels of their lives, but when it comes to food, they're so limited. Vegetarianism is a different subject, but [certain people] don't eat organ meats, and too many things sound 'icky' or too spicy," says Virbila.

Other challenges faced by critics are admittedly sometimes an amusing diversion. "I remember when *Chicago* magazine invited four or five of us down to cook a meal for each other. There was Pat Bruno [from *The Chicago Sun-Times*], Phil Vettel [from *The Chicago Tribune*], people from the two alternative newspapers here, and myself. I made a salad. I have a nice vegetable garden in my backyard, so the salad had just been picked about two hours before," says Dennis Ray Wheaton. "It was great fun, and we were all very nice to each other."

Some of the challenges of the job stem from the public's extraordinary interest in food. "It's interesting the social cachet that a critic has," says Wheaton. "I find I don't like to go to cocktail parties. It drives me nuts when people come up and ask me all of their 'What is your favorite restaurant?' questions. Even around a university crowd, what I do seems to be more interesting than what other people do who are making all of these wonderful discoveries in their laboratories. Everyone thinks it's the most wonderful job in the world. I get to do all the time what most people do only on special occasions. Most of it is just hard work, sitting at a computer writing, transcribing tapes, taking notes, and trying to think about this stuff. And believe it or not, it's sometimes not fun to go to three French restaurants in a row, if you have to. It gets overwhelming.

Some kinds of meals aren't meant to be eaten too often," Wheaton points out.

Some situations that would be the fantasy of any other diner are the stuff of critics' nightmares. "One of the biggest challenges is trying to get out of freebies," says David Rosengarten. "The policy at *Gourmet* is absolutely no freebies. I've only ever had a few problems with this. For instance, one Saturday night I was out for a review and asked for the check. So the waiter came back and told me his boss said it's complimentary. I said, 'Well, do me a favor and tell him that I really appreciate him offering to do this, but...'. And again he came back and said 'I cannot give you the check.' I was beginning to get annoyed because I was eating with other people, and about to get into a fight over demanding the check. So I said to him, 'I don't think you understand—if you don't give me a check, I'm going to lose my job.' And he said, 'I don't think *you* understand. If I give you the check, *I'm* going to lose *my* job!' So finally I said, 'The customer's always right?' So he gave me the check. Hopefully, he didn't lose his job."

Since most chefs and restaurateurs like to show respect or hospitality to visiting V.I.P. guests, critics or not, how would critics like to be acknowledged, if at all? "I think some kind of restrained recognition is okay, with the understanding that you aren't to be intruded upon," says Patricia Unterman. "I suppose a little show of concern at the end of the meal might be just right—with restraint, however."

What about a chef coming over to the table? "I always loved that," Unterman admits. "I thought it was really thrilling when I was a customer. Now, I don't know. I think if they could do it when you're sitting there with your little espresso or you're finished and kind of winding down, it would be nice to see the chef, especially if it were a wonderful meal, to tell the chef how great you thought she did."

Retiring Critics

Elaine Tait spoke of her plans to retire in 1998 after more than thirty years as *The Philadelphia Inquirer*'s restaurant critic. She explains what she'll miss most about the job. "I'll miss being able to go to the best restaurants in town a month or two after they open, and the sense of discovery and the excitement of whatever's going on there because I'll never be able to afford that," she admits. "But I won't miss having to go out as often as I do. Certainly I've enjoyed it, but you get awfully tired sometimes. I won't miss the physical exhaustion of it."

Tait also reveals what she'll miss least: "Hurting people's feelings. I really hated to do that. If you knew me as a civilian, you would know that I'm never the one who says, 'Hmmm, this cake could have been a little more moist.' Socially, I would eat anything and not complain about it. But I also know that that's not what I'm paid to do professionally."

"I think I was one of the first people to mention Frontera Grill in The New York Times. *Someday, when all of this is over, I'd really like to sit down with chefs like [Rick Bayless] and a few others and just talk. But for now, I can't have any kind of contact at all."*
—Dennis Ray Wheaton,
  Chicago

Three

Is Judging a Restaurant a Matter of Taste?

"Gourmandism is an act

of judgment, by which we

give preference to things

which are agreeable to

our taste over those

which are not."

—Jean-Anthelme Brillat-Savarin,
The Physiology of Taste

The manner of reviewing restaurants in America is as diverse as its practitioners. While a general industry ethic has evolved that holds that reputable reviewers are to adhere to certain standards—such as paying for their own meals, basing their judgments on more than a single visit, or maintaining some degree of anonymity—this isn't always the actual case.

In addition, the criteria on which restaurants are judged vary from publication to publication, and sometimes even from critic to critic at the same publication! Judgments, too, are rendered in different ways, from quantitative ratings of stars or forks, to simply qualitative descriptions of the dining experience. The length of the review also varies, as does timeliness. And when the restaurants being reviewed range from multimillion-dollar enterprises to very modest storefronts, the Eurocentric star system provides an increasingly difficult challenge.

"Restaurant reviewing seems to me, without question, the least understood, the least researched, and the most difficult of the critical arts," says William Rice, food and wine columnist for *The Chicago Tribune*. "There are no textbooks. There are no schools. And beyond that, if I review a movie, the people who go the next night are going to see exactly the same performance. But in a restaurant—even on the same night I'm there!—somebody sitting two tables away ordering much the same food could well be having a very different experience. A dining experience involves your head, as well as all your senses. And some critics, over the years, have tried to opt out of that and

review only the food. But I think, particularly in this country and in this era, that's a cop-out.

"At the same time, nobody has to take a course to be a critic. Nobody has to know food. In the old days, the restaurant critic was quite likely the wife of some assistant city editor who spoke French. It was very subjective, and everybody eats, so anybody could be a restaurant critic. A newspaper wouldn't think of taking somebody out of the pool and sending them to cover City Hall or Senator So-and-So's speech! But a movie critic or a restaurant critic? Anyone who's willing to do it! And that really hasn't changed very much," observes Rice.

Certainly, no tests are given to judge a potential critic's food knowledge. Alison Arnett, restaurant critic for *The Boston Globe*, says, "It frightens me even now because I'm not a trained chef, and I've never worked in a professional kitchen before. So, while I certainly know enough about cooking to be able to understand when a chef tells me how he's made the food, I try to approach criticism from the role of a diner."

Gregory Roberts, restaurant critic for *The Seattle Post-Intelligencer*, says that his reviews rely very heavily on reportage. "Beyond that, I'm not even qualified to say, 'This bouillabaisse has tomato in it when the classic doesn't,'" he admits. "Beyond the facts, as far as judgments go, that is subjective, and you have to have a certain amount of confidence in your ability to judge. Generally, if the preparation allows the ingredients to speak, and they're good ingredients and the flavors come through clearly, then that's good. But there are many dishes that don't really do that. Stew-like dishes, or dishes with rich sauces, have another character all together, where the whole is greater than the sum of the parts. Then, you fall back on subjectivity."

Honesty and fairness are the critical starting points, according to Los Angeles restaurant critic Merrill Shindler. "Any critic can look at any dish and say that it is the best or the worst, and can very easily justify it: 'This is a marvelous dish' or 'What a stupid mess,' 'It's worth any price' or 'It's about three cents worth of food and they're charging $4 for it,'" he says. "So what it really gets down to, for me, is: Does the restaurant have heart? Does the staff care? It will never justify bad food, but I'm concerned with the whole experience."

Because their position is so potentially powerful, critics should be capable of handling this responsibly. "My own facetious take on it is that a potential critic should be given a psychological test," says William Rice. "The ego causes more problems than anything else because this position holds a lot of power. And no one, in a sense, questions it. Once you've got this badge that says *The New York Times* or *The Chicago Tribune*, nobody but the chef—who everyone assumes is disgruntled—is going to sit there and say, 'This guy's never cooked anything in his life,' or 'This guy grew up eating hot dogs and has never had paté.' Nobody knows that one way or the other. You're the critic, and you're there at the behest of a publication that justifies this expense on the grounds of consumer protection. So it's built in, when you start, that you're going to have an attitude."

How It's Done

Generally it is seen as unfair for a critic to review a restaurant after, say, a single visit on opening night. But this is a delicate balance. While critics might try to take into consideration the fact that it will take a new restaurant weeks, and perhaps months, to begin running smoothly, some have a mandate to cover the news of a restaurant opening while it is still news.

"Le Bernardin got four stars in the first three or four weeks after it opened," remembers Gael Greene, restaurant critic for *New York* magazine. "I had told [owners] Gilbert and Maguy LeCoze when they were getting it ready that I never came to a restaurant before three weeks. Craig Claiborne had told me many years before, when I'd interviewed him for *Look* magazine, that he always waited at least three weeks to give people a chance to get the service organized. The second day Le Bernardin was open, I got a phone call about the restaurant, 'It's so fabulous. The service is perfect. The food is incredible. It's so amazing that it could be like this the second day.'

"I think I appeared the Monday of the second week, and Maguy was furious: 'What are you doing here? You told us you never review before three weeks!' And I said, 'Well, I've been getting these phone calls, and everyone says you're ready,'" recalls Greene. "But today people are going even before the doors are open. Some people are writing things based on a pre-opening tasting. And with the new *Time Out* magazine and the new expanded [*New York*] *Times*—which seems to have twenty-five people covering food—the competition is so intense [to be the first to review a new restaurant]. I've already reviewed two restaurants this month that were so new that one is still in preview prices. If it hadn't been a good review, I wouldn't have done it. I could never defend a bad review in the first few weeks."

While no industry etiquette is cast in stone, certain guidelines are passed down informally. "I learned a lot from the Kelsons [*Chicago* magazine's founders and original editors]," says Dennis Ray Wheaton, chief dining critic for *Chicago* magazine. "Details like the whole professional side of reviewing—making multiple visits, staying anonymous, not going on Mondays because it's typically the chef's night off and it's not fair, and not judging too harshly if the service fails just a bit on a huge, busy Saturday night.

"The thing about a restaurant is that it's a different experience every time you go there. We usually wait six weeks until after it's opened. And if we go sooner than that, say to a really hot restaurant, we'll tend to disregard problems, like waiters who haven't got it together. Or if a dish was a problem we'll try the same dish later on, and if it's good, we'll disregard the first one," says Wheaton. "So I don't grade on a curve; I grade on a vector. If you're doing really well by the end of the 'semester,' you're in good shape with me!"

The New York Times has developed its "Diners Journal" column and *The Los Angeles Times* its "First Impression" column as a way to alert readers to the opening of a new restaurant without providing a full-fledged review.

"There are very few restaurants that could withstand a review in the first couple of weeks," says S. Irene Virbila, restaurant critic for *The Los Angeles Times*. "I'll wait two or three months until reviewing them, eating there over a period of several weeks."

Finding Restaurants to Review

Ideas for new restaurants to review come from a variety of sources. Tips come from readers, from industry insiders, and from press releases. Arthur Schwartz, restaurant reviewer for WOR Radio in New York City, remembers receiving "huge piles" of restaurant press releases every week when he was the critic at the *New York Daily News*. "Once, after I'd been away for three weeks, the post office delivered me two official U.S. mail sacks, and most of the mail was restaurant press releases of one kind or another," he remembers. "I'd say there were at least 15 new restaurants that had opened while I was gone, another 15 or 20 were telling me that they were going to be opening, and another 15 or 20 were telling me that they hadn't opened yet, even though they thought they were going to."

"I get ideas from all over," says Phyllis Richman, restaurant critic for *The Washington Post*. "Restaurants send me information, people call or write me with tips, I spot them on the street, I hear talk and gossip, especially from people in the food business or restaurant realtors.

"Jean-Georges Vongerichten told us that Ruth [Reichl] ate at Jean Georges about seven times during the review process. Some critics are really trying to understand what a chef is trying to do. And we respect that."
—George Germon and
   Johanne Killeen,
   Al Forno

I've always felt, right from the start, that depth of knowledge of your subject matter is the most important thing. That was something that I worked on and still do work on, if I don't understand where a dish is coming from. Over the years, I've done a huge amount of traveling and eating at the source.

Will you ask a chef about a dish?

I rarely ask the chef. I do my own research. I find out what the ingredient is. I look at cookbooks. If I'm really stymied, I'll ask the chef. But I try to separate myself as much as possible.

Why is that?

I don't want to be swayed by personality. I want there to be a clear division between myself as an eater in the restaurant and the chef in the back of the house. I know myself. I'm all too likely to identify with the back of the house, coming from the back of the house myself.

Is the chef's vision considered in criticism?

Really, what's important is how that vision ends up on the plate. It doesn't matter what the chef's idea was, what the concept of it was. You don't want to make excuses for it. What's important is how it was executed and how it comes off.

Are there principles for judging quality?

I feel that the most basic level is the quality of the ingredients. If that fails, why go on? I think execution is very important, too, as is consistency. I don't think the chef's taste or vision is criticizable, if the principles are there and the ingredients are good. I like family-style food, and I have a personal prejudice against highly composed food, but if a chef is doing it well that's perfectly fine. Things have to succeed within their own context. And I think that's the most important consideration.

How do you judge creations you've never experienced before?

After so many years in this business, there's very little in terms of ingredients or flavors that I haven't come across before. Even if people come up with the oddest things, I always kind of understand where it's coming from. Then you can only judge based on whether it worked, whether it tastes good. I suppose that's purely personal. But I think there are certain guidelines there, too. You look for balance in a dish. You look for clear flavors to come through. You look for some distinguishing quality. You know when things are muddled or things are fighting—and you can tell when it all comes together. That's our art, I guess.

Do you have a formula when you review restaurants?

I am a dinosaur when it comes to that. I'd say that, for me, 95 percent is food. I know that now many other critics and diners consider the setting and the service as very important to the meal. But for me, if I don't get something good on the plate, it just doesn't do it for me. My prejudice is clearly with food. I tend to overlook bad service. If it's really horrible, of course, I'll comment, but I don't think that's the heart of it.

What do you mean by 'bad service'?

You know, if someone is completely bumbling and the food has chilled on the plate before it gets to the table, or if someone screws up the table and then doesn't handle it. If someone just confesses to it and says, "Oh, you're right, I screwed up," and it was an aberration, then I don't think twice about it. But I resent those situations where they pretend that it didn't happen.

Have you ever taken the opportunity to articulate your prejudices for your readers?
I think I've been in this town so long that my readers pretty much know what my prejudices are. They probably can read between the lines and say, "Well, she doesn't like that; that means I'll love it." If I were a newcomer and starting out on a job, I think I would write a column like that to articulate what I think.

How do you define what excites you in a dining experience?
I'm a complete omnivore. I get as excited by a great Chinese restaurant as I do by a steakhouse. I have very few food prejudices. My prejudice is only for freshness. I'm ingredient-prejudiced—that's the one thing that turns me on or turns me off.

Do you run across bad ingredients very often—especially with the bounty of California?
Many times a restaurant kitchen buys good ingredients, but they don't handle them right. They get old. When they reach the table, they've been ruined. You can taste that they haven't been treated with respect and love.

What is an example of that?
I'm very conscious and worried about all the tartares which are so popular now, such as tuna tartares and scallop tartares. Seafood has to be so impeccably fresh. I am so sensitive that if it's even a little bit old, I can't eat it. It ruins it for me. Oysters are another good example. Every time an oyster is opened, the oyster-opener has to smell it. It's absolutely essential, because an oyster has to have that grimy sea smell. I can't tell you how many times I've been served a plate of oysters and had to spit out two of them. In those cases, it's clear the kitchen doesn't know how to handle the ingredients. So excellence goes beyond getting your hands on the best ingredients. It also has to do with the sophistication of the kitchen and its understanding of how it should deal with them. It goes to the next level.

How do your two careers [as a critic and restaurateur] influence each other?
They happened simultaneously and have been amazingly enriching. If I eat a great dish in another restaurant, I'll come back and say, "I think we ought to do something like it [at the Hayes Street Grill in San Francisco]." I'm completely influenced or open to that. Running my restaurant, knowing exactly what's available in town, and knowing exactly at what level things should be, have made me quite understanding, but also tough when it comes to judging the quality of ingredients.

So, you'll know when it's impossible to get good strawberries, for example?
I know how silly it is for a restaurant to put a strawberry dish on the menu when it's completely the wrong season or the wrong time [such as after a hard rain, when strawberries have absorbed too much water and are likely to be mushy and bland].

Is cost a factor?
Cost, to me, is practically irrelevant. Food costs have almost nothing to do with how much any item costs. So much depends on the level of the table top and the level of the restaurant, the location, and the service. I think customers are much more sensitive than ever before to environment and to decor. They know that when they get a $4 million decor, they are going to be paying quite a lot for that plate of strawberries.

Do you have a typical reader in mind?
I write for someone like me. I just aim high and talk about the things that interest me. If it reaches 1 percent of the people, maybe the rest of them will learn something.

- "I almost **never go out on weekends** because it's too crowded, and it interferes with other things." —Alison Arnett, *The Boston Globe*

- "**I like to go alone**, so I can concentrate on what's going on. I'll notice the interactions with other diners and get to see how they treat single diners." —Alison Cook, *Houston Sidewalk*

- "I've always thought that **two or three people** was a good number for dinner because once you get into four, what you have is a party. Everybody gets to talking, and you can't control it. It's like a team of runaway horses. **I try to take someone along with me who is going to like that type of restaurant.** If it's a restaurant where there are going to be children or it's a playful place, you might want to take somebody young. If it's very geriatric, take your mother!" —Elaine Tait, *The Philadelphia Inquirer*

- "The first time I go, we'll just order things that look interesting or the **signature dish**, to 'get it out of the way.' The next two visits, I'll try to get **a balanced view** of whatever the restaurant does." —Penelope Corcoran, *The Arizona Republic*

- "I have a total of **eight different meal experiences** in that, counting myself, there will be eight people who visit, and there will be **no duplication of items** if the menu is big enough. And I realize that at most restaurants, by the time I get there the third time, I'm going to be digging really low in their menu. At how many restaurants is the eighth-choice entree very good?" —Gregory Roberts, *The Seattle Post-Intelligencer*

- "As a restaurant owner, I know that it takes six months before a restaurant can even hit its potential. And, in my heart of hearts, I know that a good restaurant, after a year, will be much better. But unfortunately, there is huge pressure from my editors and from the public to get those reviews as soon as possible. **I wait at least a month** and then, knowing what it's like, I discount or don't even think about some of the mistakes that happen." —Patricia Unterman, *The San Francisco Examiner*

- "**A restaurant has to have the capital to stay open three months**, and that's important. Secondly, if I love it, then at three months, they will be able to handle the onslaught of customers who show up. It's my responsibility to the reader." —Penelope Corcoran, *The Arizona Republic*

Or chefs or restaurateurs might call just to chat. This has been a very slow season [1997] for restaurants in Washington; there haven't been many significant restaurants opening. So I've been looking farther afield for places.

"Sometimes it's hard to find a restaurant worth reviewing," Richman admits. "I'll wind up reviewing places that are really not significant or interesting enough to warrant the public space. I think people don't realize how hard it can be to find a restaurant to review. I'll go to four restaurants in a row where the chef is leaving, or just left, or they're changing the menu next week, or there's some other reason why I can't review it. Or I'll be trying to get to a number of different restaurants I haven't tried, and none of them will work out. It's not that any one of them is impossible to review, but none of them quite seems worth a second and third visit. And so I'm stuck with having to make several visits in a hurry. I'm often scrambling to find the right restaurant to review that week.

The Coach House in New York City, which was founded in 1948, closed in 1993.

Mimi Sheraton	Bryan Miller
1982: ★★★★	1982:
1985:	1985: ★★
1991: ★★★	1991: ★

Former *New York Times* critic Mimi Sheraton's 1991 ★★★ review of The Coach House:

"One of the city's very few continuing classics, albeit one that has lost just a bit of its original glow."

Black bean soup: "The justly-famous black bean soup."

Rack of lamb: "Done rose-red and crusted with parsley, garlic and bread crumbs."

Wine list: "[American wines] are as well chosen as his French bottles; Italian wines are banally represented, but perhaps they are unnecessary in this context."

Desserts: "As irresistible as ever."

Then *New York Times* critic Bryan Miller's 1991 ★ review of The Coach House:

"Be wary when a restaurant is described as an institution, which often signifies that its main attribute is being old."

Black bean soup: "Tepid and lacking flavor one evening, hot and gutsy another night."

Rack of lamb: "Poorly trimmed of fat but succulent."

Wine list: "Nearly half of the [California] wines I ordered were out of stock. No vintages are listed, and for French wines, producers are not identified."

Desserts: "Still excel."

"A restaurant has to have something to say. There has to be something that distinguishes it from the great mass of restaurants. It's not easy to quantify. It's kind of like falling in love—you just know when you're there," says Richman. "Sometimes it's really good cooking. Or an interesting menu. Or even a single dish that nobody else is doing. Or some special ingredients. There's a French restaurant out in Maryland—a perfectly ordinary, decent French restaurant—that served the best herring that I've had in this country. It's like being a reporter and having a pretty dull interview with somebody until you happen to ask just the right question that opens up something unanticipated and extraordinary."

To find interesting, out-of-the-way restaurants in Los Angeles, Jonathan Gold, restaurant critic for *Los Angeles* and *L.A. Weekly*, drives around twice a week. "I try to cover every major street in the county every four months, to see what's open," he says. "It's as much a culture column as it is anything else. And it's really interesting to

"I once went to an Ethiopian restaurant that a taxi driver had told me was the best one that all the taxi drivers go to. It was a perfectly ordinary Ethiopian restaurant, but it turned out that they served breakfast, so I went back again for an Ethiopian breakfast and wrote about that."
—Phyllis Richman,
  The Washington Post

I go out almost every night on a restaurant review for *Gourmet*, in order to review three restaurants a month in New York. Of course, *Gourmet* is a national publication, and so it doesn't need to keep readers up to date on what's new and *bad* in New York. *Gourmet* wants a review to be of a place that the reviewer heartily recommends. That means that not only do I write about three restaurants every month, but I've got to *find* three restaurants that I heartily recommend. So, that means there will be seven, eight, nine, ten restaurants that I don't use.

I really believe that the way to be most helpful is for the reviewer to taste a very large percentage of what's on the menu. I can always tell when somebody's reviewed a restaurant and they've only been there one or two times. I can tell the bullshit factor. First of all, you see how few dishes they're referring to. You get the sense that they haven't sat there enough to grasp the overall picture of the restaurant.

I usually visit a restaurant five times. I have perceptions that I definitely think of as "first-time perceptions"— they're the kind of superficial physical perceptions. I feel that every time I'm there, I'm peeling away another layer of the skin of the onion, and I'm getting a little bit closer to the reality of the restaurant, to its center. It's usually not until my third or fourth visit that I say, "Eureka! I finally understand what's great about this restaurant, or what's bad about this restaurant, or what people need to know."

There is something unique about every single restaurant in the whole world. My goal is to communicate what that uniqueness is—on a theoretical level and also on a very practical level for diners, so they can go in with the big idea of what the restaurant is about, as well as make certain choices about the menu.

Ultimately, for a review, I want to give readers a "culinary roadmap." I want people to read the review and then be able to order the best possible meal. This doesn't usually mean just giving them a laundry list of my favorite dishes because so many restaurants today change menus so often. I have to be able to apprehend whether this chef is a whiz with grilled fish, or whether he's a disaster at stuffed vegetables. I have to see the big patterns. I read a lot of restaurant reviews, and it seems that these days the trend is more about the place, the crowd, the scene, and all that kind of stuff. I might take a stab at that or imply those things. But for the most part, I've got 1,000 words in a review and I want to devote as many of those words as possible to trying to understand what this chef is doing, and what parts are going to especially appeal to readers or are parts they should avoid.

On the first visit, I like to go knowing as little as possible about the background of the restaurant and the chef, to just have a real brush with the food before I'm influenced by these other things. By about my third or fourth visit, everybody is on to me; they've seen me take my little notes. It's at that time that I start asking questions, and, if I'm lucky, the answers will help hasten the epiphany.

I do go out with different numbers of people. In every group of five visits, I try to go once by myself. I find that when I'm sitting there by myself and I'm bored to tears, then I'm amusing myself with my thoughts—and I get better thoughts than when I'm trying to be social. So, by my fourth or fifth visit, which is usually by myself, somehow it all comes together.

Of the five visits, I might go two or three times with one other person. My favorite size of group is three. I find that four or more is chaotic and if there are four of us, by the time the last dish gets around to me it has degraded. With three, there's no degradation. It's even better with two in that sense, but the problem with two is that you're that other person's company and you've got the pressure of conversation. Three is great. I'll say to the two of you, "Listen, I've got to take some notes for the next three minutes. Just talk amongst yourselves."

But the fact is that I can't always arrange a threesome. Most often I do it with two and order like we're six. I mean, I order a lot of dishes. When I order, they always say, "This is going to be a lot of food. We could divide the portions," and I always say, "No!" It's the bane of my existence. I want to see the dish and what it's going to be like. I've got to get some sense of portion or quantity. And all the time I'm fighting waiters and chefs who are saying, "What's the matter? Don't you like the food?" because I never eat everything on the plate. It's true; I try not to eat very much of each dish. Most of the time when I go to a restaurant, I never order an appetizer, a main course, and a dessert. For me, it's a waste of energy for what I'm doing. When I get to the restaurant, I try to plow in and get as many things going on the table as possible. Three- or four-hour dinners are not unusual for me. Actually, I set a record recently at Le Cirque: 6 hours and 15 minutes, in a non-reviewing situation. I should contact Guinness!

see where there are little Korean neighborhoods that didn't exist six months before, or to see a neighborhood grow from one Cambodian store into three Cambodian grocery stores and a restaurant, or to see certain Mexican neighborhoods in East Los Angeles get sleeker and more upscale. It's amazing. You get this picture in your head of a living, breathing city, and you try to get to know every part of its fabric."

Hasn't he found ways to discover new restaurants without burning through so much gas? "Recommendations from readers are bombs nine out of ten times," says Gold. "The best thing they can do is steer you toward a neighborhood that you hadn't thought of before to find a good restaurant. But another good place to find things is in ethnic newspapers. I can't read them, but sometimes they'll have a restaurant name in English, or they'll have pictures of the specialties. It's almost like detective work. I'll even go into a Laotian grocery store and ask, hope against hope, if a restaurant has opened yet."

David Rosengarten, New York restaurant critic for *Gourmet*, doesn't find unsolicited tips of much help, either. "I know when not to pay attention [to tips]. You get a sense of people's palates, and who not to listen to," he says. "I got a letter, for example, from somebody who wrote, 'I've had the best meals in New York City at Two Two Two on West 79th Street,' and there was something about the way it was written and the things she said about the food that I felt I couldn't trust. I ended up there later, and my instinct proved right.

"I also have extensive files of reviews I've clipped from publications ranging from *Time Out* to *The New York Times*, to neighborhood publications like *The East Side Reporter*," says Rosengarten. "Tonight, I'm dining as Mr. Kelly at an Italian restaurant on Second Avenue [whose owners have since left to open Pierino in TriBeCa]. About five people told me it's great, and Ruth [Reichl] also mentioned it on her radio show on WQXR."

Would You Review Our Restaurant, Please?

Penelope Corcoran, restaurant critic for *The Arizona Republic*, says she has received phone calls from publicity agents asking, suggestively, "What does it take to get a review?" "I want to say, 'A million dollars would be nice,'" she laughs. "But I explain that I work incognito, and

"Somebody just tried to bribe me within the last few months. They were willing to pay me a weekly stipend to mention their restaurant on the air once a week."
—Arthur Schwartz,
  WOR Radio

that they can send me a menu. Clearly, there is that perception out there [that it takes a bribe to get reviewed]. And other than at major newspapers, who knows how these things get done?"

"I'm always getting these letters from little places, mostly, saying, 'Present this letter for a dinner or lunch,'" says S. Irene Virbila. "And I get calls from restaurateurs or PR people who don't quite understand [how this process works]. You'd think that after all these years, they would understand that you don't invite the restaurant critic to have lunch or dinner with the owner of the restaurant."

Tom Sietsema, restaurant critic for *Washington Sidewalk*, says he has received gift certificates for $100 to $200 from restaurants. "I wanted the restaurants to know that I wouldn't use them, so I would call and explain that we had expense accounts and that this is not how we did our reviews. And they'd tell me, 'Well, give it to your friends.' And I'd just explain, 'I can't do that, either, but thanks very much,'" he says. "The restaurants are usually not very good ones, or sometimes they're better-known ethnic restaurants where perhaps in their home countries these things go on."

Doing Their Homework

The review process starts even before you call for a reservation, according to Elaine Tait, restaurant critic for *The Philadelphia Inquirer*. "There's a balance of types of restaurants that you want, so if you've just reviewed a very upscale Italian restaurant, you're not going to want another one the next week," she says. "You're basically looking for something to keep readers interested, so they don't know what to expect from you."

This often involves juggling the reviews of restaurants of varying ethnic cuisines. Before—or while—reviewing a restaurant whose national or regional cuisine they're not familiar with, the most diligent critics make it a point to do some homework. This can take the form of everything from cookbook research, to consulting with colleagues or natives, to buying and tasting raw ingredients.

"When we started getting a lot of Asian restaurants, nobody really knew much about [Asian food] and there weren't many texts," remembers Tait. "So I went to Asian markets and bought ingredients like lime leaves and *galangal* and tasted them so that I could recognize their flavors.

"I had a friend who was a Hare Krishna, and she taught me a lot about Indian food," says Tait. "I learned a lot about spices and the blending of the spices, and she would cook all these wonderful things from Lord Krishna's cuisine. But it's very labor-intensive, and I've never had the time to do it myself.

"On one trip to Berkeley, California, I bought some 'goat's foot mushrooms,' and some other oddball things so that I could identify them," recalls Tait. "And one year I spent the entire summer cooking different kinds of fish all summer long. It helped me to identify what freshness tasted like and what the textures were like. I also came to understand better ways of cooking fish, that some lend themselves to grilling and others to poaching."

Tom Sietsema finds his research easier in Washington, DC, than in other cities where he has worked. "I'm lucky here because if I want to explore a cuisine that I have never tried before, I can call the foreign embassies and say, 'Hey, could I take your cultural attaché out to lunch?'" he says. "But I have to remember that I have a mostly American audience, and I have to filter those foreign tastes through an American perspective."

Restaurateurs who try to do the same don't necessarily win points from critics. "I was just at a Thai restaurant that was clearly very popular with Thai people, but pretty ordinary otherwise," says Phyllis Richman. "Then I realized that people at other tables were eating different things and had Thai menus, so I got a copy of one and gave it to a translator, who looked at the name on the menu and said, 'Oh, I like this restaurant a lot!' So I asked her, 'What do *you* order there?' While the menus overlapped quite a bit, a few dishes were different. I guess the restaurant is afraid that Americans won't like them. But it was odd because the manager has worked in some pretty prominent restaurants, so you'd think he'd be savvy enough to know that Americans would like to try some of these things. For example, there's a pig's foot dish cooked for a couple of days, a spicy catfish dish, and some tripe dishes."

"Over the years, I've used the original Time-Life *Foods of the World* books a lot. When it's something I don't know, I'll take along somebody who's lived in that country and I read up on it. And I have a lot of old cookbooks and foreign cookbooks," says Richman.

Dennis Ray Wheaton has also learned a lot from natives about evaluating a cuisine. "There was a lot of controversy here over the Chinese restaurant [Ben Pao] that [Rich] Melman opened. We have never listed that restaurant, and I really panned it when it opened," says Wheaton. "I took some friends who were very good Chinese cooks to the restaurant, who commented as the dishes came out: 'This soup is not the right temperature,' which is very important in Chinese [cuisine], and 'This sauce was cooked by somebody who doesn't understand the cuisine.'

"There are different criteria in different cultures," explains Wheaton. "The first time I ever had a fried egg for breakfast in Japan, it was served at room temperature. It didn't occur to them that it was important that the egg be hot when it was served. And in Chinese cuisine, a lot of foods' softness and glutinous textures are really important, which turn Americans off as 'slimy.'"

Alison Arnett has had mixed success with the same approach. "I've found that sometimes it's difficult if you bring someone who speaks the language. For example, I've found that the Chinese are very, very polite and hardly ever tell you what they *really* think," she says. "But sometimes I'll take along Nina Simonds, who writes Chinese cookbooks."

Jonathan Gold believes that the best education comes from dining out itself. "You learn more about [various cuisines] by eating them. It's surprising how much you can learn about a cuisine by eating in a restaurant that serves it 30 times," he says. "In mainstream restaurants, you're used to being able to ask somebody what's good or what the best thing on the menu is or what the chef's specialty is. But you can't do that in most Asian restaurants because they've almost always been burned by people who don't like the 'real' food. So they're suggesting things they think you will like, and a lot of it's clichéed.

"In that case, you make them translate wall signs, and that's almost always good. You can stand around and point and say, 'I want some of what that man has at his table over there,'" he says. "But the best thing is to do your homework. When you're going into a Shanghai style restaurant, if you have some idea of the contours of the cuisine, then it becomes not so terribly difficult."

"I get around the country to about 25 cities a year," says John Mariani. "And I'll call my colleagues [for tips]. For example, I'll call Bill Rice [at *The Chicago Tribune*] in Chicago, and I'll say, 'If you were

"Food is one of the world's most powerful drugs. Last night, I was eating guinea pig—and I've never before had an experience that was more like LSD. It was absolutely bizarre."
—Robert Sietsema, *The Village Voice*

- **Karen Berk**, Los Angeles *Zagat Survey:* "The tiniest little fish that were brought to us in a restaurant in Kyoto, where it looked like there were thousands in the bowl; and tiger, at a game dinner at the Jonathan Club in Los Angeles."

- **Alison Cook**, *Houston Sidewalk:* rattlesnake, alligator, fish eyes

"Since I live in Texas, hard by Louisiana, rattlesnake and alligator do not seem all that exotic to me. I will say I have never found rattlesnake worth eating, other than as a curiosity: it has all the charm of an old boot, usually. Alligator can be quite winning—especially in a Creole sauce piquante, the way the late, great Buster Holms' joint in the French Quarter used to serve it. It was in Thailand, however, that I once ate something that required a real faith. Two Thai friends took me to an open-air restaurant on the beach at Rayong. We were served a glorious-looking whole fish called Batsa. The 8-year-old daughter of one friend very solemnly dug out one of the fish's eyeballs and presented this delicacy to me, since I was the guest of honor. I knew what the occasion called for, so without flinching I popped the eyeball into my mouth. I swear it tasted a bit like chicken liver. But it was the chitinous lens that made me feel I was ingesting something truly alien."
—Alison Cook, *Houston Sidewalk*

- **Penelope Corcoran**, *The Arizona Republic:* "Rocky Mountain Oysters." i.e. deep-fried pig, buffalo, cattle, and turkey testicles; rattlesnake; fried grasshoppers; alligator; and Japanese mountain potato (which she describes as "not weird, but unpleasantly snotlike")

- **Jonathan Gold**, *L.A. Weekly* and *Los Angeles:* braised goat penis; Filipino duck eggs three days from hatching; pig uterus; testicles of a bull that had fallen in the ring to the matador

- **John Mariani**, *Esquire:* congealed duck blood at a restaurant in Chinatown, New York City; spine ganglia and unborn calf ravioli in Bologna

- **Ruth Reichl**, *The New York Times:* ant eggs, armadillo, snake and snake blood, stingray burritos, worms fried in lard

"I've had some pretty weird things in New York City, too. Recently, I had a pasta dish with blue cheese, basil, and grapes. Nobody can make things as awful as experimental young chefs who think they're being clever!"
—Ruth Reichl, *The New York Times*

- **Phyllis Richman**, *The Washington Post:* snake bile wine, chocolate soufflé served as first course in China; ortalans (which she describes as "weird and wonderful")

"Poi is pretty weird, if you ask me. And in China, we were once served a fish that was caught and cooked so rapidly that it was still flapping when served—and the gills were still going when we'd eaten it all off the bones."
—Phyllis Richman, *The Washington Post*

- **Arthur Schwartz**, WOR Radio: Sea slugs ("sometimes euphemistically called sea 'cucumbers,' right out of the water, raw, at the 'city of refuge' on the 'big island' of Hawaii"); grasshoppers; ants, locusts; milk straight from the teat of a cow

- **Dennis Ray Wheaton**, *Chicago:* cured grasshoppers; roasted duckling brains

"The most wonderful-tasting exotic thing I've ever eaten—and that includes fugu several ways at the incredible Ginza Sushi-Ko in Beverly Hills—was a dish I assisted Mexican cuisine authority Diana Kennedy in preparing at her home in Michoacan. She had found that morning in the local market bright blue chanterelles native to the local mountains. She braised them in fresh cream from her own cow and we folded them in homemade blue masa tortillas for a sublime turn on sauteed mushrooms in crepes that demolished George Carlin's old line about there being no good blue food."
—Dennis Ray Wheaton, *Chicago*

in Chicago for two days, where would you go?' And he'll give me four places, and two of them work out."

How Many in Your Party?

Deciding how many visits to pay to a particular restaurant with how many people over what period of time is practiced as more of an art than a science. Certainly, a publication's budgetary restraints dictate the level of thoroughness a critic can employ.

"The first time I go, I'll let it be just a normal dinner: going out with friends, where everybody orders what they like, except we don't repeat," says S. Irene Virbila. The "dibs" system that worked so well on elementary school playgrounds also has an important place at a critic's dinner table: "Whoever says it first gets to order it. And other times, I'll let people know what I want them to order.

"Sometimes I'll go just with one person, when it can be very calm, and I can pay attention not so much to the food, but to what's going on in the room and how the other tables are being served and a lot of quiet observation because I don't have to be in a conversation that much," she says. "Sometimes I'll go with as many as six people, but if it's complicated food, that's about the limit to both pay attention and not be too obvious."

"I'll visit a restaurant at least twice," says Patty LaNoue Stearns, former restaurant critic for *The Detroit Free Press*. "During the first visit, I usually just take it all in. I usually don't take notes, because I want to just concentrate on everything I would experience if I were just going in and not reviewing. And I try to pretend that I am just 'Joe Diner' coming in. During the second visit, I have a tiny notepad that

I keep in my lap, and usually I'll take notes when no one's observing me. And I have a tape recorder with me, so that when I'm leaving, I'll go over the experience with whomever is with me, and we'll talk about the decor and the service. My husband often goes, because I often rely on him in the middle of the night for details!"

Ruth Reichl, restaurant critic for *The New York Times*, finds that her choice of dining companions definitely has implications at the table. "There are certain 'job obligations,' people in the office I'll eat with. But my favorite thing to do is to just take old friends, so you don't have to think about them," says Reichl. "Tonight I'm taking some colleagues of my husband's out, so I'm going to have to be 'on,' in addition to having to think about the food. Tomorrow night I'm taking some of my editors out, so I'm going to have to be 'on' again. The most relaxing thing is to just take your oldest friends out so it doesn't matter."

Some critics specifically mentioned that they prefer not to dine with opinionated food-lovers. "People would think that a restaurant critic would be going out with foodies all the time, but in fact, it's very relaxing to go out with people who are not foodies at all," says S. Irene Virbila. "Foodies are exhausting because they tell you everything they think about everything! And if it's not good, then the evening's ruined. You have to go out with people for whom it's going to be entertaining regardless of how the meal turns out."

First Impressions

A restaurant never has a second chance to make a good first impression. "A restaurant tells you the minute you walk in the door what it's trying to do," says Elaine Tait. "It's how they greet you. It's a feeling, like when you meet a new person. In a person, it's body language. In a restaurant, there's a smell, there's an energy level. There are so many things going on that you could probably review some restaurants without even tasting the food. There's a confidence level sometimes that tells you to expect great things—it's the posture of the server who takes you to your table. In terms of the noise level, there's what I call a 'happy hum' in restaurants, or there may be an icy silence. If you go into a restaurant that is really, really quiet, you know you are not going to have a wonderful evening. The food's not going to be great because if it were, there would be somebody out there cooing.

"I let the restaurant tell me what it's trying to be," she says. "If it's trying to be grand or it promotes itself as being very upscale, with 'one of the top chefs from New York,' then I'm going to want them to prove to me that it really has something. Whereas if it's really quiet and kind of creeping in the back door, I let that be my measure of what I'm looking for."

Despite all that can be learned on a first visit, a critic should go to a restaurant at least twice before reviewing it, according to John Mariani, restaurant critic for *Esquire*. "Sometimes you can go to a restaurant that's so good—and if you've got four people, and you order four appetizers, four entrees, and four desserts you can tell—and there's no sense in coming back. But if a place is problematic in any way, or you've got a really lousy waiter...I would never go in print as saying, 'This place has terrible service' on the basis of one bad waiter on one bad night. That's not fair. I don't think you have to go six times, maybe not even three or four times, necessarily. If I'm eating 16 or 20 dishes, I'm getting a pretty good assessment of this restaurant's strengths."

Even after multiple visits, it still amazes Alison Arnett how consistent restaurants tend to be. "I'll make a note of something, and when I re-check my notes from my previous visits, I'll realize that I wrote the exact same things," she laughs. "And it will range from the music being too loud to the service being off in one specific way or another."

Review Criteria

Do all restaurant critics use the same criteria to rate a restaurant? Is there a general pattern in the 'formulas' employed? "No," insists Gael

HOW DO CRITICS REVIEW A RESTAURANT?

Critic	First Visit	Number of Visits	Party Size
Alison Arnett, *The Boston Globe*	3 weeks	2+	4+
Caroline Bates, *Gourmet* (California)	6 months	2-3+	3-4
Penelope Corcoran, *The Arizona Republic*	1 month	3	4
Gael Greene, *New York*	2-3 weeks	2+	2-4
Phyllis Richman, *The Washington Post*		2-6	2-4
David Rosengarten, *Gourmet* (New York)	6 months	5 (1 alone)	2-3
Patricia Unterman, *The San Francisco Examiner*	1 month	2+	2/1st visit 4/2nd visit

"A friend of mine, who is a Michelin inspector, told me that one star is a great bourgeois restaurant, two stars is probably the best there is, and three stars is just cinema."
—Arthur Schwartz, WOR Radio

Greene. "For me, it's totally impressionistic. It's based on, would I want to come back? Did I adore it? Is it beyond anything I've ever tasted? Is it really great at the price? If I lived here, would I come more often? It's about that kind of reaction. And if the service is not ideal, it's much less important to me than the food."

What's the most important factor in a review? "Way over half of it is food," says Dennis Ray Wheaton. "Next comes decor, and then service, and the whole experience of dining there. If I'm rating a restaurant three or four stars, most of that is going to be on the food, and then up or down half a star according to whether the service or setting kept up with the rest of the experience."

Sometimes criteria vary slightly by city, due to local factors such as climate. "When I was at *New Times* they didn't operate with any kind of rating system, so I had to develop my own criteria there," says Penelope Corcoran. "In my personal view, food is the most important thing, followed by service, followed by atmosphere. Because Phoenix has pleasant weather all year-round, people don't spend as much on the interior as they do in, say, Toronto, which is a cold-weather climate where everyone's indoors for nine months."

Different critics use different criteria when reviewing restaurants. Even *The New York Times'* critics over the years have given different weights to various factors. In 1982, Mimi Sheraton deemed food 85 percent of the experience. (By 1991, she'd revised that number to 75 percent.) Bryan Miller weighted food at 80 percent, while for Ruth Reichl it logs in at only about 50 percent of her evaluation—depending!

- *The Boston Globe* (**Alison Arnett**): "The food is certainly 60 percent. I also like to give some feeling of what the chefs were trying to do, and whether or not they did. Service is typically worth a half-star, up or down."

- *Chicago* **magazine:** "Stars are assigned primarily on the basis of food quality; menu selection, service, ambiance, and value are also considered."

- *The Detroit Free Press* (**Patty LaNoue Stearns**): "Ratings are not meant as a comparison of restaurants but as an evaluation of how well individual ones accomplish what they set out to do. Food, service, and setting are all considered."

- *Gault-Millau:* "Rankings reflect only our opinion of the food. Other important considerations—the decor, service, wine list, and atmosphere—are commented upon in each review. What is on the plate is by far the most important factor. The quality of produce is among the most telling signs of a restaurant's culinary status....Freshness is all-important, too, and a telling indication of quality."

- *L.A. Weekly* (**Jonathan Gold**): "It's *all* about the food. I find that I'm actually a little overgenerous on third-world cooking, and I tend to be bitchier on high-end chefs' restaurants. If you have a bad dish and it costs you $4, it's different than if you have a bad dish and it costs you $20. It's something else because of the level of pretension."

- *Gourmet* (**David Rosengarten**): "Mood, tone, theme, setting, harmony—dining and the arts share the same crucial elements. Critiquing restaurants is similar to reviewing books, music, and theater."

- *The Los Angeles Times* (**S. Irene Virbila**): "In my heart of hearts, I think food is 100 percent of the experience—unless somebody is astonishingly rude. I know I'm not the typical customer, so I have to balance that. But personally, I'm not that upset by slow service, unless it's just absurd."

- *Michelin Guide:* Awards between 1-3 stars for cuisine. Judged on quality of cuisine served, as well as dining value. ***: "Exceptional cuisine in the country, worth a special journey." **: "Excellent cooking: worth a detour." *: "A very good restaurant in its category." M: "Other recommended carefully prepared meals."

Evaluating Food

No matter how heavily food is weighted as part of the experience, how do reviewers go about evaluating it? When something's good or bad, it doesn't necessarily have to do with authenticity, observes Jonathan Gold. "While going through Malaysia and Singapore a couple years ago, I always ordered *rojak*, which is one of my favorite dishes, and noticed that it was never as good there as it is here," he says. "It could be because it's generally a street-food dish, and so [the vendors were] not likely to get the best quality produce. The quality of fruits and vegetables tends to be a lot better in the U.S. than it is almost anywhere, including France."

- *New York Daily News* (**Daniel Young**): "A great restaurant is like great sex: everything is perfect. You feel like you belong; you feel important. You're treated well. The flavors are vivid. Everything is stark, really defined. The music is not loud. It has an arc to it. And it's great if it's under $20."

- *The New York Times* (**Bryan Miller**): "A three-star establishment must excel; a four-star must excel and inspire."

- *The New York Times* (**Ruth Reichl**): "To me, the best food in the world is no good if you're miserable while you're eating it. I think it's half food and half everything else. Maybe food isn't even 50 percent, because so much else is really important, including certain comfort factors, which matter a lot. If it's noisy, it matters. If you're cold, it matters. If the booths are uncomfortable, it matters. Then again, sometimes it really depends. If you're at a steakhouse, the steak is probably 80 to 90 percent of it."

- *The New York Times Guide to New York Restaurants* (**Mimi Sheraton**) (1982): "Food is the primary and overwhelming factor in arriving at a rating....I would say it accounts for about 85 percent of the total rating. Cleanliness and service are also important....I place the least emphasis on decor....Price is another important factor in determining a rating. One has a right to expect certain skills and ingredients at one price that are not expected at another." *Mimi Sheraton's Favorite New York Restaurants* (1991): "One important consideration in arriving at these ratings is price; I expect more and allow less margin for error in an expensive restaurant than in one that is moderately or low-priced. Food counts for about 75 percent of my ratings, with atmosphere and service making up the rest."

- *The San Francisco Chronicle* (**Michael Bauer**): "Our job is to remain impartial, to analyze—and then ignore—any hostile feelings we might be having. We pick apart the food, the service, and the ambiance in an almost clinical way. Then we put the puzzle back together again to try to capture the mood and spirit of a restaurant."

- *The Seattle Post-Intelligencer* (**Gregory Roberts**): "As a critic, since I go back so many times and am focused on the food, I abstract that out of the experience when I'm working so everything else is relatively neutral. I tell people it's like real estate: the three most important things in a restaurant are 'the food, the food and the food.' To me, everything else is what can drag a restaurant's rating down."

- *The Wine Spectator:* "40 percent for food, 30 percent for wine, and 15 percent each for service and ambiance."

Patricia Unterman of *The San Francisco Examiner* believes certain objective standards can be used when evaluating restaurants of any kind. "I look at everything from freshness, to the handling of ingredients, to the pristine nature of what gets to the table to the clarity of the food," she says. "I'm sure that 90 percent of the people who eat out aren't even thinking about it. That's why I think one of my primary purposes is to educate, to keep telling people what is important."

Would Unterman add "authenticity" to her list of objective standards? "Yes, in some ways. If, in fact, the dish is presented as an authentic Vietnamese dish, it has to live up to a certain standard of preparation. The restaurant must use fish sauce, for example. They

TESTING A KITCHEN

What does Dennis Ray Wheaton of *Chicago* magazine like to order to test a kitchen? "More than a certain dish, I like to try different styles—to make sure I get a grilled dish, a roast dish, a sautéed dish. That way, you can tell what the different cooks inside [the kitchen] are doing—and whether they've got a really great person in the sauté station, but the grill guy can't get it [together]," says Wheaton. "And then I get variety: different fish, meat, vegetables. I often try not to get the cheapest or most expensive dishes, unless the cheapest happens to be a vegetarian dish. If there's one dish that's just way out of line in price, lobster or whatever, that doesn't seem central to the restaurant, then I'll ignore that."

Type of restaurant	Will order to test
Fine dining	consommé, organ meats (Arthur Schwartz)
	crème brulée (Penelope Corcoran)
	game birds (Arthur Schwartz)
French	escargot or paté (Penelope Corcoran)
Hong Kong-style Chinese	won ton noodle soup (Penelope Corcoran)
Mexican	tamales (Penelope Corcoran)
Steakhouse	hash browns (Ruth Reichl)
	shrimp cocktail (Ruth Reichl)
	steak (Ruth Reichl)

cannot substitute soy sauce. They have to understand the pantry and use it correctly," she says. "I think that's a problem with fusion cuisine and crossover cuisine: they are using ingredients out of context, and the result isn't as good as if you ate the real dish."

Arthur Schwartz agrees that the standard of freshness applies to all cuisines and all restaurant situations. "Why go to a place if the food is not fresh? I don't care what the cuisine is. And I would say that in most cuisines, every dish has to have a balance, some kind of harmony to it. In different cultures, the harmonies play different tunes, but the food still has harmony," he says. "And, of course, there is the level of care in cooking. You can start out with a great ingredient, but if you do not treat it with care, the result isn't as great."

Critics' Biases

Restaurant reviewers are human beings with human biases even though many try to be as objective as possible. "I like an awful lot of stuff," Dennis Ray Wheaton admits. "If you didn't, you wouldn't work in this business. You really have to at least appreciate it."

But clearly, not every critic is going to like every style of cuisine or restaurant equally well. And naturally, that is a concern to those who are affected. For example, some chefs and restaurateurs considered former *New York Times* critic Bryan Miller to have favored French restaurants during his tenure. Sensing their biases and preferences, some restaurants will actually try to cater to critics on their menus. When another New York critic was perceived as liking cheese, one Manhattan restaurant added a cheese course in the middle of being reviewed. (The tactic backfired when the server misidentified the cheeses served.) And New York cooks joke about the offal dishes they keep on their menus because critics always order them. (Arthur Schwartz admits, "I'll order it because I like having a chance to have something different!")

"I have a hard time with a few odd foods, probably because of my cultural background. I was raised in the South, and I remember watching my mother and aunt kill chickens as a kid. I don't do well eating cockscombs or things like that; I've seen too many chicken heads lying on the ground!" says Dennis Ray Wheaton. "And I'm not fond of brains. I had them recently in an Italian restaurant, and my Chinese friend appreciated them much more than I did."

Elaine Tait admits that she was never a big dessert eater. "For a lot of years, I was bored by desserts: ordinary cakes and pies and things," she remembers. "I've apologized to pastry chefs all over the place. But now, desserts are really interesting. They're creations. They're visual; they're multi-ingredient. And for a lot of people, they're a big part of their enjoyment of a meal now. So I've tried harder to write more about them and to call more attention to the pastry chefs and what they're doing."

Sometimes biases are in favor of certain foods or flavors. "I find that most of what I really like are regional American restaurants, which are very hard to find in L.A.," says Jonathan Gold. "To be obvious, places like Phillippe's, or there's a place called M&M Soul Food in Watts that's amazing and has terrific braised oxtails."

Merrill Shindler, Los Angeles restaurant critic, concedes that his favorite style of cuisine is Japanese: "On the west side of town [in Los Angeles], there is a little Japanese district called Sawtelle, with Japanese noodle places and lots of good sushi places. If I weren't writing about restaurants anymore, I would probably eat there most of the week. With Japanese food, the focus and intensity of flavor is very satisfying."

Other times, biases may be based on physiological differences in sensory perception. "One thing you learn is that some cuisines are just intrinsically more interesting than others," says Jonathan Gold. "I am definitely prejudiced against Filipino food, for example. I think [former *New York Times* restaurant critic] Raymond Sokolov put it well when he once said something like, 'Filipino cuisine is often undervalued by Westerners, usually those who can't differentiate between thirty-seven different levels of sour.' That's it!"

Ruth Reichl would agree. "I believe that we all have stronger and lesser acuities for different things," she points out. "I happen to have a greater acuity for acidity and oils. It's not a happy thing to have. I will taste a peanut that's gone bad before anyone else can taste it."

Similarly, Alison Cook, restaurant critic for *Houston Sidewalk*, has discovered over the years that she loves tart and bitter flavors more than her readers do. "I love big, exuberant flavors in general. What works for your palate just works!" she explains. "A critic can't please all palates."

But pleasing critics' palates doesn't always require big flavors or innovation. "I could be very, very impressed and write a very favorable review about a restaurant that doesn't have a single dish on its menu that you couldn't have found on a menu fifty years ago," says Gregory Roberts. "If they do a great job with steak, and if they grill fish perfectly, and their mashed potatoes are wonderful, and their service and atmosphere is up to snuff, I'll write a positive review. And I think some critics wouldn't because they're looking for the cutting edge.

"A lot of the media goes for what's hot and what's in keeping with current food trends," Roberts observes. "I think we all understand why fashion is fashion, and what that is. Fashion in clothes is all about looking different than you did before, and standing out and distinguishing yourself. But I'm not sure why food should be that way, and it does seem to be that way."

At least one longtime critic has developed a bias against restaurant fare. Arthur Schwartz admits, "After eighteen years of reviewing restaurants, I'd rather be at home. I don't appreciate restaurants the way I appreciate eating at home. I actually never wanted to be a restaurant critic. I wanted to write about cooking and food as a window into culture and as a social comment, but nobody took you seriously as a food writer if you weren't a restaurant critic."

But the vast majority of critics expressed a real passion for most of the food they encounter while eating out. "I am biased toward whatever I happen to be eating at the time," enthuses Robert Sietsema, restaurant critic for *The Village Voice*. "I try to keep as open a mind as possible, and if you asked me what is it that I hate and can't stand to eat, I would have to say boring food—like instant mashed potatoes or McDonald's. There is so much interesting food available at any price that there's no excuse to eat boring food."

Judging Ethnic Restaurants

"I've been to Portugal, West and North Africa, and I've been all over the Caribbean, but I've never been to South America or the Far East. I'd love to go to those places. But you don't really need to go out of New York City to experience the whole world. You can get it all right here," says Robert Sietsema.

"What's neat is seeing how the food changes when chefs come to the United States—both because of the ingredients available, and the way people change when they become acculturated," says Sietsema. "Context makes a big difference. Food tastes different if you're sitting in the middle of Africa than if you're sitting in an African restaurant in Harlem.

"So many people have misapprehensions about going into some of these small ethnic restaurants where the food is so cheap," Sietsema, who is recognized for his ability to discover new ethnic restaurants, says. "A lot of New Yorkers wouldn't set foot in some of those cab-driver hangouts on Lexington where the Indian food is incredible.

"I have relatively few disappointing meals. Anyone who regularly explores restaurants develops a sixth sense as to whether a place is good or not just by looking at the place, and looking at the menu, and talking to people who have eaten there. There are a million different ways to identify a good place before you go into it," says Sietsema.

How does Sietsema approach a restaurant he has never been in before? "I'll look at how full the restaurant is. And I'll look at the faces of the other diners to see if they're enjoying themselves. If they have soup dribbling down their chins, or happy smiles, that's a good sign," he says. "Sometimes you'll go into a restaurant, and everyone's looking like it's horrible, and they want to get out of there as fast as possible."

Sietsema always asks himself the same question after a meal, no matter the price. "Is it worth the money?" he says. "Sometimes it is, and often it's not. We always have to be thinking, 'I have this expense account, but would anyone else want to pay this kind of money?' It's more of a moot point when you're eating at cheap places where anyone could afford to eat. But it's up to a critic to unmask places where you eat and find that the food is horrible, and sometimes they're very expensive. The more you pay, the better it ought to be—even though I claim that for every $60 or $70 meal, you can get food just as good for $5 somewhere else in the city."

Jonathan Gold will ask himself certain questions when making his evaluation. "Are the flavors clear? Strong? Are the ingredients fresh? Is it something you want to eat? A well-cooked piece of fish is a well-cooked piece of fish, whether it's at a Cambodian restaurant or at Campanile," Gold explains. "But there's a Cambodian method of cooking fish called *hao muk* which steams the fish until it's essentially the consistency of pudding, which would obviously be a flaw if you had it someplace else. So, when you're reviewing restaurants of any kind, you've got to figure out what the restaurant is about and what the chef is trying to do—and then hold them to their own standards."

Are there any cuisines Robert Sietsema hasn't yet tried? "Yes, and there are two different categories," he explains. "Some countries don't really have their own ethnic cuisine. Some don't claim for themselves any unique dishes. There are lots of countries where the good cooking goes on at home, and there's not much of a restaurant tradition. One example of that is Puerto Rico, which has amazing food, and many, many interesting dishes, like a shrimp and rice stew, *asopao*, which is absolutely delicious, yet you can rarely get that at a restaurant. And there really are not that many Puerto Rican restaurants in the city, and there are even fewer if you go to Puerto Rico. That's just one wonderful cuisine that's hard to find. There are certain Eastern European countries, too, that don't have a dining-out tradition, like Latvia and Lithuania. The food is eaten in the home, and to go to a restaurant is considered a useless expense.

"Then there are the restaurants we don't have because the immigrants have never come here, specifically to New York. There are a lot of Pacific Rim places where they have the restaurants in California, but we don't have them here. Ditto with California, which doesn't have many African restaurants, whereas we have the world capital of West African restaurants outside of West Africa.

"I consider myself like a prosthelyte for all these different foods," says Sietsema. "Beef tongue is something that's eaten in tacos all the time, and yet many people recoil at the idea of eating beef tongue. I find it to be absolutely delightful, especially when it's stewed with chile peppers. But the idea is to give people the feeling that there are many more foods than they've ever tried, and that the world is filled with amazing and interesting foods. By eating foods from around the world, you get a much better understanding and appreciation of other cultures. You meet people on their own turf. I've never found anybody in an ethnic restaurant—even when they often don't speak English, and I don't speak their language—to be angry or mad that I came in there. They're usually very grateful that someone took an interest in them other than their fellow countrymen."

More than just readers are curious about critics' experiences at ethnic restaurants. "I was eating by myself at a Vietnamese restaurant in Monterey Park, and I was the only non-Asian in the restaurant, and probably the only non-Vietnamese," recalls Merrill Shindler. "And the people at the next table kept looking over at me until finally one of them asked, 'What are you doing here? You're not Vietnamese!' And I said, 'Well, I like Vietnamese food.' And he said, 'I never heard of a white person who liked Vietnamese food. How do you know about our food?' It was so funny. It was wonderful. Then they looked at what I was eating and said, 'You order pretty good. You know Vietnamese food pretty good.' And then they passed me something to taste from their table and said, 'Here, you should try this!'"

"I don't believe in Italian food or French food or California food. I only believe in good food and bad food."
—Sirio Maccioni,
  Le Cirque 2000

(Con)Fusion

While judging ethnic cuisine might call for one set of standards, evaluating 'new' cuisine is a different thing altogether. "When you're critiquing fusion cooking, for example, you can't go by the criteria of the cultures," says Dennis Ray Wheaton. "Once you're bringing five-spice powder into a French dish, or whatever, you have to ask yourself, 'Does it feel balanced, the elements of sweet and salt and sour and bitter?' It's got to have some kind of harmony that works for you.

"I find that a lot of soy flavors and some Japanese flavors seldom work in a Western tradition. All of a sudden you just get this wash of taste that just tastes like miscooked Japanese food," says Wheaton. "That stuff is really tricky."

Merrill Shindler finds it interesting to consider how a critic judges quality. "I don't have a clue. I don't know what water 'should' taste like, or what anything 'should' taste like," he says. "Some years ago, I was on a panel at UCLA, and someone asked us, 'How do you know if the food served at a Greek restaurant is good or not?' One of the panelists said, 'Well, I've had these dishes a hundred times before, so I know what they should taste like.' And I was flabbergasted. I would never in my life be so egotistical to say that I know what something *should* taste like!

"Indeed, the very essence of California cuisine has been taking what things taste like and turning them upside-down. If Wolfgang Puck was going to be a traditionalist, he never would have put shrimp or smoked salmon or caviar on a pizza. He'd still be making pizza with pepperoni on it. So, it's sometimes getting away from what things 'should' taste like that makes them interesting," Shindler points out.

"One of the things you'll find on menus is Caesar salad with grilled shrimp or grilled chicken. So I could get on my high horse and say, 'This is baloney. Caesar salad doesn't have either!' But you know what? Some of them taste terrific! It's a great innovation. The idea that food stopped dead someplace is ludicrous," says Shindler. "So, play with your food! Do interesting things with it! That's fine with me."

On the other hand, even restaurateurs believe that experimentation can go too far. "You can't put things together simply to shock people, like serving crème brulée with ginger," says Sirio Maccioni, the owner of Le Cirque 2000 in New York City. "You know, I hate to have an injection when I go to the dentist, so I have a dentist who takes a piece of ginger and puts it on my gums and I don't feel anything for fifteen minutes. Try putting a piece of ginger in your mouth. You'll lose all sense of taste. So, to put shredded ginger in crème brulée—I don't even want to try it!"

Chris Schlesinger, the chef-owner of the East Coast Grill in Cambridge, Massachusetts, points out that some dishes on his menu featuring unusual combinations of ingredients are often mislabeled as "fusion" experiments. "Because food writers might not have seen those ingredients together before, they automatically assume it's fusion," he says. "However, the combination of tomatoes and coconut milk and peanuts is a classic combination in northern Brazil. But how can you expect somebody to know that?"

When critics judge food, their gut reactions count. "I think there's an instinct there, when things work, and when they don't work," says William Rice. "And you don't necessarily have to be trained to get that. Sometimes doing a wine-tasting presentation for a luncheon group, instead of talking the aroma or this or that, I'll start out by saying simply, 'There are two wines in front of you. Taste them both. And now I want everybody who *feels* that wine A is more cohesive and so on to raise their hand, and then wine B.' And an astonishing percentage— just approaching it on a sensory level, and not being asked to explain or defend themselves or to use a specific language—get the 'right' answer. And for a lot of stuff, there is no 'track record,' so what else are you going to do except use visceral reaction? You can't look it up in a book!

"With fusion, which has largely meant 'Oriental/Occidental' in the past, no area in the world is going to go unmined eventually," says Rice. "And if critics aren't qualified to criticize Japanese and Norwegian food, how in the hell are they going to be capable of saying, 'I know everything there is to know about Norwegian/Japanese food'? A lot of it has to be based on your own sensibility. Hopefully, there will be an openness there and yet, at the same time, a sense when things get 'wacky' and there's too much going on.

"One of the great problems for a critic in this day and age is you go to Charlie Trotter or Norman Van Aken or any number of these chefs and the food is so complicated that I, frankly, have a hard time the next day," says Rice. "I know I liked much of it, and I know I had certain mouth experiences, but trying to reconstruct what was in a particular dish is difficult. And beyond that, if I go back to the restaurant, the dish is not on the menu any longer because the chef has moved on!"

Writing the Review

Providing a set-in-stone opinion of an ever-changing product like a restaurant provides many challenges to a reviewer, particularly given other considerations like the timing of the review, as well as the paucity of space many reviews are allocated.

"I try to wait almost three months before reviewing a restaurant, but it depends on the restaurant," says Ruth Reichl. "With Le Cirque [2000], I waited. I wanted to give them six months. They opened at an odd time, and the summer's dead, so you don't want to do a major review in the middle of July or August. It doesn't make sense because everybody's out of the city. You think a lot about holidays. One of the reasons I'm reviewing [Smith & Wollensky, to which she gave two stars] is because the four other places I was planning to do are not going to be very positive reviews, and you don't want a real bummer to come out the day before Christmas! It just doesn't seem right."

Encapsulating the experience while conveying basic information also involves a careful balance. "People want to know, 'What is it like?' 'Is it worth the money?' 'Am I going to be welcomed, or am I going to have a struggle?' 'How does it feel?' 'Do I really have to get dressed?' Is the service fast or slow? Is the kitchen is impossible? But there's only so much space [in my column]," says Gael Greene.

In deciding what to convey in the space they're allotted, some critics put a premium on "translating" the restaurant experience for readers. "I always try to put the restaurant in perspective, giving an idea of what this developed out of in New York City or what the actual food is like in its home country," says David Rosengarten. "When I reviewed the Moroccan restaurant Lotfi's, I talked a little bit about Morrocan food in general, and I put it against that Moroccan context. I've reviewed Limoncello and discussed the state of pasta eating in New York and why it's so bad and so inauthentic. I like to gently give my views of what the standards are and then judge the restaurant against that backdrop. Now when you've got people who are acclaimed restaurant critics, and they don't know what the standards are or they have wrong information about it—that's scary. It's a wonderful moment in the history of American gastronomy for people to learn a lot and to jump levels ahead in their knowledge, but if the people that they trust are telling them the wrong things, that can't happen."

The Medium Is the Message

In addition to a publication's determining a critic's power through its circulation, its target audience and frequency will determine the restaurants selected for review, not to mention the tone the criticism will take. "I think that a monthly magazine and a newspaper have different functions in writing about restaurants," explains Caroline Bates, the California critic for *Gourmet*. "I think it's almost an obligation for a newspaper to report on everything that's happening in their particular city or area—or to do the best they can to give a relative idea about what is good, and maybe even help a place. The downside of newspapers is that they tend to report on it as a 'new' event, after the restaurant is open a month, and most restaurants can't get it all together for several months. Yet the restaurant wants the publicity, too, I'm sure; they don't want to wait six months before they're reviewed. And I think that's a difficult call for a critic on a newspaper.

"At a monthly magazine—like *Gourmet*, and I assume others—we have such a long lead time that we can't be bringing the news to readers in the same way," says Bates. "So I don't think there's any point in writing about something that is not good or that hasn't shown that it's a place that people may enjoy."

Critics take their magazines' distinct readerships into consideration in a number of ways. "Among the magazines I write for is *Esquire*," says John Mariani. "The *Esquire* reader is a male, thirty-five to forty-five. He's a guy who's not consumed or obsessed by food, but he travels a lot and wants to know what's new. He needs some advice on tipping or how to bone a fish. That's the *Esquire* man.

The New York Times Star System

★★★★: Extraordinary
★★★: Excellent
★★: Very Good
★: Good
[0 stars]: Poor or Fair

When I took the job [as restaurant critic at *The New York Times*], I told them that I was profoundly uncomfortable with [awarding stars]. I'd never given any kind of stars before. And I have always gone out of my way to say, "I don't know if this is right or wrong, but this is my opinion." I've always tried to inject the personal into [my reviews] for that reason. It's why I object to the *Zagat* reviews, because there is no person. I want to know the person who is passing on this opinion, so it's not an Olympian viewpoint. When push came to shove, I was told, "You have to give stars." So I do my best.

I know what a four-star restaurant is: it's perfect. It's very high-end, a special occasion restaurant. That's easy. And I've worked out for myself what a three-star restaurant is, which is either a failed four-star restaurant or it's one that is perfect in its class but not trying to be the place to go for your fiftieth anniversary—like **Bouley Bakery** or **Honmura-An** or any place that really does an extraordinarily good job without pretension.

I have no problem with those two [four- and three-star ratings]. But below that, I just sort of muddle it out. I usually don't know until I'm done writing what I'm going to do. Some time in the course of the writing, it makes itself apparent.

Basically, you have four [starred] categories, and then nothing. So you've got five [ratings], which is not very much to pigeon-hole thousands of restaurants into. And it seems to be a disservice to the restaurants to even try. We don't do it for movies or theater or anything else. People make up their own minds.

An alternative could be just having four-star restaurants. Or, for a handful of restaurants, for the grand special occasion, you could give a star to those five or six places you'd want to go to. So you wouldn't get rid of the cachet of the star,

"Stars put too much value on 'fine dining'—and don't always signify the 'best' restaurants. Star systems tend to value service and decor."
—Alison Cook,
   Houston Sidewalk

"*The Wine Spectator* reader is obsessed with wine. He is crazy about wine and obviously loves food in good restaurants so, consequently, if there's not a great wine cellar there, I'm not going to write about it. *The Wine Spectator* gives awards to thoroughly meretricious restaurants, but it's not for the food. It's simply for the wine list," he says. "I'm not going to write about a crappy restaurant with a great wine list, but if I do want to write about a good restaurant, it's got to have a significant wine list. It doesn't have to be huge, but it has to be significant in the sense that it's part of the story.

"For *Diversion*, a magazine for 'doctors at leisure,' I assume that, despite their moaning about making less money than ever because of the HMOs, doctors have a lot more money to throw around than most of my other readers," says Mariani. "They're probably better-traveled and can afford to go anywhere, so I take that into consideration.

but you'd get rid of that whole muddled middle. Everybody was horrified when I gave **Honmura-An**, which is a fairly perfect restaurant within its own aspirations, three stars. Basically, I think you have to judge restaurants on what they're trying to do, and whether they succeed or not. This means that it's possible to have a four-star hot-dog stand—which I believe is the case, but not within this system. In the system that *The New York Times* has set up, you couldn't.

To me, Honmura-An really did what it tried to do pretty perfectly, and I would have given it four stars, but it didn't quite fit into their system. I mean, I could have done it, but I don't feel that this system is mine. I came into a continuum, and I'm just the person occupying the seat for a little while. Any institution is much bigger than I am. For Honmura-An to merit four stars under this system, it would have to be much grander. It's a second-floor walk-up, so it would have to have an elevator. Its aspirations would have to change.

A more interesting distinction is that between a two- and a three-star restaurant versus a three- and a four-star. I wish I had a clearer answer. [Former *New York Times* critic] Mimi Sheraton was much more didactic than I am, and much more sure of herself. I don't have an innate sense of rightness about it. I often go hoping it's going to be a three-star restaurant, and then a number of things go wrong, and I just can't.

On other occasions I've refrained from giving a restaurant three stars because I thought that it would send people in with such a chip on their shoulders that it would ultimately be very difficult for the restaurant. I worried that people who always rush to three-star restaurants would go into some wonderful little place and just hate everything about it. So I'm very cautious about giving that [rating].

For example, I really loved **Union Pacific**. But it's just not ready for it. They need the time. It will be a three-star restaurant, I think—possibly four stars. But it's just too young; it couldn't handle it right now. They're much better off having customers come in and say, "She wrote a three-star review, but only gave it two stars." That way, they come in on the side of the restaurant, as opposed to coming in and saying, "Oh, she gave it three stars, and they can't get the food out of the kitchen."

The period right after a review is always a hard time for a restaurant anyway. You don't have to think about this when you're a restaurant critic at *New West*, but you really have to think about when you're the restaurant critic at *The New York Times*. It carries with it so much weight that you have to be responsible in thinking about what the impact on the restaurant is going to be. That's something an art critic doesn't have to think about.

Although I review the best hamburger joints in America for *Diversion*, I'm more likely to do something on fine dining."

The Star System

Summing up one's evaluation of a restaurant in stars, or any symbol, can be daunting. Assigning a set rating to a constantly changing experience "is like trying to pin a butterfly down," Corby Kummer, the restaurant critic for *Boston* magazine, once observed. Not a single critic sang unreserved praises for the star system.

"I do have mixed feelings about it," says Patricia Unterman. "I'm 99 percent food-sensitive. If I eat a perfect taco someplace, I'll just want to give that the highest rating. But then, of course, other people think, 'Oh, a three- or four-star restaurant' and find it's a little shack, so they think, 'This woman is nuts!' Because there's that division between what's perceived as a four-star system and what's perceived by the public. Our star system here has been influenced by the Michelin system, which I think really codified what that meant.

"I always say, 'This is the most perfect Chinese noodle house. It's really perfect, and it's getting three stars.' It may be a dump, but I don't care. The way most people do it now is to divide stars for food and service, and just give an overall rating. There are so many of these complex systems. I just give stars for food, and then there's a box at the beginning that always mentions ambiance, so people aren't caught unaware," says Unterman.

Dennis Ray Wheaton admits, "We'll often wait a little while before we list the star rating [in *Chicago* magazine] to see what effect the magazine's [non-starred] review has on the restaurant. Some restaurants can't handle the wave that's coming in. They know right before the review comes out that it's coming out because of the fact-checking done. We'll keep an eye on the restaurant, and maybe go back and check it again in a while to see whether they've been able to handle the business and that the chef hasn't left. We're generally cautious before we finally list our rating."

When Tom Sietsema launched *Washington Sidewalk*'s restaurant area on the Internet, he saw the awarding of stars as a way to make *Sidewalk*'s reviews stand out from those of other Washington, DC, media. "*The Washington Post* and *Washingtonian* magazine—both of which are forceful presences here in town—do not use stars, so I thought we could distinguish ourselves in that way," he says.

"I think the market almost demands [stars]. I also think that stars force a writer to be more honest. You cannot waffle. You have to come down: Is it two or three stars? You can't hide behind anything. And while you do have people who just look at the stars and probably won't read the text, it does give weight and significance to a review when you use stars," says Sietsema.

How do reviewers arrive at their star ratings? "I kind of imagine myself at a party, and having someone ask, 'Oh, you've been to that new restaurant. How was it?'" says Gregory Roberts. "And what you'll want to say in response represents the rating. Here, four stars is 'It's exceptional.' Three stars is 'excellent,' two stars is 'good,' and one star, 'fair'."

Starless Reviews

Why do some critics not award stars? How do they perceive the star system and its power? Are they freed or hindered by not using them?

The Los Angeles Times doesn't award stars, for restaurants or movies. "Not for anything—the philosophy is that people should read the review," says S. Irene Virbila. "And restaurants are so volatile. I might go one week, and the chef might leave three weeks later, and those stars will stick until I get around to going there again, so it can be very misleading. If it was a different world, it would be great to have stars, but nothing is stable."

"I've always avoided giving stars," says Jonathan Gold. "I like to set places in their cultural context. The idea of saying one cultural context is greater than another one is inherent in the star system. The entire point of it is not just to say that one bite of food is 'better' than another bite of food, but that one context—specifically, almost always, a luxury context—is better than another one. It seems wrong."

"I hate stars," says Robert Sietsema. "They're stupid. To begin with, you would need a lot more of them to characterize a restaurant, so they're useless. Reading a review is, first of all, a practical experience and, second of all, a literary one. You first read it, and you get information you need about the restaurant and decide if you want to go there. Stars are not enough to evaluate whether a restaurant is good or not. All they can do is generate a frenzy among people who don't care what the food tastes like anyway."

"The only time that I've ever used ratings is when I did either a steak piece, where everybody got bulls' horns, or my favorite French restaurants, where everyone got mouths, signifying contentment—where things were easily comparable. And even then, I was never able to just give three; I had to give 2 1/2, and 3 1/2. So I'm glad that in the beginning Clay [Felker, *New York*'s editor] did not ask for stars," says Gael Greene. "I thought that, number one, it is very hard to award stars and, number two, people were going to have to read it! But, of course, they don't always; they read the first paragraph, or the last paragraph. Or they read the blurbs. But I felt that I could give a subjective picture of a restaurant and tell people more about it, so that they're not just judging whether it's good or bad, but whether it's for them.

"The other side of it is that it's easier for people to talk about restaurants in terms of stars," says Greene. "Even *New York* magazine will sometimes write, 'Such-and-such is a four-star restaurant,' and I will say, 'Well, who said so?' I think we should not be referring to other publications' ratings. But it's a shortcut, and it's very useful."

Phyllis Richman has never awarded stars at *The Washington Post*. "My predecessor had a star system, but I just refused to do it," says Richman. "And I had a real fight on my hands. It took a while for the *Post* management and the readers to get used to not having stars. In fact, a few years ago, I was planning to do a dining book for the *Post*, and I brought up the subject of stars. I said that if we were going to award them in the book, we also should do it in the column, and the editor didn't want stars in the column. So I was relieved to find that it had really taken hold.

"There are some places in the world where you could fairly award stars," says Richman. "If you're doing French restaurants in France, they're sufficiently along one continuum that you could reasonably use the star system. We have such a variety of restaurants, and types of restaurants, and purposes of restaurants, that there's no way to fairly compare a pizza parlor with a grand Scandinavian smorgasbord. There are too many dimensions. Secondly, when you give stars, people tend to just look at the stars and read the three- and four-star reviews and skip the others.

"I think every star system is unfair," Richman asserts. "Some are more unfair than others. I think that Ruth Reichl does it about as well as you can do it because almost all the restaurants get two stars. There has to be some really strong reason for a restaurant to get three stars, and some outrageously extraordinary reasons for it to get four stars. Generally, the star system begins to cheapen as you tend to give more and more restaurants higher ratings. So, unless you start out very tough, you could wind up with everything decent being at the top of the heap.

"[With the star system,] you can't transmit enough information. It's a very fine measure for very crude material, so it's bound to be misleading. You can't transmit in that symbol that 'Here is a terrible restaurant that happens to have one great dish' or 'Here is a restaurant that is pretty good, but it's inconsistent.' And how do you compare that with a restaurant that is sometimes wonderful and sometimes terrible? Or how do you compare the food at a hole-in-the-wall Thai restaurant with the food at Jean-Louis? The star system often ends up reflecting price, unfairly, and tends to favor European restaurants. There are a thousand things rolled into it," she says.

"I've tried for years to come up with something that I would consider useful symbols—something that indicated how far it would be worth travelling for this restaurant, or for whom it would be a good restaurant," says Richman. "I've spent many hours in the middle of the night trying to devise this system, but I haven't come up with any that I think is useful. I'm always playing with, 'How would I rate these on some continuum?' or doing concentric circles. But all of them are just minimally useful."

Alternative Star Systems

Some publications and critics have created systems that try to take a restaurant's intentions into consideration. For example, *The Detroit Free Press* has a unique method of awarding its stars. "We go by what the restaurant sets out as its goal," explains Patty LaNoue Stearns.

> *"You should be able to have a four-star pizzeria, if it is great —you can explain that it is a pizzeria."*
> —Sirio Maccioni,
>   Le Cirque 2000

"It's another difficulty for me, because I have no idea what their goal is. You have to go in several times and figure out what market they're aiming at, what they're trying to hit, and judge it based on how well they do that. At first, it was kind of difficult, but now I've gotten into the groove. It's pretty rare that I would give a one-star review—unless I got food poisoning or something."

Those traveling to Detroit should keep this in mind—while a one-star review from *The Detroit Free Press* is a definite tip-off to stay away, a one-star review from *The New York Times* might in fact steer you toward a charming, though unpretentious, restaurant in Manhattan. "It's a very oddball rating system," admits Stearns. "But that's the way we do it at the *Free Press,* which actually uses a four-star system for all of its reviews, including movies, theater, symphony, and restaurants. This was established a couple of years before I took over. It caused a lot of pain at first because writers like to sit on the fence."

In addition, restaurants are not awarded stars "on a curve," but rather on the basis of how well each achieves what it set out to do. "You might walk into a four-star Middle Eastern restaurant and find counter-top dining, yet wonderful, fresh Middle Eastern food and wonderful service," Stearns explains. While other major American cities might have only a handful of four-star restaurants, Detroit under this system has "dozens," according to Stearns. "Some four-star restaurants are extremely special, like Tribute and The Lark, but because of our system, they have the same ranking as the Kabob Village."

Penelope Corcoran was able to develop her own rating system when she joined *The Arizona Republic*. "When I came to the paper, they did operate on a star system, which I changed to forks to make a break from the previous restaurant critic. I just didn't want it to be stars. Stars are *The New York Times*," says Corcoran. "And I wanted it to be three gradings: food, service, and atmosphere. I did it for the reader because everybody has different criteria for choosing a restaurant. Some people are totally into atmosphere. Some just want great service—and if the food is good, fine. But for some people food is the most important thing, and they will forgive a lot else.

"Within this criteria, there is some flexibility. Even though food is the most important thing to me, if service is truly awful, I'm not going to recommend the restaurant," points out Corcoran. "A place could have great food and absolutely horrible service, and it would be a negative review—or at least I would skew the review to writing about the service because people need to be informed of that."

The Chicago Tribune employs a dual-rating system. "Phil Vettel's reviews are stars, and the 'Cheap Eats' reviews are forks," says William Rice. "That may be too subtle for some people, but there's meant to be a distinction there.

"How does one review the storefront restaurant one week and the palace of gastronomy the next week, and somehow come up with star ratings for both? The answer is that it couldn't possibly be done except on a wildly subjective scale," admits Rice. "There is no objective scale of criteria you click off that would allow the storefront restaurant to emerge with a high rating."

	Chanterelle	Restaurant Daniel	Jean Georges	Le Bernardin	Le Cirque 2000	Lespinasse
Excellent Service	"…[T]he perfection of the service." "It is the service that gives the restaurant its reverent quality."	"The service that night was smooth and sweet…. It was formal, thoughtful, and not at all stuffy."	"Extremely professional staff….All over the room, waiters [are] intent on nothing more than their guests' pleasure."	"When you reserve a table at Le Bernardin, you can count on being seated promptly [and] served beautifully…."	"Each time, the staff has been too nice."	"The service makes you feel that you belong there."
Simplicity	"[David Waltuck's] hallmark is a kind of serious simplicity."	"The simple luxury of a large yellow potato mashed with lots of butter and fresh truffles."	"He introduced simplicity to four-star cooking…. His food continues to be essentially simple…"	"This superbly simple dish is fresh and vibrant." "Halibut is simply poached…."	"It is subtle, but brilliant." "It is not the sort of dish that makes a chef famous, but it makes me very, very happy."	"Mr. Kunz is even inspired by simple bistro dishes."
A Point of View	"Mr. Waltuck… seems to cook to an inner tune."	"Daniel Boulud… seems to be cooking for himself."	"Mr. Vongerichten… has found a new, earthier direction."	"The key to Le Bernardin's food has always been that it allows each fish to express its personality."	"Although [chef Sottha] Khunn does not show off; his food quietly makes a statement."	"Gray Kunz is ahead of the curve."
A Surprise!	"Who else would pair oysters with sauerkraut?"	"The soup is…so expressive of lobster that if you close your eyes and take a bite you are surprised to find your mouth filled with liquid."	"The surprises do not end with dessert…. An enticing rhubarb tart astonishes you with a garnish of candied celery."	"Each dish offers its own surprise."	"When he sets gossamer slices of tuna atop a plate of pasta puttanesca, it is so right it takes me a moment to realize that it is utterly original."	"Nothing at Lespinasse ever tastes the way you expect. It is a surprise to dip your spoon into this mild-mannered soup and experience an explosion of flavor."

	Chanterelle	Restaurant Daniel	Jean Georges	Le Bernardin	Le Cirque 2000	Lespinasse
Confidence	"Mr. Waltuck is not a show-off chef, but he has extraordinary confidence."	"Daniel Boulud…is working with a new confidence."	"In his quiet way, Jean-Georges Vongerichten is creating a restaurant revolution."	"Mr. Ripert seems to be having wonderful fun in the kitchen."	"The food is not flashy, but it is astonishingly good."	"Mr. Kunz uses these herbs and spices with extraordinary confidence."
A Grand Finale	"For a finale, bite-sized eclairs are passed around the table."	"[We] were charmed by the finale, a plate of petit fours…."	"Before he sends you out the door, he showers you with chocolate, macaroons, homemade marshmallows, and candied rose petals."	"Desserts, for the most part, are light and dreamy."	"The pastry chef, Jacques Torres, is a technical wizard….His desserts are too perfect; even his souffles don't fall."	"Even the petits fours are exotic."
P.S. It doesn't hurt to have beautiful flowers…	"The flowers are gorgeous."	"The flowers were fabulous."		"Flowers are everywhere."		

Four

The Evolving Definition of "A Great Restaurant"

FOOD

"Stock is everything in cooking....Without it, nothing can be done."
—Auguste Escoffier (1846–1935)

"[My cooking] is not about complicated sauces. My style of cooking involves combining ingredients that harmonize because of their quality, freshness, aroma, and flavor."
—Alice Waters, Chez Panisse

"To replace traditional basics of French cooking (such as time-consuming stocks and butter-thick sauces), I use building blocks: juices, vinaigrettes, flavored oils, and broths. With these building blocks, everything can be prepared with a thrillingly fresh point of view."
—Jean-Georges Vongerichten, Jean Georges

AMBIANCE

"If the divine creator has taken pains to give us delicious and exquisite things to eat, the least we can do is to serve them with ceremony."
—Fernand Point, La Pyramide (1897–1955)

"For our British designer Joyce Evans, fantasy is what life is all about."
—Patrick O'Connell, The Inn at Little Washington

"I am here to create new sensations in the dining room, on the table settings, and in the food."
—Gray Kunz, Lespinasse

SERVICE

"The customer is king."
—Hotelier César Ritz (1850–1918)

"The customer is usually right."
—A six-foot tall statue of a chef holds this sign in the lobby of Richard Melman's Lettuce Entertain You offices, Chicago

"We put our guests second."
—Danny Meyer, Union Square Café and Gramercy Tavern, and winner of the first James Beard Award for Outstanding Service

It's clear that what defines aspects of excellence in dining—from food, to service, to ambiance—has changed over the years in the minds of some of its most respected practitioners. So have opinions regarding the best way to achieve excellence. In the preceding chapter, restaurant critics spell out how they make their judgments about an establishment. However, chefs and restaurateurs themselves often have very different ways of approaching what they do. Indeed, restaurants have evolved to a point where some

exist for reasons other than turning the highest profit or pleasing every customer who walks through the door.

The whole intention behind certain restaurants is often greater than the sum of the parts being divvied up in restaurant reviews. In light of this, a review system that has its roots in the European *Michelin* system for rating primarily French restaurants on certain standards seems sorely obsolete when applied to the contemporary American restaurant scene. While restaurants are frequently evaluated on a similar four-star scale in the United States, the restaurants being compared to one another might differ not only on their quantitative rankings on food, ambiance, and service, but also in important qualitative ways that currently escape quantification.

An increase in stars has historically been associated with a correspondingly high level of complexity (food), formality (service), and opulence (ambiance). The stories of restaurants' efforts to achieve a greater number of stars seem tied mostly to improving a restaurant's luxury trappings. For example, the compelling book *Burgundy Stars* by William Echikson tells the tale of chef-owner Bernard Loiseau's efforts, including taking out a $3 million expansion loan and sprucing up his dining room at La Côte d'Or in Saulieu, France, to earn his third Michelin star and the associated financial rewards.

The situation wasn't so different in the United States. "I think that the United States, for a long time, looked at food experiences through a Francocentric point of view," points out Chris Schlesinger, chef-owner of the East Coast Grill in Cambridge, Massachusetts. "People thought that the best restaurants in town were the ones with the tuxedoed waiters, the kind of places where your parents might get corrected if they tried to pronounce a word and got it wrong."

Yet some of America's best chefs clearly aren't playing that game. It is more a quest for perfection than profits that motivates them. Look at the chefs who have received the James Beard Foundation's highest honor as Chef of the Year: Rick Bayless (1995), Daniel Boulud (1994), Larry Forgione (1993-tie), Thomas Keller (1997), Jean-Louis Palladin (1993-tie), Wolfgang Puck (1991), Jeremiah Tower (1996), and Alice Waters (1992). Palladin's now-shuttered Jean-Louis at the Watergate is the only one of these chefs' restaurants that could have been described as opulent. The others head restaurants whose dining rooms are certainly attractive, but where the primary emphasis is almost always on the food.

Since, after many years, diners have come to associate certain star ratings with certain levels of luxury, the star rating system does not appear to have kept pace with measuring a restaurant's excellence, given the changing intentions of the new breed of chef-restaurateurs who now serve as their driving forces. These chefs' drives for excellence might lead them to make very different decisions regarding where to invest in their restaurants' development. They are more likely to procure ever-better ingredients for their kitchens than to upgrade the china in their dining rooms.

In addition, the implication for critics' readers has been that an "objective" set of standards with which to judge a restaurant exists. This might have once been the case, such as in the days when fine restaurants were all expected to serve the same classic French dishes. But today, restaurants run the gamut—and, in reality, a critic's judgment cannot be anything but subjective.

Restaurants' Intentions

Certainly, restaurant reviewers understand that restaurants exist for different reasons. In general, however, they appear more adept at categorizing establishments from the point of view of the consumer, as

"The old variety of chefs used to be blue-collar, working-class kids coming up in the apprentice system. They're now much more sophisticated, and they have much better backgrounds. They can think in abstract ways, much more than just with their hands and mouths. A lot of them can sit down and think of these things in pencil-and-paper ways. With the increasing celebrity of chefs, there's been tremendous change."
—Dennis Ray Wheaton,
  Chicago

Restaurant criticism evolved into largely a consumer advocate orientation. Newspapers seemed to take the position, "If our readers patronize this restaurant, will they have a good experience that's worth the money charged for it?" Because this implies a personal judgment, what's "worth it" to one customer might not be "worth it" to another customer, let alone a reviewer.

"So much of this is perception," admits John Mariani of *Esquire*, of evaluating a restaurant. Some leading chef-restaurateurs agree:

"What is the nicest color, blue or red? Blue is not nicer than red, but you may prefer it. The same thing is true with restaurants. A critic may simply like one more than another, for no real reason, and give three stars to one and only two stars to another on that basis. And that's not right."
—André Soltner, former chef-owner, Lutèce, New York City

"I think what is good is kind of open to question, but what is bad is known. So, whether this is a really good Cambodian pickled pig's ear as opposed to one that is second rate is a matter of opinion. But if it's a really bad one that's spoiled, that's easy."
—Mark Peel, chef–co-owner, Campanile, Los Angeles

"The attitude of too many critics seems to be, 'We've got the answer, and here it is! Three stars, one star, no stars!' And with the variety of cuisines being reviewed, I wonder, how are they going to know all of these different things? I feel that readers should just understand that a reviewer is a person with an opinion—and hopefully with a background of enough depth to have the right to espouse that opinion—but still it is only one opinion."
—Norman Van Aken, chef-owner, Norman's, Coral Gables, Florida

"To judge a bouillabaisse *is to have eaten a* bouillabaisse. *To judge any dish, you need to know the origins and essence of the dish: what it should be and what it should taste like in its truest form."*
—Bradley Ogden, chef-owner, Lark Creek Inn, Larkspur, California

"Chez Panisse is a very good restaurant, but it tends to be situationally set up for such great expectations that most people do not think it's a very good restaurant. They walk in, and there's no reception, no bar, no fancy dining room, no choices, and hardly any good service. And they confuse eating great food with the rest of the dining experience. Some people say, 'Oh, I went to the restaurant, and I was very disappointed.' And I'm sure that they've had good food, but the point is that it's not a bad restaurant."
—Mark Miller, chef-owner, Red Sage, Washington, DC

evidenced in their basing their ratings primarily on food, service, and ambiance. "We have two separate elements in restaurant dining right now," explains Elaine Tait, restaurant critic for *The Philadelphia Inquirer*. "The first is the 'I'm going to go there because it's fast, easy, and it doesn't cost me too much, and I don't feel like cooking or I don't know how' restaurant. The other is the 'I'm going there because I'm bored and let's see what they can do to amuse me with food' restaurant."

How do leading American chefs and restaurateurs, on the other hand, classify the variety of intentions behind their restaurants?

"It is my mandate that diners have what I hope to be some of the most serious food in the world, in an atmosphere where they don't feel embarrassed to roll up their sleeves to eat. I think being a chef-restaurateur puts me into a different perspective than that of a chef," says Norman Van Aken, chef-owner of Norman's in Coral Gables, Florida. "It's the sense of both freedom and responsibility as 'Siamese twins.' Yes, you are absolutely free: no one can tell you what to put on your menu or your wine list, or what your waiters should wear. But it also becomes your responsibility to stay in business, and to create experiences that make people want to come back again and again and again.

"Each person's experience is different because each person has his own reality, values, and worth," he explains. "Norman's will never be a restaurant for 'the whole family' where everyone from grandma to a five-year-old can expect to get food that is going to be 'safe.' That's not my mandate. You can't be all things to all people. So if you're continually try to figure out what customers want, you're just dancing with a phantom. Because customers are constantly morphing, you have to figure out who *you* are and what *you* want, from your toes to the top of your head."

Daniel Boulud, chef-owner of Restaurant Daniel in New York City, agrees. "I am sensitive to the opinion of a customer, but I still believe that the only experience you can really give to your customer has to be your own feeling and your own expression," he says.

Rick Bayless's career evolved out of a love for a particular country and its cuisine. "I needed to put together what I knew about great cooking and about Mexico, and out of that could come something that would give Mexican cooking the respect it deserves," says Bayless, chef-

"What accounts for the quality of our food is that I didn't come up through the ranks. I didn't start cooking in Mexican restaurants and say, 'Hey, I can do this better.' I learned about food, good food, all kinds of good food. I don't think you can be any better at all than what you know about food."
—Rick Bayless,
Frontera Grill and
Topolobampo

owner of Frontera Grill and Topolobampo in Chicago. "In the United States, it's clearly not represented very well. Mexico does not have a restaurant culture. The restaurants there often serve, for want of a better word, 'tired' food, made haphazardly, in large quantities. No one expects any more than that in Mexico, and they don't go out for a good meal. So, if you're going to present Mexican cuisine in a fine dining environment, you have to figure it out from another perspective. You have to look at the integrity that is on the plate in Mexico, and translate that to what you know about restaurants in the United States. That's what we do in our restaurant.

"Even though I'm a real traditionalist, people laugh at what I do in Mexico sometimes," Bayless admits. "They'll say, 'You can't serve that *mole* with lobster. It's always with pork.' But it's delicious with lobster, and since I wasn't raised in that thinking, I come at it with a different perspective."

Norman Van Aken credits Alice Waters and Jeremiah Tower's regional menus at Chez Panisse as important influences on his cuisine. "It gave me positive reinforcement about the idea of distinguishing my cuisine by doing a regional American approach emanating out of south Florida," he says. "And I felt, 'This is really where I need to go.' When I moved back to Florida in 1985, I started to prune out all the other influences on my cooking. Before that, I might have loved to do a Greek menu or a Provençal menu, but I had to stop myself and say, 'Wait a minute. My job is to find out more about the flavors that are here, and mother countries that helped propel them to be here.' So I started reading more consciously about Spanish, Caribbean, and Catalonian food in an effort to school myself because there was almost no written history—especially in comparison to the volumes written on French, Italian, and Asian cuisine.

"There is, on top of the menu [at Norman's], a line that says, 'If the map of the world were a tablecloth and I could choose any place at that table, I would sit at the southern tip of Florida, at the nexus of North America and the Caribbean. My plate would touch Cuba, the Florida Keys, the Yucatan, the West Indies, the Bahamas, and South America.' That's my mission statement, in a sense," Van Aken explains.

Gray Kunz, executive chef of Lespinasse in New York City, finds his cooking has evolved through minimizing the number of ingredients in a dish. "And I give them a twist with spices. It doesn't diminish the cooking, but it makes the dish more approachable," says Kunz. "Today it's not the number of ingredients you put on the plate, but the *quality* of ingredients you put on the plate that counts."

Quality of Ingredients

As chefs continually strive to improve their very different cuisines, they all realize a common truth: the quality of their food is dependent upon the quality of the ingredients they use. As Rick Bayless emphasizes, "I certainly don't think that you can be any better than your ingredients."

Daniel Boulud agrees. "Every day we try to search for extremely good ingredients and good flavors. We always strive to bring some excitement to the customer," says Boulud. "The drive is different today because chefs are restaurateurs, whereas before more restaurateurs didn't have such a dedication to food. The front of the house used to sort of hold a place together, but now it's the back of the house. It's a big difference because nobody is more dedicated to food than the people who cook it."

Leading chefs' dedication is evidenced by their concern about ingredients—starting with how they're produced. "There's a lot that goes into the creation of a dish, and it begins in the ground," attests Alice Waters, chef-owner of Chez Panisse in Berkeley. "First of all, it's what variety of vegetable you're going to be planting, or what strain of chicken you're going to be raising. Then it's how you're going to be doing this, hopefully without herbicides and pesticides and in a way that naturally fertilizes the plants or feeds the animals. It's when this is being picked, and then, ultimately, how quickly that gets to

the table because, for me, food is about aliveness. *Cooking* is a very small part of it."

Chefs' Relations with Farmers and Purveyors

Chefs' concerns about obtaining the highest possible quality have naturally led them to get to know and subsequently develop relationships with various farmers and purveyors. "We would not put certain things on our menu unless we thought that they were really, really great," says George Germon, chef–co-owner of Al Forno and Provincia in Providence, Rhode Island. "We boycotted fish for years. We simply wouldn't put it on the menu. And we've talked to the media about our belief that the industry has got to change somehow. Here we are, living in the Ocean State, and we couldn't get a fresh piece of fish!"

Germon's partner Johanne Killeen remembers, "A fish supplier from New Bedford came in years ago and said, 'Well, you know, fish really isn't at its best when it's right out of the water.' And we kept saying, 'Come on! In Italy and France and Asia, we've watched them take

it out of the water and cook it on the spot.' And he said, 'Well, I'm telling you, the texture is different.' And when we started dealing with live fish, a lot of those words starting ringing true with us. The texture *was* different. And it was a hard sell to our customers."

"So, we started researching, Why is the fish different? Why is it softer? Why doesn't it flake off the bone?" says Germon. "And we found out that it had to go through *rigor mortis*. Then, we had to find out from our Asian friends how it goes through *rigor mortis*,

RESTAURANT CRITICS' CHIEF BEEFS REGARDING FOOD

- **There can be an enormous difference when the chef's not in**. When I review, I try to make sure that the chefs are actually going to be there, just to give them the best chance. But you can't imagine how often the chef is *not* there. I have to figure that on Monday and Tuesday [chefs' most frequent nights off], no chef is in the kitchen. And I'm flabbergasted that sometimes I'll call a restaurant two weeks after it opens, and the chef is out of town or on vacation already!

- **Oversalting food is a big problem.** Even if chefs aren't cooking, they're tasting sauces, but I find so many times that sauces are over-reduced and salty. This often happens when nobody is paying attention or monitoring that.

- **Desserts can be too cloying.** I've heard that the Los Angeles palate is much sweeter than the San Francisco palate, and that dessert chefs always adjust their recipes. But you should be able to taste something other than the sugar. I think this is very clear when you go to Vienna and taste Austrian pastries, which are undersweetened compared to French or Italian desserts. The best dessert chef we have in Los Angeles is Nancy Silverton, and Campanile has very understated desserts. In fact, they're so understated that a lot of people probably don't realize how good they are. It's not like there are ten pastry chefs out there imitating her. They're not imitating her at all, which I find interesting.

- I think food should look beautiful and appetizing, but I see a lot of very **unappetizing looking food** in the attempt to make it showy. I'm beginning to have a lot of trouble with all this food molded in PVC tubes: sometimes it looks like somebody's *Popular Science* project, or somebody's gone crazy in an arts and crafts store. "Let's put this here, and we'll have this shooting out here." It's all about the mechanics and the startling effects, but it should also have a taste that makes sense.

- Free-spirited **creativity** has a lot of advantages; it's just that it often goes too far. This is a particular problem in high-priced restaurants where diners shouldn't have to pay for amateurish experiments. I'm cautious whenever the description of a dish runs to two lines.

- I feel that you can play with cuisines, but it can be a problem with some young cooks who **don't know what the real dish is before they start elaborating**. It really bothers me when people take names like "aioli" and apply it to different things. You have to interrogate the waiter sometimes: "How exactly is this made?"

"I didn't know that by finding the people who were growing those things or were catching those fish that I would become connected in a much deeper way with people, with my community. That was a revelation. I had people I could count on, and they could count on me. I spent more time with friends, and around the table, and all of these things that I had wanted came because I was looking for real food."
—Alice Waters,
   Chez Panisse

and how it could happen more quickly. So, it was a great education. And [our fish supplier] Foley had a lot to do with that. He opened our eyes to what fish is all about."

Charlie Palmer is also committed to freshness. "I have a diver, Chris, off Long Island now who gets my oysters for me," chuckles Palmer, chef-owner of Aureole in New York City. "He calls me from his cell phone: 'I just caught two bass!' I tell him, 'Look, Chris, don't even call, just bring it. Whatever it is, I'll buy it.' He's the kind of guy who gets a kick out of putting the stuff in his car and getting it to New York while the fish still has *rigor mortis*. He's a nut. But there are literally hundreds of these people, and they need to have our support; they're doing something special, and they have to make a living somehow."

This mutual dependence has forged strong bonds. "We have a trust with the farmers, and for us that is the most sacred thing," says Daniel Boulud. "The person who grows the tomatoes will bring us about twenty different kinds during the summer. We know that we can trust him for the quality. We ask for the best, and we want to make sure that they can provide us with the best, so if they are 15 cents more or a dollar more than somebody else, we will agree to that as long as we get the stuff right. But we will not agree to be overcharged for something of a lesser quality."

The concern for quality and having the greatest amount of control over their ingredients has also led some chefs to grow their own. "We

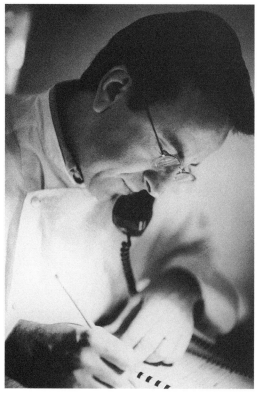

have a co-op garden we call 'The Basil Brothers,'" says Charlie Palmer. "We started a garden in Amaganton, which is owned by Lorne Michaels [the producer] of *Saturday Night Live*. When we went to him to ask permission to use his land, he said, 'Absolutely. But there are two things: I want it to be organic, and I want to be able to pick vegetables whenever I feel like it.' Done. We grow whatever we feel like growing for ourselves, with eighteen varieties of tomatoes, top hat garlic, all kinds of herbs, six kinds of basil. We have all kinds of beets, including candy-striped beets this year. We have sweet corn, too. It's been great."

Rick Bayless sees the commitment to working with farmers and purveyors to obtain the best ingredients as the mark of a great restaurant. "Great restaurants in Georgia, North Carolina, Texas, and Arizona are all doing very different food," Bayless attests. "But the great ones are all relating to farmers, the crops that are being grown there, some of the area's history, ethnic make-up, and all that kind of stuff. This is how we are developing a regional cuisine that is purely American. And as a country, that's where we need to be."

Sacrificing Variety for Quality

The drive for quality has also led chefs to embrace seasonality, which usually goes hand-in-hand with obtaining the best possible ingredients. "When we were in Italy, we saw that when mushrooms were in season, every course had mushrooms," says George Germon. "And we thought, 'Why shouldn't we do the same thing?' So we decided to do it."

"Now we're cherry freaks at the height of cherry season," says Johanne Killeen. "We're doing cherry sauce for ice cream, cherry tarts, cherry cakes." Germon adds, "We use cherries as pickles, too. So when an ingredient's season hits, that's exactly what we do."

Killeen admits, "I think people who don't know about the restaurant might find it unusual. But people who are our regular clientele look for it, and wait for it. They want to see that sort of thing. So, when corn and tomatoes are out, everybody is as excited as we are!"

Menus used to change seasonally to feature the best products available that season. Now, managing quality demands daily attention. In the past, a key aspect of many restaurant reviews was the citing of particular dishes recomended by the reviewer. This practice, too, has become outmoded in many cases since chefs change their menus more frequently. Many restaurants now print new menus daily, a practice which offers chefs the flexibility to serve only the ingredients that are at their very best that day. Such menus also prevent chefs from having to serve inferior ingredients simply because they're listed on a more permanent printed menu.

"People want to have raspberries in January and chestnuts in July. That's the problem in the United States: people cannot wait. There should be a law that you use products only seasonally."
—Sirio Maccioni,
 Le Cirque 2000

Many people are beginning to be connected with the farms around them. I was just back at a place in New Jersey that had its own garden and picked everything from it—this was a wonderful experience.

Lots of restaurateurs are caring about this now: **Al Forno** (Providence, Rhode Island), **Frontera Grill and Topolobampo** (Chicago), **Campanile** (Los Angeles), **L'Etoile** (Madison, Wisconsin), and **Zuni Cafe** (San Francisco)—and many, many more.

I think it's ultimately going to be more and more critical that they do that. A lot is happening in the food supply in terms of contamination. People are going to be more and more interested in knowing where their food comes from.

At Your Service

"I think the level of service in America is perhaps the biggest problem right now. Today, there are no rules at all. Being pleasant is about as much as a customer can usually ask of a waiter. But waiters should be real professionals, and customers should respect them as such."
—André Soltner,
  formerly of Lutèce

Does a $75 Broadway theater ticket give you the right to instruct the cast to provide a happy ending? Should ordering a chef's *prix fixe* menu at the same price give you the right to make alterations to the chef's vision? Every chef and restaurant draw the line in a different place.

Recent movies have parodied customers who make special requests of a restaurant. While Danny DeVito's character in *Get Shorty* demonstrates his clout by ordering and being served an egg-white omelette not on the menu at a trendy restaurant, John Cusack's gun-toting assassin in *Grosse Pointe Blank* got into an argument with a coffee-shop waitress when he tried to order the same.

Aren't customers always right anymore? "They are, unless they are being at all abusive to anyone on our staff or anyone else dining in the restaurant, or if they do not honor a reservation," says Danny Meyer, owner of Union Square Cafe and Gramercy Tavern in New York City. "Our business is not about lecturing you on what our standards are. Our business is about delighting you. If you are good enough to tell me what delights you, and I'm dumb enough not to do it, then I deserve whatever I get. The only other time a guest is wrong is when they don't come to the dining experience wanting to be delighted, or they're unwilling to share what would delight them. That I find very frustrating. At that point all we can do, if we've screwed up, is apologize and feel bad because that's not the outcome we wanted."

Through years of serving New York customers, Sirio Maccioni, owner of Le Cirque 2000 in New York City, has learned that excellence in service is "invisible." "Service is something that should happen without your realizing that it is happening," he says. "Service is not the waiter saying, 'I'm your waiter tonight.' Well, of course you are. Why else would you be here? But everything depends on whether you are a *good* or a *bad* waiter."

Good waiters wouldn't dream of asking a table, "Is everything all right?" says Maccioni. "It is already too pretentious to even suggest that everything is all right. Maybe the person at the table does *not* think that everything is all right! People want to have someone ask, 'Can I do anything for you?' These are magic words."

Because service is provided by people, hiring the right people is the first step in being able to provide it. "I can't do it all myself, so I have to start by hiring talent," says Rich Melman, founder of Lettuce Entertain You Enterprises in Chicago. "I like to deal with a certain type of person—one who cares, and has some intelligence and integrity. Many things go into the equation: you hire the right people, train them in your methods and philosophies, and then keep them happy and keep developing them. It's easy to say these things, but difficult to do. I'm always dropping the ball somewhere along the line. But you pick it up, apologize, and keep trying your best."

"Trying your best" has come to mean pleasing individual customers as consistently as possible, and the variety of customers' personalities has resulted in a flexible style of service. "A good waiter will read the table," says Jeremiah Tower, chef-owner of Stars in San Francisco. "They have to sniff out anniversaries and birthdays. I tell servers to sense the table and find any hook to get to talk to these people. If he sees a present, is there a birthday or anniversary going on? If there's a red rose on the table, what's the occasion? That immediately has to be communicated to the manager or chef. Are they adventurous? Then the waiter can mention that we offer flights of wine, vodka, scotches, and cognacs, which can be fun and educational."

Karen and David Waltuck, co-owners of Chanterelle in New York City, share this philosophy about what it takes to provide excellent service. "What's great about our service is that it can be formal, or less formal, because it's able to adjust to what people want," explains David. "We try to hire people who are interesting and not of a particular look or age group or anything like that. We look for people who are perceptive and who understand what kind of place this is, what this food is about, and what that means in terms of how they carry themselves, how they serve people, and how they can learn to anticipate what others might want without calling attention to the

"Everyone still talks about 'food and service,' but in New York, it's 'service and food.' It's the hottest subject in New York restaurants— who is treated how? That's what really matters, and what really builds a customer base, more than the food."
—Corby Kummer,
    formerly of *New York*

fact that they are noticing things. It's unobtrusive, but it's very, very meticulous.

"The whole thing that comes through is that it's not service by robots. It's done intelligently," he explains. "There is definitely a style behind our staff's ability to adjust and change and go with the flow, but it's not rote."

Gordon Hamersley, chef-owner of Hamersley's Bistro in Boston, operates in much the same way. "Our servers have to approach every table and figure out what they're going to do, given our mission statement of being proper, professional, and friendly. The extent to which they pull it out really leaves an impression on people," he says.

"But because our approach allows them to be themselves and let their personalities come through a little bit, there's a chance they may blow it," Hamersley admits. "It's easy to be cold and machine-like. It's hard to be a human being and also provide great service. I think the standard-bearer for this is Danny Meyer, whose staff is always friendly and professional at the same time. They are incredibly helpful, and they know the food and they know the wine.

"Through the years, my respect for the front of the house has gotten much greater," he says. "It's a real dance out there, and there's a lot to go wrong. The kitchen is relatively controllable, but the front of the house, who knows?"

Mark Peel, chef–co-owner of Campanile in Los Angeles, believes that all customers who walk through the front door should be treated cordially. "You may never have been here before, but that doesn't mean you couldn't become a regular customer, or that you aren't somebody extremely important in your field. If the chairman of General Motors walked into Campanile, I wouldn't recognize him," Peel admits.

This is especially important in Los Angeles, according to Nancy Silverton, co-owner of Campanile. "Some of the people in Hollywood are used to a certain type of treatment, and if they don't get that treatment or don't get a certain table, they just won't return," she says.

How to Have Eyes in the Back of Your Head

Many diners are not aware of the lengths restaurants sometimes go to in order to ensure them of a pleasurable experience. French chef Alain Ducasse earned three *Michelin* stars for Louis XV in Monte Carlo in

1990, after the restaurant had been open less than thirty-three months, and three stars for his eponymous restaurant in Paris in 1998, becoming the first chef in Michelin history to head two three-star kitchens. One of the managerial secrets behind his talent for being in more than one place at once involves the use of video cameras to monitor his kitchen staff.

Sometimes great chefs think alike. Daniel Boulud doesn't wait for waiters to report to him in the kitchen what's going on in his four-star dining room. Instead, discreet video cameras are located throughout the room, and he simply checks the video screens in the kitchen. "It gives us more control over the communication, mostly," explains Boulud. "We definitely know what is happening at each table, at what time, at what point. For example, we never [start preparing the order for] a table before it's clear, so we constantly check, and we might note if someone needs another ten or fifteen minutes. Efficiency in this business is most important to success, I think. When I am back there, I don't want to be in the dark. It is very important for me to be constantly in tune with the front of the house.

"I am watching the waiters, too, and the way they serve, the way they clear. If I see a customer is finished and there's been a lapse, I want to make sure that the waiter is on top of it. This way, I can send someone to tell him to clear," Boulud explains. "I stay in the kitchen, but still I am in touch. And, with the phones, I constantly call the *maitre d'* and say, 'What's going on with this table?' or 'It's 8:30. So-and-so is supposed to be here. Where are they?' We have the sheet of all the reservations in the kitchen. There are copies everywhere—in the dining room, in the kitchen, in pastry—so everyone knows during the whole evening what is happening."

Gray Kunz agrees that a strong link between the front and the back of the house is very important to providing diners with a seamless experience. "When you feel that you've made a great dish, but you don't have the conviction that that dish is going to go out with the same kind of enthusiasm by the waitstaff as that with which you cooked it, then that's only half of what you have done," he points out.

"We have a system set up where we give everybody, the cooks *and* the waiters, copies of the recipes. We also give a

Danny Meyer, owner of Union Square Cafe and Gramercy Tavern in New York City, was the first recipient of the James Beard Award for Outstanding Service, and is widely considered by his peers to have re-established great service in American restaurants.

How did you develop your own definition of excellence in restaurant service?
When I was in Rome working as a tour guide, I spent a lot of time by myself, at restaurants, coffee bars, or markets, being around people and enjoying food. There's something wonderful in some of the family-run trattorias—just pure hospitality. They were not so much run as businesses but as places to take care of regulars. When I saw the kind of treatment I was accorded as a single diner in some of these places, I said, "That's great. That's something I want to do for people."

What's your philosophy?
The guest is everything. No, actually the staff is everything. **Caring for each other comes first. We put our guests second.**
    If all of us—starting with me, and including the dishwashers, cooks, waiters, office people—don't feel respected by each other, we're not going to be able to give great care to our guests anyway. So that's where hospitality starts. And then second, it is our guests. Third is our community. Fourth is our purveyors, and fifth is our bottom line. And we talk about that with everybody who works here, and that's how we prioritize decisions.
    Everything is based on caring. I've been to restaurants famous for service where this is missing. For example, I went to a restaurant with my wife and we were seated at a banquette between two other couples. First, the manager disciplined the *maitre d'* in front of everyone, and then he bucked us up to a "better" section. How do you suppose those other couples on either side of us felt when they essentially said, "You guys stay here in coach while we bump these people up to first class"?

How would you define great service?
If you ask twenty people what great service is, you'll get twenty different answers. I come from St. Louis, where service is absent if they don't provide a giant spoon with your pasta, if the waiter's not wearing a tuxedo, or if they don't make the fettuccini next to your table on a sterno flame. It's absent in California if the waiter doesn't introduce himself or herself. It's different everywhere.
    What I think we do better than everyone else is hospitality. I make a big, big distinction in my own mind between "hospitality" and "service." I think of hospitality as delivering the emotional goods as far as caring for and welcoming people. I think of service as being the technical aspects of doing this in as lovely a way as possible.
    You can't be a great restaurant unless you first have great hospitality and then great service on top of that. You've probably been to restaurants where the wine was decanted flawlessly, and the *maitre d'* seats you flawlessly, and the food timing is flawless, and yet something is missing. That's because the hospitality is missing.

How do you manage your staff to provide hospitality?
Through three things: selection, training, and managing. **Selection is 80 percent of the game, training is 15 percent, and managing is probably 5 percent.**

The basis for success in this business is great hospitality. But the basis for being able to deliver great hospitality are an employee's emotional strengths, that which we could not teach them if we had all twenty years of our lease. These are the foundation of everything else employees are going to do in this restaurant. Whenever we make a mistake in hiring, we didn't do a good job of judging one of five traits. Prospective employees should be 1) extremely **nice**, 2) **intelligent**, 3) infused with an extraordinary **work ethic**, 4) **empathetic**, and 5) **emotionally self-aware**. When one of these five characteristics is absent, that person is probably going to be unable to provide the kind of hospitality we are looking for.

These are not simple things. How can I interview you and really, truly know how nice you are, how smart you are, how willing you are to put in a good day's work, or how important it is to you emotionally that a guest is having a good time? How can I know how emotionally aware you are of yourself if you wake up on the wrong side of the bed, and what you're going to do about it? You're responsible to know that it's going to affect the other people you work with. Are you going to go for a run? Are you going to talk to a shrink? Are you going to go to the gym? You've got to do something.

I did make training 15 percent, because, given point number one of staff hospitality, I'm not taking care of them if I don't give them the tools they need to succeed. If I don't train you on our wine list, it doesn't matter how nice or smart you are. You're not going to feel prepared if you don't know how to sell a bottle of wine to a table.

I don't really have to manage anyone who has these five traits, because I have someone who knows what we're trying to do. **We're in the business of giving people an emotional massage and filling their bellies.** And they're going to have fun doing that, and I don't have to babysit them doing that. It's all there.

What's the relationship between hospitality and value?
I consider value a huge part of the equation and absolutely a subset of hospitality. There is a French expression that "there is a rapport between price and quality." How much quality you are giving for each dollar you're asking for is a matter of hospitality. In other words, are you on my side or not? When I go to a restaurant, I feel like I'm being ripped off if I don't feel like you're on my side. I don't feel like you care for me; therefore, it doesn't feel very hospitable. On the other hand, giving great value is a wonderful expression of hospitality, and it's going to make people want to come back and spend more money in your restaurant. That's a big part of my philosophy.

What's behind your active involvement in the community?
Hospitality is an absolute. It's not something you get to pick and choose, as in "I'll be nice to a regular customer but not to a member of my staff." I don't trust that hospitality.

Last summer, we sent our staff to teach at Washington Irving High School, which is in our neighborhood and is 90 percent minority. Ultimately, I thought that would help our staff see that hospitality is something that can be applied. We had staff members teaching hospitality to these kids not only in class, but in action, serving lunch in the cafeteria. They got to look at the difference on people's faces who usually get fish sticks and tater tots, and watch how people melted when they were smiled at and spoken to.

This is also true with our purveyors. We give lip service to the fact that we're only as good as our weakest ingredient. All restaurants want the best piece of tuna delivered on the first delivery at the best price. But do you get that because you flex your muscles and say, "You'd better do this, or I'm going to go elsewhere," or "You'd better do this because this is the Union Square Cafe"? Or do you get it because you respect what these guys do for a living, and because they *want* to do business with you?

The benchmark of excellence in service was once, "The customer is always right." For years, a fast-food jingle lured customers with the promise "Have it your way." However, today many leading chef-owners believe that customers need to trust that a restaurant has their best interests at heart, even in refusing them their requests. **Mark Peel**, the chef-owner of Campanile in Los Angeles, explains:

Round I

We put a pulled-chicken sandwich on the menu, which was tossed with aioli and served with bacon. Delicious. The first day of the menu, someone comes in and says, "I'll have the chicken sandwich, no aioli, no bacon." It comes back to the kitchen with the message: "This is the worst chicken sandwich I've ever had." Well, of course it is! The second day, the same thing happens, and we were told "You know, this is our favorite restaurant in town, but that was the worst chicken sandwich we ever had." So we made a rule: The next time anybody alters that chicken sandwich, let them know that they won't enjoy it because it needs the mayonnaise and the bacon.

Round II

The next day, sure enough, it happens again. We're not sure how the waiter explained that it would be better if he ordered something else. But the customer apparently was horrified and got really angry and screamed profanities at both the waiter and the *maitre d'*.

Soon thereafter, Campanile received a letter from the diner addressed to "The Management." "Gentlemen:" it, "I had one of the most unpleasant and inexplicable dining experiences of my life in your restaurant this afternoon.

"At a business lunch, I ordered the chicken sandwich on your menu; I asked your server to bring it without the mayonnaise since mayonnaise makes me ill. After some time, the server returned and explained to my disbelief that the chef refused to serve the sandwich without mayonnaise. One of my lunch companions asked to see the manager of the day, who explained, without even bothering to ask me why I wanted the sandwich prepared the way I did, that the chef did not feel that the sandwich without mayo 'was reflective of the food at Campanile,' and also exclaimed, 'Why, there are thirteen other items on the menu.'

"Everyone at our table was, frankly, stunned. **Since when does a chef's aesthetic sense take precedence over the wishes of the customer?** Everyone else at the table was ready to leave, but I urged them to stay and finish what they had ordered. Although the chef of Campanile had ruined my lunch, I was not prepared to ruin anyone else's. I ended up going hungry.

"In twenty years of dining in Los Angeles, I've never encountered anything like this in a restaurant. The Burger

"When people leave a restaurant and the food was good, but they've had bad or indifferent or haughty service, they have not *had a good time."*

—Dennis Ray Wheaton, Chicago

brief description of what the dish is. It's a very tedious process," says Kunz. "What I finally found out was that they need to buy into my idea, and that I need to sell them my idea. When I sell them my idea well, they sell it even better to the customers. But it took me some time to figure out that not everyone likes everything I do.

Because the presence of the waitstaff contributes a great deal to the dining room's ambiance, Kunz goes so far as to instruct his staff in comportment. "As far as body language is concerned, I tell them, 'Don't slouch, and don't drag your feet,'" Kunz says. "How certain people move in the room can put you off, as can the way they bend over to explain what something is. If a waiter walks with his napkin under his arm, that's not very appealing. It works to your advantage to

King across from my office treats the customer with more consideration than Campanile. **It seems to me that this is wholly inappropriate, not to mention unbelievably arrogant, for a chef to dictate the manner in which a customer's food is prepared.** It's even more incredible that the manager of the restaurant backed up this kind of preposterous behavior without batting an eye.

"I assure you I will never dine at Campanile again and will relate this disgraceful story to anyone who proposes dining there."

Round III

The following week, Peel sent this reply:

"I received your letter concerning an incident over a chicken sandwich. I checked with the *maitre d'*, the waiter, and our sous-chef, who was in charge of the kitchen at the time, to find out what had gone wrong. No customer should be dictated to or forced to eat anything but what they want.

"Since we have had the chicken sandwich on the menu, we have had more than a few instances where people have ordered it without the aioli, a mayonnaise-based sauce, and then sent it back because it was too dry. And they were right; without the aioli, the chicken sandwich, being all white meat, is too dry. Served that way, I doubt you would have liked it. I certainly don't. So it is not just that the sandwich served dry is not reflective of our food, it is that the sandwich served dry is a lousy sandwich. **We are not trying to force you to eat something you don't want; we are trying to offer you something that will make you happy and is the best we can do.** That, obviously, was not communicated properly and for that I apologize.

"Having said that, I must mention that when there is a problem in a restaurant, the use of loud, obscene, and abusive language is not usually the best way to get it resolved. Our staff can and does make mistakes, but they do not deserve to be treated in the demeaning manner that you displayed. Should you ever return here we will do everything to make your dining experience enjoyable. We will also expect you to behave like an adult. Until then, you should continue to dine at Burger King across from your office."

Peel comments: "I think you have to accommodate your customers because we are here to please them. And you won't survive unless you do. That's the basic rule of every business, whether you're selling chicken sandwiches, rolled steel, or crack cocaine. You have to make your customers happy, or you are not going to stay in business. But on the other hand, I think there comes a point where you have a duty to your staff to support them when a customer is clearly wrong."

---

make your own corrections on things before they come to the attention of a reviewer.

Come On, Get Happy

Despite a restaurant's best efforts, service can sometimes falter or simply fail to please. What's the best way to turn things around? Mark Peel says, "If we have their phone number, I will introduce myself and say, 'I understand there was some kind of problem.' That usually gets them started. The best thing is to let them vent because sometimes they're still angry. But when they're done, just having complained directly to the owner, they feel much better."

"Sometimes the best thing that can happen in a restaurant is a mistake because it presents an opportunity for the restaurateur to 'make nice.' If you really make it up to people after a mistake, they almost always come back."

—Arthur Schwartz,
  WOR Radio

In General

- I pay attention to the greeting at the door because too often customers are ignored when they first come in, or parties of women are treated differently than parties with men. —Patty LaNoue Stearns, *The Detroit Free Press*

- I think service is such a bad area of so many restaurants. It falls down in so many different ways. I have not paid much attention to a number of restaurants in Los Angeles because **there's no point in sending people there if they're not known** or a 'name.' They're not going to be treated well. —Caroline Bates, *Gourmet*

- My newest pet peeve is when you're seated and they come right over and want to know what you want to drink right that second, so you tell them—and then **it's ten minutes before they bring the drink**. —Penelope Corcoran, *The Arizona Republic*

- **The attack of the pepper mill**. A lot of top restaurants now put pepper mills on the table rather than having the looming pepper mill suddenly emerge over your shoulder!" —Arthur Schwartz, WOR Radio, New York City

Excessive Familiarity or Effusiveness

- I don't like **overly chatty or overly friendly** servers, although I do like friendly service. I draw the line when they tell me personal things that I just don't care about, such as anything that's going on back in the kitchen. I really don't want to know, unless there's a big hold-up. —Patty LaNoue Stearns, *The Detroit Free Press*

- **Waiters who introduce themselves,** tell you their favorite dishes, and congratulate you on your choices as being brilliant. —Gael Greene, *New York*

- **Waiters who praise your order** with "wonderful choice" or "brilliant choice." There was a wonderful cartoon in *The New Yorker* a few years ago where somebody says, "Okay, I'm going to place my order—and I *don't* want you to review it for me." —Dennis Ray Wheaton, *Chicago*

Excessive "Service"

- **Restaurants that try to overwhelm you with service that isn't really a service,** such as by pouring your water every time you take a sip. —Phyllis Richman, *The Washington Post*

- Last night, we were in a very good restaurant, and I think perhaps six times the waiter said, **"Is everything all right? Are you happy with what you have?"** demanding a response. I hate that. I don't want to be interrupted or to have to reply. That would never happen in a serious French restaurant, where they would only say, "Please let me know if I can get you anything." Then you don't even have to respond. And if they say, *"Bon appetit"* or "Enjoy," I don't mind that. I think that's fine. —Gael Greene, *New York*

- I don't need **gimmicks**, but it seems that a lot of restaurants feel they have to have one [citing a restaurant where the waiters actually hand out business cards]. —Patty LaNoue Stearns, *The Detroit Free Press*

"Customers are a little confused about exactly what they want. They used to complain about not getting enough attention, and now it's the reverse."
—Alison Arnett,
The Boston Globe

Gray Kunz has found the same to be true at Lespinasse. "I judge the restaurant on the critiques that we get, and I want to know what happened with anyone who is not satisfied," he says. "With the unsatisfied customer, all they really want is to know that someone cares. When I call, there is almost a 99.9 percent chance of turning them around. Those criticisms are very often justified. But even when they're not, they're still the customers. I know it is more detrimental

Downright Rudeness

- When Bice first opened in Chicago, they had a real **attitude problem**. In Chicago, that doesn't work very well. I called for a reservation, and the woman on the other end immediately said, "I have to put you on hold; somebody important is on the other line." —Dennis Ray Wheaton, *Chicago*

- I had a waiter touch me on the shoulder and say, "I have to tell you the specials. Could you **stop talking**, please?" —Gael Greene, *New York*

- I hate **rude waiters**. Palio [in New York City] has a really talented chef, but the dining room has some of the rudest waiters I've ever encountered. At one point, I got wine that was corked and told the waiter, who replied, "No, it's not!" —Ruth Reichl, *The New York Times*

- I've only had really **snotty service** a few times in my life, and one time I wrote a column about it: "Somewhere out there in the city there's a waiter wondering whether I forgot to leave him a tip. I didn't." —Elaine Tait, *The Philadelphia Inquirer*

- For years, I have been going to a restaurant that once received the James Beard Award for Outstanding Service, where they do not know me. If you're not known, you might get a good waiter. But only if you're "known" are you given "**the treatment**." And I've had **terrible service** there over the years.

The End Game

- Servers who ask, "**Are you still working on that?**" or "Are you still picking at that?" It's so gross. All they have to ask is, "Would you like me to clear now?" —Gael Greene, *New York*

- Sometimes I think that busboys are paid by their activity. They take the plates one by one, so maybe they get paid by the plate. There seems to be a pattern now of restaurants **taking away the plate of anyone who is finished**, and I think it's rude to leave other people eating while you're clearing the plates of some of the people at the table. I'm also annoyed when restaurants abandon you at the end of the meal. Of course, I hear a lot of complaints in the other direction, too: **they rush you out**. Sometimes that happens, but in my position I'm sometimes relieved to be rushed out. —Phyllis Richman, *The Washington Post*

- One of my pet peeves is **the frequent difficulty of getting the check**. A very important thing that's neglected is the timing of the meal. That needs a lot of work, even in some of the best restaurants. You're sitting there with your dirty plates in front of you, you finished eating ten minutes ago, yet sated with food, dulled by the wine, and nearly asleep, you have to go look for the waiter and try to get the check. It's ridiculous. They should make it possible for you to leave expeditiously and congenially. —Robert Sietsema, *The Village Voice*

to have one unhappy customer walking out of here than it is beneficial to have fifty satisfied ones leaving. Word travels fast."

The Setting

In certain restaurants, improving the ambiance has entailed toning down formal touches that some diners might find too stuffy. "For me,

> *"A great restaurant is a place that makes you think that you're being treated as well as one of the restaurant's regular customers."*
> —Arthur Schwartz,
>   WOR Radio

Deafening Decibels

- The **noise level** is the thing I hate most. A lot of restaurants these days seem to want to have that noise, to make it seem like there are more people than there are. I've complained about it in many, many reviews. Especially as they get older, I really believe that baby boomers will start demanding better acoustics. Noise is perhaps the number one complaint I receive from readers. In fact, many of the times I've written about the problem in specific restaurants, they've gone back and put noise-dampening material on the ceiling. —Patty LaNoue Stearns, *The Detroit Free Press*

- **I really dislike noisy restaurants** because your senses kind of shut down, and it's much harder to taste wine. That may be one reason why there's this fashion for noisy restaurants. Everybody says it's because it feels very animated, but it's also because you can't taste and you're not focusing on the food as much. —S. Irene Virbila, *The Los Angeles Times*

- Music is often too loud and too intrusive, and **they play too much "Gypsy Kings."** But a record producer told me why: it's lively and upbeat, but you can't really hear the words, so it doesn't stop you in your tracks. —Alison Arnett, *The Boston Globe*

Smoke Gets In Their Eyes

- **I hate cigars** because you can't taste the food. It's so irritating to the nose. —Alison Arnett, *The Boston Globe*

- Especially with the cigar craze, I think smoke is horrible. I hate **having to walk through smoky bars to get to the dining area.** I have an acute sense of smell, and if something hits me wrong, it can bring down the whole experience. —Patty LaNoue Stearns, *The Detroit Free Press*

it all goes back to making customers feel special because those are the ones who are going to come back," says Hubert Keller, chef-owner of Fleur de Lys in San Francisco. "There are young clientele who are going to remember an experience for many, many years. And even if they can't afford it twice a month at that time, they might be able to come a few times a year. I think those are the customers, when I come out [in the dining room], who say, 'Oh, we had such a good time, and we are just amazed how friendly the waiter was with us!' And you can sense that they were surprised because they'd been thinking, 'They must be pretty stuffy in there.'"

Keller took steps to make the restaurant more approachable. "We changed things when I took over the restaurant, starting with writing the menu completely in English," says Keller. "At that time, every French restaurant menu was written in French. But it's little steps of intimidation that bring the ambiance down. We cut out the waiters' tuxedos a few years after that."

In other cases, a restaurateur has the express intention of celebrating a particular culture and its customs. "I believe that the food I do is very much rooted in culture, so you have to get a sense of that culture," says Rick Bayless. "If I were to put sombreros on the walls and do all types of shenanigans that relate to the stereotypes of Mexican food in the United States, I would end up with people misunderstanding everything that I was putting in front of them.

"A case in point is the kind of music that we play," says Bayless. "We play all Latin music, and it is very far-reaching. It does not just relate to the music of Mexico, but, oddly enough, it relates to the music that is popular among Mexicans. A lot of that music is not even created by Mexicans, but by people from Cuba, the Dominican Republic, or Spain. But it's popular in Mexico. When we put on certain music, especially the Gypsy Kings, people recognize it and say, 'This isn't *mariachi* music; it should be *mariachi* music.'

"On the flip side of that, sometimes we put on indigenous music from southern Mexico, which is very annoying to listen to, just a drum and a flute. It sounds sort of New Age-y and definitely tribal, and some people will complain, 'How do you expect me to eat my food while I'm listening to this?' Well, it's all part of the whole package. And probably everything that we put in front of you is not going to be exactly to your taste, either," Bayless says. "But I feel that it's important for us to represent it all, yet not in any stereotypical way."

Charlie Palmer found that a restaurant's ambiance predisposed diners to have the best possible experience. "The River Cafe [the Brooklyn restaurant known for its skyline view of Manhattan] was a great stage to work on. I always loved the fact that we had this fantastic view," says Palmer. "I began to understand that if you can make people feel happy and comfortable, you have a much better chance of making them really love what you're doing. [At the River Cafe] they're sitting in this immensely romantic room, with this great view of

"A pretentious restaurant is not one that has Bernardaud and Baccarat and Cristofle. Some of the most pretentious places I've been in have been simple little places in California that scream, 'Look how simple I am!'— and they're boring as hell."
—Jeremiah Tower
  Stars

Manhattan and the water. They're in the mood, so if you just do what you're supposed to do, you're in pretty good shape."

Sirio Maccioni says he infused the spirit of Barnum & Bailey all over the entrance to Le Cirque 2000, with huge baskets of fruit cascading down stairs. "Why? To remind people that this is a restaurant, a fun place, a meeting place," he says. "St. Patrick's is across the street, but *this* is not a church. So I put color in to take away the austerity. I've tried to create a comfortable restaurant for a New Yorker. There are not enough queens and czars to fill a restaurant! You need other people."

Creating a comfortable ambiance in a restaurant involves attention to the smallest details. Terrance Brennan, chef-owner of Picholine in New York City, points out that it took him ten months to get decorative show plates and bread plates designed, produced, and shipped to the restaurant. "I gave the designers a fabric sample I liked, and they came back with a design. Then we went back and forth about colors. 'It has to have more of the olive color; this is light green,' and 'It has to have more purple in it; this is just too blue,'" he recalls. "I've been trying to get hand-blown cruets because I really wanted a beautiful olive oil on the table since I don't use flowers. The first guy who was supposed to do it was a three-month investment of my time, but then he couldn't do it. Now that project's been going on for seven months.

"I've got a big custom mirror that I'm working on, and I've ordered pottery from France that's taken three months. It's really frustrating that everything's taken so long. I opened the restaurant quickly, in six weeks," he says. "Now, to take it to the next level, it seems a lot more difficult. It takes a lot of my time. At least it's nice that diners have responded to the changes, and that the press has noticed as well."

The Whole Experience

The experience of a restaurant goes beyond its quantified ratings in a guidebook. It encompasses not only food, service, and ambiance, but everything a diner encounters consciously and unconconsciously. Leading chef-restaurateurs agree that food is only the starting point—albeit a crucial one. "The entire experience is triggered by flavor, which to me is the emotional component of a dish," says Rick Bayless. "That's what is going to make you remember it very well. Texture can do that to a certain degree, but I think more than anything it's flavor. What we can offer in the United States now, because we have this wonderfully developed restaurant culture, is the full experience: ambiance, service, the way the table is set, the music, and the flavor."

Former chef-owner of Lutèce André Soltner believes he's biased about food's importance. "For me, as a chef, I'm very prejudiced. Food is number one," says Soltner. "But it's not 100 percent. The ambiance, the spirit of the restaurant, is very important—everything from how the reservations are handled to the greeting you receive when you arrive. If you walk into a restaurant and are not greeted well, it's already over."

Other chefs underscore the importance of service and ambiance. "There are always some people who are unhappy with you," says Hubert Keller. "You cannot always please. But I do feel that when someone comes through the door, the front of the restaurant—the ambiance, the way you're treated—is at least 50 percent of the experience. We are in a region [San Francisco] where the food is extremely important, and probably, being a chef, I should be the one saying that, 'It's 100 percent about food.' But it's not. I think food is 50 percent.

"Very often, if there's an incident, it's because diners were not well-treated, or there was some rudeness. Automatically, the food is going to taste bad, too," says Keller. "Mistakes in the kitchen can be fixed, but a problem with the front is very hard to fix. That's why it's so important. People can walk out of here extremely happy with the experience, even if there was an incident. It's all in the way it's handled. You have to figure out what's best. What works for one table

"The challenge we have as chefs is to give our guests a good table—the opportunity to have a fabulous food memory that will be triggered the next time they have those flavors. They will remember something that is integral to their own experience as a human being."
—Rick Bayless,
   Frontera Grill and
   Topolobampo

doesn't work for the next one. That's where the professionalism of the floor comes in," attests Keller.

No small part of providing a great restaurant experience involves finding your audience. "It's odd. What's happened is that we've developed a natural clientele [at Gramercy Tavern] over time," observes Danny Meyer. "Those who feel at home return, and they tell other people who are like them about the restaurant. At the outset, however, it's like dragging a prime net through the ocean. You catch every fish out there, and three-quarters of them are fish that you didn't mean to catch and don't belong in your net. Right now, I think Gramercy is doing better than ever, and it's by-and-large showing itself to its more natural audience."

Self-Defined Success

Once a reputation for excellence has been earned, it gives restaurants the luxury of defining their own success.

"The success of Union Square Cafe and Gramercy Tavern is ultimately not what Ruth [Reichl] or any other restaurant critic does for it," argues Meyer. "I think we have enough of a sense of self at this point to know what we want, and to know that if we didn't do well, it's because we didn't do well and not because someone else had to tell us that. And if Gramercy Tavern never gets four stars, that's okay—as long as we're being true to our goals. Everything we do is for ourselves and our customers. The critics don't make any difference because I think by the time a critic comes, the dice are rolled already."

Daniel Boulud is the chef cited most often by the chefs we interviewed as the quality benchmark for cuisine in America. With the success of Restaurant Daniel, which holds four stars from *The New York*

Times, Boulud could easily coast on his success. "Right now, I feel I could definitely stay here [at Restaurant Daniel] and maintain my place by sort of cruising on it," he admits. "Financially, I'm almost coming to the surface, after five years of investment, so I could start to get the benefit of that investment over the next five or ten years by just protecting what I've created. And instead, I am beginning everything all over again [by purchasing and creating a new restaurant in Le Cirque's former site]."

Boulud's attitude underscores the intentions of America's leading chef-restaurateurs. The personal rewards of challenging himself and his restaurant to continually improve and redefine quality is worth the risk to Boulud and other chef-restaurateurs like him who are driven by more than profits or stars. "I am cautious, but I am trying to achieve a performance which I will be very happy with," he explains. "So I am not worried. But I don't know what is going to happen when I move there. I know that I am going to make a four-star status restaurant," he says with pride. "But will it be four stars to the critics? Who knows?"

"I never did what I did for the critics. I do it for myself, for my customers, and for my staff. If the critics don't get it, so what? Is your restaurant full? Do you have a high turnover? Can you look at yourself in the mirror every day? Who do you do what you do for?"
—Norman Van Aken,
  Norman's

Five

The Power of a Review

"If you've invested $1.25 million

in a project and certain people

can crush you like a bug if they

have a bad time, you're a fool if

you're not trying to find out who

these people are, what they look

like, and when they're in."

—Bob Kinkead,
Kinkead's

In what other field is it possible for a business's fortunes to rise or fall on a single person's opinion? Chanterelle opened as a tiny, 30-seat restaurant in New York City's SoHo in November 1979. It earned a favorable review from *New York* magazine restaurant critic Gael Greene a month later and a two-star review from *The New York Times* not long thereafter. Within eight years of opening, the restaurant went on to secure the *Times's* highest rating (four stars) in 1987. "The minute we heard the news, we screamed—and then we served the whole dining room champagne," recalls co-owner Karen Waltuck. "From then on, the phone never stopped ringing."

The Waltucks knew that 1989 would be an eventful year. The restaurant's success prompted a move in March to larger quarters in TriBeCa, where the number of seats in the dining room doubled. And the Waltucks welcomed their daughter Maria in May. "It was an enormous change," remembers David Waltuck, chef–co-owner. "And because we'd been closed for nearly five months between locations, we started out in the new place with a whole new staff."

On revisiting the restaurant's new location in TriBeCa, Bryan Miller, restaurant critic for *The New York Times*, commented, "The sublime integration of flavors and textures that once marked Mr. Waltuck's cooking is not always evident....[The current entrees] are all skillfully prepared, but nothing you could not find at a half-dozen other places in town for half the price." Miller's June 1989 verdict: two stars.

Chanterelle's phones went dead overnight. That year, New York City was already in the midst of an economic downturn. "More than 10,000 people on Wall Street lost their jobs downtown [where the restaurant is located]," remembers David. And between the damning review and the economic slump, the owners of Chanterelle feared for their restaurant's life.

But the restaurant held on, and managed to persevere. "We had to be a lot more careful about salaries and expenses in general," David remembers. "And there were no more vacations," adds Karen.

Bryan Miller re-reviewed the restaurant in *The New York Times* less than two years later, commenting, "Since Chanterelle was reviewed in 1989, the kitchen has become more focused and increasingly inventive." He boosted Chanterelle's rating a star.

In December 1993, Ruth Reichl reviewed Chanterelle. She wrote, "[Chef Waltuck's] hallmark is a kind of serious simplicity, each plate built with layers of flavor that resonate with each other. You get the impression that he has tasted each dish over and over, refining the ingredients until they are in perfect harmony." The Waltucks happily celebrated the holidays that season with the return of their restaurant's four-star status.

A Review's Impact

While critics also play important roles in other fields, including film, theater, and music, for example, the impact of a restaurant review is felt for years as opposed to months or weeks.

Restaurant reviews are often framed and displayed at a restaurant's entrance, sometimes misleadingly, even years after publication and through changes of both the chef and the ownership. Whereas dozens of critics might review a nationally released movie, giving it a fighting chance of reaching its audience, historically, some individual restaurant critics have held almost monopolistic power in certain markets.

Stories of negative reviews closing down restaurants are legendary in every city. One New York City restaurateur reminisces, "La Coupole [in Manhattan] used to be packed with 350 diners. But the night after Mimi Sheraton's [no-star 'poor'] review in *The New York Times*, the 350 diners became 60 diners. And then, soon after, La Coupole closed."

In San Francisco, "The Pink Section [of *The San Francisco Chronicle*] could either make you or break you," says Jeremiah Tower, chef-owner of Stars in San Francisco. "Restaurateurs expecting a good review learned to find out in advance when they'd be reviewed so they could hire more staff the Saturday before because it could literally make you full overnight. And if it trashed you, you might as well shut the door."

Certainly, the potentially devastating power of a restaurant review has given pause to chefs and restaurateurs. But restaurant critics don't necessarily agree they have that much power. "I don't think I close

"It's very hard to look at reviews in an objective way. On some level, it shouldn't matter what a review says because you know what you're doing. On the other hand, there is a personal impact. If something is in print, it takes on a life of its own."
—Karen Waltuck,
 Chanterelle

down restaurants. I think they close themselves down," says Phyllis Richman, restaurant critic for *The Washington Post*. "But certainly a lot of restaurateurs who have closed feel that I'm responsible for it. And that's painful. Because even when it's somebody I think is a miserable S.O.B. and doing a terrible job, it's still uncomfortable to take people to task publicly."

Penelope Corcoran, restaurant critic for *The Arizona Republic*, doesn't believe she can close any restaurant that isn't already struggling. "I know I can affect people's business, but mine is just one opinion. Plenty of people are loyal to a place no matter what I say. And some people will go and check it out just to prove me wrong," she says. "So, I don't think I can kill a place. If I write about a place that's truly lousy and struggling, it might be a nail in the coffin, but I don't feel I killed it."

Other critics have been known, or rumored, to vex careers. "I know that chefs have been fired after certain reviews," admits Elaine Tait, restaurant critic for *The Philadelphia Inquirer*. "And that's the part of my job I never liked. Pino Luongo opened a Coco Pazzo in Philadelphia, which I reviewed, and it was terrible. I mentioned that I had been to the Coco Pazzo in New York and that it had been delightful. But this one was not at all like it. The ingredients were of supermarket quality or worse. After my review, Luongo ended up firing half the staff immediately. By the end of the week, he had fired the rest and brought in a new staff and a new chef."

Still, their perceived power is one reason certain leading restaurant critics try to temper their criticism. Gael Greene explains, "I have made it my policy not to review small restaurants that aren't good. They'll either sink or swim on their own. I won't write a negative review of a place unless it's falling apart, and it's an old institution on

- **Alison Cook, *Houston Sidewalk*:** "When I was younger, it used to thrill me to write a bad review! But after more than twenty-five years of reviewing restaurants, I seem to have acquired the quality of mercy."

- **Gael Greene, *New York* magazine:** "I was speaking with [the chef of one Manhattan restaurant] who was so proud of his products, and I thought, 'This is terrible because I'm going to say that the food is just nothing much.' And, of course, he was devastated. The place could not be more filled, but the review was totally about 'This is the happening place of the moment on the Upper East Side.' And it is. Most of the diners there are totally content with what they're eating. It's only if you really care about food that you have to say, 'This is not food that I want to eat.' So I did feel sad because he was so proud."

- **Ruth Reichl, *The New York Times*:** "It doesn't feel good being mean, ever. If I had it my way, I would probably never write mean reviews. But your obligation is to be truthful. Plus, readers like mean reviews. You cannot have credibility unless you're occasionally tough. But I think some people might do it with glee. I *don't* do it with glee."

- **Phyllis Richman, *The Washington Post*:** "While it's not difficult to write a bad review, when I'm uncertain I probably err on the kinder side. But when a restaurant is clearly bad, that's easy enough to write."

- **Patricia Unterman, *The San Francisco Examiner*:** "I've written bad reviews only when I've felt like I'd been poisoned. Then I feel like I have a public responsibility to say, 'This kitchen is not together. They're sending out rotten food.' And that causes huge libel problems. I did this with two Italian restaurants. One was one of the city's oldest restaurants, and I couldn't believe the food the kitchen was sending out. I was just appalled seeing things like rotten chicken being served. And the restaurant is still in business!"

- **S. Irene Virbila, *The Los Angeles Times*:** "It's always with a heavy heart that you have to write a bad review. It's so public: it's 3 million people on Sunday! In order to do it, you just can't think about that. You've got to write it as close as possible to what you would tell a friend about the place."

- **Dennis Ray Wheaton, *Chicago* magazine:** "I usually try not to think about [the power of this position]. There's no point in it. I do worry about it if I'm going to say something that might hurt somebody. That's the time one must be very careful, so I'll go back and double-check and triple-check the facts."

S. Irene Virbila adds: "I think restaurateurs may have the perception that critics are out there gunning for them, but I can't tell you how exciting it is when you find some place that you really love. It is a thrill, and even more so if it's a place that's struggling and doesn't have the savvy or the resources of some of the big places. A great restaurant is something to celebrate, but you don't get to do that very often."

the way down or a new place that's extremely hot or fashionable or much-promoted. Then, of course, I think they're fair game."

A Symbiotic Relationship

Just as scientists have learned that their mere observation of an experiment can affect its outcome, critics learned that they have an integral effect on the restaurants they review.

As some critics have discovered, even a great review can kill a restaurant. "I put a restaurant out of business once with a good review,"

Penelope Corcoran admits. "I really loved the food, and part of the dilemma of my job is that a lot of the time I go to places that are empty. I write accurately about my experience, but there's a 'before' and an 'after.' If I go in and describe the restaurant and write a rave review, everything changes! Suddenly, 200 people show up that day. This poor Shanghainese couple couldn't handle it, and they were up all night making Shanghainese dim sum! It was very sad, for them and for me."

Elaine Tait knows the feeling. "It's always a scary thing with small, unpretentious restaurants," she says. "You can ruin them with a good review by getting mobs of people in there that they can't handle. Or if you give them a good review, they get all puffed up and think they have to be better and grander. Then they raise their prices, and it's over. So, you write the review very carefully, and you assume that people will read it as carefully as you wrote it: 'This is a small place, with only one server, and if you come the day that this review runs, you will probably not end up getting a meal because it's going to be too busy.' You have to write it with the precision of a legal document, just to make sure you don't ruin the place."

John Mariani, restaurant critic for *Esquire* magazine, points out that an enthusiastic review from a powerful critic can literally change a restaurant. "Let's say a critic raves, 'Oh, they're so nice to everybody,' and 'the cassoulet was just perfect.' After a three- or four-star review like this, a place will be overwhelmed. And on Saturday night, you can't get in," says Mariani. "So the customer thinks, 'I could barely get through on the phone, and once I did, I couldn't get in until 9:30!'

"Also, suddenly the restaurant kitchen doesn't have ten orders for cassoulet; it has ninety orders because the restaurant critic said it was incredible," he says. "So, the reviewer has a lot of power, good and bad. But it's not the same restaurant the next day, anyway. It's never the same place because the place that used to be serving 90 customers a night suddenly has to serve 150 customers, twenty-four hours later, with no increase in staff, and the same size kitchen."

When Good Things Happen After Good Reviews

To be fair, just as critics can break a restaurant or a chef, they can make one as well. Anne Rosenzweig, chef-owner of Arcadia and The Lobster Club in New York City, remembers, "Mimi [Sheraton of *The New York Times*] reviewed me when I was at Vanessa seventeen years ago as the brunch and dessert chef. She said that it was an okay restaurant, but if you had brunch or dessert there, it was spectacular. Two weeks after the review, the chef was fired, and I was hired. So I used to joke, 'I got my job through *The New York Times*,' which was also the tagline of the *Times*'s classified section's ad campaign.

"Six weeks after we opened Arcadia, Bryan [Miller of *The New York Times*] reviewed us and gave us two stars," says Rosenzweig. "That was fine because it was back in the 1980s when a review like that was able to keep us packed, with the phone ringing off the hook, for two and a half years."

Daniel Boulud found the same to be true when he first opened. "We were busy before we got reviewed because many of my customers didn't need the *Times* to tell them to come to Daniel. But after our first review, we were *extremely* busy," he says.

"On the other hand, if it had been a four-star review, it would have created a madness, and things were already mad enough with the opening," says Boulud. "I think it was almost a blessing to receive two stars at that time because it allowed me to really be what I wanted to be. I remember saying to my staff, 'You know, if we're going to be a two-star restaurant, then we are going to be the best of them!'"

The economic impact of a strong review can be substantial. After Picholine earned its third star from *The New York Times*, business increased by 25 percent. "We were busy anyway, but it filled out Monday nights and it filled out our second seating a little bit better earlier in the week," says chef-owner Terrance Brennan.

In the best of all possible worlds, the positive impact of multiple reviews is maximized. "In Washington, DC, what you want to have happen ideally is for Phyllis [Richman] to review you first, and then six or seven months later to have [Robert] Schoffner [of *The Washingtonian*] review you again," says Bob Kinkead, chef-owner of Kinkead's in Washington, DC. "That way, by the time [the impact of] her

"I think reviews can help restaurants get customers. Chez Panisse has been helped in so many ways by reviews. We need a lot of people to come through this restaurant to make it work, which means there has got to be a constant flow of reviews out there and people coming in who have never been here before."
—Alice Waters,
   Chez Panisse

review is dying out, he gives you another pop. And that's exactly what happened for us at 21 Federal. We were lucky."

Encouraging Dining

One of the most important powers ascribed to restaurant critics is the ability to create excitement about restaurant dining in general. "Journalists generate great enthusiasm for dining out," says Mark Peel, chef–co-owner of Campanile in Los Angeles. "If you don't have a good, strong food media—love them or hate them—you don't have the same level of enthusiasm."

Part of this involves encouraging diners to visit new restaurants. "People don't have the time or energy or don't want to risk the money, so they need to be alerted to information about a new place before they're willing to take a risk. When you have a weak food journalistic community in a city, the whole restaurant community settles into a rut," Peel says.

Peel's partner Nancy Silverton praises the enthusiasm of New York City's food media. "I read *New York* magazine, and I do think Gael Greene is a terrific writer. She makes everything sound so delicious that sitting here [in Los Angeles] I always think, 'My God, there are so many unbelievable restaurants in New York!'" Silverton says. "When I go there, some of them may be every bit as good or bad as what we have, but there's not the same amount of enthusiasm here. And I think that, between Gael Greene and Ruth Reichl, everyone knows that New York City is really an eating town."

Positive recognition bestowed upon a restaurant can swing significant dollars its way. For example, coming out on top of *Gourmet*'s restaurant survey for the city of Miami prompted an influx of hundreds of thousands of dollars into Norman's, a Coral Gables, Florida, restaurant, during a time of year when chef-owner Norman Van Aken expected business to be slow. Van Aken says, "I was able to buy a new stove and build up my wine cellar [with the windfall]."

But the biggest difference is whether a critic chooses to report on a restaurant or not. Phyllis Richman argues, "I think that simply getting mentioned in the media is important for restaurants, so that may be a greater area of responsibility than the actual review."

Most chefs and restaurateurs realize that their relationship with the food media is symbiotic. "I think that everything that gets print-

ed—big, little, good, bad—everything helps," says Johanne Killeen, chef–co-owner of Al Forno and Provincia in Providence, Rhode Island. "Even bad press is great," adds George Germon, Killeen's partner. "When they spell the name right and give the address!" finishes Killeen.

"One of the most important things [about press coverage] is that people don't remember anything they read or see or hear accurately," observes Jeremiah Tower. "It's all immediately edited. So, in a restaurant review, the headline is probably the most important thing. Over the last two weeks, dozens of people have commented to me about a recent article in *The San Francisco Examiner*. And you'd think they'd all read a different article! They really latch on to only one or two things, and they all seem to be different things."

"Two reviews I wanted to do were nixed by my editors, and later I read in Florence Fabricant's column [in The New York Times] that the chef had left one of the restaurants, and the other one was closing. They were both restaurants I wanted to celebrate as having upheld standards, places where you could still go to have a wonderful time and a wonderful meal. That's something I felt I could have made a difference about, and I was enormously frustrated. I am under pressure to review things fast."
—Corby Kummer,
  formerly of *New York*

Are All Media Created Equal?

When we interviewed leading chefs about the media with the strongest influence on their restaurants, we had expected chefs to mention their local city newspapers. However, without exception, it was *The New York Times* that top chefs from coast to coast cited.

"[*New York Times Magazine* columnist] Molly O'Neill featured Fleur de Lys in an article about upscale restaurants serving vegetarian cuisine. And it was bigger than we ever thought it would be," admits Hubert Keller, chef-owner of Fleur de Lys in San Francisco. "Then I was featured in an article called 'Rebel with a Cuisinart,' or something like that. The *Times*'s photographer said they wanted something different, so I suggested that we go to the produce market early in the morning. I told the photographer, 'If *The New York Times* wants action, I think we can get lots of action. The guys I'm working with out there would be thrilled to help. We can build something with vegetables or produce.'

"I could sense on the phone that it wasn't what they were looking for. I don't know why I said it but I added, 'And we can throw a motorcycle in there if the vegetables are not enough.' He asked, 'What kind of motorcycle?' I said, 'I was just joking.' He said, 'No, really, what kind of motorcycle?' I said, 'It's a Harley-Davidson.' He said, 'Let me call the *Times*.' When he called me back, he said, 'They love it.' But then I didn't like the idea, because I have a certain clientele, and I thought Harley-Davidson was just not their thing. But when the article came out, more people remembered the motorcycle than what was actually written in the article!

"The same day, there was a James Beard Foundation party in Napa Valley," Keller remembers. "As soon as I walked in, everyone said, 'Congratulations!' and 'Where did you get that motorcycle?' No one could believe it was mine! But everyone had already seen *The New York Times Magazine*."

Among the critical opinions in various cities, the power of each can vary from city to city. "A lot of people I know buy *Chicago* magazine just for the dining guide," says Dennis Ray Wheaton, chief dining critic for *Chicago* magazine. "And I've been told that *Zagat* does less well in Chicago than it does in most major cities because of *Chicago* magazine [which lists hundreds of recommended restaurants along with their addresses, phone numbers, and recommended dishes in every issue]. We're even more up-to-date because we call every restaurant every month and make sure all the facts are still accurate and that the chef hasn't left."

Nationally, airlines' in-flight magazines are found to be influential. Jeremiah Tower saw "very powerful" results from a five-page, full-color article on Stars that appeared in an in-flight magazine. "So many people flying into San Francisco read these magazines, and there are no unfavorable articles about restaurants in them," he observes. "A wonderful article in one of these magazines is about as important as it gets."

Tower also points out the importance of *Gourmet* magazine. "Through the 1980s, a review in *Gourmet* was a good restaurant-filler," he remembers. "At Chez Panisse when we were reviewed in *Gourmet*, it would not only fill the restaurant, but people would come in with the review on their laps and want to order what was in the magazine arti-cle—which, since the menu changed daily, was a bit difficult."

Getting Reviewed

Sometimes even an initially disappointing review can work out for the best. "Bryan [Miller] gave me two stars, and I remember screaming at him on the phone over it," admits Charlie Palmer. "We had become pretty good buddies at that point. And then, after giving me three stars at River Café in New York City, he turned around and gave me two stars here [at Aureole]. It wasn't a bad review. I just thought he was going to give me three stars, and it was going to be great. I knew what we were doing here was better than what we were doing at the River Café, so it just didn't make any sense to me at the time. It still doesn't!

"[But, in retrospect] it was probably the best thing that could have happened," concedes Palmer. "We had to build our customer base one by one, by starting a relationship and taking care of them. When it became 'their' restaurant, they'd send their best friends. It's almost like they want to protect the restaurant; they don't want all the 'riffraff' coming in. So, they send the kind of people who are going to be sup-portive, and then when there's a dip in the economy, the restaurant still has a great clientele."

"I don't get chummy with chefs and restaurateurs because they don't under-stand when I have to say something negative."
—Alison Cook,
    Houston Sidewalk

PATRICIA UNTERMAN OF *THE SAN FRANCISCO EXAMINER* ON SPOTTING A CRITIC

Have you, as a San Francisco restaurant critic-*and*-restaurateur, ever been at your restaurant when a critic was in the house?
I must have. But in the heat of battle when you're in the kitchen, they're really hard to spot. They have to be picked up by another diner or the waiters them-selves. I've been picked up tons of times when another diner will tell the waiter that I'm there.

What do you tell your staff to do when a critic is recognized?
I tell them to find out what table it is, and to give them the most intelligent, most attentive, best possible service. And I tell them to have the chef on duty walk through those plates so they are just perfect when they get to the table.

What about having the chef walk over to the table to greet the critic?
No, because I don't like it myself.

Would you ever have the kitchen send out additional dishes as a welcome?
Oh, God, no, because I hate that. I just have them play it as if the critic were a regular customer.

Chefs admit they've also learned a thing or two over the years from critics' opinions. André Soltner, former chef-owner of Lutèce in New York City, remembers, "Gael Greene wrote an early article about Lutèce that was very good, but she criticized a few things, including the raspberry *soufflé glacé*, which she said was good but 'grainy.'

"I was a young chef then, and I immediately said, 'What the heck is she talking about, 'grainy'?! My *soufflé* is done in exactly the classic way!' But the next day, after I'd calmed down, I sat down and ate my *soufflé glacé*. And I said, 'Damn it. This lady is right! It *is* grainy!'" says Soltner. "And it made me go back and figure out how to improve it. If she had said nothing, then for the next twenty years maybe I would have made the *soufflé* grainy!"

On another occasion, after Lutèce had held four stars for many years, "We lost a star [in *The New York Times*]," says Soltner. "I was not angry about it, even though I was shocked at first. Everyone in the kitchen was shocked. And for about two months, we didn't cook with love. But I said to my people, and to myself, 'She's not wrong.' Maybe I didn't agree with everything she wrote, but on the other hand, maybe we had taken [our four-star status] for granted. After two years, we were re-reviewed and received four stars. So, I think she helped us very much."

Nancy Silverton credits a critic's comments with prompting the redesign of Campanile's dining room. "When Sherry [S. Irene Virbila of *The Los Angeles Times*] first reviewed our restaurant, she gave us a really wonderful review, but she mentioned that the back dining room as being really drab," says Silverton.

"If you get a bad review, it's easy to say, 'Oh, they don't know anything,'" she says. "But the truth of the matter is that I think they *do* know something, and that they keep you in check. As long as restaurant critics aren't prejudiced as reviewers, then I think you've got to take what they have to say."

William Rice, food and wine columnist for *The Chicago Tribune*, believes that one of the great problems for restaurants is that they rarely understand their own success, which allows critics to serve an important function in helping to pinpoint the reasons for it. "Restaurants are afraid to examine it. They think, 'I've done this and it works, so I'd better not change,'" he says. "When you walk through your dining room every night, with a few customers saying, 'Great meal!', you begin to believe it! So when a critic comes in and comments that the sauce was cold, the meat was overdone, and the bathroom was dirty, the immediate reaction is, 'Who is this son of a bitch? My customers love my food! Nobody's said anything!' It's very defensive on the part of the restaurant.

"Now the critic may identify the steak as a T-bone, and in fact it was a sirloin. But instead of pointing at that and saying, 'See, he doesn't know anything,' it's important for a restaurant to try to step back from a review and see what's being said that might be useful. And a 'dirty bathroom' is one of the best examples that I can think of because no customer is going to talk to you about that. But nobody's going to forget it, either."

That's *Not* Entertainment!

Several chefs and restaurateurs express resentment that some critics make a mockery of their business by treating the job of restaurant reviewing as an opportunity for sarcasm or low-brow humor. "Too many restaurant critics seem to think that restaurant reviewing is entertainment. And, by giving it stars and symbols, the reader is given a shorthand clue that it's seen as entertainment," says Joyce Goldstein, former chef-owner of Square One in San Francisco. "However, I don't believe that people's livelihoods should be other people's entertainment. When a restaurant gets slammed badly, forty people might lose their jobs. It affects the economy. I'm not saying you shouldn't say bad things. It's more a matter of *how* you say them, how *often* you say them, and the *spirit* with which you say them.

"You could say a dish is ill-conceived and explain why you think that's the case. Certain flavors might not work together, or might curdle or conflict, or might be out of balance. You can point this out, and people can agree or disagree with you," says Goldstein. "But to say that something tastes 'like dishwater' or 'an ashtray'? Come on! I don't see the place for that. I think a critic can say that a dish had 'an overly smoky taste,' or that a broth 'was so thin as to not be very flavorful,' or 'lacking flavor almost altogether.' You could find a lot of ways to say it. But to say 'dishwater'? That's a sign that critics are merely reveling in their power."

Norman Van Aken is also upset by some critics' approaches. "They should stop being so f—-ing cute," he complains. "Despite any valid criticism, their basic premise should be that they care. However, that is not what comes across with many critics these days. It's more

> "When you look at a restaurant review today, they don't say that there are going to be some things they like and some things they don't like. Instead, they go after the bad stuff with a machete, saying how disappointed they were."
> —Joyce Goldstein,
> formerly of Square One

the well-turned phrase, the double entendre. It's being cute. And they talk about chefs being self-indulgent!"

Mark Miller, chef-owner of Red Sage Grill in Washington, DC, and Coyote Cafe in Santa Fe, believes that, as businesses, it is unfair that restaurants are not judged along business lines. "I think *Consumer Reports* is fine because it's testing products that are essentially all alike on an absolute basis. How long does the battery last? How many miles per gallon does this car get?" he says. "But when you get into restaurants, you're getting into things that are not basically the same product. A dining experience is always a subjective experience; you cannot objectify a personalized experience. As much as you can describe it and critically analyze it, the basis of eating food is personal.

"My main objection to all the criticism that goes on in food is the quantification that is used as the basis of it: how much it cost, how long it took," says Miller. "The dining experience is entirely qualitative, and it's situational and individualistic. So, what most critics are doing is like measuring sex. A purchase is denoted in terms of what it is; whether it's a battery or a car, you can define what you're buying. But in food, or sex, you can't define it. What is good sex? How many kisses is it? *When* is it? *How* is it? It changes in terms of the situation and the person and the mood—as does the definition of good food."

What is 'A Good Review'?

Chefs and restaurateurs are filled with praise for critics who can capture a dining experience insightfully and articulately. Nancy Silverton is the first to admit that the most fulfilling review is not necessarily the 'best' review. "What means the most to me is when a critic 'gets' the spirit of Campanile," she says. "They don't try to make us anything that we're not. But [critics] Sherry [S. Irene Virbila], Jonathan [Gold], and Ruth [Reichl], in their own ways, for different reasons, have all said, 'This is the restaurant where I would eat on my night out.' And that's what I always wanted to be. None of them has ever said, 'Go to Campanile and you'll be blown away by their creativity' or 'You'll taste food that you've never tasted before.' But just the fact that they've all said, in their own way, 'This is the place that I relate to most in my own heart,' has been the most flattering to me."

Joyce Goldstein agrees. "Some of the food press really get it," she says. "I think someone like Patty Unterman, who has worked in restaurants, gets a feeling for the enthusiasm of the owner and the kitchen. Even if she doesn't love all the food, she tries to give you the excitement of being there. Other people don't give you that excitement, and sometimes you don't sense that they are even enjoying their job. They start with a physical description, and they move on with the menu, and then the service, and then the wine list— a set pattern. You never get the feeling that they just got carried away, or that they had a really good time or caught

on to the spirit of a restaurant. It's a job, with people taking themselves terribly seriously. I like to see education of the reader, explaining something about the food and its origins. Sometimes reviews cover that, but more often they don't."

Feedback to Critics

The responses critics receive to their reviews vary widely. "You'd be amazed," sighs Penelope Corcoran. "I've had James Beard Award nominees freak out. I've had mom-and-pop places be totally gracious. It really depends on how evolved the individuals are, and how much they can set aside their egos to hear what could be improved."

S. Irene Virbila, restaurant critic for *The Los Angeles Times*, agrees. "Sometimes I've gotten great letters from chefs which say, 'I thought you were correct. I did have this problem.' I've received some very heartfelt, intelligent letters, and others completely upset," she reports. "I'm surprised when it's a very mixed review, and a chef will still write and say, 'Thank you for taking the time to come in and consider our restaurant.' And part of that is that any publicity is good publicity. Sometimes they'll say, 'We're looking at these problems.' And that's a good thing. After all, I will go back at some point."

Some responses tip reviewers to the aftermath of their words. "I got a letter from Ocno, which is a hot new restaurant in [Chicago]," says Dennis Ray Wheaton. "It said something like, 'Thank you for your review. We've been mentioned in several publications, from *The Chicago Tribune* to *Vanity Fair*, and business has increased every time. But when the piece in *Chicago* magazine came out, we had a huge onslaught of people.'"

Phyllis Richman says that reactions to reviews are all over the map. "Some think that any criticism is a personal attack. Some of them are grateful for getting feedback. Some of them think that, whatever you say, since you're the critic, it has to be right. Some think that since you're the critic, it has to be *wrong*. Some say, 'You don't have the faintest idea what you're talking about, and you're trying to get me,'" she laughs.

A negative review of an all-time favorite restaurant is enough to start a stampede. Tom Sietsema, restaurant critic for *Washington Sidewalk*, recalls, "One of the largest public outcries I got was on my eighth review, when I took on Canlis, a well-known steakhouse in Seattle. Whereas everyone before had just drooled over themselves, giving it four stars, I gave them a one-star review—and I got over 350 letters. *Very* personal letters. Half of them hated me, writing 'I would hate to be your spouse,' 'How could you?', 'I'll bet you have a miserable life.' And the other half were people writing, 'Finally, someone told the truth!' Then they related stories about how they had gone there and spent their hard-earned money on a prom or special anniversary just to have a horrible experience.

"I was even accosted at a cocktail party over this review, and had to leave the party," Sietsema admits. "This guy was a lifelong Canlis lover and had just made reservations to take his wife there the next week for her birthday. What was I going to say? 'What a lousy place to take your wife'? Restaurants are a very personal thing. No one likes to be told their favorite restaurant is a dog."

See You in Court

Within legal channels, a restaurateur's last resort might be to file suit against a critic. "I was sued once, in the 1980s," says Alison Cook, restaurant critic for *Houston Sidewalk*. "I'd written a very negative review of La Colombe d'Or [in Houston] after eating there five times and finding only a couple dishes that were decent. The owner stormed into our offices, and I was advised to hide behind a desk! He'd been a lawyer, so he ending up filing suit, and I had to go to trial. In the end, the case was thrown out, but it took five days of my life. I learned that while hyperbole may be a good literary device, it's not good to use around litigious restaurateurs."

"Pino Luongo has threatened to sue me several times," adds Arthur Schwartz, restaurant reviewer at WOR Radio in New York City. "He'll claim there's some factual error, which is about the only way you can sue a restaurant critic. But, because it is criticism, you are allowed your opinion."

Sometimes It Gets Personal

Restaurants' frustrations over their lack of recourse to a negative review are sometimes expressed in inappropriate ways. "A PR person called me after I'd written a very negative review of [a seafood restaurant]," recalls Alison Cook. "I got chewed out for a while, and then I was told, 'But it's not like the owner's going to have your kneecaps broken or anything.' And I was once hung and burned in effigy [at a party held at] a bad Chinese restaurant that didn't like the review I wrote. I always regretted that I didn't attend, but I heard the food at the party was still just as bad as when I'd been there."

More than one critic cited thinly veiled threats from reputed mobsters. "It was a scary experience. One guy kept me on the phone for four hours," admits one critic, who asked not to be identified on this topic. "I didn't sleep for a week."

Other threats allowed little room for ambiguity. *San Francisco Examiner* restaurant critic Patricia Unterman remembers, "I was eating in this really popular place [The Flying Saucer in San Francisco] with a completely open kitchen, and taking notes in my lap. I could see the chef was staring at the table, and he finally came out from the kitchen, hot and sweating, with a chef's knife in his hand and a look in his eye. He said, 'Are you Patricia Unterman?' And I looked at him and then the knife and said, 'No.' He began ranting and raving: 'Oh, these people like Patricia Unterman. They don't understand what it is like to be a French chef! I started cooking when I was fourteen, and I apprenticed, and I don't know how they can say these things about me....'

"The meal had been good, and I wrote about the whole incident. I remarked, 'I don't know how to write about the service, you know, given the death threat,'" says Unterman. "But the chef sent me a huge bouquet of roses when the review came out."

Death threats are not the only frightening responses that restaurant critics get when their opinions are published. "I've gotten some pretty vicious messages," says Phyllis Richman. "Years ago, a guy called me and told me very graphically and violently what he wanted to do to me, and he hung up. But he had told me who he was! So I called him back, and his son answered. When I asked for the father, I was told, 'He just left.' And that was it—until I found out the next day that the restaurant burned down. It's creepy sometimes."

While trying to represent their readers, some critics have found themselves drawn into battle. "I received several phone calls from customers who had been extremely upset by the owner of a local restaurant. One woman had been reduced to tears," remembers Penelope Corcoran. "I wrote about it in a column, and the owner went ballistic on me. He made threatening phone calls, saying he would 'throw me out on my ass' if I ever came to his restaurant. Then, he had a campaign where he developed table-top [displays] with my likeness, and wrote that I 'take money' and I'm 'bulimic.' We had to get the lawyers to take care of it. I was scared because he was definitely unstable."

Critics have found some restaurateurs only 'fair-weather acquaintances.' "I reviewed a restaurant out in the suburbs that I liked quite a bit, and one of the things I liked was a dish with mussels," remembers Elaine Tait. "The restaurant sent me a note saying that they were so complimented that I liked the mussel dish that they were naming it after me because I was 'the premier restaurant critic in the United States.' About five years later, I went back to the restaurant, and the dish was awful. There wasn't anything I could say that was good about the place—it was that unusually bad. Well, the owner got so angry that he took out an ad in the *Inquirer*, and he said that I was unqualified and that no one should believe me. But he wasn't satisfied with that. He wanted to debate me in front of the local restaurant association. So I said, 'Fine, I'll be happy to, but I'll need a slide projector.' When I was asked why, I said it was because I had a letter from him saying that I'm the most qualified restaurant critic in the country, and I thought it might be fun to project it while we're talking. I never heard from him again.

"Another time, I had a rock thrown through the window of my home," remembers Tait. "We were living in the country, so it couldn't have been casual. First we heard a noise, but he must have missed the window. Then an hour or two later, he came back and threw a rock so hard that it went through the window, across the room, broke the paneling, and ricocheted halfway back across the room again. My reaction was to put my typewriter in front of the window, turn on all the lights in the room, and sit there with the rock in my hand, thinking, 'Come back. I want to show you how frightened I am!' Obviously, they wanted me to sort of know who it was, and I did because of certain circumstances, both timing and because they knew somebody else who knew me. But they're out of business now."

Aren't there better ways for restaurateurs to respond to reviews? Gael Greene believes there are. "From time to time, a restaurateur will either take out an ad or write a letter and say, 'Your critic ate a scallop and thought it was a peach, and we never served this dish or this could not have happened because of such-and-such,' she says. "So they do have a chance to respond. But they don't really have as strong a response as the review, and there's no way to get around that."

Greene's own critical review of Harry Cipriani's eponymous restaurant in the Sherry Netherland Hotel in New York City resulted in his writing a letter to the editor of *New York* magazine, which the magazine published. In it, he asked that Greene "remove the condom from her tongue" so that she could more accurately taste the food when reviewing. "I guess he just revealed his breeding," sighs Greene. "I think perhaps there was something to be said by Cipriani, but he would have had much more dignity if he'd said something in a biting, clever way instead of a vulgar, stupid way.

"I was more shocked that *New York* magazine ran [the letter] than that he wrote it….I couldn't believe that *New York* would use that language in the magazine. I also wrote an answer to his letter, but *New York* didn't run it. When I asked why, I was told, 'Oh, well, you weren't correcting any facts, so Kurt [Anderson, the former editor] decided not to run it.' So I said, 'What should I say? That I *wasn't* dressed like a clown? That I *didn't* have a condom on my tongue? Is *that* what you wanted me to correct?

"Shortly thereafter, I was in Venice. I was really hungry for a hamburger after all the seafood and black squid ink risotto and so on. And I love the hamburger at Cipriani. So, I walked in the door, and there was Cipriani himself serving somebody," says Greene. "It was very soon after the review that he wasn't too fond of, so I just turned around and walked out. And there was no hamburger that night. We had pizza," she adds, wistfully.

Greene understands how some people can take criticism so personally. "I am the worst person at being criticized," she admits. "If you write about me, and you say one thing that's critical, and it's in 10,000 words of how wonderful I am, I will fasten on that and wonder, 'What did I do?' and 'Why did you say that?'

"I remember when I was going around the country doing a book tour for my novel *Blue Skies, No Candy,* and I was wearing a slit skirt and ankle-strap platform shoes. I thought it was pretty sexy," recalls Greene. "But somebody wrote a story about how 'dowdy' this person was who had written this erotic novel. And everything else in the article was fine, but I thought, 'How could she say that?' Then again, she also said that my shoes were 'pumps.'"

Hide and Seek

Ruth Reichl's photograph was posted in the kitchens of more than one of the Manhattan restaurants where co-author Andrew Dornenburg has cooked professionally. One even offered a $50 reward to any staff member who spotted her. A sharp-eyed waitress who recognized a slight resemblance to the wide-angle photograph that *The Wine Spectator* published shortly after Reichl started won the money.

Because restaurants have a great deal at stake, they go to great lengths to spot critics. Tavern on the Green circulated a memo to the restaurant's staff regarding Ruth Reichl, *The New York Times*'s restaurant critic:

March 20, 1995
Attached you will find a photocopy of a picture of Ruth Reichl, the restaurant critic for *The New York Times*. Please be advised that some of the aliases she makes reservations under are listed on the photograph. They are: Hollis, Shore, and Johnson. I am sure there are others.

We understand that Ruth has very curly hair, shoulder length, that it usually looks rather uncombed, and that she pushes the hair in front of her face so that people won't recognize her. Please watch for Ruth or anyone who fits this description, and make sure that everyone is informed if a person who looks like this is dining at Tavern on the Green. She will probably be writing about us.

It should also be noted that she only travels in parties of two or three. She does work weekends, so she can appear on a Saturday or a Sunday, brunch or dinner. Her advance person is a gentleman about thirty-eight years old, who usually comes in and checks the front desk and lobby area first, and then waits for Ruth either in the cocktail lounge or at the table.

Ruth uses a tape recorder to record her thoughts during dinner. If you see a woman in the dining room who fits the description speaking into a small tape recorder, most likely it will be Ruth. Occasionally, she goes into the ladies' room to do her taping, but she also does taping at the table as well.

The photograph has already been circulated to the entire dining staff—captains, waiters, busboys, front desk, etc. Anyone who needs additional copies, feel free to ask.

• • •

A manager at Tavern on the Green later noted, "Also, aside from the description of Ruth Reichl in the previous memo, I have found from restaurants she has already reviewed that she sometimes wears her hair in a ponytail, but it is still curly. She is short and always dresses in black. Another thing that may help you recognize her: I have been told that she is always smiling. She smiles a lot."

The cat-and-mouse game is partly what hurts the chance of any kind of "normal" relationship, not to mention the huge imbalance of power between critics and the restaurants they review. Still, some critics are close to or friendly with certain chefs or restaurateurs. Otherwise, relations can be strained, so critics claim they prefer to have none. On the other hand, a restaurateur's business is to find out who the critics are. Bob Kinkead recalls, "I was at a food convention with Jasper [White], and he knew who Phyllis [Richman] was and I didn't. So I made him introduce me to her so I'd know who she was when she came into the restaurant.

"If you've invested $1.25 million in a project and certain people can crush you like a bug if they have a bad time, you're a fool if you're not trying to find out who these people are, what they look like, and when they're in," says Kinkead. "Phyllis Richman came into 21 Federal about two weeks after we opened, and I was up at the front

"I think if I were a restaurateur, I would pretend I didn't see me. I'd just make sure that everything was as perfect as possible. When you feel you're not known, you're so much less self-conscious, and you can enjoy the evening and talk and not think that people are looking to see whether you're smiling or swallowing."
—Gael Greene,
New York

door looking at the reservations book when she walked in the door. So I was able to say, 'Hello, Ms. Richman. How are you?' And I let my staff know, 'Phyllis Richman is at table twenty-five. Make sure you memorize what this woman looks like!'"

Gordon Hamersley, chef-owner of Hamersley's Bistro in Boston, recalls the time Legal Sea Foods' owner Roger Berkowitz introduced him to Alison Arnett at a social event. "I had no idea what she looked like for the first two reviews," Hamersley admits. "So I kind of joked, 'You're kidding—let me get my camera!' But I was already snapping pictures of her mentally! And it also happened that my two sous chefs were both at this event, so I just dragged them over and introduced them to her, too. And it was really good for them to meet her. Critics are very important to our lives, and they can take on proportions that are fantastical unless you actually see them for the human beings that they are."

Sometimes running into a critic is natural, and may even be beneficial to the process. Daniel Boulud remembers, "One time when Ruth Reichl was in, I was doing my tour of the dining room, and I was not going to skip her table. I said hello, and she had a question about the sauce on the wild hare. She said, 'There's something intriguing in the sauce. What could it be?' I told her how we finish it with wine, spices, and a little bit of bitter chocolate. She thought, 'Ah, chocolate. That's it!' But if I hadn't told her, maybe she would have always been intrigued by the real depth of that dish, because you cannot describe the depth of a dish's flavor unless you know how it's made."

Terrance Brennan recalls keeping a particular dish on his menu at Picholine for months, just so Reichl would have an opportunity to review it. "I knew my roasted chestnut soup was a superb soup, and I really wanted her to try it," Brennan admits. "And it was a good thing I did. She ultimately mentioned in the review that it was 'the most perfect winter dish' she's ever eaten."

Church and State

The difficulties associated with dishing out—or taking—criticism have led to the unspoken practice of arms' length relations between most critics and restaurant chefs and owners. While notable exceptions exist, most critics try to maintain this separation of "church" and "state."

"If you have a sense of how much the person is trying, it does make it harder [to levy criticism]," says Gael Greene. "I often call the owner or the chef of a restaurant when I'm looking over my notes and ask questions: 'What was in that dish?' 'Where did you work before?' 'How did you come to do this?' And then you find out what they had in mind. I think what they had in mind versus what they've created is always interesting."

Alison Arnett, restaurant critic for *The Boston Globe*, agrees. "Always, at the end of a review process, when I'm writing, I call and talk to the management and chef," she says. "Otherwise, how would you know everything? I'll ask them to describe how they do a particular thing, and I think it's good to know what they put into it—how much intensity, or education, or whatever. I think it's important to talk with the person who makes the food."

Sometimes this step in the review process yields a plea from the restaurants for Arnett to return. "I've had some Indian and Chinese restaurants tell me, 'No, no, no, come back and I'll give you the *real* food! Come be my guest!' It's very sweet, but it doesn't help," she says. "It makes you think, 'What are most people walking in your door getting, if it's not what you can really cook?'"

Ruth Reichl found moving to New York City, where she knew few chefs and restaurateurs, a professional boon. She says, "When I was writing about food in San Francisco, I'd done a number of pieces for which I interviewed chefs. I'd written a piece about the opening of Michael's in Santa Monica, and one on the opening of Chinois [on Main] for which I spent almost a year with [chef Wolfgang Puck] and Barbara [Lazaroff] very closely. I knew Mark [Peel] and Nancy [Silverton] very well. I knew a lot of chefs down in Los Angeles. And I don't approve of it.

"I feel like I was lucky when I came to New York, because I knew almost no one. And I don't want to be friends with anyone. You do not want to have someone's face in your head while you're writing. You don't want to disappoint people that you care about. The less you know, the better off you are," says Reichl. "The truth is, I'm the advocate for the consumer. I'm the representative of the person who's spending money, and it's my obligation to be as fair as I can. And that is hard to do when you're getting feedback from them. It's easier when you don't have to struggle with yourself over that."

"I'm not known by a lot of chefs. I usually don't go to food events or dinners. You're a different figure in the community if you go to them. You become a force, and not just a critic. And then you don't look at it from the outside."
—Alison Arnett,
 The Boston Globe

[Im]Balance of Power

Chefs and restaurateurs view critics as their biggest champions, or their greatest detractors. One of their gravest concerns is that, once a review is published, they can do almost nothing to counteract its impact, even if its accuracy and fairness are called into question. In that case, although they can ask for a retraction, there is no certainty that there will be one—or if there is, no guarantee that it will appear promptly. More than one leading chef cited instances of having jeopardized relationships with critics by disagreeing with them either publicly or privately. Some have detected retribution in subsequent reviews, as critics in major cities often become long-term fixtures on the local restaurant scene.

Some chefs and restaurateurs seriously question whether the media always apply the same journalistic standards to what appears in their food pages as they do to the rest of the news they report. "When you open and you're very busy, there are always people who are angry that they can't get in or can't get a reservation when they want," says Anne Rosenzweig. "You don't recognize how important they are, so they're angry. A letter, or maybe more than one letter, went to Bryan Miller [of *The New York Times*] saying, 'Those people at Arcadia are so greedy. They put in all these extra tables, and now it's too squeezed.' Meanwhile, we had never done anything! As many tables as we opened with on opening day, we have no more, and no less, fourteen years later. If we had put more in, you wouldn't have been able to move, and if we had put fewer in, it wouldn't have been economically viable. So it was absolutely not true.

"Meanwhile, some [writer] on the *Times*'s financial desk decided to write about wonderful restaurants that get ruined because they get

RESTAURANT CRITICS' LONGEVITY	
Critic (City)	Tenure
Elaine Tait (Philadelphia)	35+ years
Gael Greene (New York City)	30+ years
Caroline Bates (California)	25+ years
Alison Cook (Houston)	25+ years
Phyllis Richman (Washington, DC)	20+ years
Patricia Unterman (San Francisco)	20+ years

reviewed. The writer asked Miller about it, and he apparently mentioned Arcadia and the 'extra' tables and, without fact-checking, *The New York Times* published it.

"I was devastated that I was portrayed in such a light," says Rosenzweig. "Customers I liked came in and said, 'Did you see what the *Times* wrote about you?' Then I had customers saying 'Are you really greedy? Did you really do this?' It hurt me, and I felt it would hurt my reputation and my business. So I called up the editor and said, 'No one fact-checked this story, which is very damaging to me. I don't know who the reporter is. What's going on? Please, I'd really like a retraction. It's not true.' A week went by, and nothing happened.

"Then I got a call in the middle of dinner service one night from Miller, saying, 'Anne, what's the matter? It's not that big a deal.' That's when I figured out that he was the source. And I said, 'Well, Bryan, it's a big deal to me. And it's a big deal to my staff, who feel hurt by it, and to my customers, who are suspicious of me now.' I said, 'What about journalistic integrity and truth?' I think that was what he didn't like, so that was basically the end of the conversation," says Rosenzweig. "About a month later, they printed a tiny little retraction which, coming a month later, is next to meaningless."

Even in a non-review situation, restaurateurs are understandably concerned how their restaurants are portrayed in the media, especially when an article for which a restaurant is interviewed develops a life of its own. "The day we opened [Gramercy Tavern], the cover story of *New York* magazine had a picture of our matchbox with four stars below it, asking, 'The Next Great Restaurant?'" reports Danny Meyer. "Of course, 99 percent of the people who saw it felt we were proposing ourselves as the next four-star restaurant, which was not the case.

"We were told that the article, for which we were cooperative, was supposed to be published by another magazine [*The New Yorker*] six months after the restaurant opened, as kind of a 'how to open up a restaurant' piece, as opposed to a hyperbolic cover story in *New York* the day we opened," Meyer explains. "I got so many calls from people who said, 'I never knew you were so cocky!'"

Has the award-winning restaurant Al Forno in Providence ever received bad press? "*Rhode Island Monthly*," cites Johanne Killeen, Al Forno's chef–co-owner. "They *hate* us. About four or five months ago, they sent a reviewer over who had no concept of what live, fresh fish was all about. It was a *horrible* review. She nit-picked about every-

"It's horrible to give a bad review. I hate it because I know how vulnerable restaurant owners are. They have no platform to answer back. They're helpless. And once it's out there, it's almost impossible to take back."
—Patricia Unterman,
The San Francisco Examiner

thing, and she said that the fish was 'mushy.' We were very discouraged about that."

"Still, the review brought people through the door," adds Killeen's partner, George Germon. "Yes, it did," she concedes. "It was a great controversy for a while, and people love controversy and to take sides. So people would come in and say, 'I wrote a letter to that magazine. Who do they think they are?' You'd have that, and you'd have other people saying, 'Well, they deserve what they get. Who do they think they are?'"

Sometimes the press that hurts most involves sins of omission. "A restaurateur in Randolph [Massachusetts] had been to our restaurant many times, and took a lot of the stuff from our menu and put it on his menu, including grilled pizza," says Killeen. "When *The Boston Globe* decided to do an article on grilled pizza, they interviewed *him*. He told them, 'This comes from the Jewish ghetto in Rome,' and the *Globe* printed it. I called Sheryl [Julian at *The Boston Globe*] and said, 'What's going on? You know that's not true.' She said, 'Well, I'm sure George [Germon] told me ten years ago that's where it came from.' I said, 'Sheryl, I can stake my life on the fact that George never said that to you. We've had influences from everywhere, but the grilled pizza is

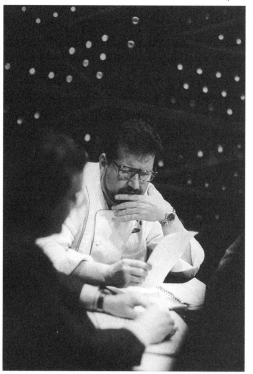

George's creation.' She just backpedaled and backpedaled, and of course the paper didn't do anything. But I couldn't believe that they would print that in the first place, even if they were confused about the dish's origin, knowing that we had been doing it for fifteen years longer than this guy. Why wouldn't they fact-check?

"We get screwed because food is not taken seriously," Killeen continues. "We can say, 'It's just food,' in that it's just food compared to brain

I'd like to tell young chefs and restaurateurs that it is within their rights to expect fair, honest, and informed criticism. And if they don't find it, they should complain to whomever the critic is working for. I think that some critics out there really don't do a very good job, and that people are intimidated by them and think that they have no recourse. But they do, if enough people complain.

If somebody's a bully, you should complain. You should! But make sure you know what you're talking about, and then complain. Sooner or later the message will get through to that person's employer.

I don't think there should be an adversarial relationship between critics and the people in the business. I think that if somebody is unhappy with a review and has a legitimate gripe, they should feel free to tell you. And they should also know that you are not going to go 'get 'em' for saying so. Jack McDavid [of Jack's Firehouse in Philadelphia] was always saying to me, "I don't always agree with what you say, ma'am, but I defend your right to say it."

"The more power a publication has, the more knowledge its restaurant critic should have."
—Bradley Ogden,
   Lark Creek Inn and
   One Market Restaurant

surgery. It's *not* brain surgery. But we're *not* saying 'It's just food, and it's nothing.' On a national morning television show, a former employee of ours who has a cookbook made grilled pizza. When asked about it, it came out as 'his' idea. On national television!

"Yet another guy in Florida was interviewed about serving grilled pizza, and a former employee sent us the article," remembers Killeen. "The guy is from Rhode Island and opened his restaurant a year or so ago. He was asked, 'Where did you get the idea for grilled pizza?' and he replied, 'It just came to me one day.'

"And we can't do anything," laments Killeen. "We went to see a lawyer about this, and were discussing copyrights and patents, but we were told we can't copyright grilled pizza. He said, 'You cannot copyright a recipe. You can copyright a painting because it's a creative process, and you can copyright prose, but you cannot copyright a recipe.'"

"But it has to change somewhere," insists Germon. "What happens now in cooking is that nobody really knows where the reference point comes from. Right now, anybody can get on national television with a dish and say, 'Yes, I created this. This is mine.'"

Chefs on Critics' Credentials

Because of the food media's power in recording culinary history and arbitrating standards in the restaurant business, chefs and restaurateurs are outspoken on the subject of the credentials that should be required of restaurant critics. One chef laments, "Sometimes I resent that after working for decades in this business, I have to wait for marks like a schoolboy, and from people who know barely one-tenth as much as I do about cooking."

"Some great food critics out there know their stuff inside and out and up and down, and they teach us. But who knows how other people got into this?" asks Johanne Killeen. "Because they eat? Does that mean they can criticize what someone is doing?"

"Food critics should, perhaps, be licensed," muses Norman Van Aken. "They should have a certain amount of knowledge—or at least the public should be made aware that they don't. 'I'm Harvey Bigmouth, and this is my opinion. I've never been to cooking school, and I've never cooked, but you might like what I have to say, so read my column or listen to my radio show' or whatever. Fine. But there should be a little disclaimer up there. The public, unfortunately, subscribes to these stars ratings and blindly follows them without forming their own opinions."

Jeremiah Tower believes a critic should be a trained writer and a trained intellect. "They should know something about the field, or they should at least like it," he says. "And they should be able to cook, or know something about how a restaurant is run. They've got to have seen great service somewhere, both formal and informal. And they've got to know something about value, what the things on the table cost. Some critics feel that any dish over $18 is a rip-off.

"A critic should be someone who is a professional and knows something about the business, but who has discipline. You have to have the intellectual discipline to be able to write about all kinds of cuisine. So if you don't know Indian food, you'll have someone teach you about it so you can provide that service for Indian restaurants," says Tower.

"You need to know about food to be a food writer, or a restaurant critic," says Mark Peel. "Russ Parsons [*Los Angeles Times* food writer] started out as a sportswriter and he, on his own, got the training and the knowledge he needed to do the job. But a lot of people don't. Instead, it's as if they were pulled from other parts of publication almost as an afterthought."

"Reviewers should be well-educated," agrees Bradley Ogden. "They should have worked in kitchens, and they should know how kitchens are run and how a business should operate. Some do, but many don't. They should have that knowledge before they're able to write about restaurants."

Still, chefs understand that no critic is an expert on everything. "It's okay to point out, 'I don't know enough about this, so I brought a friend with me for dinner who is knowledgeable about it.' That, I think, is a good thing. Or, 'I called the restaurant later to find out about this.' Or, 'I went to the library and got a book on Vietnamese cooking and found this out,'" says Joyce Goldstein. "But when you are cranking out five reviews a week, you don't have time to do research. So, to me, that is the difference between criticism and reviewing. Reviewing is 'You went, you ate there, and you had a good time, or not.' And then there is criticism, for which you actually do your homework. How many newspapers, cranking out stuff on deadline all the time, pretend to do that?

"To me, a review is getting the facts right," says Goldstein. "I have seen reviews in which the manager, the owner, and the chef's name were spelled wrong! Did you tell us a little bit about the food, the scope of the menu, the price range? It's information. It might mention a couple of things one liked and a couple one didn't, but it doesn't take itself so seriously. Criticism implies having a scale of knowledge and having a range of things that serve as a basis of comparison. It involves a certain level of intelligence, a frame of reference, a big picture, and some depth behind the words."

Ideal Review Process

What is the best approach for a critic to take in order to evaluate the food? Is the point to evaluate what a restaurant is capable of when operating at its peak—or what the average diner is likely to experience?

"Occasionally I order a tasting menu, but generally I'm tasting a cacophony of things. A problem with the way a critic works is that seldom can I tell people whether a dish is going to be interesting all the way through, or whether it's going to get boring after four bites," says Phyllis Richman. "I don't often know what it's like to sit down and eat simply that dish. I think it's a drawback for the reader. But there's no way that you can do this job thoroughly. You can't go in and have one meal just by yourself for each possibility on the menu. It's definitely an imperfect art."

Elaine Tait muses about the benefits of a European approach. "I would love to see a situation where you continue the tradition of the

> *"When anyone gets such a bad review that everyone talks about it across the nation, they say, 'Well, they should have been one of us; they should have worked in a restaurant.' But no one ever says that when they get a great review. In fact, no one says anything about restaurant critics' credentials when they get a great review."*
> —Jeremiah Tower,
> Stars

anonymous critic, but also have a critic for fine dining restaurants who behaves in the European manner, where you call the restaurant and announce, 'Eight of us are coming in at eight o'clock on Friday night, and we want to spend $80 a person. Do your best.' And then you can grade them, giving them the advantage to show their best, as opposed to this sort of defensive 'Where can we find fault?' attitude. It won't happen because it's too expensive. But the review system is stacked against the chef, even though probably 90 percent of the reviews written in this country are favorable," she says.

Sirio Maccioni, owner of Le Cirque 2000 in New York City, would like to see a similar system. "I know the limitations that they have, coming only three or four times to my restaurant. In a restaurant like this, they should say, 'Let me see what you can do,'" he says. "But they don't. They go to restaurants and have three appetizers and three main courses."

Critics' approaches to the review process are sometimes antithetical to a chef's intentions. "What bothers me about critics is that they don't eat the whole meal, generally," says George Germon. "We lose out a lot of times because of high-impact cooking. You can put two or three tastes of something in your mouth, and you could fall off the chair, but if they'd had a fourth or fifth taste, maybe they would have found the dish too overwhelming, too salty, too cloying. And because our food is subtle, this is where we lose out. It's the purity that's in it. When I eat something, I don't like to muddle it. I don't like to eat fish with meat. I wouldn't want to cross over to [my partner] Johanne's plate and say, 'Let me taste that.' I want to taste what this person was trying to do, and get the whole experience. What are the condiments on the plate? Do they enhance or take away from the food? We care about those things."

Johanne Killeen adds, "And just like tasting wines with certain foods, where certain foods will make the wine taste off, certain foods will make other food taste off. Once, a critic came in as a party of five and ordered five main courses. Everyone took one bite, then passed the plate—and the review is based on that kind of experience! I mean, maybe there is one person out there who can synthesize all of that, but I think for a good and fair review, the critic should come in and have an experience, maybe with one other person, and come back and have another experience and another experience...."

Daniel Boulud agrees that a critic should try to understand an individual chef's intention. He comments, "Critics may have great knowledge of food and an understanding of the classics, but to interpret a

CHEFS ON KNOWING CRITICS' BIASES

Alice Waters, Chez Panisse: "I think you really need to know the reviewer and what his or her tastes are. I'd like them to just put it out on the table by having a little disclaimer at the bottom of the review—you know, 'I'm reviewing restaurants, but my ideal meal is pasta and salad.' I think that a reviewer should describe his prejudices, his likes and dislikes. If he likes cheap wine, he's not going to be able to evaluate the fancy bottles on the list. That way, you know when you're reading the review that when he mentions wine, it's not his strong suit, so you can read past it if you like."

Anne Rosenzweig, Arcadia and The Lobster Club: "They all have their quirks. There are things they do like. There are things they don't like. There are things that happen in the dining room that get them upset. We're all quirky. There are things we hate or absolutely love and somebody next to you would go 'What? Are you kidding?'"

Norman Van Aken, Norman's: "How many words is an average, full-length review? And how many times a year do they come out with reviews? Add it up, and that has got to be, probably, two full-length novels! You're going to know that person's predilections, for sure. I think it's inevitable."

"Any critic is welcome to spend time in my kitchen."
—Norman Van Aken, Norman's

particular chef's dishes is very difficult." For this reason, Boulud believes critics should try to better understand chefs and what they are trying to achieve through their food. "Not too many writers know how to deeply write about somebody because too few have any deep knowledge of the person they are writing about," he says. "That's why many reviews all read the same."

Boulud believes it would behoove critics to spend time in the kitchens of the restaurants they review. "When you taste something complex, as a whole it may be a great sensation, but sometimes you don't know if it's only 5 ingredients or 15 ingredients that go into the dish to make it that way," he says. "I think for critics, it's almost necessary to plunge into a restaurant kitchen and see the actual life of a dish, to really see what depths a dish actually undergoes in preparation."

Mark Miller believes that critics should get to know a chef's preferences. "The chef always starts with those things that please him—always. So without knowing what is pleasurable to him, it's hard to put it into the proper context," he says. "Some chefs are like surrealist artists, who are great thinkers. Jean-Louis Palladin [of Napa in Las Vegas] is a great thinker. Some chefs are whimsical, like David Burke [of Park Avenue Cafe in New York]. And [David] Bouley [of Bouley Bakery in New York] is a kind of scientist, but a little more sensual than that. Jeremiah [Tower] is much more dramatic. Alice [Waters] is much more generous. Women are much more into their own bodies than men are, and men tend to be much more concept-driven in their food. But how many critics write about this?"

In communicating a chef's intention, Miller believes critics should be comprehensive, and not selective. "I think a good review should not pick dishes, but should publish the entire menu," says Miller. "I think the menu tells something about the way the chef thinks, his progression of courses, his flavors, his belief in seasonality, and the way he puts foods, flavors, and colors together."

Many chefs would like to see a more interactive approach used in reporting on restaurants. "I think the chef, or the owner, or possibly both, should be allowed a certain number of words to share their mission statement," says Miller. "The chef should say what his food is about. The restaurateur should say who the target audience is. The designers should say something about what they did. A review should convey who they want to have come to the restaurant."

In addition, Miller believes the public should be informed of a critic's beliefs and prejudices. "I think that at least once a year, critics should state their philosophy about food," he says. "And once a year, they should reflect in a few thousand words about the meaning of their food experiences in the last year, what they got out of it, and what that means in society. They should prove to the public that they can actually think about food. And I think they should go to culinary schools, like the Culinary Institute of America, and give lectures on their philosophy of food criticism."

An interactive dialogue on restaurants can be encouraged other ways, according to Joyce Goldstein. "I read the Sunday *New York Times Book Review* section, and it's interesting because sometimes the people who are reviewing have an ax to grind. Sometimes they've written a book about a similar subject and don't fully agree with the author they're reviewing. Sometimes the author's findings are a revelation for them. But there's a context there. And you can read the correspondence that happens as a result of the review, so there is actually a dialogue that takes place.

"I think one of the delicious things about criticism is the letters to the editor and the things that come afterward because that is how you get smarter. The whole point is to learn more, to open up a dialogue," says Goldstein. "I love reading those letters to the editor. Sometimes they say, 'How could you have let so-and-so review that book?' And you think, 'They obviously knew that, and they let that person review that book anyway. They had an agenda, too.' And then you get the author's letter. It's exciting, and you learn something.

"Well, you don't get that in restaurant reviewing," Goldstein continues. "How often do you see a dialogue? It could be from the chef or the owner who feels that [the critic] didn't understand the food. I know people have claimed that dishes have been criticized that have not even been cooked in the restaurants. That tells me there's some sloppiness, or someone coming in with an agenda."

The Role of Price

The arts critic who mentions a performance in the context of the price paid for admission is a rare thing. However, given the roots of restaurant criticism as a consumer service, the subject of price is often raised. How do chefs react to this?

"The '$25 and Under'-type of reviews bug me a little bit," admits Rick Bayless. "By their very name, they're saying, 'Don't take this too seriously.' Nobody says, 'We're going to give four stars to a restaurant that is doing what it set out to do perfectly.' That's a problem. Because then you say, 'Okay, the table wasn't as nice at this cheap place as it was at another place, so it doesn't deserve as many stars.' The French, for example, really value table-setting: the china, the glassware, the silverware, the tablecloth. I'm not sure if that's the way to look at it. I think it's more a matter of whether a restaurant is doing what it set out to do perfectly. I think we could have a better understanding of American food if we could do it that way."

Norman Van Aken considers the way in which critics approach the subject of price. "They might approach it from the standpoint that, within a certain atmosphere, $29.95 might be a lot for a catfish dinner, considering the placemats were paper and the waitress's name was Dixie. Or they might think that $29.95 was okay because they were in a place where they were served on china with silver, or something like that. But it needs to be on a register where it all makes sense together," he says. "Too often they use perjorative terms like 'expensive.' To me, 'expensive' is completely subjective. I'm expecting to spend hundreds of dollars on lunch on Wednesday [at Restaurant Daniel in New York City], and believe me, I think every cent will be well spent."

"I always think there's more joy in finding a wonderful meal at a reasonable price. And I think it's arrogant, and a mistake, when an ordinary new restaurant charges as much as a very good, established restaurant. It would be better to start out somewhat more modest, and to see what the response is. Seeing a tiny little restaurant start out with $10 desserts really annoys me."
—Gael Greene,
  New York

Terrance Brennan doesn't believe critics always understand what's behind a restaurant's pricing structure. "They ask why chicken costs $26, but it's not the chicken—it's the china, it's the staff, it's the twenty people behind the scenes who are slicing and chopping. Fine dining is very labor-intensive, and labor is a high cost. A recent article about wine asked why everyone wasn't charging $6 for a glass of wine! [The writer didn't understand that] we sell only two things. That's *all* we make money on. And we have a staff of sixty-eight people. How are they going to get paid if we don't make money on wine?

"Food writers need to know what goes on behind the scenes and what goes into a restaurant of this caliber to make it all go," says Brennan. "I think that if the customer knows that something is a luxury ingredient, it is easier for them to be comfortable spending their money on it. What's not known is all the prices of all the little herbs and baby lettuces that are used, not to mention the wines used in the sauces. I spend $3,000 to $4,000 just on cooking wine every month. I think the four-star restaurants in New York City are underpriced if you compare them to the best restaurants in Europe."

Sirio Maccioni agrees. "While critics today say that everything here is 'too expensive,' they go to France, and say, 'Oh, we're in paradise! We had the dream lunch and the dream dinner.' But in Paris, it's a *minimum* of $200 per person if you're careful, while they come here and say we're 'too expensive' when we have a *prix fixe* lunch for $35 per person with everything included! This is not fair, and it is misleading. When Europeans come to my restaurant and I give them the bill, they say, 'Oh, thank you very much!' They all think we gave them a special discount!"

Chefs and Restaurateurs on the Star System

Danny Meyer's peers often cite him as one of America's most respected restaurateurs. But neither of his well-regarded restaurants, Union Square Cafe and Gramercy Tavern, holds a four-star rating from *The New York Times*. "Back in the days of Bryan

Miller and Mimi Sheraton, the star system was much different in New York, primarily in that the fourth star was used and, more importantly, the 'Satisfactory' and 'Poor' ratings were used," says Meyer. "Today, the 'Satisfactory' and 'Poor' ratings are never used, except maybe once every two years. As a result of that, and because the fourth star is not used that often, it's basically a three-star system: one star is 'not very good,' two is 'what's expected,' and three stars is 'very good, but not perfect.' Back in the late 1970s and early 1980s, a two-star rating was considered a very good review. Consequently, getting two stars just ninety days after we opened the Union Square Cafe was a big deal.

"Today, that's considered average and not something that people strive for," Meyer explains. "Last week, a Chinese restaurant got one star, and its review read like a one-star review used to read, which was, 'This is a really compelling restaurant to go to. They're not doing anything wrong; just don't go there expecting formality or fanciness or technical flawlessness.' One star was never used as a punishment unless it was a demotion from something else. Union Square Cafe and Arizona 206 were the first two restaurants that broke the barrier that a three-star restaurant had to be a formal restaurant. It was the first time that they looked and said, 'Well, the word next to it is 'Excellent,' not 'Formal.' That was in 1989, and we haven't been reviewed since."

Other restaurateurs are well aware of what most diners characterize as a "four-star restaurant." Rick Bayless says, "When most people read reviews, they read the stars, and nothing else. I'll bet they get people at four-star restaurants who have never even read one word of the review but just saw that it was four stars and go to the restaurant with the idea that they are going to have their 'perfect' meal. And maybe they will, because the china and the silver are exquisite, and the service is great. So maybe they will have the perfect meal no matter what is put in front of them because it meets all the criteria they think are important for that kind of restaurant.

"I would die if I opened a restaurant, and it got four stars," says Bayless. "That's the kiss of death as far as I'm concerned because everybody is going to come in expecting their 'perfect meal' on the plate. But what does that mean? How many times can you hit that? People might come into our restaurant and say, 'I didn't like a thing.' So what—if what we did, we believe we did perfectly well. If we made a mistake, then that's our fault, but if we did it all right, and customers say they didn't like a thing....Well, everybody's got different taste. You

"Stars are just the quick, easy way of judging everything. How many people even bother reading the reviews after they see the stars, though? 'Two stars. Why should I bother reading this column? Skip it. Where's Garfield? What's my horoscope?'"
—Norman Van Aken,
  Norman's

have to account for people's taste but, at the same time, with a four-star rating, everybody expects it to be perfect according to what *their* rules are."

Reading the Stars

Many chefs and restaurateurs say they would prefer to see more restaurant reviews appear without an accompanying star rating. "The quantification is the part that I object to," says Rick Bayless. "It's not uncommon in Chicago for someone to read a review by one of our local reviewers that has one negative thing after another after another, and then to see it given three out of four stars. Or sometimes a glowing review will come out, with one star. What is *that* all about? I don't understand it."

Anne Rosenzweig agrees. "It's interesting, because they don't give stars in theater or movie reviews, at least not at *The New York Times*. I think [star ratings] are kind of screwy sometimes. Occasionally you'll read a really wonderful review of a two-star restaurant. Sometimes you'll even read something that's not that good, and it has three stars! That's when I ask myself, 'Whoa, what planet am I on?'"

Second-guessing the critics' ratings has become a sport for self-professed restaurant lovers. Do many chefs play along? "Well, maybe there *are* some three-stars that should not have three stars, and some two-stars that should be three-stars, and some four-stars that should not be four-stars, and some three-stars that should be four-stars!" laughs Daniel Boulud.

André Soltner plays the game, too. "When Jean Georges, for example, got four stars [from *New York Times* restaurant critic Ruth

Reichl] I thought, 'Well, that's the only thing she could have given it!'" Soltner professes. "I had eaten there the week before, and I thought, 'If this guy doesn't get four stars, then I don't know *what* you have to do to get it!'"

Months before Le Cirque 2000 received its four-star rating, Soltner also judged it as deserving nothing but: "I've eaten there three times already, and it's been great. Nobody in the world can do better than that!" Soltner expressed surprise that the restaurant, which had been open for more than four months at the time of our interview, had not yet been reviewed. "In my head, I ask myself, 'How come?' It must be something."

Star-following among chefs is more akin to avid sports fans' following batting averages than determining which restaurants to try. "I'd never decide whether to go to a restaurant based on how many stars it got," says Daniel Boulud. "I'd go because I like the place, or because I like the chef. The stars would be completely irrelevant. A review might help you to rediscover a restaurant, or discover a new one. But for the most part, I always go to the same bistros, like La Goulue or Trois Jean, or Gotham Bar & Grill on a Sunday night."

Stars do function as a shorthand for readers, according to David Waltuck. "Most people who read restaurant reviews are not very discerning," he observes. "If there aren't stars, they are not really clear on what to think. They might remember the first couple of sentences and the last couple of sentences, and sometimes they'll even remember enough about the review to know whether it's a restaurant they might like. However, ratings take away the possibility of people making up their own minds."

Gordon Hamersley doesn't like the fact that a star rating reduces the idea of a restaurant to a certain number of stars. "In six months, nobody is going to remember the nice things [Alison Arnett] wrote about her fish or her waiter [in *The Boston Globe*]," he says. "All they're going to remember is, 'Oh, Hamersley's Bistro got X number of stars.'"

Charlie Palmer believes starless reviews allow both the reader and the restaurant to take a review the way they want. "I've heard people say, 'I got a great review!' Meanwhile, I'm thinking, 'Gee, I read that, and I didn't think it was that great. I thought it was a pretty *bad* review,'" chuckles Palmer. "It's funny how people perceive what they read sometimes."

"I hate it when people write negative things about me, but thank God they're writing about me in the first place. Thank God restaurants today are thought to be important enough to occupy space in newspapers and magazines."
—Chris Schlesinger,
   East Coast Grill

Six
Exploring the Art of Criticism

"All the arts are brothers;

Each one is a light to

the others."

—Voltaire (1694–1778)

Today there are more options vying for our disposable income and limited time than ever before. We depend on critics to make more informed decisions to enhance our satisfaction and even pleasure regarding everything from which computer to buy to which movie to see. At the same time, the dramatic rise in the number of restaurants has elevated the societal role played by restaurant critics. Not only do they help readers decide among the myriad options available to them, but they provide advice on getting the most out of these experiences.

Dennis Ray Wheaton, chief dining critic for *Chicago* magazine, remembers, "I taught a course for about three years at Northwestern University on 'The Social Role of a Professional Critic.' I'd start out every class by bringing in the previous Sunday's *New York Times's* entertainment section, which includes plays and movies. I'd take a red marker and circle every advertisement that listed the critics' raves about a performance, and there might be 80 or 90 of those blurbs. Then I would ask the students, 'What do you think this is about?'

"This exercise made clear that the role critics have is as very important gatekeepers between the public and the people who are pro-

ducing these cultural works," Wheaton explains. "It doesn't matter if you're *Consumer Reports* magazine reviewing a new car, or writing restaurant criticism or art criticism or whatever. For urban professionals—which is whom I think of most of my readers [of *Chicago* magazine] as being—there are too many choices out there. Personally, I read ten times the movie reviews as I see movies, and probably fifty times more book reviews than books.

"I've heard there are 100 CDs of Beethoven's Ninth.

How do you know which one to buy? You've got to read a review of it. You've got to find somebody's opinion you trust. When there are this many choices, part of our role is to say, 'This is my viewpoint, this is the way I do it, and I like this one.'"

Goals of a Review

Critics typically have multiple goals in mind when writing their reviews. Some approach it from a sense of responsibility for being the standard-bearers for restaurants. "I think raising the general level of taste is very important," says Dennis Ray Wheaton. "The Kelsons [*Chicago* magazine's founders] had a lot to do with raising Chicago from a meat-and-potatoes town into one of the best restaurant cities in the country. They said that when they first started reviewing restaurants, a good restaurant in Chicago was one that wrapped their baked potatoes in foil! By the time they left, there were Le Perroquet, Le Francais, Gordon, and other influential Chicago restaurants."

Penelope Corcoran, restaurant critic for *The Arizona Republic*, agrees. "Part of my mission here, I feel, is to raise the level of restaurants [in Phoenix]. The only way I have to do that is to send people to the places that I think are doing it right. Now, that's entirely subjective, but it's based on taste that's been cultivated through travel and eating in other cities. Part of the reason I wanted this job is so that when I said, 'Hey, you really have to go to this restaurant,' people would go! And I love that. I have every hope that we will only continue to be a better city in terms of dining."

Gregory Roberts, restaurant critic for *The Seattle Post-Intelligencer*, believes that critics ideally give people information they can use to decide where they're going to spend their dining-out dollars. "For many people, that is a significant outlay," he says.

Tom Sietsema, restaurant critic for *Washington Sidewalk*, agrees: "An important part of our job is to educate or enlighten readers by pointing them in the direction of good food, and to shine the spotlight on really good work."

Is That Entertainment?

As restaurant dining becomes seen as a form of entertainment, and restaurant reviews often appear alongside reviews of concerts, movies, or plays, many restaurant reviewers feel the tug to ensure that their reviews are entertaining as well. "It varies with the kind of restaurant, but a great part of the intention is simply to entertain, because most people will never get to that restaurant," explains Penelope Corcoran. "In addition to that, it's to reveal 'What is this restaurant? What's it about? What's it like?' The appreciation is part of it—appreciation of the art, whatever art it is seen as. I do tend to take a consumer viewpoint because the person I'm writing for is the reader, and the reader might be looking for entertaining reading, or for a place to eat. I'm trying to tell that reader what's worthwhile, what's not worthwhile, how to get the best out of it."

"In these last five years, restaurants have become entertainment," says Alison Arnett, restaurant critic for *The Boston Globe*. "So you're looking for much more than just a good meal, which has to be the beginning point or the end point. People, particularly when they're paying good money, go out to be entertained, and that has more to do with the way they feel when they're at the restaurant. So you might write a little about what the other people there look like, or the way something hits you, like the light or the layout or sometimes the art

work. But particularly often with ethnic restaurants, you have to strip that away so you can say what's important about a restaurant without judging it on the surface. But for a lot of people who are out for a big night, they want to know, 'What will it feel like when I walk through the door?'"

Limitations of a Review

As readers' interest levels have risen over the decades, restaurant reviews have gotten longer and more detailed.

Craig Claiborne's first restaurant reviews in *The New York Times* were merely 100-word write-ups. Today, Ruth Reichl's 1,200-word reviews in the same paper are setting a new standard in restaurant critique by placing reviews in a sociological context. More reviewers are going beyond listing recommended dishes to try to give readers the experience of being at the restaurant themselves.

Other critics complain that restaurant reviews are a very restrained and restrictive format. "I've always thought of it as akin to baroque music, within which you create variations," says Phyllis Richman, restaurant critic for *The Washington Post*. "I hardly ever use the first person in my reviews. Perhaps it's out of some traditional journalistic priggishness on my part, who knows? But I think it's appropriate that there be a distance and a sense of objectivity in that distance. I think that the review shouldn't be about me. It should be about the restaurant, and the way that the reader can best approach the restaurant.

"In restaurant reviewing, you have the food, the service, and the environment. Within the food, there are relatively few adjectives or ways of describing food without getting too technical," says Richman. "I've been the *Post*'s critic for twenty-two years, so obviously I've had to find new ways to describe and write about food. How many ways can you say 'crisp?' You're stuck with 'hot,' 'warm,' and 'cold;' 'crisp,' 'soft,' 'moist,' 'juicy,' 'tender.' And there's a limit to how much you can write metaphorically."

Dennis Ray Wheaton agrees with Richman's assessment of the limitations of language when it comes to restaurant reviewing. "I really find it difficult to find the right words to describe such subjective sensations," he says. "English is not a very rich language in those terms. Spanish has the difference between *caliente* and *picante*—the difference between 'heat' and 'spicy.' We say 'spicy' or we say 'hot,' and we can't distinguish between those two. I find it very frustrating at times. In terms of using analogies, it's sensory, so it's really easy to find other sensory experiences, from music, to sex, to all sorts of things like that."

Gregory Roberts says he tries to avoid words like "fabulous" and "terrific." "They're just pure qualifiers that don't say anything," he says. "What does it mean to say that this salmon is 'terrific'? I think I should say it's 'perfectly cooked' or that 'the champagne vinaigrette

"So many new restaurants are opening that New York magazine is now supposedly not going to review anything that has already been reviewed in the Times, and vice versa. That means that the public isn't even going to get the advantage of having more than one opinion on a restaurant. They are writing about them as social happenings. A new editor killed my review [of Verbena in the Daily News] because the restaurant was already a year old, even though we'd never reviewed it."
—Arthur Schwartz, WOR Radio

A database search of *The New York Times* restaurant reviews over the last few years provides an interesting sense of what reviewers reported:

WHAT THE FOOD IS LIKE
The Top 20 Most Frequently Used Adjectives

Number of
Mentions

Flavorful	321	Excellent	190	Perfect	131
Good	303	Wonderful	180	Hot	124
Appetizing	299	Tender	165	Soft	124
Delicious	248	Special	156	Pleasant	118
Fresh	225	Warm	143	Simple	118
Crisp	217	Dry	137	Unusual	109
Rich	193	Spicy	132		

WHAT REVIEWERS THINK OF THE RESTAURANT
Frequency of Judgment

Who says critics are negative? The judgment verb used most often was overwhelmingly "like," followed by "love." There was only one mention of "dislike" and two mentions of "hate" referring to aspects of the restaurant being reviewed.

Like	334	Hate	2
Love	149	Dislike	1

*"I like all these dishes so well that it is a shock to find one I absolutely **hate**.*
The flavors in the chilled cantaloupe soup with curry-roasted shrimp are as jarring as the wrong wine with
blue cheese, a taste that lingers unpleasantly in the mouth."
—Ruth Reichl, restaurant critic, in a review in *The New York Times*

plays off the richness of the salmon.' The art critic here helped to put that thought into my head. What does it mean to say that 'This is a beautiful painting'? Does that tell you that it's by a great artist? No. You have to say that 'The painter's women look like real women and not just decoration,' or something like that."

Educating Eaters

"There is also an educational function, in teaching people about food and even educating restaurants about what works, what doesn't work, and what's worthwhile," says Penelope Corcoran. Dennis Ray Wheaton agrees. "Especially with ethnic restaurants: 'This is how you

> *"As much as I like the room, I could easily **hate** it if the food were not so good and if the restaurant were not so well thought out. But the food is as fresh and as well conceived as the room, healthy but delicious, thoroughly modern yet with a clear heritage."*
> —Eric Asimov, restaurant critic, in a review [of Republic] in *The New York Times*

WHAT CRITICS ARE EATING
The Top 20 Most Frequently Mentioned Foods

Chicken	236	Chocolate	188	Lamb	138
Greens	228	Onion	184	Potato	127
Mushrooms	204	Tomato	177	Beef	124
Cream	194	Bread	171	Pasta	122
Fish	191	Salmon	156	Pork	122
Garlic	190	Lemon	149	Tuna	120
Cheese	189	Steak	147		

How They're Cooking: Seven of the Most Frequently Mentioned Cooking Techniques

grilled	256 (leading chefs' #1 favorite cooking technique*)
roasted	223
fried	213
sauteed	100 (leading chefs' #2 favorite cooking technique*)
steamed	98
baked	63
braised	57 (leading chefs' #3 favorite cooking technique*)

*Based on leading chefs interviewed for our book *Culinary Artistry* (1996)

approach this kind of cuisine, this is what to look for in it, these are the elements of it, and this is why it's so interesting and enjoyable,'" he says. "A few years ago, there was a short spurt of Moroccan restaurants in town, a cuisine in which I had no experience. I spent a month buying Moroccan cookbooks and cooking everything I could, just to try to get a feeling for how the cuisine works."

In educating his readers, Jonathan Gold, of *L.A. Weekly* and *Los Angeles* says, "The two things I do well are to evoke a sense of community, and to give a description. You can be as pornographic with a description of a stew as Henry Miller ever was with anything.

"I like to think of my subject as Los Angeles, and that I write about it through food. It's easier to evoke a neighborhood sometimes through a place with good steamed fish, and those sights and smells, than it is formal interview pieces," says Gold. " People let their guards down around food."

"I write for someone who goes to a lot of restaurants," says S. Irene Virbila, restaurant critic for *The Los Angeles Times*. "But that public is so diverse. You can't be writing just for people who have eaten in all the restaurants: part of the job of the critic is to explain why this is good, and why this isn't. What's hard is to find a balance [between critique and education]."

Joyce Goldstein, former chef-owner of Square One in San Francisco, says, "I would like to think that the job [of a critic] is to educate, but too many critics think it's their job to entertain. See, right there, we are at a crux. Can you entertain and educate at the same time? Yes. Ruth Reichl does it. Patty [Unterman] does it. But not many people do so."

Comparing Criticism

Because dining is so "immediately sensual," San Francisco critic Patricia Unterman would most likely compare it to some kind of performance art. "It just grabs you and changes where you are," she explains. "It might be like a sex show. Of course, that's Gael Greene's territory, so I'm not going to step on that," she jokes. "But it's so immediate. There's no division between the stage and you. You're part of the performance."

This has implications for restaurant criticism, in Unterman's opinion. "It makes it so personal. It's more personal than practically any other form of criticism," she says. "It's very intimate. These people are doing it just for you."

A Dramatic Flair

Some of the restaurant reviewers we interviewed said that they'd found it interesting to discuss their works with other types of critics. Elaine Tait, restaurant critic for *The Philadelphia Inquirer*, remembers, "I told our drama critic that I measure a restaurant against the expectations it seems to want to create. And he told me that he measured every dramatic presentation against the best Shakespeare! It made me think of a little seafood restaurant that I've written about a few times called Buoy One. You pay your money before you get your food, they give you a clam shell, you sit down on a hard bench, and they bring you your food. Now I guess it's about a $6 fish plate, but back in the beginning it was a $1 fish plate. I didn't measure that against Le Bec-Fin [one of Philadelphia's highest-rated restaurants]; I measured it against any other place that would charge that little, and I thought they were terrific. I don't think you can measure every restaurant against the best," says Tait.

"Yet the drama critic believed that you can't *not* do that. And I realized that it was very different, and that I felt sorry for all those poor amateur theatrical groups who'd ever gotten nailed by him," Tait laughs. "Clearly, some critics feel they must speak from the top of the mountain, and only talk about those places that are terrific by certain classical standards."

David Rosengarten, New York restaurant critic for *Gourmet,* has a doctorate in dramatic literature, and is just as focused on finding the essence of a meal as he was the meaning of a play. "I was a student of theater as well as a professor, and then this very sensual love of food got married to the kind of intellectual pursuit that I was involved with in theater," he says. "I found food a very interesting subject to pursue in the same manner and, in fact, it's the intellectual side of food that I like best. If you're just in it for the physical side, that can get wearying after a while. If it were just that I loved food and eating and tasting, I'd be wanting to check out pretty soon. But I use my mind more than anything else. I'm sitting, watching,

MARK MILLER ON THE "PROGRESS" OF AMERICAN GASTRONOMY

I gave a speech in New York a few years ago to an audience of food writers and critics, and I said, "The reason we don't have good criticism is because we don't have good critics." A food critic is a person who, by experience, knowledge, intuition, or sensibility, has a greater ability to discern quality and knowledge of an experience. Given that definition, most food critics today aren't qualified. They don't necessarily have higher sensibility or a better palate. They don't necessarily understand the history, the psychology and the social setting of food or the dining experience.

At the time of the speech, I had Janet Maslin's review of *Thelma & Louise* from *The New York Times*, which was written by looking at woman as anti-hero, and women and violence in the history of American cinema, and how it paralleled the awareness levels of women and violence in America. That was used to describe what made *Thelma & Louise* a good film—not how many lines either Geena Davis or Susan Sarandon spoke, or how long they were on the screen, or what the ticket cost.

Art reviews try to make the audience aware of the artist's intent. That is where restaurant critics really fail. They do not allow chefs, as artists, to create and communicate a philosophy, either through their work or through their words, and they themselves don't understand what the chefs are doing because in many cases they've never talked to them! Instead, they put chefs on a marketplace platform as merchants who are selling services as compared to somebody else's. By doing that, they basically break down the meaningfulness of their work because it's not seen in the larger context of its entirety, which is important.

The intent of one chef may not necessarily be the intent of another chef. For example, some chefs are trying to please high-class audiences. Other chefs hate that audience. Some don't like to [kowtow] and purposely keep their food at a base level, where it's kind of sloppy with really big flavors. That's what they *want* to do with their food, yet someone comes in and criticizes them for it. We all have to accept what the artist did, and we have to take it in as a whole. We're not allowing restaurants to create a work of art because we're telling them that we don't want to see certain things. Critics aren't putting things into a larger, philosophical context. So the experience itself becomes less, in that it has less meaning. We're not going to have great cooking in the future if we limit it to these things.

Critics justify reviews with the logic that, "We're protecting the audience who is going to spend this large amount of money." If we're going to talk about chefs as businesspeople, then why don't we publish all the lawyers who lose cases in *The New York Times*? Why don't we publish all the doctors whose patients die in *The New York Times*? If we're talking about protecting people who spend a lot of money for services in the marketplace, then why don't we talk about all the contractors who are being sued by clients? If you're building a million-dollar house, that's much more serious than going out for a $50 meal! This [consumer protection] ideology does not hold true.

Going back to my speech, I said, "We don't have any food critics. Therefore, we don't have food criticism. And therefore, we don't have a food audience." We're not educating anybody about food; we have a bunch of people eating steaks out there.

You learn about dance by reading dance reviews, and you learn about art by reading art reviews. The art critic usually tells you the basis of what you're looking at, and why he or she thinks it's a great work of art. But it's always placed in a larger perspective. Food critics say, "Well, the larger perspective is that I eat out a lot." I think a lot of people go to a restaurant because a critic writes about it. But they order the recommended dish, and they don't 'get' it. So, they never really have the experience. What the critic needs to do is let them in: What *is* meaningful about the experience? What *makes* it a great dish? What makes it a great *restaurant*? A great writer about art can make a painting come alive for everyone; writers about restaurants should do the same.

We've got Chez Panisse, and twenty years of American regional food, and great chefs doing interesting things. Here we are talking about diver sea scallops and cuisines of different ethnicities with lots of great chefs out there now, and, all of a sudden, it boils down to putting a big piece of meat on the plate [referring to the current boom in steakhouses]? It's not even prime steak—it's just big and it's there. This is dining in America? This is what it's come to? This is the result of twenty years of so-called food criticism and education and CIA graduates and the American Institute of Wine & Food and the IACP [International Association of Culinary Professionals] and God know what else? This is it?

It proves my point: We don't have food criticism. We don't take food seriously, and we don't write about it seriously. Not yet.

hypothesizing what the chef and what the restaurant are all about. It's very exciting—even more so than trying to figure out what [playwright Henrik] Ibsen, who was the subject of my dissertation, was all about," says Rosengarten.

"Food *can* be intellectual, but it doesn't have to be intellectual. If you're becoming a chef and learning to make risotto, that's basically a craft and there's nothing intellectual about it. But think of the restaurant as an art form, and to me it's the same thing as watching a movie. You look to see what the director intended to do, and how it came out.

"When people review movies and books, they also break out of the form to say, 'What this tells us about the world is. . . .' It goes onto that other level. Sometimes reviews are wholly discussions of other issues rather than discussions of the book or the movie. But it's always been a more technical discussion that I was interested in. I wanted to know 'What is this playwright doing as a playwright?' So, I think there's a lot of intellectualism in just discussing an art form as an art form without making reference to the world.

"Now, let's ask the dangerous question here: 'Can a restaurant make reference to the world beyond restaurants?' Can you say that the cooking of Daniel Boulud causes a kind of melancholy, or that his food is a metaphor for something else? That's a tough one.

"To me, the thing most clearly artistic about restaurants is the cooking," says Rosengarten. "Lots of elements of a restaurant are artistic, clearly, but at least the ones that appeal to me as most artistic and most intellectual are the style of the food, the cooking, and the choices that the chef is making. Not enough critics are looking at that very carefully."

Dinner and a Movie?

Is there any other critic's job a restaurant critic would want? "Every once in a while, I say I want to trade jobs with the movie critic," admits Phyllis Richman. "I did one movie review, actually. I reviewed *The Godfather III*, suspecting it of subliminal propaganda for the U.S.D.A., because everyone who ate healthfully survived, and everyone who ate junk was murdered! So even with movie reviews, I use food analogies. Then again, in this movie, the murder weapon was a cannoli!

"I do think that in a lot of ways, it would be easier to be a movie reviewer. You're using only a few of your senses; you don't have to invade your body with your work. It's not as long hours. And mainly, it's the same movie that everybody sees, so it's easier to be accurate. You know what the reader is going to see, so you can write about the same experience," says Richman. "Whereas with restaurant reviewing, you're trying to predict what some unknown reader with unknown tastes and an unknown appetite will experience. Everyone sits in a different part of the restaurant. Everyone gets different service. Everyone

experiences a different part of the menu—and the food changes. The chef may have left. The chef may not be feeling well. The chef may have the day off. So, you're predicting—and a prediction can be much more accurate with a movie or even a theater review."

Ruth Reichl has spoken with Janet Maslin, *The New York Times* film critic, about the differences between restaurant and film criticism. "We talk about it a lot. Her job is really hard, and it sounds so easy," says Reichl. "I used to think, 'Oh, I'd happily just sit and watch movies,' but she *doesn't* just sit and watch movies. She reads the book, she sees the movie, she sees the movie again. And she wouldn't want to do my job. She'd never want to eat out as much as I do!"

Jonathan Gold also points out that other forms of criticism differ from restaurant criticism in significant ways. "If Arnold Schwarzenegger makes a bad movie, and you write a bad review of it, then it's fine. It's expected as part of the process. But you're dealing with multimillion dollar organizations," says Gold. "Whereas if a restaurant opens and you give it a scathing, negative review, what you're doing is closing down a small business that's really not doing any harm to anybody. I will sometimes take potshots at places, or write negative reviews—I can't not. But I don't take any pleasure in it, whereas I take real pleasure in writing bad album reviews."

A Taste for Music

Some restaurant critics are actually experienced in other forms of criticism, including Jonathan Gold, who still writes about music. "I find that the hats I wear when I'm reviewing a record or a book are completely different from the one I wear when reviewing a restaurant," he says. "But it's similar in the way that you're trying to decipher the context and the conceit, and see how the musician, author or chef follows it all the way through."

Penelope Corcoran, a former music critic, says, "I reviewed music back in the days of vinyl, and there were certain things I'd listen for on an album. Was there one song that grabbed you? How many? Was the album an integrated whole? Did it go beyond that one hit, with the whole becoming greater than the sum of its parts?

"This same kind of thinking can be applied to a meal," says Corcoran. "Ordering a restaurant's signature dish is like listening to an album for the hit. In both cases, you're wondering, 'Is there more to the experience than that one thing?' Some restaurants take time to figure out. Likewise, I've had to listen to some records five times before all of a sudden they'd kick in and become one of the best things I'd ever heard! The most recent is Beck's album *Odelay*. It's an album you listen to once, and you think, 'Hmm. . . interesting.' But there's so much detail that the more you listen to it, the more that detail comes out, and you come to realize how it works as a whole.

"I stopped being a music critic because I loved music, and listening to bad music was destroying me."
—Penelope Corcoran,
  The Arizona Republic

What makes a good restaurant critic? According to David Rosengarten, New York restaurant critic for *Gourmet*, "Three categories are important: **Knowledge** about food, **judgment** of food, and **writing style**. I find that some writers are way up on style and way down on food knowledge and judgment, and some are vice versa." Other critics share their views:

"I like **[Eric] Asimov**'s pieces for *The New York Times*. He's got a nice niche cut out doing that. And **Jonathan Gold** says some very intelligent things."
—Dennis Ray Wheaton, *Chicago*

"**Seymour Britchky**, I think, taught us all how to describe food. Of all the critics, he'd look at a dish and try to figure out what made it work or not work."
—Jonathan Gold, *L.A. Weekly* and *Los Angeles*

"It's incredibly hard to convey the whole restaurant experience in one paragraph, or an entire dish in one sentence. But do you know who's great at that? **Gael Greene**."
—Alison Cook, *Houston Sidewalk*

"There has been a serious deterioration in the quality of restaurant critics just in the last two years. It starts with *New York* and *Time Out* magazines, which are both getting away with having staff know-nothings doing restaurant items. The public doesn't always know the difference between a feature item and a critical restaurant review—or between a staff writer from *Time Out* doing a round-up of ice cream parlors and **Gael Greene** doing a round-up of ice cream parlors."
—Arthur Schwartz, WOR Radio, New York City

"**Michelle Huneven**, who writes for *Buzz* now, mostly, is interesting. She is a novelist (author of *Round Rock*), and takes almost a 'Raymond Carver approach' to restaurant reviewing."
—Jonathan Gold, *L.A. Weekly* and *Los Angeles*

"How many restaurant critics in the country are there whose prose you'd read for pleasure? Two? Three? Most restaurant criticism, for better or for worse, is the same people eating the same dishes and doing the same things. If you look at a **Bryan Miller** column, it was as dull as a column of stock quotes. But I think **Ruth [Reichl]** is doing a good job."
—Jonathan Gold, *L.A. Weekly* and *Los Angeles*

"Just recently another columnist at the paper asked me if I read other restaurant critics, and I don't. When I was first trying out for the job at *New Times*, I gathered some reviews, including some of **Bryan Miller**'s. I dissected them for structure and what needed to be in there. Miller had a very formulaic style, so you knew when that paragraph on wine was going to pop up! Some people really loved that because they knew exactly which paragraph to go to for what they wanted, and the predictability was helpful to them."
—Penelope Corcoran, *The Arizona Republic*

"There are a lot of good restaurant critics now; and there weren't always. I think **Ruth Reichl** is a wonderful writer. **Sherry [Irene] Virbila** is very good. **Jeffrey Steingarten** [of *Vogue*], who in some ways does reviewing, is a fine, fine writer. **Corby Kummer** is terrific. **Bill Rice** is a great food writer, not just a restaurant reviewer. I think **Gael Greene** has been a master for years. Gael was an inspiration [when Richman was first getting started in restaurant reviewing]; she was an original. **Craig Claiborne** was inspiring too." And in Washington, DC? "**Tom Sietsema**, who's at *Washington Sidewalk*, is a protégé of mine, so of course he's terrific."
—Phyllis Richman, *The Washington Post*

"I often think **Ruth [Reichl]**'s writing is the most interesting part of her column because often I don't like the same kind of food. But I know what her biases are, and I read it with that in mind."
—Arthur Schwartz, WOR Radio, New York City

"I think **Ruth Reichl** is the benchmark of restaurant criticism today. She knows a lot about food, but she gives you a real textural feel. Sometimes it's for the room, sometimes it's for the way the restaurant fits into the fabric of the city's social life. And she's incredibly good at describing food, which I think is definitely the hardest thing."
—Alison Arnett, *The Boston Globe*

"I'm fond of **Ruth [Reichl]**. She's a warm, lovely person, and I don't feel competitive. The same with **Bryan [Miller]**; it's always been just another person writing with another opinion. Other people in the past were maybe much more cutthroat, but I don't feel that with either of them. Once in a while something is just more important to [Ruth] than it is to me."
—Gael Greene, *New York*

"Critics' styles have varied a great deal. For example, **Mimi Sheraton** would never tell you that Sharon Stone was dining at San Pietro today, or if she did, she'd put it in such a way, like 'San Pietro was fawning over some Hollywood star, while they gave me the worst table in the room.' **Gael Greene** would say, 'All the trendetti are coming out to San Pietro,' and would mention that Sharon Stone had the risotto."
—John Mariani, *Esquire*

"I think what **Robert Sietsema** is doing at *The Village Voice* is interesting.
He's really good about ferreting places out."
—Jonathan Gold, *L.A. Weekly* and *Los Angeles*

"To me, the writer in this country who scores highest on all counts is probably is **Jefferey Steingarten**.
I think he's a wonderful writer; he does more research than anyone else in the field."
—David Rosengarten, *Gourmet*

"I think newspaper criticism is quite good in L.A. at *The Los Angeles Times* [where **S. Irene Virbila** is the critic]. And I think **Phyllis Richman** [of *The Washington Post*] has had a big impact in her area; I think she writes very informative articles. She knows a lot about food, and she gives me a very good feeling for what a restaurant is like."
—Caroline Bates, *Gourmet*

"I think that other critics in [San Francisco] are so overworked because they've cut the editorial sides of the newspapers down to next to nothing. All these people have responsibility for too many articles, and they don't even stop to think about what they're saying or what it means. I think the level of writing really reflects that now. Plus, at the *Chronicle*, the editor of the food section is also writing reviews, so there is a huge crossover. One day he's calling chefs to do features on them, and the next minute he's in their restaurants supposedly writing criticism. It's a very, very bad mix. I think in some ways there's more of a conflict of interest in that than there is in someone having their own restaurant and writing about restaurants."
—Patricia Unterman, *The San Francisco Examiner*, and owner, Hayes Street Grill

"Similarly, T. Cook's [one of Corcoran's favorite Phoenix restaurants] makes an overall impact, such that you don't even have to look at the details to say, 'Wow!' But if you go multiple times and you start to look at the details, you're just as blown away by the design on the tiles on the floor as you are the precise julienne cut of the vegetables," Corcoran says. "It's a level of richness: How much *is* there? How much can you continue to see or hear or experience each time?

"In cutting my teeth as a music critic, I had to listen to tons of stuff—stuff that I hated, plus different styles of music I wasn't familiar with and had to bone up on. You can make the analogy to the different kinds of cuisine I've had to learn more about," she says. "Then an interesting question becomes 'How do you review a restaurant whose style of food you don't like?' And I don't know how to answer that. Fortunately, there's really nothing that I detest or don't like. I wouldn't be able to have this job if there were. Going back to the music analogy, maybe country music isn't my thing, or maybe salsa music isn't my thing. But I can listen to it, and I can still figure out what is good about it, or what doesn't work about it. And maybe that's the mark of the ability to critique: the ability to step back from your own personal likes and dislikes, and say, 'This may not be my favorite kind of music or food or whatever, but they do it well.'"

The Role of *Zagat*

Given the subjectivity of criticism in any field, aren't more opinions better than just one? This was the thinking behind the establishment of the People's Choice Awards, which debuted in 1975 as an alternative to the Oscars, Emmys, and Grammys in honoring entertainers in film, television, and music, respectively. Awardees are chosen by neither critics nor industry insiders, but by a survey of Americans conducted by the Gallup Organization.

Similarly, the *Zagat Survey*, as its name suggests, provides restaurant recommendations based on the results of "thousands" of local *Survey* participants in forty markets across the United States, from Miami to Seattle. Tim Zagat has been quoted as saying, "If you ask large numbers of people for their shared experiences, at least on things like restaurants and hotels and cars and the things they're familiar with, you're likely to get a better answer than if you ask one expert who is very often biased one way or another."

Perhaps not surprisingly, restaurant critics don't agree. "I think *Zagat* is useless except as a handy reference for addresses," says Patricia Unterman. "First of all, I'm not interested in what people write in because I want to hear the opinion of someone I respect. Popularity is not necessarily a test of quality, as far as I'm concerned."

Penelope Corcoran concurs. "My problem with *Zagat* is that who

knows who's providing their opinions?" she says. "When I go to other cities, I use it for addresses, and I read what it says. But it's not reliable, so I use it only as a cross-reference. And I probably weight it about one-third in a group of three different sources. It is only one indicator from one group of people who think they know about restaurants, so that's the big grain of salt I take it with."

Other critics also credit the *Zagat Survey* as a useful address book when traveling. "*Zagat* is good that way from the standpoint of its information," says Elaine Tait. "But you have to look at it carefully and interpret it for yourself. It's also good as an idea starter, and as a way to 'shop' for a restaurant."

While chefs and restaurateurs also credit the survey as being an useful address and telephone directory for restaurants, they share restaurant critics' mixed views on the validity of the *Zagat Survey* results.

"Who reviews for *Zagat*?" asks Rick Bayless, chef-owner of Frontera Grill and Topolobampo in Chicago. "It's people of a certain socioeconomic group who have certain likes and dislikes, and it's not the most heterogeneous group. There's going to be bias, even though it's trying to be more populist in its approach. Look at the Chicago *Zagat Survey*. Some pretty tired restaurants in town always come out at the top. But they're apparently doing something that [*Zagat* surveyors] like."

Bob Kinkead, chef-owner of Kinkead's in Washington, DC, argues that results are unreliable nationally. "They don't provide a good benchmark of how a restaurant is because they're not consistent from city to city," he says. "I once made a chart of each city included in the *Survey*, and assigned each a 'handicap.' New York was the benchmark city, so if a city's reviews were pretty accurate, it was only -1 or -2. However, there are cities that were -7! Baltimore and Phoenix were about -5. I think DC was -3. San Francisco and Chicago weren't too bad. But Los Angeles has a huge handicap: they think that all their restaurants are sensational, and they're not. I tried to look at it like, 'If a certain restaurant was in my city, what would its rating be?' In some

cases, one restaurant would be off the charts in a particular city, but in another city, it couldn't exist."

Joyce Goldstein believes that each city's *Zagat Survey* takes on the view of its editor. "The editor can choose good comments or bad comments, or make you the object of a joke—all depending on how the comments are selected," she says. "I think it's sometimes a little glib." Goldstein says she doesn't look at *Zagat*'s food ratings. "I don't care," she says. "I go to a restaurant because someone whose opinion I respect has recommended a place. I probably would never go to a restaurant just based on reading about it in *Zagat*—not in a million years."

Merrill Shindler, a restaurant critic who co-edits the Los Angeles *Zagat Survey* with Karen Berk, points out that the *Survey* represents solely the input of the participants. "There are restaurants for which the results are completely out of line with my thinking," he says. "For instance, Chinois on Main ranks as the number two restaurant [in popularity] in Los Angeles. To me, it has good food, but the noise level is horrifying, and the service is questionable. It's like being in the middle of a nervous breakdown! I don't mind noisy, but it's beyond noisy. It's annoying. So I personally wouldn't rank it that high.

"Participants rate the restaurants on a scale of 0 to 3 points, which turns into a 30-point scale through some strange Zagatian alchemy that is never explained. Participants are given no guidance other than that 3 is best, 2 is next, 1 is next, and 0 is the bottom," Shindler points out. "When you have 7,000 or 8,000 people surveying restaurants, you are going to get a pretty good result. In fact, the results tend to be within the parameters of most critics."

Is it possible to spot a restaurant that is trying to inflate its own score? "We have all sorts of ways to prevent that," says Shindler. "Every ballot is examined, and if you get twenty people saying, 'This is the best restaurant in town,' you'll know. Also, we have a test group of 200 people whose opinions we trust, so if the test group rates a restaurant 20 for food and the restaurant comes out with a 26 for food, we know to look at the ballots to see what's going on.

"It might happen, but very, very rarely," Shindler assures. "When you have 7,000 or 8,000 surveyors, even if the restaurant owner and his cousins fill out forms, it's not going to make a difference. What's 2 or 3 in 100? It doesn't really change things. So I think the results are pretty honest."

Despite some misgivings about the *Zagat Surveys*, chefs and restaurateurs acknowledge their influence. Jeremiah Tower, chef-owner of Stars in San Francisco, says, "They're incredibly powerful. Often private parties and business reservations from out of town will mention that they know about Stars from *Zagat*. Hotel concierges also seem to rely very heavily on *Zagat* in their recommendations to guests."

Does Tower use *Zagat* himself? "All the time," he says. "I find it especially useful in New York because there are just so many restaurants to choose from and only a limited amount of time. Where can you get a meal at 1 A.M.? Which restaurants are open on Sunday? It's also indexed by neighborhood, so you don't even have to know any geography."

"I think it's indispensable," says Chris Schlesinger, chef-owner of the East Coast Grill in Cambridge, Massachusetts. "The *Zagat Survey* is broken down cleanly and usually includes one little criticism, so you know what you're going to run into—whether it's a little too noisy or has long lines or whatever. It's useful to the public."

Where has *Zagat* succeeded? "We don't have another guide that covers the United States," points out Hubert Keller, chef-owner of Fleur de Lys in San Francisco. "That's why I think *Zagat* is so popular. When you go to New York, you take *Zagat*, and when you go somewhere else, you bring *Zagat*, and soon you have a little collection of your three or four *Zagats*. They have achieved some of what *Michelin* achieved, in that *Michelin* has everything. The United States is so big that before *Zagat* there was no national restaurant guide. But they achieved it."

Still, at least one chef-restaurateur believes *Zagat*'s influence could be improved: "The basic idea behind the *Zagat Survey* is pretty good, but it would help if they used an auditor. It would give the *Survey* a lot more credibility."

The Restaurant "Oscars"

"The James Beard Awards bring the whole industry into the limelight, which helps the industry a lot."
—André Soltner,
   formerly of Lutèce

With the founding of the James Beard Awards, the culinary arts became the first nonperforming art with its own nationally televised awards program, akin to the Oscars given for excellence in film. "The mission statement of the James Beard Foundation is to elevate the culinary arts alongside the other fine arts and, in a sense, to create respect for them as a *bona fide* art form," says Len Pickell, president of the James Beard Foundation in New York City. "The Foundation saw that actors have the Academy Awards and Tony Awards, and musicians have the Grammy Awards, but that there were no similar awards for chefs. We wanted to create an award for which peers would nominate and vote for peers."

In addition to its awards program, considered perhaps the highest honor bestowed to American restaurants, chefs, and other culinary professionals today, the Foundation seeks to identify and spotlight culinary promise. "What we're really doing for the community, other than establishing a scholarship program, is providing a showcase for chefs to come and demonstrate their talent," says Pickell. "Today, three times as many chefs want to come to the Beard House as we can accommodate.

"One of the earliest Webster's definitions of a chef was a 'servant.' The James Beard Foundation's goal is to someday have it say 'artist.'
—Len Pickell,
   The James Beard
   Foundation

"I believe that we've also created more awareness in the country for fine food and beverage," he says. "Of course, we're not the only reason. It's just happening. I think there is a big awakening going on in the United States, with average consumers beginning to appreciate food and wine. French chefs and restaurateurs, both in France as well as in the United States, truly feel that in terms of quality and excitement, New York is now the restaurant capital of the world."

While many leading chefs and restaurateurs support the work of the James Beard Foundation, no powerful institution is without its critics. "The criticism has been, 'If you don't do an event to raise money for the Beard House, you will never win an award,'" says Pickell. "This is the complaint of people who don't win, and there's not even a shred of truth in that. The people who nominate chefs have no clue who did or didn't raise money for the Foundation. And it's amazing how quickly sore losers turn around when they win the following year."

John Mariani, restaurant critic for *Esquire* magazine, who has chaired the Restaurant Awards Committee of the Foundation, explains, "The Awards rely on twelve regional judges. We then send out the nominations to another ten regional judges. The nominations come in from anywhere; anybody can nominate anybody. And then we discuss them, as we narrow them down to fifteen in each category: Southwest, Northwest, Best Chef, Best Pastry Chef, et cetera. These get sent to the ten regional judges, who give their input and help us narrow it down to five nominations. And then the ballots are sent out to several hundred people."

Mariani also puts to rest similar criticism of the Awards. "Some people might wonder if the James Beard Awards are on the up-and-up," he says. "They might think that if you don't appear [at the Beard House] or don't give money to the Foundation, you'll never be considered. It's not at all the case. It's a double-blind. When I was chair, I didn't even know who the winners were until the night before the Awards!"

Chefs have appreciated the publicity surrounding even being nominated for a James Beard Award. "As a nominee, you suddenly get national publicity. People congratulate you when you go to their table in the dining room, so you know that they are here because of it," says Hubert Keller.

Keller half-jokes that it's better to be nominated again every year than it is to actually win, as he himself would know after having been nominated for the Best Chef: California Award for several years in a row. "When it comes to publicity and its impact on business, it's better. The public, in general, just gets fed information, but they don't know the details. All they know is that they're seeing your name because you were nominated again, and so they come in for dinner and say 'Congratulations!'

Turning serious, Keller adds, "I think the James Beard Award is the highest, most prestigious achievement in this industry, so, of course, you're unbelievably happy when you win."

"All the arts are brothers; Each one is a light to the others."
—Voltaire (1694–1778)

The Pulitzer Prize's self-described function is "documenting 80 years of American intellectual and artistic excellence in journalism, letters, drama, and music." There is an annual award for distinguished criticism, which has historically been awarded to critics of music, books, architecture, television, art, theater, film, and dance. As of 1998, it has never been awarded to a restaurant critic. We found it instructive to interview distinguished critics in other fields to glean their insights into the review process.

Tim Page
Music Critic of *The Washington Post*
Tim Page was born in 1954 and grew up in Storrs, Connecticut, where he was one class behind chef David Bouley at E.O. Smith High School. Page has written thousands of articles on music, books, and culture, and won the Pulitzer Prize in 1997 for his work as chief classical music critic for *The Washington Post*. He was the host of a radio program devoted to new and unusual music on WNYC-FM, and was a founder and first executive producer for BMG Catalyst. Recently, he has spent a great deal of time attempting to revive the reputation of American writer Dawn Powell (1896–1965); he has edited her diaries, her letters, and a collection of her best work, and has just finished a biography *Permanent Visitor: A Life of Dawn Powell* (Henry Holt, 1998).

Do you have more than a passing interest in restaurants?
I've always fantasized about being a restaurant critic, except I know I'd have to eat too much food that I don't like. Still, it would be nice to bill my restaurant tab to the paper.

How would you approach critiquing restaurants?
I would obviously try to learn as much as I possibly could about the background and style of cuisine. When I sat down, I'd try to keep that all in mind. But, on a funny level, I'd also try to forget everything and just enjoy and fully respond to the experience. Then I would go back and bring in my critical faculties: "Well, I loved this meal, but did I love it because I happen to love this meal in general? Or did I love it because the restaurant did something very special with it?" Samuel Johnson, who is my great hero as a critic, once said that the main duty of a book is to make you want to read it through. I suppose with a restaurant it would be to make you want to come back.

In my writing, I always try to distinguish between what is objectively quote-unquote "good," and what I like. Both are important. If I'm served *tête de veau* [calf's head] at the best restaurant in the world, I'm going to be horrified. On the other hand, you could give me something like simple roast chicken, and I'd probably be completely delighted. If you know that somebody has just done an absolutely virtuoso job at something, obviously that has to be acknowledged. But I—and here I differ from some critics—don't like to be the cosmic, universal stamp of approval.

I used to read Seymour Britchky a lot. I enjoyed his stuff because it was extremely readable. Now, perhaps, his reviews are more journalistic than critical. What was interesting was that he'd review somebody who did Beef Wellington, and he'd say something along the lines of, "It was as good a Beef Wellington as you can possibly imagine, although it should be banned from the menu." I think that's a very valid way of reviewing. If you really actively dislike something, state your prejudices, and then say, "But, boy, he did it really well!" or otherwise if that's the case.

How do you bring up personal preferences if you're trying to be objective as a critic?
Most critics, for some reason, feel they shouldn't bring those up, perhaps because the approach is not "scientific" enough. However, there are some real masterpieces that I respect as masterpieces, but I don't really *like* them very much. For me, it's *Pelléas et Mélisande* by Debussy. Analyzing it on any level, it is an amazing work of art. It changed the course of music. But I'm just bored to death through it, even though I've seen it enough, analyzed it enough, and am well enough trained that I recognize that it's a masterpiece.

On the other hand, take some piece like Busoni's crazy piano concerto in five long movements that's over an hour and has a male chorus at the ending. The piece is all over the place, and it simply does not hold together. And yet, every time I hear it, I come out of there cheering, "Yeah!" And you have to take visceral response into account if you're an honest critic.

Do you try to maintain a consistent set of standards when reviewing?
You should judge a restaurant like Lutèce by different standards than the nice little trattoria that just opened on your corner. If you're going to that little trattoria, and there's some promise and the food's cheap and they're friendly and some stuff is pretty good, you might want to recommend it. But if you're going to Lutèce and you're blowing over $200, you've got to hold up different standards. I don't think when something is that well known and costly it should be reviewed in a vacuum, particularly if it's bad.

Likewise, if Luciano Pavarotti comes to town to sing something at the Metropolitan Opera and he's prepared and does a really terrific job—or, for that matter, a mediocre job—you should mention it. But if it's a scared young tenor making his debut at the Met, you're likely to be a little more lenient. You'd say, "Mr. So-and-So strained his voice at times, but there were distinct signs of a lyrical gift," or something like that. If you go to one of these awful stadium concerts where Pavarotti faxes it in, sings through these big amplifiers stuff like *Ciribiribin*, doesn't know the words, and is turning the pages and essentially sight-reading as he does it, give him hell!

Part of our gig, too, is to uphold standards. So there is a line that you walk. There was a huge scandal [in the mid-1970s] when John Canaday, who was then *The New York Times* restaurant critic, gave Maxwell's Plum four stars when the food was nothing special. People just flipped! It's reprinted in a paperback book called *The 1976 New York Times Guide to Restaurants*, and he qualified it there, saying something like, "I can hear you saying now, 'Four stars? Are you out of your mind?' No. Four stars, absolutely—because I'm always happy when I leave." That's taking it a little far, in my opinion. Four stars should really mean something. It should be the best, operating at the best.

The worst restaurant critic I ever read was a woman named Myra Waldo, who used to publish guides. They're really shocking. She'd say things like, "This is an interesting place to go. Some dishes are good, but others are not so good. I would have given it more stars, but the prices are too high for the quality of the food." And that was the review, which, of course, told you nothing. Moreover, her whole attitude was that price should not only be *a* factor, but should be a very *central* factor, so all these little places that weren't very good were getting high marks from her.

This is difficult, and it's obviously impressionist, but my attempt is to judge a concert to some extent by what I think it tried to be, and what worked and what didn't work. If it's a brand-new opera, presented by some cosmically big opera company, I'm going to be a little tougher than with some scrappy young kids putting on something in a loft.

Do you have benchmarks of excellence?
I heard Frederica von Stade do *Cherubino* in Mozart's *Marriage of Figaro* so many times, and with such amazing appreciation of what she was doing, that it would be unfair for me to go to the Met and listen to someone else sing that music and think, "Oh, well, those days are gone...." On the other hand, there's no doubt that it affected my sense of standards. It's like once you've had that special taste—one could call it that sort of "drop your fork" experience—it's ridiculous to pretend that you haven't had it. Clearly, it would be grossly unfair of me to go to a concert and every time I hear *Cherubino* which I'm going to hear a lot, say, "The *Cherubino* was good, but she was no Frederica von Stade." That memory is in my head and there's no way I could really get out of it—and there's no way I'd really *want* to get out of it. It's part of my training.

Another example would be hearing Herbert von Karajan leading the Vienna Philharmonic at Carnegie Hall about seven or eight months before he died, when he started a *Schubert Unfinished* so softly that it seemed to emanate from the walls. It was a sound that none of us who were there could ever forget. And it was so glorious, so absolutely glorious! A young friend of mine was sitting next to me, and I said, "I want you to always remember this. Even if you never hear anything like this again, now you know it can be done."

(Continued on next page)

I like new music, and I like experiments, but I also cherish the classical tradition. A perfect classic performance of a classic can be terrific, too.

Do you ever have a tough time choosing the right words?
Here we enter into tone. Virgil Thomson, who is one of my great mentors, once said that he could write a favorable review that could make the subject want to come over and punch him out, and an unfavorable review that would make the person want to invite him over for dinner! He said it was all a question of the right words and how you use them. And I pretty much agree. You take a different tone for things. I always have this sense when I start writing a review that a pretty well-formed review is already buried within me somehow. And I just work at it until it comes.

The easiest kind of review for a budding critic to write is of something awful because then you can bring out all your epithets and be really nasty and sarcastic and all the things that people think critics are in general! Infinitely harder is trying to find something fresh and new to say about a masterpiece or something that was really terrific. What do you say? "It was great. I loved it." That doesn't tell you anything. So it becomes very difficult.

Critics have to walk a careful line. On the one hand, it's ridiculous to say, "I'm with *The Washington Post* or I'm with *The New York Times*, but I'm *really* just another audience member." You're not. You're going to be writing stuff that reaches tens of thousands, maybe hundreds of thousands, depending on how interested people are in your work. On the other hand, that's exactly the way you should write: as an enlightened, informed, unprejudiced member of the audience, as somebody who was there and had an opinion.

For instance, a lot of older journalists say that you should never use the first person in your reviews, and that it's egotistical to do that. I think it's exactly the reverse. By making it clear that you are one person who says, 'This is what I heard, and feel free to agree or disagree with me,' you get rid of some of that awful, imperial, Godzilla stomp of *The New York Times* or *The Washington Post* saying, "This was terrible." Amazing as it is to me, there are people out there who wait to express their opinion until they've read the critic, which is, in my opinion, really timid. That's not what we're there for. We are here to give one opinion on the work, which is assumed to be a reasonably informed and judicial opinion, but we're not writing the tablets of God, you know? Unfortunately, because of the clout inherent in writing for a major newspaper, I try very hard to soften [a review] by using the first person, especially if it's something that I thought was really lousy, but even if it's something I thought was really wonderful. I think that's the opposite of egotistical.

I've always believed in writing in the first person. When I'm stating certain facts that's one thing, but when it gets down to something like "The tempo dragged," I much prefer to say, "There was a slow tempo, which I found overly blah-blahblah. . . ." Obviously, especially if this is a really thoughtful and smart musician, the guy's probably given this some thought. I reviewed Peter Serkin's version of the *Goldberg Variations* here about four years ago. Now, Peter Serkin is about the smartest pianist alive, a wonderfully trained musician who never does anything that is less than thoughtful, and I know that from previous experience with his work. And I hated his *Goldberg Variations*; I thought it was a misconception from start to end. So, what do you do in that case? I said something like, "Peter Serkin is an enormously thoughtful pianist, and we are bound to take anything that he offers us seriously." And then I launched in. It was a somewhat severe review, but it was a review that at all points credited this musician with his basic importance.

To some extent, you "grade a bit on the curve" unless somebody's really upholding enormous standards. Even then, somebody can have a really off night. The problem is when laziness and stupidity set in. Then you've got to deal with that in a different way.

Do music critics get feedback from the people they review?
Oh, occasionally—and almost always unhappy [feedback], usually from people who are angry with your review. They mostly write hurt letters, but sometimes they write "screw-you" letters, which is their right. And I don't hold those letters against them the next time I hear them. You can't. A lot of great artists in the world are difficult and monomaniacal. If we're going to start judging art or any kind of creation by what kind of person created it, we're in serious trouble.

Why are so many former music critics now restaurant critics?

We tend to be hedonists. It's one of the reasons I'm careful with my drinking, because so many music critics end up alcoholics. There's something about the "Eat, drink and be merry" thing that appeals to our breed. Plus, there's that epicurean sense that "You're here, this is your life, you ought to enjoy it!"

David Shaw
Media Critic, *The Los Angeles Times*

David Shaw is the media critic at *The Los Angeles Times*, and has won a number of awards for journalism including the Pulitzer Prize for Distinguished Criticism in 1991. He is the author of *The Pleasure Police: How Bluenose Busybodies and Lily-Livered Alarmists Are Taking All the Fun Out of Life* (Doubleday, 1996). He has also written for many magazines, including *Cosmopolitan, Esquire, GQ, Rolling Stone*, and *Smithsonian*.

What makes for good criticism?

Critics, in the true sense of the word, are people who write short pieces applying their own critical standards to what they're reviewing. Eighty percent of food criticism is just a catalog of dishes. But there are some very good restaurant critics who have good taste and good judgment, and who are good writers.

How would you critique the state of restaurant criticism in America?

Some restaurants are "critic-proof," in that they'll do well no matter was is said about them, just like a few years ago an Arnold Schwarzenegger movie would gross over $100 million no matter what the critics said. I don't think Tavern on the Green in New York City has ever received a great review, and yet it's one of the highest-grossing restaurants in the country.

I wrote a two-part series in [*The Los Angeles Times*] in 1980 on restaurant reviewing, which mentioned the general ignorance of many restaurant critics. I interviewed the critic from one of the suburban dailies over lunch [where the restaurant determined the menu]. When the main course came, he commented that it was "delicious beef, er lamb, er pork," when actually it was duck. I used that example with his name on the front page of the paper, and he was, and remains, livid.

I think most restaurant critics spend far too little time on wine. They usually limit it to whether the wine lists are fairly priced or not. But given the limited space they have to work with, they tend to feel more qualified to focus on the food. The other weakness is that too many do not give a feeling of the overall experience. I know it can be difficult to strike a balance on this.

I'm biased, because I'm friends with all of them, but I think the three best restaurant critics in America are Ruth Reichl, Sherry [Irene] Virbila, and Phyllis Richman.

What do you find makes a good restaurant critic?

First, they should be good journalists. They should also be very interested in and passionate and enthusiastic about food; I think the best critics are not negativists. And they should probably have some cooking training, either professional training or experience working in a restaurant, so that they know something about food preparation and service. I find that restaurant critics who cook have more acute palates, and are better able to discern what the ingredients are in a dish or why something didn't work.

How can a diner get the best restaurant experience?

Any restaurateur would probably tell you that complaints regarding service probably outnumber complaints about food by ten to one. Not everyone know what a perfect *quenelle* is, but customers *always* know when someone's been rude to them!

In France, I've never been treated badly in a restaurant. But in this country, if you're not known, some restaurants will treat you like shit. It's important to develop relationships with restaurants, either the *maitre d'* or the owner or who-

(Continued on next page)

ever's on the door. You should ask a lot of questions and be adventurous when it comes to the food. And you should go with some regularity because then a good restaurateur will get to know *you*.

Sometimes I'll invite friends to dine at a restaurant with me, so I can introduce them to the *maitre d'* or the owner. Then it's up to my friends to remind them again when they go in on their own that they were introduced the last time they were in with me, and so on. When you develop relationships, it infinitely improves the experience.

Allan Temko
Architecture Critic, *The San Francisco Chronicle*
Allan Temko, architecture critic at *The San Francisco Chronicle*, was awarded the Pulitzer Prize for Distinguished Criticism in 1990. His books include *No Way to Build a Ballpark and Other Irreverent Essays on Architecture* (Chronicle Books, 1993) and *Notre-Dame of Paris* (W.W. Norton & Co., 1996). He lives in Berkeley, "around the corner from Chez Panisse."

What do you think of the quality of food in the Bay Area?
We've always had superior cooking in San Francisco. [Alice Waters] caused a stir—people call it a revolution—by having only the freshest ingredients. Today, that doesn't seem so rare because a lot of restaurants have wonderful ingredients.

There's a lot of pretentious cooking here, but some of it is pretty good. Honesty is a good thing in architecture, and it's a good thing in cuisine. You don't like things falsified by sauces that are not appropriate. Simplest is best. And there's structural honesty, too. I hate food that is trying to seem like more than it is. Just as the wine should not be better than the food, I think the [restaurant] building should not be too much better than the food. You want things to be "appropriate." You want the design to be in harmony with the food and the setting. In a plain-spoken country restaurant, whether in California or some place like Provence, you don't expect luxury and yet the food can be delicious.

Presentation of food is quite important to me. Aesthetically, I like certain Asian cuisines because of the beauty of the presentation, both color and form. But I also like "daily food," just for its honesty.

Do you see similarities between food and architecture?
A building obviously has a utilitarian purpose, unless it is a building that has a purely symbolic purpose, such as the Jefferson Arch in St. Louis, where its real purpose is spiritual. I think there's an equivalent in food. Something that is not meant to nourish you can be a beautiful and elating thing. In that sense, food and buildings are the same.

The role of tradition in architecture and cooking is a possible parallel, especially now that we have preservationists whose adoration of the past verges on necrophilia! I once said, "In San Francisco, anything old is good." And Berkeley is worse. Architecture has brought that on itself because a lot of contemporary architecture isn't as good as the buildings it replaced. And I always thought there was a contradiction between good cooking and *nouvelle cuisine*'s three tiny carrots on a plate.

Architecture and cooking really merge in the early houses of Frank Lloyd Wright around the turn of the 20th century, up to 1910 when he really was, perhaps, "the greatest architect in history," which is what he called himself. He was the first to open the kitchen to the dining area, and he was the first one to consider servantless houses. These were new architectural problems. Otherwise, I don't see a very close parallel. Cooking may more closely resemble painting or music, which, too, is evanescent.

What is the importance of ambiance in a dining experience?

I learned a lot about food from living in France and going to great restaurants there. When I was young, Le Grand Véfour [a pre-revolutionary, late 18th century setting considered one of the oldest—if not *the* oldest—restaurant interiors in Paris] was a wonderful restaurant, featuring a cuisine of great brilliance in this grand setting. [It still holds a Michelin two-star rating.] It was a real merging of architecture, or at least décor, and food.

It's wonderful to be in a beautiful room. You forgive much. The Palm Court of the Palace Hotel in San Francisco is one of the great skylit rooms in America and probably in the world from that period. It's just been restored marvelously by Skidmore Owings & Merrill. Once, when my parents were alive, it [housed] the best restaurant in San Francisco. Then it declined.

I was eating there one day with Scott Newhall, the editor of *The San Francisco Chronicle* who was a California aristocrat and a great guy—the best editor I ever had. We were ordering lunch, and he said, "I don't see *faisan sous cloche* on the menu." He asked the waiter, who didn't even know what it was. Scotty looked across the table at me, and said, "Get your ass back to the paper and write an editorial decrying the removal of *faisan sous cloche* from the menu!" And he was serious! I said, "But I haven't had lunch yet!" And he said, "I don't give a damn. Get a sandwich!" So, I went back, and it became a rather legendary editorial. They're unsigned, but one takes care to sign them between the lines.

There are other fine rooms all across the country in which the décor is probably better than the food. In San Francisco there is The Clift Hotel, and Boston's Locke-Ober restaurant is also a marvelous environment without being great architecture. I don't think a room has to be a great monument architecturally, as long as the cuisine fits the room. Brasserie Lipp in Paris is a very interesting place because the room seems made for *choucroute garnis*!

What are the elements of good restaurant design?

I think the design of restaurants is very important. The lighting should flatter people, especially women. Women wearing cosmetics can look haggard in the wrong light.

You have to think of what a dinner means. It's very romantic to go out in New York. I once talked with Eero Saarinen, who had designed the Beaumont Theater in Lincoln Center. The lighting was quite nice, and when I complimented him on it, he told me, "You have to think of what going to a play is in New York. A woman might have spent the day like a warship in dry dock, getting outfitted for the evening." This was in the days before women's lib, of course. He said, "Much depends on whether you eat before or after, and it's always nice to have supper afterward. The meal is as important as going to the theater, because if all these things jibe correctly, you finish off the evening getting laid— and that's what architecture is all about."

I also like a sense of the arts intermingled effortlessly. So, food can be part of that. The Four Seasons [in New York City] is one of the best-designed restaurants, and a good example of the intermingling of the arts. Philip Johnson got a lot of good art in there, and he, of course, was a part of the architecture himself. I guess he still eats there.

I know [Pat Kuleto, the owner of several San Francisco restaurants including Farallon and Jardiniere] well. He's an interesting guy. He started remodeling restaurants with no architectural value at all, and gradually he got into the design business. The lighting is very important in some of his restaurants, as are open kitchens. The latter can be very successful, because the aromas are wonderful. They give an air of deliciousness that was once limited to humble restaurants.

How would you approach reviewing a restaurant?

The food would be paramount; great food can transcend ordinary environments. However, usually people who serve outstanding food also have a good sense about the design of their dining rooms.

The end goals of architecture criticism at *The San Francisco Chronicle* range from stopping the freeways, to getting height limits, to preserving views, to trying not to let the commercial and real estate worlds overwhelm the city. Some might think that a single restaurant can't affect the city that much, so why battle over a restaurant? But a single restaurant can be important to certain people.

Seven

The Customer: From "Caveat Emptor" to "The Golden Rule"

"People go to restaurants for hundreds

of reasons, and food is only one of them.

Smart diners find a few restaurants they

like and cultivate them because the

experience is so much nicer when you

get to be known. A great restaurant

makes everyone feel welcome."

—Ruth Reichl,
The New York Times

Do customers play a role in whether or not they have a great dining experience? Absolutely, say chefs, restaurateurs, and restaurant critics alike. And since the rules have changed so much in the last twenty years, customers might need to re-learn the right way to do so. The 1970s and 1980s seemed to engender a kind of "buyer beware" atmosphere of "us against them" between restaurants and their customers. When the last of this outdated antagonism, founded in suspicion, finally gives way to new relations based on mutual trust and respect, customers will find themselves enjoying the dining experience even more.

Phyllis Richman, restaurant critic for *The Washington Post*, recalls a time in the not-too-distant past when certain restaurants intimidated diners. "Especially French restaurants," she says. "But they're not intimidated now, or at least not as often." Added to the air of intimidation were suspicions the media itself raised. "For a long time, I've been very troubled with the rationale for restaurant criticism in this country," says William Rice, food and wine columnist for *The Chicago Tribune*. "It's generally provided by large-scale publications, newspapers, and magazines as a 'consumer service.' So the whole point of view was that an anonymous advocate for consumers would go in and

discover these dirty bastards cheating you."

Rice cites other publications that fueled such consumer beliefs. "Look at some of the early restaurant books, such as *Winning the Restaurant Game*. The whole presumption is that [restaurants are] out to get you. They're going to take money from you at the door, serve you yesterday's vegetables, and pour you some kind of crappy wine because they can pronounce it and you can't," says Rice. "In the 1970s, there was this mood of 'us' and 'them.' They were foreigners, they had accents, and we couldn't understand them, so there was a tremendous intimidation factor."

Times change, and there's not much left that can intimidate increasingly sophisticated diners. Hubert Keller, chef-owner of Fleur de Lys in San Francisco, believes the difference is at least in part because customers have been educating themselves about food, perhaps more than ever before. "They read the magazines now, so when you mention something like Israeli couscous, you don't surprise them anymore. In fact, they're more surprised if you *don't* have it," says Keller. "When two or three kinds of breads are on the table, people get 'spoiled' by that. They get used to better and better things. As a chef and restaurateur, now *you* have to keep up with *them* to a certain extent, which I think is fabulous."

"I think the level of food knowledge with customers has gotten better and better," agrees Charlie Palmer, chef-owner of Aureole in New York City. "Ten years ago, the customer wasn't really educated about food or wine, which comes with experience and travel. If a restaurant served frozen Dover sole, that's what customers ate. Nobody questioned it. But if you serve people frozen Dover sole today, a lot of them are going to know the difference."

John Mariani, restaurant critic for *Esquire* magazine, observes that American diners are much more sophisticated. "They're much better traveled, much more demanding—and not just demanding for the wrong reasons. They probably know a lot more about wines than the Europeans do at this point."

What Role Do Customers Play?

"A great restaurant is one that can make greatness happen," says Jeremiah Tower, chef-owner of Stars in San Francisco. "Great restaurants aren't superb all the time, but they offer the potential for diners to have a great experience." Customers can take advantage of this potential by trying to play a more active role in ensuring that greatness will happen for them. "The customer has to bring something to the restaurant," says Tower. "Sometimes before dinners out, I've gone by the restaurant in the afternoon to speak with the *maitre d'* or the chef and plan the menu. Actually, at one point that was the norm.

"Customers have a big responsibility to make their evening as good as it possibly can be, but they're usually pretty timid," Tower observes.

> "I believe that you should go to a restaurant often, you should be known, and you should get a wonderful meal. Part of the dining experience is the personalization. In criticism, anonymity creates antagonization from the beginning, that of the audience versus the chef. It brings an experience which should be personalized and rewarding and generous down to one of consumerism. In doing this, we've totally destroyed the sociability factor of dining."
> —Mark Miller,
>   Red Sage and Coyote Cafe

"I think the more famous the restaurant, the more intimidated they are. That's why Danny Meyer is so good with Union Square; it's one of the best examples in the United States of a very serious restaurant that doesn't look serious and is not intimidating."

One of the customer's first responsibilities is to choose the right restaurant. "Know why you're going to a restaurant. Is it romance? Is it business? Is it celebratory? Or is it because you like tripe?" says John Mariani. "If I'm hosting a very important business meaning, I'm not going to go to Balthazar [a trendy New York restaurant], where I may not even get in and it's noisy. Also, make sure you know what it's going to cost, and don't make a fuss about it. If you don't want to spend more than $40 per person, then don't go to certain restaurants."

"I get asked a lot for restaurant recommendations," says Penelope Corcoran, restaurant critic for *The Arizona Republic*. "And when I get asked, 'What's the best restaurant?' I unfortunately can't answer that question directly. Do they want the best Mexican restaurant? Or the best restaurant in Scottsdale? Or the most romantic restaurant? There are so many categories that I try to ask a series of questions to get down to exactly what it is they're looking for. The closer you can get to *defining* what you want, the better your chances of *getting* what you want."

When you're selecting a restaurant, particularly in another city where you're less familiar with the market, even critics recommend consulting more than one restaurant guide. "I think cross-referencing is of the utmost importance," says Corcoran. "I would never go by just one guide. I usually get *Fodor's*, which typically gets a local restaurant critic to edit its dining chapter. And I'll use *Zagat* as a cross-reference, but a much lower-weighted one. And I'll find a third reference, like *Frommer's*, a restaurant menu guide to that city, or the local newspaper's guide, or I might go online and use *Sidewalk*. But I usually try to go with a local critic's opinion. When I get to the city, I'll ask the locals questions. I don't automatically trust other people's opinions because I have to know what it is they value. When they give me a recommendation, I'll dissect it."

A big payoff can come from doing some intelligence work on a particular restaurant's signature dishes, special features (e.g., cheese cart), and wine list. "Go to the strengths of the restaurant," advises William Rice. "If an area of the menu says 'chef's specials' or 'signature dishes,' unless nothing on that list appeals to you at all, it's a good place to order from the first time you visit a restaurant. Or ask for waiter input, but don't feel obligated to take it. The waiter, or the captain, is a resource for you to use as you will. Or look around. I look at food as it goes by to other tables!"

Many younger readers ask Tom Sietsema, restaurant critic for *Washington Sidewalk*, how to get great food for less. "I always tell them to be flexible for luxury restaurants," he says. "Be willing to eat early or to grab a seat at the bar for a meal. I have had some of my best meals at the bar at Stars in San Francisco or at Gramercy Tavern in New York, eating off the tavern menu. Sometimes when you're sitting at the bar, you have even better people-watching! At The Palace Kitchen in Seattle, I insist on sitting in the bar because it's so much better. And take advantage of fixed-price menus; there is nothing shameful in that."

Some chef-restaurateurs make customer feedback an integral part of running their restaurants. "Customers are given comment cards with their checks, and every morning when I come in I read all the cards from the night before," says Terrance Brennan, chef-owner of Picholine in New York City. "Most of them, fortunately, are positive.

But they might say that something was a little too slow pre-theater or a little too salty. It's a very good source of information, and I always respond to it. Union Square Cafe made it all right for a finer restaurant to use tools like that," says Brennan. "We also have a newsletter because people want to hear what's going on, and they want to feel a part of it. That, in turn, induces more loyalty to the restaurant. Union Square Cafe's newsletter apparently has a mailing list of tens of thousands."

"There are a lot of dining publics out there, which is why there are so many restaurants."
—Arthur Schwartz,
  WOR Radio

Being an Open-Minded Guest

How can a guest meet the restaurant halfway? "By going in with an open mind and expecting the best," says Gael Greene, restaurant critic for *New York* magazine. "And not going in with a chip on your shoulder," adds John Mariani. "I know so many people who go to restaurants just waiting to be displeased, believing that they're not going to get the table they want or that they don't particularly like this kind of food. They're going for all the wrong reasons," he says.

"If you're more open and enthusiastic, you're likely to have a better experience," Greene testifies. "I have a friend who is so enthusiastic that he has relationships with Nobu [Matsuhisa] and Drew [Nieporent]. He's just a restaurant-goer who dines with great passion and is full of compliments. He goes a lot, follows up, and sends his friends. He can *always* get a table at a restaurant! The ideal thing is to pick the restaurants you like and make those your places. If you're always going around to a new restaurant, unless you're Calvin Klein or Anna Wintour, you're going to find it somewhat hard to start fresh."

"When a diner comes in with a chip on his shoulder or a 'show-me' attitude, it sets up a challenge with the waiter, and that deteriorates," says Phyllis Richman. "I get a lot of letters of complaint from customers, and sometimes you can tell that they went seeking trouble."

Anne Rosenzweig, chef-owner of Arcadia and The Lobster Club in New York City, has seen this syndrome. "Some people refuse to be happy. And it's so tough to watch because everyone in the restaurant works hard to provide great food and great service. To see people so unhappy makes me want to cry. It's the kind of pressured and harried life so many New Yorkers lead, and sometimes they don't know how to relax. People in other cities somehow seem more willing to have a good time. I'm not saying New Yorkers aren't, but you see so many that come in who seem to want to have a *bad* time.

"Sometimes people walk in and are angry, unhappy, or upset. And they just don't give the restaurant a chance. You ask yourself, 'What can we do?' I think there's no greater feeling than taking an irate customer and making them happy." In other cases, a customer will go insane over one little mistake, says Rosenzweig. "You work hard to make it a beautiful, rounded, complete experience, and if one thing goes wrong, they're quick to criticize. Customers just don't seem to understand how many things *can* go wrong. And, for me, that's one of the most frustrating parts of this business."

Alison Arnett, restaurant critic for *The Boston Globe*, believes, "People should just allow themselves to enjoy the experience. Too many people are looking to be impressed, which may or may not happen. And they're too edgy about being cheated. If you go in thinking that it's a battle between you and the restaurant and the chef, you're likely to have exactly that experience."

Arthur Schwartz, restaurant reviewer for WOR Radio in New York City, agrees. "I think the general public does tend to blame everything on their one contact person, which is the waiter," he says. "I think if you are a regular diner, you should try to understand the dynamics of a place. You are a human being. You should have a little bit of Christian generosity. I have found myself, more than once, saying to listeners [on my radio show], 'Are *you* so perfect?'

"Another thing that upsets me about the dining public is the no-show problem, and their complaints about having to leave a credit card number at a very popular restaurant. People treat dining out as entertainment now, and every other entertainment venue requires you to

MARK MILLER ON CUSTOMERS vs. GUESTS

In speaking with my staff, once in a while I'll write down the words "customer" and "guest," and I'll ask, "How do you act toward, or how are you as, a customer? What do you expect in this situation? And how are you when you are, or have, a guest?" There are very different social expectations all the way down: what you say, what you bring, what you expect, how you act.

The dining public is always a customer. They're hardly ever a guest, which I think is unfortunate. In a good restaurant, you should always be a guest. And as a guest, you should have a host, which is the restaurant. You should act as a guest, and you become a good friend. A good guest is one who has a good time and is always welcomed back to a dinner party. If you're not having a good time, then you don't accept the next invitation.

To me, opening a restaurant is an invitation. It's not, "I'm going to make a lot of money off you guys." It's an invitation to the public to dine with you. And on your menu, you should publish your philosophy: who you are and what you do. That way, people can choose.

buy your tickets in advance, with no refunds," says Schwartz. "So what's the big deal if a restaurant asks you to reconfirm your reservation or to leave a deposit on Mother's Day or New Year's Eve?"

Phyllis Richman recalls, "I just got a letter from somebody who had a 7:30 P.M. reservation and got there at 7:45 P.M. The restaurant had given their table to another party and had asked them to wait for a few minutes while another table was set up for them. The writer was outraged, and the situation went from bad to worse. I believe the restaurant still should honor the reservation, which it was doing, but the customer shouldn't expect that they can be fifteen minutes late, but that the restaurant has to be exactly on time."

Artistic Vision

As a customer, you want to understand what the restaurant is trying to achieve with its food. If chefs recommend a dish a certain way, the dish was put together for a reason: to show harmony or accentuate the juxtaposition of certain ingredients. Chefs hope that you will at least try to see it their way. But a little knowledge can be dangerous. Some cus-

tomers criticize a restaurant's cuisine without fully understanding it and end up insulting the exhaustive efforts of leading chefs who are striving to serve their visions of what is "best."

"I put comfort in the surrounding and the human aspect [of my restaurant], but I put edge in the cuisine. And that cocktail works for me," says Norman Van Aken, chef-owner of Norman's in Coral Gables, Florida. "And, yes, if you want a plain piece of grilled fish, we will do that. If you want us to scrape the adobe paste off the chicken, we'll do it. I'm not going to force customers to jump into the swirling waters with me. But only up to a point," he adds quickly. "Then, it becomes, 'Wait a minute, go outside, walk across the street, turn around, and look up and see whose name is on the building. It's mine.' So I will be hung or I will be praised for whatever I do. And I am willing to take that chance."

Gordon Hamersley, chef-owner of Hamersley's Bistro in Boston, believes it's vital for a restaurant to balance its menu offerings between old favorites and new innovations not only for the sake of the customers, but for the chef's sanity. "I have to decide as a chef, 'Is this going to satisfy me, doing the same damn thing over and over again? Or do we need to go forward here?' Signature dishes of certain restaurants provide comfort to people, who come back for them again and again. We took our lemon custard off our last menu after ten years, and we've been getting cards and letters about it! But they have to bear with me a little bit. I need to be able to give our pastry chef the flexibility to come up with *another* lemon dessert. I need to be able to think about lemons."

George Germon, chef-co-owner of Al Forno and Provincia in Providence, Rhode Island, understands. "I'm sure this happens at any

restaurant where there is any level of creativity going on. You have a menu, which you have put a lot of thought into, and all you can hope is that people come in and order something that you've thought to offer," he says. "But some people come in, and they have to change it."

Germon's partner Johanne Killeen points out that sometimes requests to change the food might be veiled as dietary or allergy restrictions. "In the United States, we have this attitude that 'I can have exactly what I want, exactly when and where I want it.' And what has happened is that the rights of the creative person, which are the right to serve what I want and the right to serve it the way I want, are overlooked," she says.

"We tell our staff, 'This is the way we present our food, and we want you to let customers know, in a positive way, that this is the way we present it for their benefit. But helping people 'get it'—sometimes you can, but most often you can't," Killeen says wistfully.

"Once I was called over to a table because there were potato peels in the mashed potatoes," she recalls. "And so I'm there, being bubbly and trying to explain that it is meant to be that way and that we do it for these reasons. And the customer said to me, 'You're just trying to save on labor.' And I'm thinking, 'I've got twenty-four cooks in a restaurant that seats 110, and my labor costs are probably higher than any other restaurant in the country!'"

Al Forno takes a stand on the way it will serve meat, based on its judgment of the way it tastes best. "Our biggest bone of contention here is that we won't cook anything beyond medium rare," says George Germon. "For older people and for young children, we'll make exceptions, but otherwise, we tell people to order something else. The dirty steak [a signature dish not on the menu] comes one way: it comes sliced, it comes rare or medium-rare, it comes with the sauce on it, and it comes with mashed potatoes. We allow no alterations to that particular dish. But people come in and they want it well done, they want it with roasted potatoes, they want it with vegetables. Can't they do this or do that? And we always just say, 'No, you may not. This is the way the dish was conceived. And this is the way it is going to stay.' And it has been that way for a long time. That's one of the reasons it is not on the menu, but we sell a ton of them anyway."

Who's right? Ruth Reichl, restaurant critic for *The New York Times*, points out, "Ultimately, customers vote with their dollars. I take real exception with restaurants that won't cook food to a certain doneness. I hate overcooked anything, but I really disapprove of chefs who insist on serving rare fish to people who find it offensive because you've got them sitting captive at that moment at your table. So, if they want an overcooked piece of tuna, you ought to give it to them.

"If the chef says, 'Trust me, this just doesn't taste good this way. Why don't you have something else instead? I'll be happy to give you blahblahblah, but I really can't give this to you because I think it's really not very good,' I think that's okay. As long as there's an alternative," says Reichl. "I am not of the belief that this is high art. Ultimately, this is a service business. And anybody who doesn't believe that isn't going to stay in business very long.

"It's a miserable service business. It's the hardest service business. A billion things can go wrong. How my job differs from, say, Janet Maslin's job [as *The New York Times*'s film critic] is that Janet knows that whoever sees the movie is going to see exactly the same movie she's seen. The one thing I know is that *nobody's* going to have my experience. It's not replicable in any way. So you have to do your best to say, 'This is how it is.'

"I wouldn't own a restaurant again, for anything," adds Reichl. "You're so dependent on your waiters' moods, your chef's moods, the weather, the heat, the air conditioning—a million things can go wrong to spoil the customer's experience of the restaurant. But once they're in your establishment, I think you have to do your best to make them comfortable, without compromising your standards. And I don't think that asking someone to cook a piece of fish more than they think is good is the same as somebody asking Michelangelo to change the height of the David."

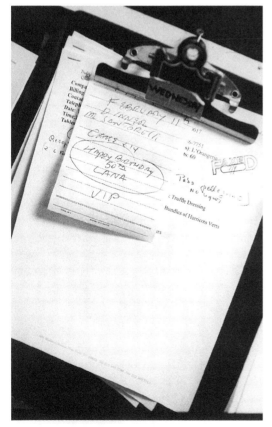

The Way to Ask

"A lot of how you're treated is how you treat others," observes Elaine Tait, restaurant critic for *The Philadelphia Inquirer*. "If you come in with an attitude, you're going to get treated badly. A whole lot of it is what you ask for, and how you complain, if you complain."

Tom Sietsema has conducted research that confirms Tait's observation. "I once inter-

viewed fifteen *maîtres d'* across the country at top restaurants on tips for getting in," he says. "One thing they told me over and over again is that if you're not a V.I.P., it really helps to be *nice*. It sounds corny, but the Midwestern farm couple who calls up and says, 'Hey, we'd love to eat in your restaurant' is much more apt to get a table than the executive who sort of barges his way in with his cell phone."

If you have special needs, such as for an all-vegetarian menu, mention this when you call for your reservation, and not at the moment the waiter asks for your order, even though more restaurants are happy and able to comply on the spot. "Call ahead, and voice your expectations," suggests John Mariani. "'This is romance, this is business,' whatever it happens to be. Try to talk to the owner, if possible, and describe to the person what your situation is: 'I've never been to your restaurant' or 'I read about it in *Esquire* magazine' or 'I hear you serve white truffles.' Just establish a rapport with the manager or *maître d'*."

"What I really like is when customers call ahead," enthuses Johanne Killeen. "They might say, 'I've got an allergy to nuts' or whatever, 'Can I eat at your restaurant?' And I'll say, 'Okay, you can have this, and you can have that, but you cannot have this because it is cooked in peanut oil.' I just got a call from a very nice woman who said, 'I don't want to create any problems, but I just wanted to call and let you know my restrictions ahead of time, and talk about what the possibilities were.' And, I thought, this is great! This is somebody with a head on her shoulders. We're happy to help people like that."

The biggest complaint I hear from readers is that they had to wait for a table. But there is no way for a restaurant to consistently avoid that. You cannot make magic. You cannot make people get up from a table if someone in their party arrives late so they order late and end up still at the table 45 minutes longer than anyone anticipated they'd be there. That's going to happen at every restaurant that's trying to turn their tables.

That's the reason restaurants in America are so much cheaper than restaurants in France—because they're turning the tables, getting a lot more customers through the door on any given day than a three-star restaurant in France. If you don't want to spend $350 per person for a meal [to "buy" the table for the entire evening, as is the case in France], you're occasionally going to have to put up with waiting. It's unpleasant, but it happens because the economics of American restaurants are different from the economics of French restaurants.

On the other hand, I do think that restaurateurs can really do a lot to avoid having people being annoyed by that. An "I'm sorry" really helps a lot. If you're going to make people wait half an hour, a glass of wine and an apology go a long way, and people tend not to get angry.

Restaurateurs and their customers are increasingly learning about each other, and it makes a better experience for everyone—on both sides.

When Something Goes Wrong

If something clearly goes wrong at a restaurant, Elaine Tait advises, "Don't whine, for God's sake. If you have a legitimate problem with something, discuss it. If you don't get any results with the waiter, perhaps discuss it on your way out. And if that doesn't work, write a letter to the restaurant with a copy to a critic that you respect. That usually does it. A lot of times, readers won't be able to get any kind of response until the restaurant gets a letter that's been copied to me.

"Stick to the facts. Don't get hysterical," Tait says. "It's like sending back a bottle of wine because you didn't like that kind of wine, rather than because it was spoiled or corked. Make sure that something really was wrong with it. If it is just something you didn't like, that was your mistake. Ask an intelligent question beforehand."

Alison Arnett has observed that readers are complaining to restaurants more and more frequently. "A lot of people want something more from a restaurant experience. It's not just that they want something *better*—they want *something*. Sometimes they want a free meal because they imagine that the rest of the world is getting comped, and

"We live in a society where restaurants, for some reason, are taking the brunt of all our complaints. While I'm sure every business gets complaints, restaurants are very easy places to go after, because there's so much that can go wrong on a nightly basis."
—Gordon Hamersley,
  Hamersley's Bistro

> "Our only real goal is to provide people with so much joy and delight that they have no choice but to come back."
> —Danny Meyer,
> Union Square Cafe and Gramercy Tavern

they want to be comped, too. Everyone wants to be treated as though they're special, but some people want to be treated *extra* special. And they'll complain if they're not."

When Something Goes *Right*

What about the times when everything goes *right* at a restaurant? A customer should be sure to let the restaurant know that, too. If the evening's wine recommendations prove especially pleasing, let the sommelier know. If the service is excellent, mention it to your server or, better yet, the manager on duty. If a particular dish stands out as extraordinary, consider asking whether you might tell the chef or the person who cooked it. (This is *not* recommended during peak dining hours, however, when the kitchen may be too busy cooking to appreciate an interruption, even if it's a compliment!)

Notes of appreciation are always welcomed. On a recent trip to Sonoma, we visited the restaurant Freestyle. When chef Steven Levine visited our table, we mentioned that we'd sent him a thank-you note a few years earlier after a very special Thanksgiving dinner we'd enjoyed when he was at Zoë in New York City. We were very surprised to learn that not only did he remember certain parts of our letter word-for-word, but he claimed he still had it!

Tipping well goes without saying. If you'd like to be remembered at a restaurant, tipping generously for excellent service goes a long way. (And if you're at the East Coast Grill in Cambridge, Massachusetts, you can even order up a six-pack of beer for the kitchen staff right off the menu!) "We basically tip 20 percent; that's the *Inquirer*'s money or my money," says Elaine Tait. "And I tip on the whole thing, food and wine. I worked my way through college as a waitress, and I feel you really can't tip too much. These people are overworked and overburdened."

Ruth Reichl has a soft spot here as well. "I was a waitress for years, and now I'm a big tipper. That experience helped make me aware of what it means to go home with an extra five dollars. It lifts your mood a little. It's not just the money—it's communicating, 'Yes, you really made me happy tonight. You did a good job.' Sometimes I really want them to know that," she says.

"Likewise, customers can say, 'Please tell your chef how much I liked this.' I don't think people do that often enough," says Reichl. "I'll often send wine back, saying 'This is great wine, this was a terrific dinner—would you tell the chef I'm saving half the bottle for him?' People in the kitchen appreciate that. Or you can say to the waiter, 'It's been great service. I know you can't drink this now, but I'm leaving it. Put it aside and drink it when you get off.'

"There was a visiting Italian chef who came to New York, and a doctor and his wife were so taken with her food that they sent her flowers the next day. And the chef was so thrilled that she never forgot that, and they've all become friends," says Reichl. "They go to Italy and eat at her restaurant, and she makes them a special dinner. The doctor made himself very well known in this restaurant. Anyone could do that and make a chef very happy. And if you're planning to visit that restaurant again, it's a smart idea—it would pay off in spades!"

The Restaurant-Customer Partnership

In the best of all possible worlds, restaurants' relationships with their customers take on a sense of partnership. André Soltner, former chef-owner of Lutèce in New York City, once told a critic, "If you walk from Lutèce to Third Avenue, you might pass fifty people, and you don't look at them. But if the fifty-first person was in school with you twenty years ago, you see them, your eyes light up, and you give them a hug and all your warmth. But for the other fifty, you didn't. This is the same in a restaurant. Imagine a customer who comes four times a year for twenty years. When you see him, you have to refrain from kissing him! And to the other customers whom you don't know, you'll be very polite and serve the same food and everything, but you cannot give them the same warmth as the customers you've known for 20 years."

When Soltner was at Lutèce, he tried to give diners the opportunity to develop a relationship: "Every night I tried as much as possible to go to see everyone at every table."

Gordon Hamersley believes that a trust is built between the chef and the customer: "As a customer, that's certainly the kind of relationship I want with a chef. I want to go into his restaurant and say, 'Give me something you love, something you're working on that's a little bit different and out of the ordinary.' Those are the kind of customers that I really like a lot, as a chef."

"After a while, customers begin to realize what you're setting out to do, and that you're serving quality," says George Germon. "I think eventually the clients who trust you the most start to have a vested interest in the restaurant. They will tell you when something is not right, and they'll tell you when something is right."

"We have great relationships with some of our customers," adds Johanne Killeen. "A fellow who comes in a lot and sits at the bar has gotten to know a lot of the staff. We were away from the restaurant once for three weeks between two different trips, including one to Hong Kong. And he said, 'You know, there was nothing wrong. Everybody did their jobs, but I could feel that you weren't here. You were away too long.' And, you know, we really appreciated that. We take comments like that very, very seriously."

Other leading chefs and restaurants also take their customers' preferences equally seriously. "I think customers would not be excited if I didn't have something different for them each time," says Hubert Keller. "So, I keep a file, and I can tell you going back fifteen years what some of my customers had on a particular night. I developed that file for our regulars, some of whom have not seen a menu in ten years! And sometimes, in ten years, they've never, ever had the same dish twice. And I'll note their preferences and allergies, so when the canapés come down at a table of four, there will be three little crab-cakes plus something different for the person I know who is allergic to crab. Details, service-wise, are extremely important. If they drink martinis, a martini shows up; they don't have to mention it. It's just part of what makes up the whole experience."

Working with customers in a personal way is more exciting for the customers and more challenging for the chefs. "If wine collectors want to bring a bottle of wine, I'll work around that bottle of wine," says

Keller. "Then, when you bring guests in, they are impressed to see that the chef has built a meal around your bottle of wine.

"Repeat customers are the ones who are basically your bread and butter," Keller adds. "They are the ones who support a restaurant and who will get you through a recession or an earthquake. When we went through all these things, sometimes people would come in and say, 'What's happening here, with the recession?' And I'd say, 'The recession stops at the door!'"

Restaurants recognize that building relationships with customers is a long-term prospect. Daniel Boulud, chef-owner of Restaurant Daniel in New York City, points out, "In the first contact, they may feel special, but there is no bonding yet. It's just a superficial connection, I would say, which is done through the food, through the service, through the quality of everything. But when they come back the second time or

third time, then, really, a bond is created. Then, we start to know what they like. We start to know a little bit what we can do for them. We know what to suggest for them."

The payoff isn't just in more satisfied customers. "You know, it's those little things that will really make you feel happy about your business," admits Boulud. "I wouldn't be happy if I had a restaurant with only visitors, and not regulars. That's a problem, sometimes, with popularity. You are inaccessible, so you become a special occasion restaurant or 'a one-night stand.'"

David Rosengarten, New York restaurant critic for *Gourmet*, uses the exact same phrase to describe what Le Cirque 2000 is *not*. "It's not a one-night stand. It's a relationship," he says. "You have to go in and cultivate it, and make yourself a member of the club. It's not hard to become a member. Sirio [Maccioni, Le Cirque's owner] really wants to be open to everybody. It's not that he's mean or is out to 'dis' people. It's just that he knows some people. So get to know *him*. At any restau-

rant where you want to develop a relationship, it's a good idea to go there frequently. And if you saw Sirio once a month, he'd know you after a while.

"If you want to become a good patron, it's a good idea to go in and be earnest and curious about the food," says Rosengarten. "Ask questions. Look like you care. Look like you're interested in that restaurant. The worst thing to do is to go in and not notice the food, so restaurateurs get the idea you're just looking for a nice place to sit and have a conversation for a couple of hours. But if you walk in and start talking, asking about the specials and what's recommended, eventually they'll think, 'This is a person who's serious about food. I've got something special I think they'll like.'"

"Anyone can have the luxury of being treated as a regular customer at a restaurant. All you have to do is go back a few times," agrees Elaine Tait. "And they'll know you, and they'll say, 'Here's your table,' and 'Here's your martini.' We live in impersonal times, so restaurants can become kind of your extended family."

As, in the happiest cases, do customers to restaurants.

WINE CAN BE THE BEGINNING OF A BEAUTIFUL FRIENDSHIP

Wine offers a wonderful opportunity for restaurants and customers to come together over shared passions. In the pages that follow, two leading sommeliers discuss how.

As wine has become increasingly important to many readers, critics sometimes include in their reviews sweeping generalizations about a restaurant's wine list, which can be misinformed. "Too many restaurant reviewers don't know anything about wine," laments Anne Rosenzweig, chef-owner of Arcadia and The Lobster Club in New York City. "We have two of the best, most exciting, most interesting wine lists in the country. But they never get written up.

"Andy [Freeman] has discovered a lot of wines that he then brings in direct from the winemaker, then it gets written about in *Wine Spectator*, and then it finds a distributor in New York. And then everybody's clamoring for it. But we've already had it for a year or maybe two years before it becomes a household name," says Rosenzweig. "But you've really got to work hard to find all of that. Right now one of the things we really love are the Austrian wines, which are really spectacular."

Larry Stone, sommelier at Rubicon in San Francisco, is the first American to have won the title of International Best Sommelier in French Wines and Spirits in a competition held in Paris. He is also the only American to have earned the title of French Master Sommelier from the Union de la Sommelierie Francaise. Stone has the distinction of Master Sommelier granted by the English Court of Master Sommeliers and is one of only five people in the history of the exam to have passed on the first attempt.

Are there any wine matching guidelines left?

People don't really follow rules anymore because food is no longer what it used to be. There are so many cuisines. I love it when people say, "Gewürztraminer goes well with Chinese food." I just want to laugh my head off! China is a huge country, with distinct cultures and cuisines. So are they saying it goes well with my squab, or with my marinated jellyfish, or with my duck tongue? What are they talking about? It's like saying, "Pinot Noir goes well with American food." It's a ridiculous, pompous statement that shows a lack of knowledge while parading as being something significant. There's so much diversity in every cuisine that no single wine would go with everything.

On the whole, Gewürztraminer does go well with some kinds of Asian food. It tends to go better with certain kinds of sweet curries from India, something with rice and nuts and maybe a little coconut, because of the exotic flavors of the wine itself and the low acidity in that cuisine.

A person can follow rules or guidelines, such as trying to match intensity of flavors and finding the acidity in the base sauce of the dish to match the acidity of the wine. It can be complex, but it will help. To say, if you're having beef, you must have Cabernet Sauvignon, or if you're having fish, you should have Chardonnay, is too general. When you say fish, does it refer to poached trout or to blackened catfish? Obviously, they're very different dishes.

What is the average customer's approach to ordering wine?

Customers can be too timid about their wine choices. They tend to go to Chardonnay, Merlot, and Cabernet Sauvignon very often and are too afraid of experimenting. After a short conversation with a good sommelier, they should feel confident trying something new, even if it's Viognier or some grape they've never heard of before. You can ask, "What's it like? How would you describe it?" If you don't like it, then at least you've expanded your horizons!

You can say you love something because it's the only thing you've ever known, but it's another thing to experience different things and say that what you started off with is what you really like the best. Chardonnay is a delicious wine, and there are a range of different kinds of Chardonnay. On the whole, they have the soft, buttery, apple and citrus kinds of flavors that people enjoy, so it's easy to stay in that one rut. But it's kind of dull, if you dine out regularly, to have the same kind of wine all the time. You're really missing out on an awful lot!

Why should a customer use a sommelier?

Wine is a very complex subject. There are thousands of wines, and even people who are specialists in the field tend to concentrate on one area or another that they like. So, for someone who's not really up on wines to try to keep track of them all, it's almost impossible. Often the most impressive wines now are the ones that practically no one's ever heard of, except collectors. So if you're trying to impress a client with your knowledge of wine, then you'd better keep up on it and spend lots of hours researching it—or simply seek help from the restaurant. The role of the sommelier in a restaurant is to help people who are interested in entertaining and in food and wine.

(Continued on next page)

Wine enhances the meal. It's more complex actually than some of the food, both on the basis of the number of wines and styles and regions, as well as being one of the most complex things that people consume. And it has been since its inception, probably since about 6000 B.C. It's an aesthetic pleasure. It also acts as a way to loosen up and talk a little bit about something other than what's at hand. It's often difficult for people to talk about the food. A growing number of people feel comfortable discussing the appropriateness of the wine, the pleasures and sensations they get from it, and the matching of the wine and the food. They can compare it to other wines they've had of its type. So it can be quite a stimulus for conversation at the table in a more relaxed way.

Sometimes selecting a wine can be intimidating for a person who doesn't subscribe to Robert Parker's newsletter or one of the other leading wine publications. The main thing when you're dining out is to try to make contact with the wine person if you want to have a good wine experience. Don't just ask for a copy of the wine list; a good restaurant might have anywhere from 300 to 1,000 selections. If you don't know what you're doing, you're going to probably find something on the list that you know already, and maybe it's something that isn't that impressive anymore.

How should a customer ask for recommendations?

If customers are entertaining and want to make wine a feature of the dinner, they should talk to the sommelier before they come and explain, "This is the dinner I'm having, these are the guests I have, this is my goal with this dinner, and this is my budget." If it's done beforehand, then it's much easier when you come in. On the phone, you can get a lot of stuff out of the way that you wouldn't want explained in front of your guests without insulting them or putting yourself on the spot.

When you make the reservation, say you'd like to speak with the sommelier or whoever's responsible for the wine list. In some restaurants, that's probably necessary because the sommelier or wine buyer isn't there at night when it's a day job. Otherwise, they'd be there from 9 A.M. until 2 A.M. every day! That way, you ensure yourself that you can talk with someone since you're not guaranteed that someone will be there when you get there. You might already have some preliminary selections made by the time you arrive.

If you don't do that, when you come into the restaurant you should arrive a little earlier than your guests, try to speak with either the manager or the wine steward or the sommelier responsible for the wine list, and get some preliminary suggestions. Sometimes you really can't pinpoint everything because of what people are going to order when they sit down. But that way, at least you're focusing on a few ideas and getting the prices and the quality level that you're looking for established beforehand.

Or, once you sit down and have a wine list and menus in front of you, even before you choose your food, it's a good idea to say to the server, "Is there a sommelier or someone here who knows all about these wines?" It's not going to make you look inept; it's going to make you look good because it's a negotiation. You're not just going to take that person's recommendation. They're going to make suggestions, and then you, in turn, have to come back and say, "Tell me more about that one. It sounds interesting" or maybe "I've had that kind of wine, and I'm not really fond of it. Do you have any other suggestions?" You're not saying that you're throwing yourself at the mercy of this person who's going to try to sell you something; it's always a negotiation.

Asking for help on a wine list doesn't show any sign of weakness or lack of skill. Last night the head of Sony came in. He knows wines and has his own collection, but he always asks me to come over, and no one thinks any less of him. And last week, the founder of Toyota brought in some of his executives to meet me, saying, "This can be an example for us, the way he runs his wine list and interfaces with clients here." In this position, you get immediate consumer response. Customer satisfaction or dissatisfaction is immediately apparent, as are design flaws. For example, if a bottle of wine is corky or spoiled for any reason, I'll take care of that part myself.

What happens when a wine is off?

Good sommeliers in Europe are trained to taste the wine before they serve it. Unfortunately, America has less of a wine-drinking tradition, so it's not as common. The people serving the wine don't always know how to taste the wine to see if it's flawed, and the guests don't always know either. So it's very important for a restaurant who has a person there who knows about wine to taste it. Before serving wine, I usually take about a quarter or a third of an ounce and smell it and taste it, and it gives me an idea of what the wine is doing. Usually about once or twice a week, I find a bottle that's either corked [ruined by a rotten cork, so it tastes of cork] or spoiled [turned to vinegar]. Last Saturday night, I had the head of a bank here who always drinks very expensive Bordeaux and he ordered a 1983 [Château] Lynch-Bages. He's had probably half a case of that wine in the last six months. But I opened it, and I didn't like the way the cork looked. I tasted it, and the wine was totally oxidized. In a normal restaurant, that wine would have been served, and the person ordering it might have caught it or might not have. After about a quarter of a glass of wine from this particular bottle, they'd probably have wondered about it and given up on it, or been faced with having to make a complaint in the restaurant, which is kind of embarrassing sometimes, or been stuck with a bottle of wine that they all hated and not known what to say to the table host.

For us, it meant eating the price of that bottle of wine, which cost us about $100 when we bought it at auction, but it's worth it. I don't ever want to serve anyone a bad bottle of wine. That's one of the risks, which is why restaurant prices have to be higher than retail: restaurants are taking responsibility for the quality and condition of the wine served.

If I taste the wine before it's served, the customer never tastes a bad bottle of wine; I just take it away. You'll find customers who were served a wine that was not in good condition who don't make a sound. When I was working at Charlie Trotter's, a couple came in on a Saturday night and said, "We just got married. We want the most expensive bottle of white Burgundy you have." When someone says "most expensive," it tips you off that they don't know much. So I asked, "Have you ever had a white Burgundy?" They said, "No, but we've heard it's the best white wine there is, and it's our wedding night, so we want something that we'll never forget." They wanted to buy the 1983 Domaine de la Romanée-Conti Montrachet, which was about $1,200 then and would probably be almost $5,000 today. I told them, "I have another bottle of wine that's really great and half the price from a top producer, and I think it would be nicer with what you're having. Also, it will be easier to get this wine on your anniversary, so you could have it every year."

It was a very busy night, so the waiter served the wine. When I saw them about twenty minutes later, I asked them, "Do you enjoy it?" They replied, "Yeah, it's good." You could see that their response was not enthusiastic—and with a bottle of wine like that, you'd expect them to be ecstatic. I asked them, "Would you mind if I tasted it? It should be really fantastic." But they said, "No, no, no, it's fine. We're just getting used to it."

At the end of the night, the waiter pointed out that they had left half the bottle of wine, with two full glasses of wine on the table. So I tasted it, and it was the most horribly distorted example of a corked bottle of wine I'd ever seen. It was so foul, it was disgusting. People who get a bad bottle of wine who don't know what it is feel that they don't want to complain because it's $600 and it will make them look like they don't appreciate the wine—that it must be good at that price.

Fortunately, they paid by credit card, so I took the wine off their bill and wrote them an apology. But they were on their honeymoon, so all week they were probably thinking, "That's it. We're never going to drink white Burgundy again!" I can just imagine the conversation at the table: "Is it what it's supposed to be like?" It smelled like sewage water that had sat around for a few weeks filling with bacteria. It was so bad, and I felt so sorry.

That's an extreme example of people not speaking up. Usually if a wine is that bad, they will. Normally, many things are almost not perceptible. Only someone who drinks a lot of wine will perceive them and will have enough confidence to say, "Excuse me, but I think that's corked," or "I think that wine was stored too warmly," or "This wine has started to turn to vinegar." There aren't that many bottles like that. The percentage of wines with corkiness has gone down, but you still might get 2 percent that are corky. And that's usually not the case. You see less than that because people don't speak up or they don't even notice. Sometimes corkiness is very slight.

How should a customer handle such a situation?
As a customer, a good way to handle this is to ask, "What do you think of this wine? Is there anything wrong with it? I'm not sure that this is right." That way, you're not setting yourself up as an antagonist with the restaurant, and all of sudden the restaurant has to demonstrate that they know what they're talking about. Is it wrong? Well, let's see. Then it becomes a search for the truth, rather than some sort of showdown at the OK Corral.

(Continued on next page)

Any good manager or sommelier would taste the wine. If there's something wrong, it could be anything. Is it corked? Did the cork fail, so the wine oxidized? Maybe there's nothing wrong with it. In that case, sometimes the manager will say, "There's nothing wrong. This wine just tastes this way. But you don't like it, it seems, so maybe we should make another selection." Sometimes you might get a wine when it's going through an awkward stage in its development, where the fruit has receded and it's not really as good as it was when you had it last, but in the future it will be, and sometimes even more glorious. You should not assume that because you had that wine or a similar vintage before that every bottle is going to be the same. That's what makes wine far more complex than beer or whiskey: it's always evolving in the bottle and always changing.

How should the order of wines progress during a meal?

Normally, in any well-thought-out dinner, you start with something simple and then go into something more intense and complex as you go along. If you go the other way, then it's either disappointing or you can't even taste the wine. If you start out with a Syrah and then go to an old Pinot Noir, you won't even taste the Pinot Noir. The memory of the intensity of the young Syrah is so great that it overwhelms the impressions from the more delicate wine. What you want to do is have a progression. If you're going to make a delicate, older wine the showpiece of the evening, you can't start out with barrel samples of Hermitage or Zinfandel. You're not going to go very far. It's like serving a pound of foie gras as a first course.

You have to pace it, such as by starting out with a delicate Riesling, then, perhaps, a Loire Valley Chenin Blanc, followed by a Chardonnay, and winding up with an older Pinot Noir. If you want only red wine, then you have to start with lighter years of other wines, such as Oregon Pinot Noirs or something lighter.

What about beer?

I'm not a big fan of beer with food. I like beer, but I view it as something more like an *aperitif*; certain beers go well with oysters. Beer works with certain cuisines, such as exceedingly fiery cuisines. But even with Thai, Szechuan, or Indian food, I think wine is more interesting than beer.

I find beer filling, and frankly it's a little boring compared to wine. There are hundreds of different beers, but they fall into fairly recognizable styles and categories, with some variations but not a whole lot. That just has to do with the nature of malt. Malt is interesting, but it's like toast: you can toast it only light or dark. But so many factors affect the flavor of wine.

There are two factors in beer. Beer is balanced by bitter hops and sweet malt. Then you can have fermentation aromas, and those overtly yeasty and sweet malty flavors don't really match most foods. Then you add the bitterness of the hops, which also doesn't match well. The yeasty notes are very coarse compared to what you get in wine. "Beer food" is pretty well-defined: it's usually fairly low in acid, fairly greasy finger-food type stuff, or sweet and oily. There was a short-lived fad to match beer and cuisine, and while beers can be good to have a conversation over, or with appetizers or fairly simple stuff like steak and French fries, when you get to something that has a sauce and is more complex, there's no comparison.

How do you judge the quality of a wine list?

Usually [critics] might make a couple of oblique references to a wine list. Some critics try to make it an important part of their review—not necessarily that they understand it themselves, but at least they realize that they should try to analyze the wine list and talk about the wine. Critics who aren't knowledgeable either ignore it or might write embarrassing things about it. They usually try to find some philosophical stand to take so that they can approach any wine list on a superficial level and analyze it with those criteria in mind, such as the size. They can take either a positive or an antagonistic stance toward size. Some will see a big wine list with a lot of variety and will say, "This is too much. This is impossible. No one can possibly get through this. It's off-putting." But someone else will say, "Oh, it's a great wine list with lots of selections!" They'll also look at the prices that way.

The main things they should look for have nothing to do with size or price. The prices should be appropriate to the quality of the restaurant. If they're serving wine in Riedel crystal, they are paying $15 a stem as opposed to $1.50, plus there's breakage at a rate of about 10 percent over the course of a month. Adding in the cost of excellent wine inventory, storage, and the service of a full-time sommelier, the wines are going to be more expensive than they are at a bistro with no wine buyer where they have twenty wines total that are served in tumblers. You really have to expect a difference in price. For a while, critics looked only at prices, and that's like asking every restaurant to be like a bistro and not have a good wine list or service. The cost has to be covered somehow.

Restaurant critics should look at what's offered, and whether there's someone there who knows what he's doing. It's a service that needs to be accounted for, so wine prices should be expected to reflect that. It's part of their job to be looking out for people who are overcharging, however. If a bistro is charging fine-restaurant prices, something's wrong. And some fine restaurants may in fact overcharge.

But critics should look at wine lists on an individual basis, and not just say, "The prices are high." I've seen people see wine lists that have expensive wines—when the prices are actually inexpensive compared to their current value— but because they are expensive, they think the wine list is overpriced. You might be charging retail or less, and they don't even know it. I was selling some wines for $75 to $90 a bottle, and I went to a retail store and saw the same wines for about $150! With some of the critics coming into the restaurant, I wasn't sure that they'd understand that having wines at $75 to $100 was actually a good value. They might say, "You have a lot of wines on your list at $100." But my clientele understands that those are good values, and that's what they're buying. And they're excited, because they can't even buy those wines yet! And here my clients see them on the list for lower than retail, but the critics don't know enough to understand that. Critics should know whether a wine is expensive for what the wine is.

On the whole, I think critics are trying to know more about wine and that they should be looking at wine with a more experienced background.

What are some of your favorite wines off-duty?
I like diversity, and I like well-made wines, and there are so many around the world. In general, though, Chardonnay isn't the kind of wine I normally drink at home because I'm exposed to it so much at work. So many of the wines I taste are samples of Chardonnay; it's an important part of what I sell.

• I like German Riesling a lot. Gunderloch is an excellent producer.

• Austrian and Alsatian wines. Prager, from Austria, is fantastic. In Alsace, Trimbach makes some fantastic reserve wines. Zind-Humbrecht and Ostertag are also great.

• I drink probably more reds, though, and I drink a lot of Burgundy and Rhones—probably more red Rhone wines than Burgundies because I can afford them more! There are some fantastic wines in the Rhone, and they're a source of great values as well as fantastic flavor, such as the wines from Chateau Rayas and Pignan. Guigal and Jaboulet are two larger producers who I think make very good quality and are affordable. While some of them are $200 to $300 a bottle, they also make wines that are $8 a bottle. Also, Chapoutier is making good wines.

• From California and Oregon, I drink Pinot Noir. From California, the top ones are Au Bon Climat and Talley Vineyards; they're two of my favorites. Hanzell, for an older style; they age remarkably, the way very few others do. And Mount Eden Vineyards is outstanding. And I should also mention Dehlinger; the Russian River in general is a great area for Pinot Noir, so there are a lot of good producers, including Rochioli. In Oregon, there are St-Innocent, Panther Creek, and Ponzi. If I drink Cabernet, I try to drink older wines: '85s right now are drinking nicely, as are some of the older wines I have, some '77s—it was a drought year and they were kind of tannic when they were young, and they're very nice now. I drink Bordeaux now and then, but not anything new, because I can't afford them. The prices on Bordeaux have gone insane.

• Also, good California Meritage wine. I love Meritage as a category. It allows a lot of control from the winemakers' point of view in terms of how the wine will taste because they're not looking to make it a varietal. They're looking to make the best out of their vineyard. Some favorites: Cain Five, Dominus, Harlan Estate, Insignia by Phelps. I'm also very partial to Rubicon. The recent ones are especially great.

Jean-Luc Le Dû is the sommelier at Restaurant Daniel in New York City.

What is the place of wine in a fine dining experience?
You can definitely have a great dinner without wine, but it does so much to enhance the experience when you have the correct wine to go with the correct food. So definitely I think it really helps to have wine as part of a great meal.

How do you approach the process of pairing a wine with a particular dish?
You have to use your imagination and your experience of what you have seen work before. You can say, "Oh, with crab I would serve a Sauvignon Blanc." But if you then learn that the crab is being served with pieces of mango and grapefruit, you really have to fine-tune where you want to go with the wine. Sometimes your first impression can be totally wrong. Then you want to try the dish with a range of wines that you think could work. A Chardonnay won't work in most cases because it is going to be too over-powering for the finely textured crabmeat. You will preserve that with something that is not too alcoholic or too big. In the end, I did stay with Sauvignon Blanc from a cooler climate area, although a young Riesling Kabinett from Germany would have worked as well—but only after making sure it worked with all of the dish's components.

A lot of white wines, like the more oaky California Chardonnays, can be a real problem with food because they are really overpowering. When you put food next to them, everything feels smaller all of a sudden. They really overwhelm the taste of the food. As compared with crab, lobster has denser meat, so you can really start to talk about oakier Chardonnays with it.

What first comes to mind when you think of matching a wine with lamb?
I like Pinot Noirs—something with an earthiness to it. Also, Syrahs and Sangioveses-based wines work well with lamb. After that, the dish's seasoning will really determine the wine you are going to serve. And if the preparation asks for it, why not a Zinfandel? That is what I did last night.

How does the cooking method influence the wine you might select?
When you're grilling something, whether it's a steak, veal or lamb, I would personally go with a young Cabernet Sauvignon from the New World. Because they have a roundness, they work well against the taste of grilled meat. With roasting, you get to play more with aged wines. You start to get slightly gamier flavors with age, like, let's say, an older St. Emilion. Or you can start experimenting with good aged Valpolicellas from Italy. You can also get this type of gamey overtone with some of the Spanish Riojas. The field is so big—there is so much to play with.

How do I use the services of a sommelier?
I think it is very simple. We are here to help. Basically, what has changed a lot in the profession in the last few years is that you have a fewer people who just went to school for it and more people who started studying it with a passion. If it is a job you feel 'forced' to do, it is boring and you can be a little snobbish about it. But if it is something you really care for, then I think you are really open to talking with people and trying to help them make the best of their meal.

When you are responsible for choosing 99 percent of the wines on the list, there must be a reason behind most of those decisions, either because you really like the wine or you think it goes really well with a dish. The wine list is a sommelier's toy box and with 450 wines at Daniel, that's a lot of toys to play around with, to help the customers have a good evening.

It is like a game. It's a little challenge when somebody asks you: "I would like to have this dish—what wine should I have with it?" And it gets so much more complicated when you have four diners who are having four different appetizers and four different main courses. You have to make a lot of compromises while trying to find the right wine for them.

What do you mean by "compromises"?
Following to a "T" the rules of food and wine pairing can sometimes be deceiving in the end, because what if you propose something that a person really hates? You can't stick with, "No, you have to have this wine because this is what goes well with the dish." I think your first concern is to make people happy with their choice of wine. You cannot force people to drink what they don't want. So you have to propose, but always listen to what the customer tells you.

If he is determined to have a Cabernet Sauvignon, you are not going to give him a Syrah?. So you try to find within the Cabernet Sauvignon family what you feel could work the best with his dish. There are spicier Cabernets. All your Cabernets have a different style, because of the soil, climate and wine-making process. Look at Joseph Phelps, which I find is a highly spicy Cabernet Sauvignon, and look at Colgin, which is a sweeter, oakier, more opulent type of wine. You can go in very different directions with those wines—even within the same grape.

How does your wine list break down at Restaurant Daniel?
It is true that we have a lot of French wines. I would say that 60% of the list is French. About 30% to 35% is American, and the last 5% to 10% are wines from around the world like Spain and Italy. That is something I am really looking at now, more than ever before. When I started, I was very much in a French mode, because that was what I knew best. But when you look around the world, there is so much going on. Right now, I taste a lot of wines from Spain, for example, because I think there is a new generation of wine-makers that are making wines that are so much more interesting than in the past. I find a lot of the old Rioja wines not very interesting, because they've spent so much time in American oak barrels, but some new Bodegas like Artadi are making terrific wines.

Do you typically serve whites with fish, or are you breaking the rules a little bit?
Pairing fish with white wine and red meat with red wine—I think it works a lot of the time, but I don't think it works all the time. Especially now, you'll find a lot of fish dishes which come with a red wine sauce. Tuna, for example, is a difficult fish to match with wine, because of the oily texture of the fish. And if you serve it with red wine sauce, you try to find a very dry red wine that is really going to fight against that fattiness, but that is not overwhelming, like an older Cabernet Franc or Nebbiolo from the Piedmont.

You have to be very careful of the sauce. The sauce may be more important for what wine to choose than the fish or meat itself. A very traditional example is when chicken is served with truffles under the skin in a white creamy sauce. If you find an aged Chardonnay or White Burgundy to go with that, I think you're in heaven! You're having a great time.

With red meat, I would say you want a red wine 99.9% of the time. There's always a weird case. If you had a veal stew in a white wine sauce with pearl onions, you *might* consider a white wine.

Are there other myths out there about wine that you'd like to debunk?
For me, one of the worst myths is that cheese should be served with red wine. I've made the same mistake myself. First of all, a lot of cow's milk cheeses are very oily. Aged goat cheese totally breaks the structure of a red wine. I don't think they work at all with red wine. If you serve a fresh or a slightly aged goat cheese with a Sauvignon Blanc, you can have a lot of pleasure. If you are having a Fourme d'Ambert or a Roquefort, I think a sweet wine is so much more interesting. I also find a lot of semi-dry wines work well with cheeses—like the 1971 Vouvray with a Mountain Shepherd cheese from Vermont I had the other day. In terms of classic combinations that work, it's very traditional in England to eat Stilton with port. I don't think there's a better match in the world between cheese and wine than the match between that.

(Continued on next page)

Would you ever comment on a customer's choice of wine?

Sure, but tactfully, by saying something like, "Maybe you'd be happier with this...." For example, our classic menu has black sea bass as the second course, and it is served wrapped in a potato crust with a red wine sauce. A lot of people will tell me, "We'd like white wine to start with the sea bass, and red wine afterward." And I'll explain nicely that the menu is more for red wine. If you explain it to them in the right way, I find that in 90 percent of the cases they'll say, "Okay—let's have red wine throughout the meal." Then, maybe you can try two different red wines—something lighter with the bass, and then something heavier and spicier with the lamb. This is when a well-stocked list of half-bottles is useful. But sometimes customers will tell you, "No, we really want our white wine." This is when a sommelier has to learn to stay quiet. But a lot of times they are really listening and paying attention to the suggestions that you make.

Do you put a lot of effort into your wines by the glass since you do so many tasting menus?

We just put in a system called Le Verre de Vin, which is this black device on the wall that vacuums the air out of the bottle and adds CO_2 to the champagne so it stays bubbly. I used to offer four whites and four reds by the glass, and now I've expanded it to about seven whites, seven reds, three champagnes, and three or four dessert wines. So I really can play with the many different tasting menus Daniel has to offer.

What do you think of the state of American wine service?

I'm impressed with a lot of the American sommeliers—they come to the field with a passion. I think Andrea Immer at Windows on the World is very talented. So is Andy Freeman at Arcadia and The Lobster Club. Arcadia has one of the most interesting wine lists in New York City. It really goes after quality. He spends a lot of time in the vineyards, and really tries to discover new winemakers and bring them to New York. I think they do a tremendous job.

Restaurants in France are still set up to have at least a ninety-nine to one hundred percent French list. While this has been changing, mostly they don't really look around at what's going on in other countries. When you are in New York City, everything is imported. We get all the French wines that we want, all the California wines that we want, and wines from other countries like Germany, Austria, Spain, and Australia, without a problem. I think we are really lucky here.

Do you think that customers understand the reasons for the mark-up on wine?

Yes. Especially in a restaurant like ours; we are on Madison Avenue, and have quite a high rent. Daniel [Boulud] wants the highest possible quality to go into his restaurant, which means we have about eighty employees for eighty-five seats. Food does not pay for all of that. Some of the mark-up of the wine is for the quality of the people who work in the back; we have people who come from France to work here. We have the best possible ingredients in the food. In addition, I spend about fourteen hours a day looking for those wines. Saturday was my day off, and I spent six hours at [wine] auctions at Christie's. So there is a lot of time spent gathering those wines and maintaining all the vintages of wines in our cellar downstairs. It's a lot of work. It's a lot of energy to try to secure the best wines. Considering this, I don't think our mark-up is out of line.

What kind of crystal glassware do you use?

We use WMF, which is similar to Riedel. There is a slight difference in the quality, but I have 30 percent less breakage than when I used Riedel. They cost me one-third the price of Riedel, and they look almost the same.

What are some of your favorite wines to drink?

I'm from Brittany. We make no wines where I come from, so I'm unbiased. I like a lot of different wines, but my favorites are older white Burgundies. Great Chardonnay really needs age on it, to show all its different facets. I also love red wines from the Priorat area of Spain, good Syrahs, red Burgundies, and I'm also very fond of the superb Chenin Blanc from the Loire Valley.

Do you have a favorite Burgundy?

Yes, among many others a Chevalier-Montrachet from Leflaive, 1983. I love this wine. It's very complex. It's fat, but fat from the fruit, not fat from the oak. It's a nice bottle of wine.

What would you like to eat with that? Would you like to have it by itself or as part of a meal?

Oh, as part of a meal. With, I don't know, something like grilled lobster—very simple, with drawn butter. That's all—no special sauce or anything. Just the taste of the lobster and the Leflaive. I'm getting hungry now!

Any other favorite wines?

American Pinot Noirs: Dehlinger, Capiaux—that's in Sonoma Valley. Dehlinger is very American, in a way: it's totally different from red Burgundies. It's very opulent—almost like sweet, roasted fruit. You can definitely enjoy it with something like grilled quail.

I really like this wine from Spain called Clos Ersamus. Its made from 80-year-old Garnachas vine on a spectacular terraced hillside. It's a big framed wine with good fruit flavors, and aromas of spices and sweet oak. That could be really nice with a braised lamb shank with some herbs and some tomatoes.

I also find New Zealand white wines very interesting. It seems that this country has areas with a great terroir, which produces wonderful wines like Kumeu River and Cloudy Bay.

Are there other aspects of wine service that are changing?

In the old days, we used to decant only older wines, to separate the sediment. I find now that actually young wines benefit the most from decanting. We are actually selling wines younger than we used to. Thirty or forty years ago, you could afford to let a wine sleep for ten or fifteen years. Now the logistics of maintaining a cellar have changed so much, and the wine making style has changed to make wines that are approachable younger—because people don't have the patience any more.

By pouring a younger wine in a carafe, you oxidize it by the contact with the air. Some say, "Oh, I have to open the wine to help it breathe." I'm sorry—if you are left in an elevator with only a little hole to breathe from, you're not going to get much air! The same is true for a bottle of wine—a nickel-size opening in a bottle is not doing anything to the wine.

If you want to let it breathe, pour it into a carafe. You'd be surprised at the changes in the wine. That's not only true for red wines, but it's also true for white wines. Put a white Burgundy in a carafe for forty-five minutes or an hour—it changes so much. It gets so much better.

Getting people to accept that you are going to decant a red wine, that's an easy thing to do. But getting customers to accept that you are going to decant a white wine starts to be a harder challenge. Maybe they have never seen that before. But I think people who have tried the experience once...after that, they understand.

Now, the only thing is to change people's minds in America about the temperature of the service of wines. There is a very big difference between France and America. In France, you will take a bottle of Coca-Cola from the refrigerator and serve it without any ice. Here you take a Coca-Cola from the refrigerator, but still you are going to put twenty ice cubes in it. I think that if you serve something that's very cold, you are going to have a wine that is not dead, but is thoroughly asleep—because the cold just suppresses the aroma of the wine. You see as it warms up in your glasses, you start to find that the wine has more complexity, more flavor. Put a wine in a very cold fridge, and then try to smell it. There is no aroma. Wait half an hour and the nose starts to open up, and you can start to get some flavor out of that wine. I find that [in America] we serve white wines too cold and that we serve the red wines too warm.

The warmer the wine, the more the alcohol starts to show through. If you serve a wine at around sixty or sixty-five degrees, that wine is still a little fresh. It's not cold. It's cool. You'll find that the alcohol is less noticeable and the fruit is more present. So I find the balance of the wine to be better.

(Continued on next page)

Do customers complain anyway?
I have my refrigerator in the back, and I set it at 45 degrees for the whites and 59 degrees for the reds, and usually it works. When customers complain, we put a lot of ice in the bucket and cool down the wine for them. I might have liked the temperature it was in the beginning, but, after all, I'm not the one who's paying for it. But it's changing—more and more people are finally saying, "Leave the white wine on the table; don't ice it."

Do you feel it is your responsibility to educate your customers about wine?
I find that if the customer wants to be educated, that's part of my role. But something I see sometimes and don't like is when you are at the table and the waiter or the sommelier will try to educate you no matter what. You are with your girlfriend or boyfriend on a date in a restaurant and you want to talk about getting married next week. And then you have that sommelier next to you, telling you about the 20 different kinds of Pinot Noirs he carries. And all you're thinking is, "Are you going to go away sometime soon?" I find that we have to be here with the knowledge to help the customer, but I don't think we should impose it.

I don't think you should ever make people feel stupid about wines, which would be easy with as big a wine list as we have. After all, they are coming to a four-star restaurant where they are going to spend a certain amount of money. They should be pampered. You should make it easy for them. We have many customers who are very highly educated about wine who often teach me things that I don't know. You can have a conversation with those people, because they share the same passion, but most people just want a good bottle of wine to complement their meal and that's fine by me.

But the majority of people just want to have a great bottle of wine with their meal, and they say, "I don't know anything about wine, but this is what I like. What can you do for me?" And we try to find that bottle for them, always letting the customer know that if the wine does not correspond to what he is looking for, we'd be very happy to change the bottle. You notice after a little while that you stop having bottles returned. Only about once every three or four months will a customer tell me, "I don't care for this wine—I would like to have this one changed." This gives the customer the sense that he is in charge of his wine.

What's the best way for a customer to handle sending back a bottle of wine?
It's just a matter of telling the wine waiter or sommelier or captain of the restaurant, "I would like you to try the wine—I'm not sure...." I would say that seventy-five percent of the time, they are right. Wine can be corked or have a problem. Our job is also to try the wines before they are served in the restaurant. Here, mine is such a high-pressured job that I don't really have time to sample all the wines. That should be part of my job, and I wish I had more time to do it. I must sample about thirty percent of the wine that I sell.

Sometimes you have a corked bottle, or an oxidized bottled. It's better for you to discover it for yourself than for a customer to notice it. We will just ask the customer, "Would you like another bottle of the same type?" If it's a corked bottle, there's a pretty good chance that it's the only corked bottle that you had in the case, so it shouldn't happen again. Or, if the wine is oxidized, "Maybe you would like to try something else?" Sometimes if it is the beginning of a meal, and the customer says, "Oh I don't really care for this wine," and he has chosen it for himself, and you try the wine and find it to be very good, instead of just changing it right away, you can propose to the customer to give it another five or ten minutes, to see what happens and to give it a chance. If 10 minutes later they still want to change that bottle, I'll change it right away. It is important to empower your customer with the right to decide.

How did you come to do what you do?
Chateau Cheval Blanc, 1964. I was 22 and at a Thanksgiving dinner with some family. I had never really drunk wine or cared for wine before. I tried this wine, and thought it was so wonderful....I just couldn't believe you could do so much with grapes, and that something so beautiful could be made from them! The day afterward, I tried to get a bottle. When I saw that it was $250 in the store, I figured I'd better start to learn about it and educate myself so that I could drink great wines without having to pay $250 for them! That's how I developed a passion for wine. I finished third [in a national wine competition] in America, and then Daniel offered me a job.

Just as wine represents the ultimate potential of grape juice, cheese represents the zenith of milk. **Max McCalman**, *maître fromager* at Picholine in New York City, helps diners at Picholine discover the pleasures of cheese.

What's behind the cheese boom?
People are eating richer foods, they're smoking cigars—it's a period of indulgence. Cheese is part of it. We can't get every great cheese into New York, but there are still quite a few to choose from. The imported cheeses seem to have been getting better. And because of the volume of cheese that's coming into the country, people are less fearful of cheese these days.

We started out with fourteen cheeses, and our cheese selection has grown dramatically due to customer demand. People would try them and then come back and say, "I've already had all of those. What do you have this week? Do you have Stilton? Do you have Roncal? Then I guess I won't have cheese." We'd been developing a reputation for offering the best cheese board in New York, if not the country, so it became even more challenging—and more fun—to offer a bigger inventory of cheeses and cheese types. When the job got to be too big for the waiters to handle themselves, I went from being the *maître d'* to the full-time job of *maître fromager*.

The finest cheeses are not cheap. Factory-produced cheeses are the least expensive, of course. But artisan types are not too high, and other artisan cheeses are definitely worth their price. The farmhouse cheeses in the British Isles are some of the more expensive cheeses as a group, but you can't make that kind of cheese anywhere else.

Cheese isn't a necessary part of the dining experience, but it certainly offers a good, delightful, sensory experience to help draw a fine dinner to a close. Along with the *digestif* aspects of cheese and the way it works on the stomach, it's a bargain. It's a lot of fun and excitement and nutrition. It's part of the "Holy Trinity" of bread, wine, and cheese.

A large fraction of what we offer here at Picholine are raw milk cheeses for which we get a lot of requests. Pasteurizing milk allows the good bacteria present in the cheese, which provide the aromatic esters that give the cheese its smell and flavor, to be killed off.

What constitutes a good sampling of cheese?
I don't want to waste any cheese. If I feel like people don't have the tolerance for cheeses that are a little "far out" either in aroma or flavor or texture, I won't serve certain cheeses. If a party is somewhat adventurous, that would direct me to offer other cheeses. It makes it interesting to offer at least four to six cheeses, so that you can cover a spectrum:

1. A cow's milk cheese, such as Stilton, which is one of the most celebrated cheeses in the world. It's one of the most frequently requested cheeses here.

2. A goat's milk cheese, such as a Loire Valley goat's milk cheese, which are some of my favorites. I have two favorite Spanish goat's milk cheeses, which are both made with pasteurized goat's milk, unfortunately. It doesn't destroy the cheeses, but I would have liked to have tasted the cheeses made with raw milk. Crottin de Chavignol from Sancerre is a classic; it's nice when someone has a Sauvignon Blanc or a Sancerre or even a white Bordeaux or a light Italian Chardonnay on the table with it, especially if it's a younger, gentler, milder Loire Valley goat's milk cheese.

(Continued on next page)

3. A sheep's milk cheese, such as Roquefort, which is a raw milk cheese that is also one of the most celebrated cheeses. I don't want to leave the impression that veined cheeses are more desirable or more my favorites.

4. A blue cheese, such as Valdeon from Spain. Some people call it Cabrales, but it's not really Cabrales. It's complex.

5. A bloomy rind cheese, such as Pierre Robert, which is also a triple-crème. It's our favorite triple-crème.

6. A "smelly" washed-rind cheese, such as a ripe Alsatian Muenster.

I arrange the cheeses in a circular order on the plate according to flavor and, in some cases, ripeness. If a party is finishing a certain wine, I might put a cheese that pairs really well with that wine closer to the start of the plate so that it would be recognized. The good thing about cheese is that you can taste several, and it doesn't have the taste-numbing effect that a wine tasting will have. People are really able to taste many cheeses and to appreciate the distinctions between them, particularly if a good range is offered in flavors and textures.

What's best to drink with cheese?
Almost everything goes with cheese. Even coffee goes well with certain cheeses, such as Gjetost from Norway, and some goat's milk and cow's milk cheeses. It gets down to balance. The sweetness of port, in contrast to some of the blue cheeses that tend to be a little saltier than non-blues, is nice.

A lot of people ask for red wine with their cheese, but many opportunities for pairing cheese with white wines of various types exist. Chardonnay pairs well with Ruth Kirkham's Lancashire and the goat's milk cheese from Spain Garrotxa.

As a general rule, I recommend the following pairings:

Beverage	Cheeses
Port	Stilton, Fourme d'Ambert
Sauternes	Roquefort, sheep's milk blue cheese
Beer	Farmhouse cheeses of England
Darker amber	Chimay cheese, a fairly delicate cheese
Pilsner-type	Classic blue from Westfield Farms in Massachusetts

I'd avoid water, however. I don't see that mixture in the stomach as being a natural. And tea is another beverage I don't feel works well with cheese.

When pairing cheese and beverages, a lot of people take the easy way out by pairing a local cheese with a local wine or local beverage, such as the Chimay with the Chimay cheese. In most instances, it's probably a logical pairing. But I think there are opportunities for pairing from many kilometers apart that are good surprises.

What are some of your favorite cheeses?
I think of these cheeses when they are *à point*: at their perfect stage of ripeness.

- My favorite made in America is Cindy Major's Vermont Shepherd Cheese. It's so beautifully crafted. It's a French Pyrénées style of ewe's milk cheese. She and her husband David have put a lot of effort into making the best cheese they can with the resources, animals, and tools that she has to work with. The texture is nice. It's consistently well-made, but each cheese has its own character, and subtle differences can be detected in flavor and texture.

- Garrotxa is a very creamy Spanish goat's milk cheese from Catalonia.

- Ruth Kirkham's Lancashire is made with raw cow's milk. It's the softest of the pressed farmhouse British cheeses. It's said that goat's milk makes the best drinking milk, but cow's milk makes the best butter—and this is a buttery cheese. The locals call it a buttery crumble. It's fairly mild, but it has a lot of undertones and subtle flavors.

- Valdéon is the Spanish blue. It's a cheese that's got a lot going on: a little bit of sweetness, a little bit of saltiness. The texture is usually not quite fluffy, but kind of creamy. Even though Valdeon is made with pasteurized cow's milk, its crystalline texture makes it a little sprite on the tongue. Another related cheese, Pena Azul, is from Peñamellera, of eastern Asturias, and is essentially the same cheese. It's a cow's milk blue cheese from northern Spain, not too many kilometers away. It's also wrapped in leaves, maple or sycamore, that allows good bacteria to penetrate the cheese and introduces good bacteria to the surface of the cheese, which adds complexity of flavor to the cheese. It's a cheese like a fine wine: you'll smell it and get an initial sensation. As the cheese settles on the tongue and touches off different taste buds, it sparks different nuances, and the finish will be different. It's a cheese that will talk to you.

- Charles Leary's Catahoula, from Chicory Farms, is a raw cow's milk, a washed-rind cheese. It's pretty powerful, but can be pretty creamy and gentle. This cheese, from Louisiana, is radically inconsistent, but I like it. The first time I tasted it, I thought it was one of the best cheeses I'd ever eaten.

- Taleggio is a cow's milk cheese from Lombardy, northern Italy. It's one of my favorite table cheeses, and one of my favorite cow's milk cheeses. It's big and buttery, with a fairly high fat content. It's a thoroughly luscious, delightful cow's milk cheese. It needs a piece of bread, usually. When I eat cheeses, I don't eat bread very much, but some of the soft cheeses need something like a piece of bread to be a vehicle.

What is best to eat with cheese?

At Picholine, we serve cheese with baguettes and raisin-walnut bread, dates, and quince paste, which makes a nice condiment, especially for the harder sheep's milk cheeses. We also serve pressed cakes made from plum and walnuts, or fig and almonds, which make a nice centerpiece for a plate of cheese.

Where can I find more in-depth information on cheese?

Many contrasting descriptions regarding cheese exist, and you've got to decide who you want to believe. For content, I like Patrick Rance's *Great British Cheese Book* and *French Cheese Book*. The content is enormous; it's panoramic in describing cheeses. For a lyrical and historical feel for the cheese world over the last 200 years, the book *Forgotten Harvest* by Avice Wilson tells the story of the lost art of cheesemaking in the Wiltshires in Western England. There's a lot in it, and it makes good reading.

Eight
Electing the Future of Dining

"The fate of nations depends on the

way they eat."

—Jean-Anthelme Brillat-Savarin

"In this country, we're just trying to

figure out our relationship with food."

—Alice Waters

Chefs, critics, and consumers will create the future of food, and of restaurants, together, based on their respective and collective decisions regarding how they'll use their talent, influence, and dollars. Chefs put forward their points of view in their cuisines, through the ingredients they select and how they choose to work with them. Critics have the power to steer customers toward those restaurants they believe to be most worthy and to serve as interpreters for the chefs' intentions. And individual consumers have more power than they might believe, since they fuel the engine of the entire system through choosing which restaurants to support.

What will the future they create look like?

Voting With Their Restaurants

Chefs' selection and handling of ingredients is a more important expression of their point of view than perhaps any other aspect of their restaurants. Alice Waters, chef-owner of Chez Panisse, has been frequently quoted as saying, "A restaurant can be no better than the ingredients it has to work with," and is credited with popularizing this philosophy.

"I think food in many ways is so much better, and the ingredients are better, than [in the 1960s and 1970s] when I first started reviewing restaurants for *Gourmet*," says Caroline Bates. "I really have to give Alice Waters of Chez Panisse tremendous credit for starting this movement of growing produce. Others were doing it, but none had the impact that she has had.

"For example, Peter Roelant of the restaurant Four Oaks [in Bel Air, California] has been growing produce for ages. He has very good ingredients, and he has different gardens around the Valley from which he gets special fruits and other produce. I think French chefs over the years often did that in Los Angeles, though I don't think they were given credit for it," says Bates. "But the increasing level of interest in ingredients has gotten growers interested in producing them. Today, everybody thinks of ingredients as being the most important thing. And, as a critic, I do, too."

Joyce Goldstein believes that a restaurant has other important opportunities to communicate to customers what it stands for. "At Square One, I could sit and talk to customers all night! If I was at the podium, people would ask, 'What kind of food is this?' or 'What do you recommend tonight?' Or I could have a wonderful chat with them about what they were having if I went over to their table," she says. "As a restaurant professional, if you're really good at your job, you have ample opportunity—one on one, every night—to make an impression on your customers and to let them know who you are, what you believe in, and what's important to you."

Anne Rosenzweig, chef-owner of Arcadia and the Lobster Club in New York City, sees a restaurant's influence as reaching far beyond what a customer will eat under its roof. "Chefs influence what our customers eat every day through kind of a synergistic circle: We serve something in the restaurant. Customers like it, get interested in it, and read about it. They go to their supermarket, gourmet store, or farmers' market and ask, 'Hey, where can I get this?' Then the market realizes, 'Oh, we've got to grow that or obtain that.' All of this helps raise the level of food."

Voting with Their Pens

Jonathan Gold, restaurant critic for *L.A. Weekly* and *Los Angeles*, believes that food is the most interesting subject there is. "It encompasses everything there is to write about," he observes. "I'd like to read more excitement about food and more actual awareness of where the reviewer is, though 'social consciousness' is probably the wrong term. Too many reviewers go to a restaurant with blinders on and see nothing but what is on the plate in front of them, or whether a waiter smiled at them or not."

Chefs and restaurateurs agree that more attention could be paid to all that a dining experience is and can be. They believe it's time for more restaurant criticism to go beyond the "what, where, and when" of the dining experience, with greater focus on *who* is behind providing it, *how* they have approached it, and, in many cases, *why*.

"When you're creating a sensual environment, you're trying to appeal in a visual way, in an aromatic way, in a tasty way, to that person," says Alice Waters. "These things aren't always noted." Waters says she would like to see restaurants both in the United States and elsewhere evaluated in terms of the purity of their food. "It should be a regular part of evaluating restaurants, noting which are buying from local, organic growers and which are not," she argues.

Restaurant criticism continues to change shape, just as the food and restaurants that inspire it change shape. Twenty to thirty years ago, if

The James Beard Foundation is a not-for-profit culinary organization dedicated to furthering the practice and appreciation of the culinary arts. The Foundation, which is located in New York City, was established in 1986 in memory of James Beard, the renowned cookbook author, chef, and educator who has been called "the father of American gastronomy." It fosters the appreciation and development of gastronomy by preserving and promulgating our culinary heritage, and by recognizing and promoting excellence in all aspects of the culinary arts.

Located in Beard's Greenwich Village townhouse, the Foundation is a culinary center for food professionals and enthusiasts, and sponsors culinary events open to the public. Every day of the week, chefs, pastry chefs, winemakers, and cooking teachers from around the country come to The James Beard House to prepare meals, conduct tastings, or lead workshops and classes. It has been described as a "Carnegie Hall" for chefs, a place for culinary artists to perform, and encourages aspiring chefs through offering one of the most extensive culinary scholarship programs in the country. Membership is open to all.

167 West 12th Street; New York, NY 10011
Phone: (212) 675-4984
Web site: http://www.jamesbeard.org

restaurants served only classic dishes, a critic could point out whether they were prepared correctly or not, and whether the results were pleasing or not. Now, as chefs' own dishes are featured on their menus and restaurants communicate unique points of view, critics' roles and practices are also changing. The best critics explore restaurants as the social forces that some have become, and strive to put a chef's or a restaurant's efforts into a context that will help diners to better understand, appreciate, and take pleasure in them. In addition, the rich and diverse backgrounds of some critics are contributing to their ability to help readers understand many aspects of the food experience, which can straddle myriad subjects, from history, to culture, to sociology.

While Ruth Reichl, restaurant critic for *The New York Times*, says she hopes to educate her readers about food, she acknowledges that it's sometimes a struggle. "When you get to indulge yourself by doing a little preaching, I think it's great," she says. "But a lot of people don't, for example, want to be told the right way to eat sushi. Once in a while you can say, 'Don't dip the rice in the soy sauce!' Maybe once a week, you can slip a nugget in."

For restaurant criticism to reach its potential, it will require the serious support of leading media. John Mariani, restaurant critic for *Esquire* magazine, questions whether that support will be forthcoming. "Sometimes doing this [job] as well as possible is a matter of learning as much as possible," observes Mariani. "But are the leading media who employ restaurant critics willing to send them to France and Italy

"[In restaurant criticism], I'd like to see more of the quality of writing and intellectual thinking that goes on in The Wall Street Journal *or* The New York Times. *If they want to take food as an art form, I want people who write about architecture or dance or fiction or poetry to take food as seriously. Otherwise, if they want to write about restaurants from a consumer standpoint, then they've got to be a lot more fair. They've got to let the chefs say something, publish their menus, and generally give the public more information."*
—Mark Miller,
  Red Sage and Coyote Cafe

and across the country with the same frequency that they send their fashion columnists to the collections in Milan, London, Paris, or wherever they have to be? If there's a heavyweight fight—such as 'The Thrilla from Manila'—the reporter covering boxing goes and *The New York Times* pays for it. But are the papers willing to say to their food writers, 'You should be in Paris twice a year, where things are happening' or 'Go check out London or San Francisco'? I don't think so."

Voting with Their Forks

"For me, the most important criticism comes from the people who dine here day in and day out because it is your customers who keep your doors open."
—Gray Kunz,
  Lespinasse

One of the most hopeful things William Rice has observed about consumers' interest in food is that it is so widespread. "Some years ago when I was at *The Washington Post*, I reluctantly wrote a piece about food processors," recalls Rice. "To me, they were an expensive new tool from France, and I wondered whether they would interest many readers. But the first call I got was from a woman who wanted to buy one for her son, who was a state trooper. That overcame my suspicion that only those with money were going to get interested in new culinary developments. And that's been part of the excitement in food over the years. You can't tell where the cooks are coming from, and you can't tell where the diners are coming from! And you're finding people who are absolutely passionate about food who are barely adults."

Rice believes that diners have a lot more power than they used to. "In the long run, it's the clientele who come in—what they eat and don't eat, and ask for and what they don't ask for—that's going to determine, if not your restaurant, then the restaurant your sous chef opens when he leaves to open his own place," he says. "Customers are much more important players than they used to be. Customers' attitudes, experiences, and philosophies play a much bigger part in how restaurants are formed and shaped—and even, to some extent, how critics react."

Still, Arthur Schwartz, restaurant reviewer at WOR Radio in New York City, laments that many customers are too reticent to use that power. "I wish the dining public trusted their own judgment more," he says. "They say that a movie is not made or broken by a review, and I wish that were true of restaurants. So many people are intimidated about voicing opinions about food. They think they don't know enough. That's because the food media and the food world have made it seem very elitist. I'd love to get the elitism out. After all, everybody eats."

Dennis Ray Wheaton, chief dining critic for *Chicago* magazine, has observed that the sophistication of the entire country is rising. "The whole level is going up, and the quality of restaurants in Chicago has risen significantly in the ten years that I've been reviewing restaurants," he says. "It's just getting better and better." Gael Greene, restaurant critic for *New York* magazine, agrees. "People are much more knowledgeable about food and, of course, they're paying so much money for food," she says. However, Greene adds, "There's a huge core of people who have no taste at all, and they're the ones who keep all those restaurants going that have nothing to do with food."

Americans are clearly changing in their attitudes regarding food's importance, including how much they're willing to spend for quality. "In Italy, for example, people are willing to pay a lot of money for food,

Founded on the premise that gastronomy is essential to the quality of human existence, The American Institute of Wine & Food (AIWF) is a nonprofit, educational organization with membership open to all. In 1981, Julia Child, Robert Mondavi, Richard Graff, and others founded the AIWF to advance the understanding, appreciation, and quality of what we eat and drink. The AIWF continues to promote the exchange of information and ideas to benefit all who care about wine and food, from food and wine professionals to enthusiastic consumers. The Institute has more than 9,000 individual members and thirty-three chapters across the United States, and is devoted to improving the understanding, appreciation, and accessibility of food and drink through a lively and comprehensive exchange of information and ideas in its conferences, publications, and chapter programs.

1550 Bryant Street; Suite 700; San Francisco, CA 94103
Phone: (415) 255-3000
Web site: http://www.aiwf.org

whereas here, people get edgy about spending on food. And not just for fancy food, but for the basic ingredients," says Alison Arnett, restaurant critic for *The Boston Globe*. "In France, people go to the market and spend $10 on a chicken, whereas most people here wouldn't. They'll pay a lot of money for cars, or even CDs, but not for food. I know some people in western Massachusetts who grew vegetables for a while, and they told me that people complained endlessly about the price of a perfect tomato. Now, they grow mostly perennials. Some of the same people who will pay anything for flowers won't pay for food."

A promising sign of the impact of consumers' voting with their wallets is the fact that Americans' consumption of organic fruits and vegetables (grown without pesticides or chemical fertilizers) has risen 20 percent a year since 1990, resulting in a $2.5 billion industry. "I think the proliferation of farmers' markets all around the country is the most hopeful sign. It's extraordinary how they've multiplied in the last five years," says Alice Waters.

Consumers' tastes and support have made other important inroads in food. "Look at the bread revolution, for example," says Rick Bayless, chef-owner of Frontera Grill and Topolobampo in Chicago. "In the United States, we have gone from horrible bread to wonderful bread in this country in ten years. And this is reaching into the heartland of America; it's not just in the big cities."

Educating America's Palate

An issue that chefs, critics, and consumers can come together to address collectively is improving culinary education, not simply of professionals, but of the general public. Everyone who cares about the future of food can take steps to learn more about the subject and get involved in the programs of burgeoning organizations such as the American Institute of Wine & Food and The James Beard Foundation.

"One of the problems we've had in this country in terms of food appreciation is that the sense of taste and the sense of smell are virtually ignored in the education process," says William Rice. "And with grandma going away and the advent of microwaves, it's worse because you don't even get to wander into the kitchen and smell those wonderful smells anymore. But in building a connoisseur and building taste, it's important to go back to the question of 'Why do we ignore two of the five primary senses?'"

Alice Waters agrees that it's a critical question. "The way information comes into your head is through your senses," she points out. "If we don't educate our senses, if we don't fine-tune them, then we don't get the same kind of information in there. Certain pathways are closed off. This is compounded by the fact that people are deprived of things like the touching of food, which is sold wrapped so you can't smell it. Too many people end up just microwaving their food and swallowing it without any interaction. That's painful to see.

"But now even the French are worried that they're losing their culture," says Waters. "So they're sending out SWAT teams to reeducate the kids, in the

"With all the culinary scholarships being organized, I think some of the money should be spent having students go to restaurants to taste real food, so that taste is not just a class exercise. More of the people aspiring to restaurant kitchens should experience dinners in a variety of restaurants as part of their core education. They'll also find out that way what it's like when somebody is rude, or nice, to you."
—Michael Batterberry,
  Food Arts

same ways we're talking about it here [in such programs as Waters' "Edible Schoolyard" project, described on page 234]: bringing kids into contact with a garden, and helping them learn how to cook, to taste, to feel, and to experience food in a really pleasurable, sensual way. Parents don't have the time to teach that, so I think it has to happen in the schools. It's a kind of elementary education that we all need to have."

While Waters's efforts are at the grade-school level, Rick Bayless has found that students of all ages still have something to learn. "I had the opportunity to speak at the commencement at The Culinary Institute of America recently," he recalls. "I looked at these graduating students, and realized that they're going to go in a million different directions and they're all going to affect good food. I felt it was important to let them know that the whole notion of good food in the United States has changed dramatically in the last twenty years. Even when they started getting interested in food, it was still kind of a rarity to talk about it. Now, it is much more commonplace.

"But a lot of times when you talk to culinary students you'll find that many of their food memories are around intense, artificial flavors," he observes. "One teacher at NECI [New England Culinary Institute] said she was incredibly frustrated talking about real flavors with her students because they just couldn't relate. So she got the idea to go into class and ask them to debate the merits of a Whopper versus a Big Mac, and all her students got into it in an intense way. They could debate the topic because they knew all the details of the way that each burger was put together, and that was her entree to teaching them about other flavors."

Alison Arnett shares Bayless's concern about Americans' overreliance on fast food. "So many people have grown up on it, and it wipes out so many taste elements that their palates are deadened," she says. "That's one reason why Americans like really strong flavors."

Mark Miller, chef-owner of Red Sage in Washington, DC, and Coyote Cafe in Santa Fe, agrees. "Homemakers today know fifty-one flavors, while there are 5,000 flavors or more. We may be actually delimiting our sensibility," he observes. "As this happens, unfortunately, chefs have to create food for an audience that no longer knows or appreciates what they do. And that becomes a big problem because you can no longer serve the taste equivalent of foreign films when all your customers can taste is 'Rambo.'

"Just as the 3 1/2-minute music video has become our musical attention span, Americans also have a very small taste attention span today," says Miller. "There have to be lots of fats, big proteins, and overaccentuating flavors. I'm one who falls to that—overly spicy flavors, chiles, truffles. Those have become the only flavors that people recognize. At the same time, more subtle and more interactive complexities get completely lost on the general public."

Arthur Schwartz fears that the elaborate food celebrity chefs promote in their cookbooks might unintentionally thwart home cooks' efforts in the kitchen. "Some people have become so intimidated since restaurant food has become the standard that they think they can't be good cooks or that they can't make a nice and attractive meal for themselves at home," he says. "My biggest pet peeve with American food is that we look too much to young, creative, hot-looking kids as our example of what our food should be."

To the contrary, Rick Bayless believes that leading chefs can make an increasingly important contribution to improving how Americans eat, even at home. "When I visit friends in France at their home for dinner, they buy almost everything," observes Bayless. "All the *hors d'oeuvres* are bought. They might make a main course and throw together a salad, but they'll always buy pastry for dessert. They don't make a lot themselves, but they have good things to choose from in the first place. That's where America needs to be.

"In the United States we eat out a lot, and we prepare very simple, convenient meals during the week. That segment of eating at home during the week is where chefs really need to spend some time and make a contribution because we can help bring quality to everyday cooking. So many people want to have dinner on the table in a half-hour. If the choice is between taking a bottle of our salsa and pouring

"Several generations now have been weaned on fast food. What we have the opportunity to do as chefs is to offer our cuisine to a wider range of people, so that their taste memories don't center around processed and artificial flavors. Bringing good food to the masses has to be the next step."
—Rick Bayless,
  Frontera Grill and
  Topolobampo

Alice Waters, chef-owner of Chez Panisse in Berkeley, California, has committed herself to the education of children in Northern California through her program The Edible Schoolyard, which has turned a half-acre area of asphalt at Martin Luther King Jr. Middle School into a garden that supplies the school lunch program with food. The students cultivate and cook the food as part of their curriculum.

The mission of The Edible Schoolyard is to create and sustain an organic garden and landscape that is wholly integrated into the school's curriculum and lunch program. It involves students in all aspects of farming the garden, as well as in preparing, serving, and eating the food, as a means of awakening their senses and encouraging awareness and appreciation of the transformative values of nourishment, community, and stewardship of the land.

"These programs must involve children," says Waters. "If people can get involved when they are younger, they learn how exciting it can be to get involved with food from the time it is put into the earth until it is picked and then cooked." The Edible Schoolyard has plans to expand to other schools in the Bay Area.

it over a chicken breast and baking it or going to a national chain restaurant, after a while the chain restaurant experience is not going to measure up. You're going to say, 'This all tastes so processed. I know I can have something simpler and cheaper and better at home.'"

Bayless is now offering a line of bottled salsas. "My feeling is that if it doesn't have a taste reminiscent of what you would eat in our restaurant, then I won't have anything to do with it," he says. "Mark Miller, Allen Susser [of Chef Allen's in Miami], Michael Chiarello [of Tra Vigne in Napa Valley], and other chefs are now offering their own lines of food products, and we're bringing a different perspective [to packaged foods]. Larry Forgione [of An American Place in New York City] was really the one who started that, when he founded American Spoon Foods with Justin Rashid. Bringing a chef's perspective to really good bottled things—that's where we as chefs really have to spend some time. If we can raise the level of sophistication of food on an everyday basis, that will push all restaurants to become better and better, and will help to make food great in our country."

Discerning Tastes

It is never too late to cultivate a palate, as Rich Melman, founder of Lettuce Entertain You Enterprises in Chicago, attests. "I hired a cookbook author and former food editor from *The Chicago Sun-Times* to pro-

TEACHING KIDS TO TASTE

Food historian Terrie Chrones teaches an art and cooking course called "What Did Michelangelo Eat?" at Creswell High School outside Eugene, Oregon. The course introduces teenagers to restaurant cuisine as part of its curriculum. Independent projects recommended on Chrones's course syllabus range from visiting an ethnic restaurant and trying the food to writing a restaurant review. Before taking the class, which includes dining at a fine restaurant, some students' restaurant experiences had never extended beyond fast food. By the end of the course, students had cooked and drawn their way through world history, including the Middle Ages, ancient Egypt and the Renaissance period. At the end of the course, one student admitted, "Taking this class made me taste things I never would have tasted."

"I think it all starts with desire. There are some people—at any level of income—who use food as fuel, and others who use it as a pleasure mechanism."
—Richard Melman,
  Lettuce Entertain You
  Enterprizes

vide taste instruction. For about a year and a half, she worked with me almost weekly," he remembers. "We started with caviar. It was funny because we served caviar in our first restaurant that we bought for about $6 a pound. It was the worst crap you'd ever had in your life; it tasted like ball bearings! We put it on our salad bar, for which we charged about $1.95. So I said, 'Yeah, caviar, I know caviar. You buy it in big tins, put it out on ice, and people take it and spit it out.' And she told me, 'You haven't had *caviar*.'

"That week, she prepared blini, black bread toasts, chopped eggs, and capers, and we tasted the different types of caviar. The following week, we tasted smoked salmon. Well, my wife and I had just gotten married, and after that we were eating smoked salmon every Sunday morning for about two months! It was just a matter of learning the differences, and what makes something better than something else. You'd be surprised how people pick it up with a little education.

"When you have as many restaurants as we do, there are always quality issues," says Melman. "I think it's impor-

tant to teach quality. I try to make our partners more discriminating about what quality is. I don't care if we're making egg salad or making a *soufflé*—there's a standard as to what is good, what is great, and what is spectacular."

Can education of the senses lead to pleasure? "There is no great poetry unless poetry is understood," says Norman Van Aken, chef-owner of Norman's in Coral Gables, Florida. "As our cultural diversity and the capability we have for it expands, deepens, widens, progresses, there has to be an attendant willingness to look intelligently at the restaurant experience.

"A chef with a finely honed palate would have a very different experience eating in my dining room than the average diner would have. They would have differences in the ways they perceive it. And the average diner's perceptions would certainly differ from those of the Coral Gables high school students who just visited me and asked for a tour of the restaurant," says Van Aken.

Ruth Reichl agrees that a deeper level of understanding can lead to greater enjoyment. "It's like looking at art. The more you study art, the more you bring to it and the greater your enjoyment of it," she says. "On the other hand, you don't always want to make going out to eat 'a learning experience.' But I do think that educated diners enjoy restaurants more because they bring more to the whole experience."

In addition, diners can enhance their enjoyment of a restaurant experience by approaching it with the right attitude. "Americans are just getting to the point of understanding that you can appreciate an experience in, say, a Chinese restaurant if you can get beyond the 'I don't know what it is, but I know what I like' position to try to understand what the pretensions of Chinese cuisine are," says Reichl. "I'm completely annoyed by people who judge sushi bars by the size of the sushi and are always telling me, 'You think Kuruma Zushi [in New York City, to which Reichl awarded three stars] is so great, but the pieces are so small.' It's not a great sushi bar because it gives you great big fat pieces of tuna; it's a great sushi bar because of the quality. Quantity is *not* one of the ways to judge *quality*."

Restaurant critics can play an important role in teaching readers these distinctions. "People ask me how to describe Charlie Trotter's food, as compared to, say, [Roland] Liccioni's food at Le Français [another four-star restaurant in the Chicago area]," says Dennis Ray Wheaton. "I'll say that Charlie Trotter has got an intellectual mind that he's putting into his food. The way he thinks about it, it's almost like 'edible algebra.' It's equations of things he's putting together. I have friends who really know French food quite well and love to go to four-star restaurants who just don't appreciate Charlie Trotter's food. They find it's not quite sensual enough for them. You're thinking about it more than you're tasting the *foie gras* and having it melt in your mouth. Often he'll present you with juxtapositions you've never seen before. He sometimes tries to startle people. Then he makes these wild things balance.

"Le Français, on the other hand, is a very sensual experience, spending a wonderful evening feeling like you don't have to think. You just enjoy one flavor after another. And the wait staff is so different there. They've got waiters who have been there forever, who say things like [Wheaton imitates a heavy French accent], 'The potato purée has just enough potato to hold the butter together.' When I went for dinner with my wife, we ordered Champagne and were really hungry, so we asked to look at the menu right away. The waiter gasped, 'You came here to *eat*? I thought you came here only to drink Champagne!' It was fun! You'd *never* get that at Charlie Trotter's."

Mark Miller has observed that many diners are very conversant on what the dining room and even the food look like at a particular restaurant. "But ask them to describe the flavor of the squab dish. Was it acidic, bitter, or sour? Was it rich? Where did the flavors take place? What was the progression of flavors? How long did they last? Did the Cabernet or Merlot go with the dishes? Would you have chosen a spicier wine?" he proposes. "I find they're unable to answer those questions because they didn't actually eat the dishes. They

"Whenever you eat somewhere and a few months or years later you remember what you had, that's a great meal. That's very important. If you don't remember what you had, then something was wrong. You didn't eat; you were fed."
—André Soltner,
  formerly of Lutèce

looked at them, and they paid attention to their conversation.

"When food critics don't talk about the eating experience, we end up with a dining public that isn't eating," says Miller. "We've got chefs who are basically creating works that are gravitated toward that market. Young chefs today look at *Art Culinaire* [a quarterly featuring larger-than-life, four-color photographs of architectural dishes], whereas twenty-five years ago, we were reading Elizabeth David's books, which don't have *any* pictures or illustrations. How many diners, or chefs, or restaurant critics could actually conceptualize a food experience and describe the taste and sequence of flavors—like a musician can read and hear music?"

Leading critics are starting to make a real effort to do so. "I think it's important to write about the balance of the food and whether or not the flavors come through," says Alison Arnett. "I'll try to describe how it falls in my experience, whether it's clean, hearty, robust, delicate, high on the palate. I do a lot with taste, whether one thing is balanced against another, and whether you can really taste the meat or fish. The best chefs are all working to bring out the true flavors, and we need to communicate that."

Caring Enough to Vote

What does the future hold for dining out in America? One thing is clear: we will elect the restaurants and food of our futures with the collective votes we cast today. If America chooses to eat at theme restaurants, tomorrow will look like a theme park. If we choose to voice our concerns about what we ingest into our bodies, new healthful food options will emerge. If we choose to spend a little more on organic produce that is more flavorful as well as healthful for our bodies and our planet, organic farmers will continue to thrive.

Chris Schlesinger, chef-owner of the East Coast Grill in Cambridge, Massachusetts, believes it's worth the effort. "People spend a third of their time at home and a third of their time at work, and have only a third of their time to themselves. When you go to a restaurant, you've made a choice to go there and eat there with certain people. So, just the fact of your being there with your friends, in a relaxing atmosphere, is a great accomplishment. That's what's sacred," he says. "The restaurant provides the theater for the occasion, and food gives people a reason to go there and be together and have a good time."

Ruth Reichl agrees. "The thing I love about food is that most people have very few ways to control the quality of their lives, and this is one of the places that everybody can do it," she says. "You don't have to be rich. You may not be able to buy beautiful furniture, but you can buy a good apple at the Greenmarket, as opposed to an old apple in the supermarket, and know the difference instantly. It's one of those easy ways for people to learn how to get more pleasure for themselves. You can say, 'This tastes better than that. Taste it and see!' Almost everyone responds to good food when they taste it. Most people, when given a choice, choose good food and get great pleasure from it. Those of us who care about food would like to see this country not to go to [fast food restaurants] that smell horrible or kill your soul to be in, but to go to places where food is a pleasure, and where they understand it as a pleasure," she says.

"The great thing about great food is that it can bring people real pleasure and enjoyment, *every day*," says Reichl. "And for all of us who are committed to making food even better in this country, that is ultimately the goal."

"Mary Douglas, the author of The World of Goods: Towards an Anthropology of Consumption, *is a great anthropologist whose idea is that we are what we buy, and that our choices define us. Whether we buy a magazine or a* Zagat Survey *or what a restaurant critic is saying, we're buying into something. This is how we define who we are."*
—Mark Miller,
    Red Sage and Coyote Cafe

Some of America's Leading Critics' Favorite Restaurants—And Why

What is the best restaurant in America? There is only one right answer: it depends. *Your* choice may not be *my* choice, especially if you adore French food while I prefer adventures in unusual ethnic cuisines. So much depends on individual preferences, moods, cravings, the season, the weather, and other factors that our answers today might not be the same in a month!

We asked leading critics across America to share with us some of their favorite restaurants, and why. You'll see that critics' favorites aren't necessarily the city's "finest" restaurants. What accounts for the difference? The best way we know how to sum it up: heart and soul. Critics' favorites excelled at infusing love into the experience—for their ingredients, for their food, for their customers. Even the critics can taste it!

DINING ACROSS AMERICA WITH JOHN MARIANI

If I were ranking the cities, I'd say the restaurant capital is now unquestionably **New York City**. There's nothing even close. New York is a crucible of ideas. What drives New York's gastronomy is money and people. There are people with money who are willing to pay for fine dining, which draws the best talents, as does the international crowd who comes here. And you'll find people living on top of their restaurants—people don't live on top of their restaurants in Phoenix or Denver or Los Angeles! You've got to drive forty-five minutes to get to any restaurant you'd want to go to if you live in Los Angeles. Here, people come out of their office buildings, and boom! New York has ten great chefs for every great chef in [American] cities outside New York.

Chicago is a great, great restaurant town, but it's a copycat town. I don't think it's given the world of gastronomy any singular, unique restaurant of any kind, although Charlie Trotter would probably argue with me on that. Lettuce Entertain You copies other concepts and does them as well, or better, and usually at a lower price. Okay, Rick Bayless is an exception; he did for Mexican food what no one else was doing in the United States.

San Francisco is a little ingrown at this point, in the sense that they're very pompous about their food: "We eat better than anybody in the United States, and we really are obsessed with our food and our restaurants, and we love our chefs." It gets a little precious after a while. So many of the best restaurants in San Francisco are all of the same type. They're all doing offshoots of what Chez Panisse was doing twenty years ago. The food at Stars isn't radically different from the food at Rose Pistola, which isn't radically different from the food that's being done at other places. It's not such a bad thing; if you go to eat in Rome, you're going to eat Roman food. I don't criticize San Francisco for that.

Los Angeles has the size, but I don't think it has the power anymore. L.A. lost it for a lot of reasons; the recession, the earthquakes and mudslides, all really hurt it. And it ran out of new ideas. But what really crippled L.A. is a general lethargy on the part of chefs. You can go right down the list of notable L.A. chefs who are never in their restaurants. Wolfgang Puck is the most salient example, but you're not going to find Joachim Splichal in his restaurant most nights, either. Michael McCarty spends about two weeks a month in L.A., two weeks a month in New York. Mark Peel, I think, stays in his restaurant a good deal, but the others you're not likely to run into too often. And that takes its toll.

Boston seems to have gotten a new lease on life. For a while, everybody was copying Olives and Todd English because he had such enormous success. Everybody was doing Mediterranean cuisine. Unfortunately, what Boston has lost is anything resembling what used to be called New

England cuisine, what Jasper White and Lydia Shire started out doing, and what should have developed into a regional gastronomy. It almost doesn't exist anymore. There are no New England restaurants left in Boston except Durgin Park!

Philadelphia has ten really good restaurants, and probably more will be showing up. For a long time, it was really in the doldrums. There was nothing—there was Le Bec-Fin, Susanna Foo....But now there's a lot of good stuff going on there.

In **Washington, DC**, there's next to nothing going on there anymore, and they've lost so much of their clout.

Miami's sunk.

Houston and **Dallas** are just starting to come back.

Seattle's interesting.

SOME OF JOHN MARIANI'S MOST IMPORTANT RESTAURANTS ACROSS AMERICA

John Mariani, restaurant critic of *Esquire* magazine, explains his criteria: "If there were a directive and only five restaurants could continue to exist in the United States and all the others had to close for one reason or another, I'd certainly say the restaurants below should survive."

● **Valentino**
3115 W. Pico Blvd., Santa Monica, California
(310) 829-4313
The most dedicated, serious Italian restaurant in the United States. Owner Piero Selvaggio's attention to detail, going all out for his customers, in an Italian venue is remarkable.

● **Le Cirque 2000**
455 Madison Ave., New York City
(212) 794-9292
The craziest, most absolutely over-the-top restaurant—everything a restaurant could possibly be. You may love it, you may hate it, but there is nothing that Sirio Maccioni has not considered. It's a standard-bearer of momentous proportions.

● **Le Bernardin**
155 W. 51st Street, New York City
(212) 489-1515
This restaurant has revolutionized seafood cookery in the entire world. Before Le Bernardin, seafood didn't taste that way. Nobody knew how to cook it before that.

● Chez Panisse

1517 Shattuck Ave., Berkeley, California
(510) 548-5525

In terms of its importance. It's not necessarily my favorite restaurant, but I think almost as an institution and what it stands for, which is a quirky kind of California post-'60s attitude that says, "Why can't we serve the very best? Why can't we serve what we want?" It set a mold.

● Commander's Palace

1403 Washington Ave., New Orleans, Louisiana
(504) 899-8221

For representing a very specific regional American cookery and style that is unique and has so much influence. It has great generosity of spirit, a terrific wine list, very true to its own tradition and style, and yet had a great deal to do with lightening up the traditional Creole repertoire.

CAROLINE BATES ON SAN FRANCISCO vs. LOS ANGELES

*"I think northern California has far better wine lists and,
in general, mark-ups are not as high."*

Caroline Bates is the California restaurant critic for *Gourmet*.

San Francisco's such a funny, incestuous little town. Everybody knows everybody, and I'm finding a lot of similarity up there. We have all these offshoots of **Chez Panisse**, then the offshoots of **Zuni Cafe**, and then the offshoots of the offshoots. So we're getting a lot of similar food going on, with some nice variations. But sometimes I feel I would like to eat something quite different there.

There's a second trend now: once the restaurant **Betelnut** opened, it unleashed a flood of Southeast Asian restaurants, which are kind of interesting but all pretty similar. There are a few terribly original ones, like **Eos** and **The Slanted Door**, which are being done by Asian chefs.

San Francisco has tremendous little restaurants at cheap prices. I don't know of any city like that in the country, and I think it's extraordinary that you can go and have a reasonably good meal for much less than you'd expect, such as at The Slanted Door, if you order carefully. It's in the Mission, which is not exactly an upscale dining area, but it's where a lot of the young energy has gone. And there's a little spot on Belden Place called **Plouf** where you can go in and get a plate of mussels for $10. They do mussels in ten different ways, all classic. It's a wonderful little place. And North Beach has a lot of great little Italian places. Not all of them are good, but they're cheap—and fun.

By comparison, I probably don't see the same thing in Los Angeles because I'm not living there, and the neighborhoods are so far apart. I think Jonathan

Gold has unearthed those kinds of places because he knows the city so well. But when someone who has not come out of an immigrant experience opens an inexpensive restaurant in L.A., I usually don't find it very good.

But L.A. has its own special things. In the 1970s, Japanese chefs came to L.A. who had trained at the school in Osaka and knew French technique. They did a very interesting Japanese aesthetic on French food, and it was unique. That has had its offshoots in L.A., and I don't think any place in the country had anything quite like that then. It was almost a sub-cuisine: not Japanese, not French, but its own peculiar thing. There's one wonderful little place called **(Nouveau) Cafe Blanc** in Beverly Hills, and the chef-owner (Tomi Harase) came out of that. And the guy who had **Zenzero** was one of those, and **Chaya Brasserie** was another, and the one at **Cafe Del Rey** was another.

People call it "Asian" or "fusion," but it's quite different, really; it came out of a different tradition. And I don't think that a lot of people in L.A. who frequent the places realize exactly how special that is. Now it doesn't seem so special because other people are doing this Asian business. It's often put in print, which I get annoyed with, that Wolfgang Puck started this whole thing. He did not. This was three or four years before Puck ever did Chinois on Main. Roy Yamaguchi (of **Roy's**, in Hawaii) started in L.A. and was the first person to do Asian fusion, but there wasn't a name for it back then.

GREGORY ROBERTS ON NEW ORLEANS vs. SEATTLE

Gregory Roberts left his job as restaurant critic at *The New Orleans Times-Picayune* for *The Seattle Post-Intelligencer*:

I think there's a certain type of upscale restaurant you'll find in most big cities. They're sort of contemporary American, and on the menu you'll find things like polenta, mesclun salad with balsamic vinaigrette, and seared tuna. And you can usually find a few restaurants where they emphasize fresh, quality ingredients. Both New Orleans and Seattle have those.

New Orleans has a very deep-rooted indigenous food culture, which expresses itself at every level of the food spectrum, both in homes and in restaurants. On the low end, there are dishes that are quintessentially New Orleans—grits, red beans and rice, po' boys—and on the high end, there are restaurants serving dishes like shrimp remoulade, turtle soup, and grand Creole dishes. Emeril Lagasse of Emeril's has the zealotry of a convert. He has really embraced the whole Creole and Louisiana food tradition. What distinguishes Louisiana food is the richness of flavors. It's not hot or spicy necessarily, although it can be. There's a lot of slow cooking or bottom-of-the-pot cooking or whatever you want to call it. And there's certainly no hesitancy to use fats in the mix. What that all adds up to is rich flavor. There have been a lot of cultural currents mingling there, from French, to Spanish, to African, to Italian. All these influences contributed and coalesced.

"What's striking about Boston restaurants is that there is a very strong network of chefs who are friendly with each other and have continued to be friendly even though they're rivals—and I think that makes a lot of difference in the way Boston's restaurants have progressed. There are a lot of people who have stayed here for a long time. They've become a voice in the community, through which they've become known and respected."
—Alison Arnett,
   The Boston Globe

"People in Houston spend more money on eating out than in almost any other major American city. And there are more Cajuns in Houston than in Lafayette, Louisiana! There's a common palate of liking big, hot flavors."
—Alison Cook,
   Houston Sidewalk

Seattle has dishes like seafood chowders and fish and chips on the low end. It seems that they're just now trying to develop a Northwest regional cuisine on the high end that exists beyond the ingredients like salmon, halibut and other fin fish, and oysters. Every restaurant here serves salmon; they call it "the other pink meat." Louisiana is oyster country, too, but not nearly the way it is up here. In Louisiana, they're "just oysters," but here, people are much more aware of the various varieties. Some restaurants offer samplers with a dozen different oysters on the half shell, and they'll give you a little guide to the flavor characteristics of each one. Eastern Washington has good lamb, and there are good tree fruits and agricultural produce, like asparagus and lentils. And because we're on the Pacific Rim, there's a lot of Asian fusion cuisine.

SOME OF RUTH REICHL'S FAVORITE RESTAURANTS ACROSS AMERICA

Ruth Reichl is the restaurant critic for *The New York Times*, for which she has also written about her experiences at restaurants across the country and around the world.

● **Chez Panisse**
1517 Shattuck Ave., Berkeley, California
(510) 548-5525
It's a restaurant that is absolutely about the quality of the ingredients, about the integrity of what's on the plate. It's often very, very simple. But each ingredient there is as perfect as it can be. If you have ice cream, it will be just made and just the right temperature. You might look at the menu and think, "Oh, it's just pork chops." But then you're inspired to say, "I've never had a pork chop that's tasted this good." And each vegetable is a revelation, a little explosion of flavor. It's a restaurant that's all about the ingredients rather than the technique.

● **The French Laundry**
6640 Washington Ave., Yountville, California
(707) 944-2380
What I love most about The French Laundry is that it's a restaurant that says, "Come, trust us, enjoy. We're going to give you an experience if you'll go on a ride with us." So they'll give you dozens of little tiny bites. This is very worked-over food, but it's about the entire experience of being in a restaurant: the service is wonderful, it's nothing like home cooking, and it's things you couldn't have conceived of yourself. It's a little moment in time where you're being taken care of and tasting things that you almost couldn't have imagined possible.

Ginza Sushi-Ko
218 N. Rodeo Dr., Beverly Hills, California
(310) 247-8939

It's very hard to translate a French or Italian or Japanese restaurant to America, and most don't do it that well. Ginza Sushi-Ko is the only restaurant I can think of that is as good as being in Japan. The chef is a high master of fish and gets most of his fish from Japan. You put yourself in his hands, and he gives you what's good that day. The fish is exquisite and ever-changing, and he gives it to you on plates he makes himself. He's an artist. It's all about presentation, flavor, simplicity, and seasonality. I could only afford to eat there about once every five years. It's perhaps the most expensive restaurant there is.

Nobu
105 Hudson St., New York City
(212) 219-0500

Nobu is the perfect amalgam of the Japanese and American sensibilities. It's amazing simplicity in ingredients combined with invention, which isn't a high Japanese priority. It's so exciting to be there because you never know what you're going to get. And the ingredients are *really* good.

Jean Georges
One Central Park West, New York City
(212) 299-3900

There's so much I like about Jean-Georges Vongerichten's food. I think he's a genius. I think he's one of those people who can imagine flavors that you can't, and he combines food in ways that are just a complete delight to me. I also love the way he's brought aromas back into American dining rooms. I love the fact that each dish smells wonderful. And I also like the quality of eating in that restaurant; it's a very formal restaurant that isn't stuffy.

New York Noodle Town
28 1/2 Bowery, Chinatown, New York City
(212) 349-0923

It's very hard to find really great Chinese food in America. I think people were shocked when I sent *New York Times* readers there because it's really a storefront, and it's very cheap. But they cook with *extraordinary* care and use really good ingredients. Their wonton soup is fabulous, made with really good chicken stock and ethereal wontons. And when they cook soft-shell crabs, they start with live crabs. They also make wonderful roast baby pig. Everything tastes alive there. Their noodles are great, but it's not really a place that I go for noodles; you can get good noodles other places.

The Oyster Bar
Grand Central Station (lower level), New York City
(212) 490-6650

This is a great New York institution. I don't like eating in the restaurant, but I love sitting at the counter. They make oyster stews and pan roasts right in front of you, which smell wonderful, and it's great to watch these guys doing it. They have the biggest variety of oysters and clams on the half shell that you can find probably anywhere in America. It's completely unpretentious, completely American, and completely delicious. (By the way, the greatest *fried* clams on the planet are at a little shack called **The Bite** on Martha's Vineyard!)

● **Peter Luger Steak House**
178 Broadway, Brooklyn, New York
(718) 387-7400
They have the best steak in America. I was researching an article on steak, and someone told me, "Those women at Peter Luger do things the Neanderthal way!" That's because they're still going to the meat market every day, and most people aren't doing it that way anymore because it's really expensive. But they really know meat, buy the best on the market, and age it themselves. And you can taste it. You'll taste one bite and say, "Oh, *yes—that's* why I love meat!" It's easy to find yourself picking up the bone and gnawing on it!

● **Campanile**
624 S. La Brea Ave., Los Angeles, California
(213) 938-1447
I admire Nancy Silverton's baking so much. She's one of those people with great innate taste and enormous perseverance. She'll work and work and work until something is perfect. I love the baked goods there. I also love Mark Peel's food there, too; there's always something I want to eat on that menu! It's gutsy, and not many people are doing that kind of really tasty, rustic food. There's still a place in America for more people to offer cooking like that.

● **Spago**
176 N. Canon Dr., Beverly Hills, California
(310) 385-0880
The place I've probably spent more of my own money than any other, except Chez Panisse, is Spago. I love Spago. It's so much fun. And the food is delicious. It's probably the quintessential American restaurant—it's about celebrity, and good food, and good ingredients, all rolled into one. The new one is more grown-up than the old one; it's more comfortable and just as much fun.

I dream about [Spago's] Chino chopped salad sometimes. The vegetables are from the **Chino Ranch**, which grows the best vegetables of any place in America, and maybe the world! The Chinos are amazing. They have a road-side stand in some of the most expensive land in America [fifty acres in Rancho Santa Fe, outside San Diego]. People drive up in their Mercedes to pay $1 for an ear of corn! They sell to only two restaurants: Chez Panisse and

Spago. It's an amazing family. They're all doctors and lawyers, and the guy running it has a Ph.D.

SOME OF JANE AND MICHAEL STERN'S FAVORITE RESTAURANTS ACROSS AMERICA

Jane and **Michael Stern** are co-authors of the classics *Roadfood* and *Goodfood*. Their latest book is *Eat Your Way Across the U.S.A.* (Broadway Books, 1997). They also have a monthly column in *Gourmet*.

"These are not necessarily our five all-time favorite restaurants. For example, while **Peter Luger** *[178 Broadway, Brooklyn, NY; 718-387-7400] has the best steak anywhere, we thought we'd let others pick it. We tried to choose five that do for us what we're always looking for a restaurant to do: to give us a sense of place and culture. The significance of food goes beyond its flavor to where and how it is eaten, and how it is reflective of the people who prepared it."*

- **The Farmers Inn**
Havana, North Dakota
(701) 724-3849
This restaurant is located in a farm community of about 100 people. It went out of business back in the 1980s as the community shrank. But once the town realized that without their town restaurant they had no place to gather, the community resurrected it as a nonprofit business, and people now take turns in the kitchen. So you never know what you're going to get on any particular day because it depends on who's cooking. Sometimes it's great; sometimes it's just pretty good. But that's okay, because when you walk in there, you are walking into the life of a farm community in North Dakota, and by the time you leave, you've made friends.

- **Al's Bar-B-Q**
1079 W. Taylor St., Chicago, Illinois
(312) 733-8896
We love this place. Chicago has the best street-food restaurants, and this is the quintessential street-food restaurant, in that there are no tables or chairs and you eat standing up. They claimed their uncle invented Italian beef sandwiches, which may not have any precedence in Italian cooking. Lynne Rossetto Kasper [of *The Splendid Table*] said she has had something vaguely similar in the market in Milan, but whether they got that from Al's or vice versa, we don't know. Al's is brash and has a wonderful democracy about it: you'll always find Chicago cops there. And the Italian beef sandwiches are really, really delicious. It's a perfect sandwich.

- **Polly's Pancake Parlor**
Route 117; Sugar Hill, New Hampshire
(603) 823-5575
This is a monomaniacal place that was opened back in the 1930s by "Sugar Bill" Dexter, who wanted to show off what could be done with maple syrup. At the table, you get not only maple syrup, but maple butter and maple spread and maple sugar. Plus, the pancakes are great, and made from stone ground cornmeal and buckwheat. It's a charming location, surrounded by maple trees, and very scenic. It's a lovely New England experience. (Open seasonally.)

- **Snappy Lunch**
125 N. Main Street
Mt. Airy, North Carolina
(910) 786-4931
This is one of our favorites. We'd been told about it for years, but we just made it there a few months ago. It was referred to on "The Andy Griffith Show," so it attracts a lot of out-of-towners. They have one specialty that is really fabulous: a boneless pork chop sandwich, which is tenderized, breaded, fried, and served with a miraculous relish. It's one of the most

wonderful things in the world. If you go for lunch, it's likely that fellow diners will be from out of town, but we like it even better for breakfast when it's just a local Southern cafe.

- **Phillippe's**
1001 N. Alameda St.
Los Angeles, California
(213) 628-3781
This old, cafeteria-style restaurant purports to have invented the French Dip sandwich, which is the West Coast version of the sandwich served at **Al's** in Chicago. Their sandwich is great and is served with a fiery horseradish mustard, which is the perfect compliment. The great thing about Phillippe's is that it reminds you of the charm

that California in general and Los Angeles in particular once had as a real haven for interesting, off beat people who wanted to get away from their lives back East.

 Critics' Favorite Restaurants: ATLANTA

SOME OF ELLIOTT MACKLE'S FAVORITE RESTAURANTS IN (AND AROUND) ATLANTA

Elliott Mackle was the restaurant critic at *The Atlanta Journal-Constitution* for ten years and now reviews restaurants for *Creative Loafing.* He also appears on WCNN Radio and WXIA-TV as dining commentator.

- **Bacchanalia**
3125 Piedmont Rd., Atlanta, Georgia
(404) 365-0410

This is Atlanta's best restaurant, and the people who run Bacchanalia, Anne Quatrano and Clifford Harrison, are very good. They're a very clever young couple. They're going to open a place called the Floataway Cafe. Their standards are high; they're trying to do good American food in the right way. The first time I went in there, they had Shaker Lemon Pie on the menu, and it was wonderful. It showed amazing respect for tradition. They know how to make things taste good.

- **Nava**
Buckhead Plaza, 3060 Peachtree Rd., Atlanta, Georgia
(404) 240-1984

Nava serves the best Southwestern food in Atlanta. The chef [Kevin Rathbun] was at Baby Ruth [in Houston], and while the food is good, the spice level is lower than what he cooked in Texas.

*"There are some really good chefs in the South—like **Elizabeth Terry** [Elizabeth on 37th, Savannah, Georgia], **Gunter Seeger** [Seeger's, Atlanta], and **Frank Stitt** [Highlands Bar & Grill, Birmingham, Alabama]. But, for the most part, restaurants in the South are running behind those in other parts of the country due to local Prohibition, which allowed only country clubs to serve liquor until the 1970s."*

- **Elizabeth on 37th**
105 E. 37th St., Savannah, Georgia
(912) 236-5547

- **Highlands Bar & Grill**
2011 11th Ave. So., Birmingham, Alabama
(205) 939-1400

- **Seeger's**
1111 W. Paces Ferry Rd., Atlanta, Georgia
(404) 846-9779

(http://www.creativeloafing,com/newsstand/current/eats.htm)

 ## Critics' Favorite Restaurants: BALTIMORE

SOME OF CYNTHIA GLOVER'S FAVORITE RESTAURANTS IN BALTIMORE

Cynthia Glover is the restaurant critic for *Baltimore* magazine.

"I think something that's really important to Baltimorians is value. It's traditionally meant huge portions here, but I think that's beginning to change. In the past two years, a lot more well-thought-out restaurants, and not necessarily all high-end, have opened up here, and I think Baltimorians are slowly becoming more educated on what they can and should expect for their restaurant dollar. As more sophisticated places start opening up, people's vision of what they want to pay at the dinner table is opening up. And that's really positive. The more people are exposed, the more they'll want it, and the stronger the dining scene will become."

- **Charleston**
1000 Lancaster St.
(410) 332-7373
Chef Cindy Wolf and her husband, Tony Foreman, arrived a couple of years ago and really tapped into Baltimore's Southern leanings, which is not something that anyone else was doing here, with very sophisticated low-country Carolina cooking. The thing I love about this place is that all the elements come together: the interesting menu, the great wine list, and the quality of the ingredients used are appropriate to that. It's a first-class environment, appropriate to their theme. The service level is right on the money for the price point. The whole package is right. It makes it very enjoyable.

- **Joy America Cafe**
[American Visionary Art Museum]
800 Key Hwy.
(410) 244-6500

I really like this restaurant, which is similar to Charleston, but it is much more inventive. It's one of the few places around that really carries off fusion cooking. They use Asian and Native American ingredients and make wild and interesting concoctions that really work at the table about 90 percent of the time. Chef Peter Zimmer is a rare talent, serving very unusual food for Baltimore. He served a tortilla and lime-crusted chicken with chile-chocolate sauce and a poblano potato tamale, which sounded like so many different things. But it was beautiful and well-balanced, and disappeared at our table really quickly!

● **The Polo Grill**
Inn at the Colonnade
4 W. University Pkwy.
(410) 235-8200
I have a lot of admiration for restaurateur Lenny Kaplan, who opened The Polo Grill a couple of years ago. It is a classic New American restaurant in a 'hunt clubby' environment. It serves really consistent New American staples, but always done very nicely, with the right combination of service and ambiance and everything else that supports a good chef. He just opened a new restaurant called **Lenny's Chop House** [711 Eastern Ave., Harbor Inn at Pier V; [410-843-5555], now that Baltimore is cresting that steakhouse craze like wildfire, which is a really a beautifully put-together place.

● **Corks**
1026 S. Charles St.
(410) 752-3810
Corks opened last year and has an interesting, superb, extensive wine list. You could probably spend an evening just reading the wine list: it's got a little dictionary in it of wine terms, and it mentions various vintners. It's a true education and lots of fun. The restaurant sells every bottle at $11 over cost—no matter what it is! So there are some terrific bargains to be had. The staff is very knowledgeable and has tasted much of what's on the list, which I really appreciate. They also have a really good chef who cooks simple, New American food. The food is good but without calling attention to itself so much that you can't concentrate on the wine, and it's very nicely balanced. I think they're doing something special here.

● **Pisces**
Hyatt Regency Hotel
300 Light St.
(410) 605-2835
This place surprised me. The Hyatt redecorated one of its dining rooms that has a spectacular view, which is normally deadly to anything that happens at the table! But it's very sophisticated, with lots of great little touches, and they're serving terrific seafood. There aren't that many seafood restaurants in Baltimore, but two hotels are turning themselves around to fill that breach—the other one is **Windows** at Renaissance Harborplace Hotel [202 E. Pratt St., [410-685-

8439]—and they're doing a lovely job. It's a simple menu of things like Chilean sea bass with a *beurre blanc* and braised bok choy, but very carefully prepared and beautifully cooked. I think it's a restaurant that a lot of tourists are getting to know but Baltimorians haven't picked up on yet because they wouldn't be caught dead in a hotel dining room! But it's really worth a visit.

(http://www.baltimoremag.com/wte/eats.html)

 ## Critics' Favorite Restaurants: BOSTON

SOME OF ALISON ARNETT'S FAVORITE RESTAURANTS IN (AND AROUND) BOSTON

Alison Arnett is the restaurant critic for *The Boston Globe*.

"All of these restaurants are very intent on cooking and intent on presenting cuisine that they believe in. They're serious, not in a stodgy way, but about what they're cooking."

● L'Espalier
30 Gloucester, Boston
(617) 262-3023
Not just because Frank McClellan's brilliant, but because he works to make his restaurant better all the time. It's a special-occasion restaurant, and it could become an institution and not change a lot—but I don't find that he does that. He's even started making all their breads in house. He's very earnest and less "celebrity-seeking" than some chefs are.

● Hamersley's Bistro
553 Tremont St., Boston
(617) 423-2700
I like Gordon Hamersley's place a lot. It's very consistent and has even gotten better. I could eat his food every night.

● Al Forno
577 S. Main St., Providence, Rhode Island
(401) 272-7980
You can tell that George Germon and Johanne Killeen like to eat and feed people! And in some ways, they are a little bit of a throwback. Their food is quite rich, and they use a lot of things that other chefs are getting away from. Their food is very flavorful.

● Clio
370 Commonwealth Ave., Boston
(617) 536-7200
I think that [Kenneth Oringer] at Clio is brilliant and clearly one of Boston's rising stars. Unfortunately, he doesn't always control his spices.

● **Biba**
272 Boylston St., Boston
(617) 426-5684
I like Biba a lot. It takes a lot of chances—and the chances are not always on the plating. Lydia Shire and Susan Regis's menu is always exciting.

(http://www.boston.com/globe/calendar/dining/)

SOME OF CORBY KUMMER'S FAVORITE RESTAURANTS IN (AND AROUND) BOSTON

Corby Kummer is the restaurant critic for *Boston* and *Departures* magazines, and senior editor of *The Atlantic Monthly*. He is also the author of *The Joy of Coffee*. Kummer holds a degree in English from Yale University.

● **East Coast Grill**
1271 Cambridge St., Cambridge, Massachusetts
(617) 491-6568
This restaurant is fun for everybody, and appeals to visitors as well as locals. Of the things I always look for in restaurants, consistency is pretty high on my list. And I know that when I go there, I will have friendly service, which is enormously important. It's democratic and unpretentious in a way that I enjoy and rely on. They've got a good and ambitious new oyster bar, great barbecue, and I like their grilled foods and their relishes and chutneys. But most of all, I go because I really like the place, the way I'm treated when I'm there, and the feeling of the other patrons enjoying themselves.

● **Legal Sea Foods**
(eight locations in the Boston area, including Park Plaza Hotel)
35 Columbus Ave., Boston
(617) 426-4444
This is another place all out-of-towners want to go to, and should go to, when they want really fresh fish. Executive chef Jasper White is doing a fine job, and the service is generally reliable, although it's not personal. The grilled bluefish, which is an extremely rich, oily fish, is probably my favorite thing there, along with lots and lots of oysters and cherrystones. They also have *very* good desserts, as of last year when they hired pastry chef Rick Katz. He serves Boston cream pie, which should be good and really is *quite* good there.

● **Aujourd'hui**
The Four Seasons Hotel
200 Boylston St., Boston
(617) 338-4400
At about $80 to $100 per person, this might be the most expensive restaurant

in Boston. They have a nice wine list and nice food, but it is so relaxing that it's the equivalent of a spa! The good thing about The Four Seasons is that they really pamper you with complete luxury without being pretentious about it or calling attention to the fact that they're doing it. It's my idea of a special-occasion restaurant. It's all the things you want a really elegant place to be without the pomp and the starch.

● **Hamersley's Bistro**
553 Tremont St., Boston
(617) 423-2700
I consider this in a class above all the other restaurants for its food quality. Generally, I know that I'm going to like almost anything that he serves. I really value his approach to food. My ideal is the nexus of [that of San Francisco area chefs] Alice Waters, Paul Bertolli, and Judy Rodgers. I'm always looking for local outposts of people who know Mediterranean cuisine very well, aren't completely slavish to it, but have an approach to preserving the freshness and integrity of whatever they're making and not fussing it up too much or putting too much on a plate. Whenever the most demanding food people I know come to town, I send them there.

● **Il Capriccio**
888 Main St., Waltham, Massachusetts
(781) 894-2234
For Jeanne Rogers' wines. She knows as much about Italian wine as anyone I know in this country. She's always featuring fascinating wines by the glass that I don't know, and speaks about them beautifully. It's all very small producers she herself has visited and discovered. They're wines you won't find anywhere else. I loved a wine she had from Gravner, a cult winemaker that restaurateurs wait on lists for to get his wines. I'll go there to *learn*; I think she's a national treasure. I'll go there and order lamb or the simplest meats; I'm so concerned about the wine that all I want is simply prepared food that will best complement it.

A superbly gifted chef who's going to go places is Nick Tischler at **Zinc** [35 Stanhope St.; 617-262-2323]. He's not even thirty, and he's just sensational. He was previously both [New York chefs] Charlie Palmer and David Bouley's *poissonier*. But his restaurant is hip and noisy [and didn't make my list].

A place I where I send people but don't actually go myself is **Durgin Park** [at Faneuil Hall Marketplace, in the North Market Building; 617-227-2038], which is a real Boston experience. It's huge portions, perfectly decent food, unpretentious, for not much money, and I like the cornbread, the roast beef, and the Indian pudding.

(http://www.bostonmagazine.com/restaurants)

Critics' Favorite Restaurants: CHICAGO

Among *Chicago* magazine, *The Chicago Tribune*, and the Chicago *Zagat Survey*—arguably the three most powerful forces on the Chicago restaurant scene—two restaurants clearly top the list: **Everest** and **Le Français**. While **Charlie Trotter's** is the only other restaurant to receive four stars from both *Chicago* magazine and the *Tribune*, the Chicago *Zagat Survey* ranks it a few notches down, as ninth in the city.

"In Chicago, both the *Tribune* and *Chicago* magazine use a four-star system," says Dennis Ray Wheaton. "But we tend to rate about one star lower on most restaurants than Phil Vettel [of the *Tribune*] does. Most of his two-star restaurants are one-star restaurants in *Chicago* magazine's dining guide.

"This whole star system, which I really don't like, comes from the movie industry," says Wheaton. "In the movie business, whether you're looking at Siskel & Ebert's ratings or others, a two-star movie is not very good. Three stars is worth going to see, and four stars means you've got to see it. But the way we use stars is more like Michelin does. A one-star restaurant is really worth going to; it's a good restaurant, and I'd be happy to eat at it any

WHAT IS CHICAGO'S BEST RESTAURANT?

	Chicago magazine	*The Chicago Tribune*	'98 *Zagat Survey* Rank (Food)
Ambria	★★★	★★★★	#6 (28)
Arun's	★★★½	★★★	#5 (28)
Carlos'	★★★½	★★★★	#4 (28)
Charlie Trotter's	★★★★	★★★★	#9 (27)
Dining Room at the Ritz	★★½	★★★	#7 (28)
Everest	★★★★	★★★★	#3 (28)
Frontera Grill	★★★	★★★	#13 (26)
Le Français	★★★★	★★★★	#1 (29)
Le Titi de Paris	★★★	★★★	#10 (27)
Les Nomades	★★★	N.A.	#14 (26)
Mantuano	★★★	N.A.	N.A.
Seasons	★★★½	★★★	#11 (26)
Spiaggia	★★★½	★★★	#18 (25)
Tallgrass	★★★	★★★	#8 (27)
Topolobampo	★★★½	★★★	#15 (26)
Trio	★★★½	★★★★	#2 (28)

time. There are thousands of restaurants, and we rate only a few hundred, so we do make a distinction. Currently we have only three four-star restaurants in the city, and not that many more three stars. We have a lot of good two stars, and a lot are moving up, which I'm really glad to see. As they move up, the whole level of quality gets better in the city.

"I think our regular readers know that, but I think some people tend to believe that unless a star rating is really high there's something terribly wrong. It may just not be that ambitious of a restaurant—but it's a really good restaurant."

	Chicago magazine	*The Chicago Tribune*
Brasserie Jo	1 1/2	3
Brasserie T	1	2
Hubbard Street Grill	1	3
Mango	1 1/2	3
Papagus	1 1/2	3
Park Avenue Cafe	2	3
Primavera	1	3
Yoshi's Cafe	1 1/2	3

"An almost-perfect dining experience is our four-star level. It's meant to be an elite experience, with creativity and very cutting-edge work, and special-occasion amenities. The readership of *Chicago* magazine tends to be quite affluent [and would expect that of a four-star experience]."

"I think it's only slightly the amenities that keep certain restaurants [such as **Topolobampo** and **Arun's**] from four stars. The kind of people who are comfortable at **Le Français** and those kinds of restaurants say, 'They're cramped' and 'People wear shorts.' As Carla Kelson [*Chicago* magazine's co-founder] used to say, 'At a four-star restaurant, it all comes together—everything about the experience.'"

SOME OF DENNIS RAY WHEATON'S FAVORITE RESTAURANTS IN CHICAGO

Dennis Ray Wheaton is the chief dining critic for *Chicago* magazine.

● **Frontera Grill** and **Topolobampo**
445 N. Clark St.
(312) 661-1434
(3 and 3 1/2 stars, respectively, from *Chicago* magazine)
Mexican food is the ethnic food that I know best,

and I'm amazed, for his being non-Mexican, with what Rick Bayless has learned and how he approaches it. He's got an anthropologist's take on things; no doubt his background and training in college have really helped him a lot. He knows how to analyze. He knows how to find his sources. He's one of the great jewels of this town. I've tried, and I've not found a better Mexican restaurant in the United States than his.

I could eat at this place every night, on either side (Frontera Grill or Topolobampo). In some ways, I even like Frontera Grill better sometimes because it's a little simpler and not quite as fussy. . . . I hope now that he's opening an expanded space, it might push it up to four stars. Too often, it's so crowded that waiters are bumping into tables, and there are people standing around with their margaritas getting warm. . . . The food is four-star.

- **Zinfandel**
59 W. Grand
(312) 527-1818
(2 stars from *Chicago* magazine)
Another Rick Bayless place. Chef Susan Goss does really good turns on American cooking.

- **Phoenix**
2131 S. Archer
(312) 328-0848
(1 1/2 stars from *Chicago* magazine)
I wish I could eat dim sum at Phoenix every Sunday!

- **Arun's**
4156 N. Kedzie Ave.
(773) 539-1909
(3 1/2 stars from *Chicago* magazine)
It's too expensive for me, but I wish I could eat at Arun's all the time. . . . He was a Ph.D. graduate student in political science at the University of Chicago before opening his restaurant. Arun's is almost there [at a four-star level]—I looked all over California, and I've not found a better Thai restaurant.

- **Kiki's Bistro**
900 N. Franklin
(312) 335-5454
(2 stars from *Chicago* magazine)
It's a really nice bistro in town for French food.

Of his choices, Wheaton says, "I'm thinking less of the setting and more of the food and less expensive wines that you can enjoy the food with—and still very good service."

Other restaurants he mentioned included **Emilio's Tapas Bar**, **Gabriel's**, and **Emperor's Choice** ("one of the best Chinese seafood restaurants"). We later received an e-mail from him: "In mentioning my favorite restaurants, I believe I forgot to mention one of my *very* favorites: **Mantuano Mediterranean Table** [455 Cityfront Plaza; 312-832-2600], which is the new incarnation of Tony Mantuano's great Tuttaposto. Like Frontera Grill, it is one of my most casual three-star listings. He does fantastic dishes covering the ground from Gibraltar to Gallipoli.

"I wrote an article last year on Beverly Hills. Los Angeles is the other place I know best. My wife and I spent an evening at **Ginza Sushi-Ko** [218 N. Rodeo Dr. Beverly Hills, 310-247-8939] and it was incredible. It was one of those once-in-a-lifetime experiences—at $700 for two. Fugi was in season, and he did fugi several different ways. If the blowfish hadn't been so good, it could have been to die for!"

(http://www.chicagomag.com/text/dining/cover.htm)

SOME OF WILLIAM RICE'S FAVORITE RESTAURANTS IN CHICAGO

William Rice writes about food and wine and reviews restaurants for *The Chicago Tribune*.

● **Charlie Trotter's**
816 W. Armitage Ave.
(773) 248-6228
(4 stars from *The Chicago Tribune*)
Charlie's a phenomenon. In a way, he represents a certain aspect of America and business success: extraordinary intensity, extraordinary energy channeled to certain goals, great self-confidence—arrogant, some people would say. At the same time, you take all the technical things and add money to it, and a lot of people still fail. What Charlie seems to have beyond that, which you can't buy or learn, is an intangible sense of taste and how to put food together, and a willingness to hire people who know more than he does in certain areas. Essentially, he had a vision of what a world-class restaurant should be, and admittedly with some family money and some other things, he's done it. But any number of people couldn't have done it, even with all the support in the world.

● **Le Bouchon**
1958 N. Damen Ave.
(773) 862-6600
(2 stars from *The Chicago Tribune*)
This is a particular predilection of mine from when I went to France. This is a prototypical Lyon bistro that's been lifted up and set down on a street corner in Chicago. It's a storefront with pressed-tin ceilings, poster art on the

walls, serving a fairly short menu—but it's all done by a chef from Lyon, the way he learned in Lyon. The noise level is high, but it works. If you have any nostalgia at all for the bistros of France, this place is a time warp.

- **Arun's**
4156 N. Kedzie Ave.
(773) 539-1909
(3 stars from *The Chicago Tribune*)
or
- **Frontera Grill**
445 N. Clark
(312) 661-1434
(3 stars from *The Chicago Tribune*)

They both represent an ethnic cuisine taken to extraordinary heights, in the sense of quality, attention to detail, and commitment of the owners and the staff. They're just absolutely terrific restaurants, both from an insider's point of view in the way they're run and managed, and to the customer's benefit, too.

- **Gibsons**
1028 N. Rush St.
(312) 266-8999
(2 stars from *The Chicago Tribune*)

Gibsons is a prototypically Chicago steakhouse. It's raffish, its bar is packed with people from all walks of life, its dining room is well run, its prices are quite fair, and its service is professional. Whether it's the best steak in town, I don't know. Gibsons is a place I love to take people from out of town to give them the stereotypical sense of "big-shouldered Chicago."

- **The Pump Room**
Omni Ambassador East Hotel
1301 N. State Pkwy.
(312) 266-0360
(2 stars from *The Chicago Tribune*)

The Pump Room is a relic,

an icon, that still is serving quite palatable food. It's an escape to an earlier time. I sit in there and feel like my feet aren't touching the floor in that setting. It's nostalgia, it's comfort, it's food that's quite straightforward. You can go there and have a Cobb salad, or a piece of standing rib with horseradish sauce, in this make-believe setting. It's a vicarious treat. It would not be in my top 10, maybe not even in my top 20, simply for a food experience.

(http://www.metromix.com/restaurants.html)

SOME OF DOTTY GRIFFITH'S FAVORITE RESTAURANTS IN (AND AROUND) DALLAS

Dotty Griffith reviews restaurants for *The Dallas Morning News,* and was the food editor at the paper for seventeen years.

In general:
● **Star Canyon**
[The Centrum]
3102 Oak Lawn Ave., Dallas
(214) 520-7827
This restaurant is so totally Texas, and chef Stephan Pyles does an incredible job with the food, incorporating Tex-Mex, Southern, and sometimes even Cajun touches. The Cowboy Rib Eye is probably the most ordered dish on the menu, but I love the catfish in blue cornmeal served with a black-eyed pea relish. (While his seafood restaurant **AquaKnox** [3214 Knox Ave., Dallas, 214-219-2782] is also very good, Star Canyon is Texas!)
(4 stars)

For Tex-Mex:
● **Matt's Rancho Martinez**
6332 LaVista, Dallas
(214) 823-5517
This is Tex-Mex food done as well as you'll find it anywhere—loaded with chili, cheese, guacamole, and salsa. You can tell it's good because after eating the chips and salsa, by the time your entree arrives you're not hungry anymore! But don't miss the incredible *chile rellenos.*
(3 stars)

For Texas barbecue:
● **The original Sonny Bryan's**
2202 Inwood Rd., Dallas
(214) 357-7120

It's an authentic barbecue pit: a drive-in where you can get ribs and brisket and potato salad and beans, and they'll ask if you want sauce on top. (3 stars)

- **Warren Clark's Outpost BBQ**

Highway 377, Tioga, Texas

(817) 437-2414

It's great Texas barbecue, plus you can get more unusual items like smoked catfish.

For Texas soul food:

- **Mama's Daughter's Diner**

2014 Irving

(214) 742-8646 (three stars) or

211 Record

(214) 741-6262

This is Texas home cooking at its best! You'll find everything from chicken-fried steak, to homemade rolls, to overcooked vegetables, just the way you'd expect them at a place like this! Desserts include fluffy meringue pies and wonderful cobblers.

(2 stars)

For quintessential Dallas:

- **The Zodiac Room**

Neiman Marcus

1618 Main, Dallas

(214) 573-5800

This restaurant originally debuted in Neiman Marcus's flagship store in the 1960s and was popularized by Helen Corbett as a tea room known for its orange soufflés and popovers. Chef Sharon Hage and executive director Kevin Garvin have made this a place where the food is good, too. Neiman Marcus, tired of continually denying the urban legend of its $250 cookie recipe, finally decided to have some fun and just put a chocolate chip cookie on the menu, which comes with the recipe—for free!

(3 stars)

Honorable Mention: For a chi-chi Dallas Place, **Seventeen Seventeen**, a restaurant in the Dallas Museum of Art [1717 N. Harwood; 214-880-0158], where credit goes to both chef George Brown, who was named one of *Food & Wine*'s Top 10 New Chefs of 1997, and executive chef Kent Rathbun. The food can be quite excellent, and it's an upscale, fashionable way to dine.

(3 ^{1}/$_2$ stars)

(http://www.dallasnews.com/index/dining-reviews-nf.htm)

SOME OF BILL ST. JOHN'S FAVORITE RESTAURANTS IN DENVER

Bill St. John is the restaurant producer for *Denver Sidewalk,* and also edits the Rocky Mountain *Zagat Survey.* He was formerly the restaurant critic and wine writer for the *Rocky Mountain News.* St. John holds master's degrees in economics and philosophy and a Ph.D. in theology from the University of Chicago.

*"These restaurants aren't necessarily what are commonly known as 'the best of Denver.' For example, I've not included **Papillon** on my list, which is a really nice restaurant—many might argue the best in Denver—but I wouldn't spend my own money there. These are all restaurants where I'd be happy to spend my own money."*

- **Potager**
1109 Ogden St.
(303) 832-5788
This is a laid-back restaurant that serves very good quality ingredients. Teri Rippeto, the woman who started the restaurant, bought an old laundry and ripped the walls down. It's Pan-Mediterranean food, simply prepared. One standout dish is a twice-baked Camembert soufflé. They also have a very good wine list.
(3 ½ stars)

- **Aubergine**
225 E. Seventh Ave.
(303) 832-4778
This restaurant, run by Sean Kelly, is committed to simple and pure ingredients. He doesn't just serve chicken; he serves the best f***ing chicken he can get his hands on! There's not a lot of emphasis on decor or linens, seemingly to be able to spend more on ingredients. He buys the best and prepares it simply.
(4 stars)

- **Highlands Garden Cafe**
3927 W. 32nd Ave.
(303) 458-5920
Chef Patricia Perry writes a new menu every single day, for both lunch and dinner. The restaurant is in an old Victorian house which features the artwork of friends, including a *trompe l'oeil* of a window looking out into a garden. The cooking is Pan-Mediterranean, simply prepared, but with more of a lavish emphasis on herbs and vegetables than the first two restaurants. Her menu

reads like she got so excited shopping at the market that she just couldn't stop, featuring two or three different types of fish, beef and veal, and two or three different vegetables on the same plate.
(4 stars)

- **Fourth Story**
(atop Tattered Cover Book Store)
2955 E. First Ave.
(303) 322-1824
I love the decor and ambiance of this restaurant, and I feel very comfortable here. It's on the fourth floor of The Tattered Cover, and the restaurant walls are covered with books, and there's a view of the mountains. Chef David Steinmann is an excellent chef and keen on getting the very best ingredients. He does great things with cheaper cuts of meat and makes a great osso buco.
(4 stars)

- **Domo**
1365 Osage St.
(303) 595-3666
This is my new favorite restaurant, whose name means "thanks" in Japanese. The cooking is unique country Japanese [no sushi or sashimi], and the food is delicious. Asians are into textures as much as flavors, and the cuisine here reflects it. Chef-owner Gaku Homma built a huge aikido center and meditation garden next door, and the dining room is like eating in the middle of the forest on the set of *The Wizard of Oz*.
(4 stars)

SOME OF PATTY LaNOUE STEARNS'S FAVORITE RESTAURANTS IN (AND AROUND) DETROIT

Patty LaNoue Stearns was the restaurant critic of *The Detroit Free Press*, and currently writes features for the paper.

- **Giovanni's Ristorante**
330 S. Oakwood Blvd., Detroit
(313) 841-0122
In southwest Detroit, which is not a neighborhood where a lot of people from out of town would go, there's a restaurant that has the most wonderful Italian food. Frank Sinatra would seek it out when he would come to Detroit. It's got a reputation as a family Italian restaurant that serves really authentic food, and the staff fusses over you like you're family. It's so homey and folksy.
(4 stars)

- **Northern Lakes Seafood**
1475 N. Woodward, Bloomfield Hills, Michigan
(248) 646-7900
I love this new seafood place, which is the 13th restaurant opened by Matt Prentice. It's a wonderful place to get very fresh seafood. They have a wonderful dish of steamed dumplings and really fresh shrimp and scallops with ginger. (4 stars)

- **Tribute**
31425 W. 12 Mile Rd.
Farmington Hills, Michigan
(810) 848-9393
JFK Jr. and a host of celebs dine in this glamorous, sophisticated, elegant spot that serves fine wines, foie gras, caviar, seafood specialties, wild game and Angus beef, all artfully prepared and arranged by chef Takashi Yagahashi. It's very expensive, and reservations are a must. I love it—not that I can afford to go more than once a year!
(4 stars)

- **Ja-Da**
546 E. Larned, Detroit
(313) 965-1700
It's a soul food restaurant, that has cool jazz. In fact, one of our judges, Myron Wahls, plays jazz there, in a combo on Tuesday nights. This place can be really loud, but it's a place to really feel Detroit. They have incredible ribs, the best macaroni and cheese I've eaten in my life, and whipped sweet potatoes that are just like pillows! It's comfort food, and a cool atmosphere.
(3 stars)

- **Intermezzo**
1435 Randolph, Harmonie Park, Michigan
(313) 961-0707
I love Intermezzo. It's a downtown restaurant with a view of Harmonie Park, which is probably our best urban setting in downtown Detroit. It has a really nice bar, kind of Hopper-esque, and it's packed on weekends. If we have any celebrities in town, they usually drop in there.
(3 stars)

Stearns also mentions **Harlequin Cafe** [8047 Agnes, Detroit, 313-331-0922; 3 stars]: "The chef-owner Sherman Sharpe has located his restaurant in an old mansion and makes a big deal out of every customer who comes in. He serves food that you could find in Paris and announces the menu. The service can be slow, which is why I've given it three stars, but the food and Sherman are just four-star all the way."

She also cites **Kabob Village** [13823 Michigan at Maple, next to Dearborn City Hall, Dearborn, Michigan; 313-581-0055; 4 stars]: "It has spectacular Lebanese and Mediterranean cuisine: hummus, baba ghanoush, grape leaves, falafel, kibbeh, meat gallaba, mafrouki, and arayees—and a wonderful raw juice bar.

"I gave **La Contessa Ristorante** [780 Erie St. E., Windsor, Canada, which is right across the river from Detroit, 519-252-2167] four stars. It features the cooking of Madeline Zavaglia, who lived and trained in Rome for ten years. I got a few comments from people that the service was so slow. But you can't go in there expecting fast food when the food has been prepared by hand, by a few people."

(http://www.freep.com/fun/food/reviews/index.htm)

 ## Critics' Favorite Restaurants: HARTFORD

SOME OF BILL DALEY'S FAVORITE RESTAURANTS IN (AND AROUND) THE GREATER HARTFORD AREA

 **Bill Daley** is a staff reporter and restaurant reviewer for *The Hartford Courant* and *Northeast* magazine. A graduate of Manhattanville College, he holds a master's degree in journalism from Columbia University.

● **Johnny Ad's Drive-in**
Route 1, Old Saybrook, CT
(860) 388-4032
This has been around for decades, started by John Adinolfo, and is a typical old-fashioned shoreline restaurant in Connecticut. I really love their hot lobster rolls, which is a Connecticut specialty of little chunks of lobster meat, drizzled with butter and served in toasted hot dog rolls. They've also got great batter-dipped onion rings. They know what they're doing, and they do it well.

● **The Frog & The Peach**
160 Albany Turnpike (Route 44)
Canton, CT
(860) 693-6352
This restaurant is in an Old Victorian house. They really pay attention to details, and service is friendly but professional. They don't have a liquor license, but you can bring your own wine. The classic New American food is a lot of fun with a energy and originality, and you're always waiting to see what's going to come out of the kitchen next. I had a wonderful salad with dried Michigan cherries with toasted pinenuts and goat cheese, homemade butternut squash ravioli, and a perfectly grilled chicken breast on Beluga lentils. You have a sense that there's an artistic vision in the kitchen being applied to the ingredients.
(4 stars)

● **Le Petit Cafe**
225 Montowe St.
Branford, CT
(203) 483-9791
A couple from Lyon founded this small, charming bistro on the town's village green and recently sold it to Chinese native Raymond Ip, who has French culinary training. He's kept their distinctive signature, but he's started to add more of his own touches. They do two seatings, at 6 P.M. and 8:30 P.M., and begin the meal by bringing out a selection of five appetizers for tasting and sharing at the table. I'm very fond of this restaurant, and imagine that it's the kind of place that M.F.K. Fisher, if she were alive and living in Connecticut, would love! At $21.95 for a four-course meal, it's a steal.
(3 stars)

● **West Street Grill**
43 West St.
Litchfield, CT
(860) 567-7885
In what may be the last New England village, James O'Shea owns this restaurant that exemplifies Litchfield's country elegance, complete with local celebrities at neighboring tables. I love the crème brulée and will never forget the wine the steward matched perfectly with some cilantro dumplings I was served.

● **Bloodroot**
85 Ferris St.
Bridgeport, CT
(203) 576-9168
This seasonal vegetarian restaurant was founded by a feminist collective twenty years ago in a nice neighborhood about a block from the beach. It's very welcoming, relaxed, and cozy, and eating the food, which borrows from European and Asian cooking, makes me feel warm inside. They stick to their principles, and other restaurants would do well to follow their lead.
(3 stars)

(http://interact.courant.com/taste/queries/index.idc)

Critics' Favorite Restaurants: HOUSTON

SOME OF ALISON COOK'S FAVORITE RESTAURANTS IN HOUSTON

Alison Cook is the restaurant critic for *Houston Sidewalk*.

● **Cafe Annie**
1728 Post Oak Blvd.
(713) 840-1111
I think Cafe Annie can hold its own with any great restaurant in the country. Chef Robert del Grande offers an outstanding and unusual Southwestern menu and an award-winning wine list. At times, I think his food can be as brilliant as the best at Chez Panisse.
(4 stars)

● **Irma's**
22 N. Chenevert St.
(713) 222-0767
Everything about this Mexican lunch place is personal and charming. You'll find little ladies cooking over big pots, making things like ribs in green sauce and enchiladas by hand. Plus, the room is wonderful, decorated with little tchotchkes, and it's a vibrant scene.
(2 stars)

● **Goode Company Seafood**
2621 Westpark Dr.
(713) 523-7154
Jim Goode is a great pop synthesizer of various cultural strains in this town. I love the mesquite-grilled catfish and his perfect twice-fried French fries (as are all great fries, as I learned in France).
(3 stars)

● **Pico's Mex-Mex**
5941 Bellaire Blvd.
(713) 662-8383
This Mexican restaurant was started by a guy from Monterey who went to the Conrad Hilton Hotel School. It's got great *mole* enchiladas and the best margaritas in town!
(3 stars)

● **Americas**
1800 Post Oak Blvd.
(713) 961-1492
The Cordua brothers are from Nicaragua, and Michael Cordua is the chef who has put together a creative, Central American-inspired menu. The restaurant has an incredible interior that is one of the most exotic I've ever seen. John Mariani named it his restaurant of the year. (3 stars)

● **Churrascos**
9705 Westheimer Rd. (at Gessner)
(713) 952-1988
or
2055 Westheimer Rd. (at Shepherd)
(713) 527-8300

Michael Cordua's South American steakhouses. You won't want to miss the plantain chips or the namesake churrascos tenderloin basted with garlicky chimichurri sauce.
(3 stars)

(http://houston.sidewalk.com/restaurants)

 ## Critics' Favorite Restaurants: LAS VEGAS

SOME OF MURIEL STEVENS'S FAVORITE RESTAURANTS IN LAS VEGAS

Muriel Stevens has been the restaurant critic for *The Las Vegas Sun* since 1975. She also edits the Las Vegas *Zagat Survey* and the restaurant section of *The Unofficial Guide to Las Vegas*. She has also hosted "The Muriel Stevens Radio Show" since 1968.

"No local in their right mind would ever want to go to any of the fine restaurants during a major convention because even if the food doesn't suffer—and it doesn't—the service sometimes does. I'm impressed that despite the fact that the huge hotels have captive audiences, the restaurants change their menus regularly and add new seasonal offerings, and that's one of the things I enjoy the most."

● **Coyote Cafe**
MGM Grand Hotel
3799 Las Vegas Blvd.
(702) 891-7349
I adore Coyote Cafe. It is like a little bit of heaven when you walk from the hotel into the Grill Room. Chef Tommy Birdwell is so good that I find myself almost seduced into coming back when I remember the last dinner I had there! One of the reasons I like going to Coyote is because they use things like *huitlacoche*, which tastes so wonderful that you don't even care what it is! I love it.

● **Emeril's New Orleans Fish House**
MGM Grand Hotel
3799 Las Vegas Blvd.
(702) 891-7374
It's a happy restaurant—it's very lively, and very New Orleans. Chef Michael Jordan offers the most imaginative tasting dinners, and I've never had the same one twice. If you're really in the mood to dine, it's wonderful.

● **Fellini's**
5555 W. Charleston
(702) 870-9999
Partners Bob Harry and Jim Girard took this defunct Italian restaurant off the strip and turned it into a wonderful place. Chef Chaz LaForte spent four years in Tuscany and offers a lovely menu. Everything is special, but he serves chicken Tuscan-style, flattening and serving it with salad, which is particularly good. All the breads and desserts are made there, and the restaurant features a European-style dessert table in the middle of the dining room.

● **Napa**
Rio Suite Hotel & Casino
3700 W. Flamingo Rd.
(702) 252-7702
This restaurant could be anywhere in the world. It is a chic, warm, and art-filled restaurant, and when Jean-Louis Palladin is there, you never know what to expect! No one makes soups like Jean-Louis. It's marvelous food and presentation.

● **Palace Court**
Caesars Palace
3570 Las Vegas Blvd. So.
(702) 731-7110
The *grande dame* of dining in Las Vegas—which it has been since it opened in 1963, and it's every bit as good today—is The Palace Court. If I didn't have to get dressed, I would go there more often! This restaurant is so beautiful and so elegant. Barbara Werley is the first female sommelier in Las Vegas, and one of only three female master sommeliers in the world. The food is classic yet contemporary, and very wonderful. It's enchanting.

● **Piero's**
355 Convention Center Dr.
(702) 369-2305
If I'm tired and want a few good laughs and to see people I haven't seen in a long time, I'll head for Piero's, which is a real hangout and has a host in the mold of Toots Shor, who owns the restaurant. If Freddie Glusman is there, you know you're going to have fun because he might even insult you—it's all in the character of the place! It's a steakhouse with Italian influences, and the food is very good. One day, when I questioned the price of my steak, he went into the kitchen and brought me the raw steak to show me how they trim it, and the bill that showed what he'd paid for it. And he was right. It wasn't exorbitant given what he'd paid.

● **Spago**
Forum at Caesars
3500 Las Vegas Blvd. So.
(702) 369-6300

Chef David Robins's menu changes every day, so it is never boring, and the restaurant is so wonderful to locals. No local is ever turned down at Spago, even during conventions, and the management always knows who the locals are.

(http://www.lasvegassun.com)

 **Critics' Favorite Restaurants: LOS ANGELES**

SOME OF CAROLINE BATES'S FAVORITE RESTAURANTS in (and around) LOS ANGELES

Caroline Bates is the California restaurant critic for *Gourmet*.

● **Bombay Cafe**
12113 Santa Monica Blvd., West Los Angeles, California
(310) 820-2070
It's an Indian restaurant in a little minimall. The owners are opening a new restaurant in the Crafts Folk Art Museum. Even San Francisco doesn't have Indian restaurants like this—very bright, intelligent spicing, and very fresh. They do kind of Bombay snack foods, little bites and things. It's a different menu. I love it.

● **Alto Palato**
755 N. La Cienega Blvd., West Hollywood, California
(310) 657-9271
There are places I like to go for special things, like the *gelati* at Alto Palato. They make the *gianduja* with hazelnuts from Piedmont; they do it with that level of detail. So I go there for ice cream, particularly when I don't want to eat dessert somewhere else.

● **Yujean Kang's**
8826 Melrose Ave., West Hollywood, California
(310) 288-0806
Every meal there is a discovery, even if something doesn't quite work out.

● **Jozu**
8360 Melrose Ave., Los Angeles, California
(213) 655-5600
I think it's almost "the restaurant of the year," in a way, certainly in Los Angeles. Suzanne Tracht is a very intelligent chef, and she knows how to cook so well. She's very subtle, and everything is in balance. And they have a wonderful wine list. In terms of Asian fusion restaurants, it's the best, I think, that's come along in a long time.

- **Pacific Dining Car**

1310 W. Sixth St., Downtown Los Angeles, California

(213) 483-6000

I'm not really a steak person, but I love to go to the Pacific Dining Car down-town. It goes back to 1921, and it really was a dining car. It started out as a steakhouse. And it's open all the time; it's a place that chefs go after work, as well as the produce people who have to be up at four in the morning. They have an incredible wine list and old-fashioned food—a great Caesar salad and potatoes O'Brien and stuff like that. And they're lovely people, and kind of gruff. We don't have that out here as much as you do in the East! I like that place for the personality of it.

SOME OF KAREN BERK'S FAVORITE RESTAURANTS IN (AND AROUND) LOS ANGELES

Karen Berk is the co-editor of the Los Angeles *Zagat Survey*.

"I don't always agree with my husband Michael, who serves on the Board of Directors of the American Institute of Wine and Food. His own favorites are **Patina**, **Spago** *Beverly Hills,* **Jozu**, **Valentino**—*when Piero [Selvaggio] is there, and* **Citrus**—*when Michel [Richard] is there. All of my favorites are on his longer list, however."*

- **Campanile**

624 S. La Brea Ave., Los Angeles

(213) 938-1447

(1998 *Zagat* food rating: 26)

One of my very favorite restaurants is Campanile. It's a style of cooking I love. First of all, I'm a dessert freak, and Nancy Silverton's are amazing. Most restaurants don't take the same kind of pride in their ingredients.

- **Jozu**

8360 Melrose Ave., Los Angeles

(213) 655-5600

(1998 *Zagat* food rating: 26)

It's a really good team of people. Both the chef [Suzanne Tracht] and pastry chef [Nanette Codic] used to be at Campanile, and the owner [Andy Nakano] is Japanese.

- **Pinot Bistro**

12969 Ventura Blvd., Studio City, California

(818) 990-0500

(1998 *Zagat* food rating: 25)

It's one of my personal favorites because, whether it's true or not, I sense there's less butter used! Chef Octavio Becerra is so creative. I really love his food.

- **Alto Palato**

755 N. La Cienega Blvd., West Hollywood, California

(310) 657-9271

(1997 *Zagat* food rating: 20)

The best Italian food I've had is at a place that's not perceived as being fabulous and that's at Alto Palato. I've had some dishes there that I've really loved, like their Italian tomato-bread soup. I've also had some spectacular meals at **Valentino** [which has the same owner], but I object to the fact that you have to pay double in order to have that food.

- **Spago**

176 N. Canon Dr., Beverly Hills, California

(310) 385-0880

(1998 *Zagat* food rating: 26)

The food has always been very good, the people watching can't be beat, and it's always been a top choice for taking out-of-towners. However, in its new Beverly Hills location and with its current chef [Lee Hefter] and pastry chef [Sherry Yard], it has achieved new heights and shown how a restaurant can successfully reinvent itself. [Austrian and strong Asian elements have successfully been added to its Californian menu.] I think the restaurant's design is Barbara Lazaroff's finest work to date.

SOME OF JONATHAN GOLD'S FAVORITE RESTAURANTS IN (AND AROUND) LOS ANGELES

Jonathan Gold, who has reviewed restaurants for *The Los Angeles Times*, currently writes for *L.A. Weekly* and *Los Angeles*.

- **Campanile**

624 S. LaBrea Ave., Los Angeles, California

(213) 938-1447

My favorite restaurants are those places where the chefs are completely, utterly, totally obsessed past the point of madness. Campanile is certainly one of those. Nancy [Silverton] has a certain devotion to products that's beyond belief, and she has an amazing food sense. Mark Peel is probably the best grill chef on the planet. I've never gone there and had anything that wasn't good to eat. I've had "failed food" there, but it's failed because they're actually trying things that are different. They're constantly evolving.

- **Ginza Sushi-Ko**

218 N. Rodeo Dr., Beverly Hills, California

(310) 247-8939

It may actually be the most expensive restaurant in the United States. The last time I went there, we had a $600 lunch for two. The chef is a sushi guy from Tokyo, but again someone who's utterly obsessed with product. He actually goes to Japan three times a month and brings back fish. It's seasonal in the way that only the Japanese can be seasonal: they have things that are in season for two days. He keeps a little notebook of what customers have, so you never have to have the same thing twice. And it's small, only about nine seats. He's probably the only chef of his caliber in the world who's ever moved to a smaller restaurant.

● **Michael's**
1147 Third St., Santa Monica, California
(310) 451-0843
I really like Michael's. It's always got really great ingredients. In shad roe season, they give you shad roe with a drink. They've also got an interesting wine list.

● **Spago**
176 N. Canon Dr., Beverly Hills, California
(310) 385-0880
I like the new Spago a whole lot, even though I can't get a table. I think the level of food is good, the idea that [Wolfgang Puck] is mixing the Austrian stuff in with American stuff is interesting. He's doing a lot of great "offal-ly" dishes, which people don't do nearly enough of.

● **Lake Spring Cuisine**
219 E. Garvey Ave., Monterey Park, California
(818) 985-9222
It's a New Wave Shanghainese restaurant. The chef is taking the basic flavor components of dishes and structures of Shanghai food, and he's modernizing it and bringing it up to date. They have one thing there called the "pork pump," which is sort of the totemic Chinese dish of Los Angeles; it's about two pounds of braised hog lard, with a fist-sized ball of meat in the middle. I've never been able to figure out exactly what it is. It's astonishing.

● **Jozu**
8360 Melrose Ave., Los Angeles, California
(213) 655-5600
Jozu is another restaurant I like. It's like the Asian version of Campanile. The wine list is amazing, and features a lot of small California producers.

SOME OF MERRILL SHINDLER'S FAVORITE RESTAURANTS IN (AND AROUND) LOS ANGELES

Merrill Shindler is the co-editor of the Los Angeles *Zagat Survey*, and a Los Angeles restaurant critic.

"All of these restaurants are informal, and each is very intriguing. They all have menus where I have no trouble looking at the menu and finding something to eat. You could just close your eyes and point, and you'd be happy."

- **Matsuhisa**
129 N. La Cienega Blvd., Beverly Hills, California
(310) 659-9639
(1998 *Zagat* food rating: 28)

- **Parkway Grill**
510 S. Arroyo Parkway, Pasadena, California
(818) 795-1001
(1998 *Zagat* food rating: 25)

- **(Nouveau) Cafe Blanc**
9777 Little Santa Monica Blvd., Beverly Hills, California
(310) 888-0108
(1998 *Zagat* food rating: 26)

- **Joe's**
1023 Abbot Kinney Blvd., Venice, California
(310) 399-5811
(1998 *Zagat* food rating: 27)

- **JiRaffe**
502 Santa Monica Blvd., Santa Monica, California
(310) 917-6671
(1998 *Zagat* food rating: 24)

I love the Chinese restaurants in the San Gabriel Valley; Monterey Park is the center of it. There are at least 300 big Hong Kong-style Chinese seafood restaurants out there, and the quality is extraordinary. **Ocean Star** [145 N. Atlantic Blvd., Monterey Park; 626-308-2128] holds about 1,000 people, and often they're having a couple of weddings going on at the same time you're having dinner.

SOME OF S. IRENE VIRBILA'S FAVORITE RESTAURANTS IN (AND AROUND) LOS ANGELES

S. Irene Virbila is the restaurant critic for *The Los Angeles Times*.

- **Alto Palato**
755 N. La Cienega Blvd., West Hollywood, California
(310) 657-9271
I like Alto Palato for truly Italian cooking. I get to eat exactly what I want to eat! They have

spaghetti with sea urchin that's really nice. I love the artichokes fried in flour, very crisp, like they do in Rome. I could eat two or three plates of artichokes!

- **Spago**

176 N. Canon Dr., Beverly Hills, California

(310) 385-0880

It's terrific. It's really a surprise. Wolfgang Puck has upped the ante and seems to be cooking the food that he wants to cook.

- **Guelaguetza**

3337 ¹/₂ W. Eighth St., West Los Angeles, California (another is in East Los Angeles)

(213) 427-0601

I like this Oaxacan restaurant a lot. They had the sommelier at Michael's do a little wine list for them. And I went for breakfast the other day, and it was great!

- **Mimosa**

8009 Beverly Blvd., Los Angeles, California

(213) 655-8895

It's a really tiny French bistro that really *feels* like a bistro, where you can get great platters of charcuterie.

- **Vincenti**, 11930 San Vincenti Blvd., Brentwood, California

(310) 207-0127

Maureen Vincenti, the wife and partner of the late Mauro Vincenti of Rex II Ristorante, has opened a smart, contemporary Italian restaurant, together with Rex's last and best chef Gino Angelini. He's a brilliant Italian cook, and everything here tastes utterly true to Italian cuisine.

(http://www.laweekly.com.)

 ## Critics' Favorite Restaurants: MIAMI

SOME OF BOB HOSMON'S FAVORITE RESTAURANTS IN (AND AROUND) MIAMI

Bob Hosmon, a wine and food writer for twenty years, is currently a senior editor at *The Wine News* and restaurant critic for *Miami Metro* magazine.

"For the last fifteen to twenty years, there's been a tremendous boom here. The restaurants here are getting not just national but international publicity. The turning point was when a group of young chefs started to use native ingredients, going under so many different names—from Floribbean, to New Florida, to New World."

Norman's
21 Almeria Ave., Coral Gables, Florida
(305) 446-6767
Norman Van Aken puts more of an emphasis on the Caribbean, including the larger scope of the Gulf of Mexico and even Mexico, by being inspired by ingredients and dishes from these places, from *jabanero* peppers to jerk pork. He's toned down and refined his cuisine, and produces even better food than he did in his earlier years. And he's got a very loyal audience that just named him the #1 restaurant in the area in a *Gourmet* reader poll.

Chef Allen's
19088 N.E. 29th Ave., Aventura, Florida
(305) 935-2900
[Chef-owner] Allen Susser seems to have more of a hands-on approach, in that I've never been to his restaurant when he's not been there! He does interesting things with yellowtail snapper, which to my mind is the best seafood from South Florida. He's also tried to do a lot with the marriage of food and wine, and his staff is very well trained and knowledgeable in that. In addition, he was one of the first to be quite the humanitarian chef, doing benefits for Meals on Wheels.

Mark's Las Olas
1032 E. Las Olas Blvd., Fort Lauderdale, Florida
(954) 463-1000
Mark Militello was one of the pioneers of the new Florida cuisine and was the first to receive national exposure. There was a time when if people asked me, "Where *must* I eat?" I would have said Mark's. Now, there are others who are doing an excellent job while Mark continues to do an excellent job.

Pacific Time
915 Lincoln Rd., Miami Beach, Florida
(305) 534-5979
Pacific Time is the best restaurant on all of South Beach. Chef Jonathan Eismann has created a menu of Pacific Rim-influenced cuisine, drawing on Florida seafood and ingredients and giving it that twist. He was the first to do anything like that in South Florida. He took a big gamble in being one of the

first high-end restaurants on that street, but the last time I was in on a Tuesday night, people were told there were no tables available until 11 P.M.!

● **Joe's Stone Crab**
227 Biscayne St., Miami Beach, Florida
(305) 673-0365

This is an institution here, and I think the food is excellent. Where else are people going to get such extraordinarily fresh seafood? They have their own shipping boats, and they'll cook it any way you want it. They're clearly the yardstick for key lime pie in the world. It's almost like dining in history, with the waitstaff still in black tie, even though the restaurant is informal like most South Florida restaurants. They don't take reservations, and people will wait two hours for a table at dinner! The solution is to go for lunch, when you won't have to wait more than five or ten minutes, and it's the same menu.

Honorable Mention: For Cuban food, I'll always take friends to a restaurant called **Versailles** [3555 S.W. 8th St., Miami, 305-445-7614] because it's an institution, and President Clinton has eaten there when he's in town. It's real typical mom-and-pop Cuban food, though it's not a little place. It's budget Cuban food, from a beefsteak balamia to a very good flan. There's another little Cuban place I love called **Rio Crystale**, but finding it can be difficult.

(http://www.sfl.com)

Critics' Favorite Restaurants:
MINNEAPOLIS/ST. PAUL

SOME OF KATHIE JENKINS'S FAVORITE RESTAURANTS IN MINNEAPOLIS/ST. PAUL

Kathie Jenkins has been the restaurant critic for the *St. Paul Pioneer Press* since 1995. Before that, she was a food writer at *The Los Angeles Times*, where she began her career many years earlier as restaurant critic Ruth Reichl's secretary.

"When I moved from Los Angeles to Minneapolis, I was worried about missing ethnic food, but that's the one thing I don't miss. The Italian food here is horrible; the pasta is consistently overcooked. The fine dining segment also leaves a lot to be desired; I'm constantly seeing dishes with at least one too many ingredients. Whereas in New York and Los Angeles you'll find many chefs who have trained abroad, here you'll find chefs who trained at [local restaurants] D'Amico or Table of Contents and have hardly been out of the state."

● **Shuang Cheng**
1320 Fourth St., S.E., Minneapolis
(612) 378-0208
The name means "Twin Cities" in Chinese. It's not just a great Chinese restaurant, but a great seafood restaurant, and everything is incredibly fresh-tasting. Specialties include quick Hong Kong-style seafood, like steamed lobster, whole fish, and *geoduck*, which is a giant clam, sliced and served with baby bok choy. Unlike a lot of Chinese restaurants, where when you ask for recommendations you'll hear "sweet and sour pork," the waiters are great and will remember what you had last time and encourage you to try something new. They're very passionate about the food.

● **Cheng Heng**
448 University Ave. W., St. Paul
(612) 222-5577
The fantastic food at this little tiny Cambodian place tastes like a cross between Thai and Vietnamese, with French, Indian, and Chinese influences thrown in. It's run by a family who also owns a jewelry store and print shop that are practically on top of the restaurant. There's a salad called *band xiung*, which is beef, rice noodles, pieces of egg roll, and lettuce all tossed together. It's fabulous! It's in a district called Frogtown, where the Asian community lives.

● **Lucia's**
1432 W. 31st St., Minneapolis
(612) 825-1572
Chef-owner Lucia Watson has her own cookbook *Food from the Heartland*, and that's what she serves. Her small menu changes frequently and according to the seasons. Watson's cooking lets the ingredients shine. It's basically California cooking with a Minnesota twist. I've enjoyed dishes like pork tenderloin with mashed root vegetables, and wonderful crème caramel and fruit desserts. Only half the restaurant takes reservations, while the other half is saved for walk-ins.

● **Birchwood Cafe**
3311 E. 25th St., Minneapolis
(612) 722-4474
This is a modest cafeteria-style coffeehouse with takeout. It's a mom-and-pop operation with essentially two moms: Susan Muskat and Tracy Singleton, both formerly of Lucia's. The food is very fresh, and they rely on a lot of organics and bake their own bread. And the desserts are wonderful, including a chocolate layer cake.

● **The Loring Cafe**
1624 Harmon Pl., Minneapolis
(612) 332-1617
When this restaurant opened in 1986, it was really hot—and it still is! If I

wanted to go somewhere nice for a special occasion, this is where I'd want to go. The owner is involved in theater, and everything is really dramatic. They were shabby chic before shabby chic, with a decor featuring velvet curtains, dripping candles, and silver candlesticks. There's a big bar scene, with lots of sofas and chairs. At night, there might be a saxophonist or clarinetist playing overhead. One of the dishes I had there, roast chicken with lemon-mascarpone mashed potatoes, sounds awful, but it's actually very good.

(http://www.justgo.com/twincities)

 ## Critics' Favorite Restaurants: NEW YORK CITY

WHAT IS NEW YORK CITY'S BEST RESTAURANT?			
	Ruth Reichl's Rating *The New York Times*	1998 *Zagat Survey* Rank (Food Rating)	Gael Greene's Top 12 *New York* magazine
Aureole	N.A.	#4 (28)	Top Dozen
Bouley Bakery	★★★	N.A.	Top Dozen
Chanterelle	★★★★	#6 (27)	
Daniel	★★★★	#1 (28)	Top Dozen
Gotham Bar & Grill	★★★	#12 (27)	Top Dozen
Jean Georges	★★★★	#5 (28)	Top Dozen
La Grenouille	★★★	#9 (27)	
Le Bernardin	★★★★	#2 (28)	Top Dozen
Le Cirque 2000	★★★★	(25)	
Les Celebrités	N.A.	#10 (27)	
Lespinasse	★★★★	#3 (28)	Top Dozen
Mesa Grill	N.A.	(24)	Top Dozen
Nobu	★★★	#7 (27)	Top Dozen
Peter Luger Steak House	★★★	#8 (27)	
Picholine	★★★	(25)	Top Dozen
Shun Lee Palace	★★	(24)	Top Dozen
Union Square Cafe	★★★	#11 (27)	
Vong	N.A.	(25)	Top Dozen

It's clearly a matter of opinion. However, among Ruth Reichl of *The New York Times*, Gael Greene of *New York* magazine, and the New York *Zagat Survey*—arguably the three most powerful forces on the New York restaurant scene—you'll find unanimous agreement that these four restaurants top the short list: **Daniel**, **Jean Georges**, **Le Bernardin**, and **Lespinasse**.

SOME OF THE AUTHORS' FAVORITE RESTAURANTS IN NEW YORK CITY

We asked America's leading restaurant critics about their favorite restaurants: the kind of places of which their overburdened palates never tire. A few asked us how we'd answer the question, which we found challenging but, in fairness to them, include the answer below. These are the local restaurants we eat at most often—or most wish we could eat at even *more* often!

● **Daniel**
20 E. 76th St.
(212) 288-0499
The gracious staff, the well-matched wine, and Daniel Boulud's magic touch with French cuisine envelop diners in a well-rounded restaurant experience for which all superlatives seem trite. His deceptively simple food never ceases to astonish us.

● **East in the West**
113 Lexington Ave.
(212) 683-1313
Its delicious Indian food is a draw despite the cafeteria-style setting. You can enjoy a huge platter of chicken tikka masala, chicken curry, and your choice of vegetable (creamed spinach is a favorite) over basmati rice, served with fresh-baked nan bread, for less than $6!

● **Jean Georges**
One Central Park West
(212) 299-3900
Jean-Georges Vongerichten is a wizard with ingredients and creating new taste sensations. His garlic soup with sautéed frog's legs is a dish not to be missed, and the desserts are so ethereal that your feet won't feel like they're touching the ground as you leave this extraordinary room with a quintessential view of Manhattan.

- **Picholine**
35 W. 64th St.
(212) 724-8585
Terrance Brennan was already such a great chef when we first visited Picholine that it amazes us to find that his extraordinary food keeps getting better and better. We especially love the white gazpacho (summer only), the risotto, the scallops, the cheese cart, and the chocolate sorbet.

- **Solera**
216 E. 53rd St.
(212) 644-1166
The best tapas we've ever enjoyed, in the service of the world's best bartender, Angel Jurio, and warm and gracious *maitre d'* Ron Miller. Consider making it easy on yourself by ordering a tasting plate of tapas, but don't miss the awesome fried calamari with aioli.

SOME OF GAEL GREENE'S FAVORITE RESTAURANTS IN NEW YORK CITY

Gael Greene has been *New York* magazine's restaurant critic for thirty years.

- **Daniel**
20 E. 76th St.
(212) 288-0499
I love Daniel Boulud's passion for perfection.

- **Gotham Bar & Grill**
12 E. 12th St.
Definitely a four-star restaurant in my book.

- **Le Bernardin**
155 W. 51st St.
(212) 489-1515
The world's most spectacular seafood. The problem is that strangers won't have the same experience; waiters have been rude to some of the people I've sent.

- **Mesa Grill**
102 Fifth Ave.
(212) 807-7400
Bobby Flay has an instinctive taste for food. His taste palate is very close to mine.

- **Nobu**
105 Hudson St.
(212) 219-0500
On my early visits, I tried to order but it didn't work. The way to go is *omakase*—let *them* decide.

New Favorites:
- **Balthazar**

80 Spring St.

(212) 965-1414

It's more perfect than any French bistro in France.

- **Butterfield 81**

170 E. 81st St.

(212) 288-2700

It's been newborn under chef Tom Valenti.

- **Union Pacific**

111 E. 22nd St.

(212) 995-8500

Chef Rocco DiSpirito is more focused and refined now, yet full of surprises.

(http://www.newyorkmag.com)

SOME OF DAVID ROSENGARTEN'S FAVORITE RESTAURANTS IN NEW YORK CITY

David Rosengarten is the New York restaurant critic for *Gourmet*.

- **Daniel**

20 E. 76th St.

(212) 288-0499

A contender for the best French food in America, particularly Daniel Boulud's high-end versions of French farmhouse classics.

- **Il Buco**

47 Bond St.

(212) 533-1932

Tapas bar meets trattoria in this unique, dynamic space, where the best of both worlds come together.

- **Churrascaria Plataforma**

316 W. 49th St.

(212) 245-0505

Carnivorous carnivale at this astounding night in Rio.

- **Bay Leaf**

48 W. 56th St.

(212) 957-1818

Possibly the only Indian restaurant in New York that breaks out of the Indian restaurant rut. Authentic and surprisingly delicious.

- **Nobu**

105 Hudson St.

(212) 219-0500

It may infuriate some Japanese diners, but Nobu's "logical" creativity makes perfect sense to sushi lovers with a taste for adventure.

SOME OF ARTHUR SCHWARTZ'S FAVORITE RESTAURANTS IN NEW YORK CITY

Arthur Schwartz is a restaurant critic for WOR Radio and was the restaurant critic for *The Daily News*.

● **Jean Georges**
One Central Park West, Manhattan
(212) 299-3900

Right now, there's no place I'd rather go for an important meal than Jean Georges. Jean-Georges Vongerichten is the great genius in New York. Maybe not everyone would say he is the #1 French chef, but I think he's the #1 French chef-restaurateur because I think he has a very complete understanding of what happens in the dining room. Besides that, his food is truly original but, at the same time, it's not for originality's sake.

● **Daniel**
20 E. 76th St., Manhattan
(212) 288-0033
My second choice would be Daniel, even though the room is a little crowded and noisy for me.

● **Union Square Cafe**
21 E. 16th St., Manhattan
(212) 243-4020
I always love the Union Square Cafe, and I take out-of-towners there because I think it's a very New York restaurant and very representative of contemporary American food. But it's also European enough for my European friends to get it.

● **Peter Luger Steak House,** 178 Broadway, Brooklyn, New York
(718) 387-7400

If I think of steak, I go to Peter Luger. It's a childhood restaurant for me, so it has those attachments of going there with my family. It was the one big-time restaurant where my father was well known, and where we got treated very well.

- **Pierino**
107 Reade St., Manhattan
(212) 513-0610

James Beard used to say that the best restaurant is the one where they know you best. This is another restaurant where I'm friendly with the Neopolitan family [the deRosas] that owns it, and they also make food that I love. They're absolutely fanatic about ingredients and fly in everything you need to make real Neopolitan food.

(http://www.wor710.com/n-schwar.htm)

SOME OF ROBERT SIETSEMA'S FAVORITE RESTAURANTS IN NEW YORK CITY

"I have a few restaurants that I go to over and over again, but it changes all the time. I don't like to give a specific list because it can be different from day to day, but this is my list for mid-September 1997."

Robert Sietsema is the restaurant critic at *The Village Voice;* the editor of *Down the Hatch,* an ethnic restaurant fanzine; and the author of *Good & Cheap Ethnic Eats in New York City.*

- **Curry in a Hurry**
119 Lexington Ave., Manhattan
(212) 683-0904

I'm definitely in a Curry in a Hurry mode at the moment. I especially like their *masala dosai.* And they have a chutney buffet upstairs, and free dessert, a warm and soupy rice pudding with cardamom that's really delicious.

- **Hudson Falafel**
516 Hudson St., Manhattan
(212) 242-3939

It's a little Jordanian place where I eat a lot. They have a vegetarian special that I really like.

- **Katsuhama**
11 E. 47th St., Manhattan
(212) 758-5909

It's a Japanese restaurant that specializes in these pristine, nearly fat-free pork cutlets that are deep-fried—*katsu-don.* When you go there, they try to dissuade you from coming in, warning, "We don't serve sushi!" But it's magnificent. I look forward to my every visit there.

● **Shanghai Gourmet**
57 Mott St., Chinatown (Manhattan)
(212) 732-5533
It's the cut-rate **Joe's Shanghai** (another great restaurant, at 9 Pell St., which is usually too crowded).

● **Pearson's Texas Barbecue** (formerly known as Stick To Your Ribs)
5-16 51st Ave., Queens
(718) 937-3030
Because I lived in Texas for so long, I get homesick for that barbecue once in a while, and that's the only place in town that has the real thing. Period.

"There was certainly no talk of ethnicity in my family when I was growing up. To be assimilated was the greatest goal of everyone in the middle class. I still eat the kind of food I grew up on; I love hot dogs and hamburgers and stuff. But I refuse to eat crap, which they're not if they're good. A good hot dog is like the one at **Papaya King** [179 E. 86th St., Manhattan, 212-369-0648]—two for a dollar? You can't beat them! And the best hamburger in town is, I think, at **Steak Frites** [9 E. 16th St., Manhattan; 212-463-7101]." (Authors' note: When we ordered a hamburger at Steak Frites on Sietsema's recomendation, we were told that they're usually served only at lunch and brunch. And while we enjoyed it, the manager tipped us off that *he* likes the burgers even *better* around the corner at **L'Express**!)

SOME OF JIM LEFF'S FAVORITE RESTAURANTS IN (AND AROUND) NEW YORK CITY

"There's increasingly sophisticated knowledge about other ethnic groups in general. A lot of it comes from music. There's a huge ethnic music wave, and I think the ethnic music and ethnic food waves are feeding each other. Some very important people in music started the ethnic music wave; Paul Simon, David Byrne, and Peter Gabriel started popularizing more obscure world musics. When you start to explore a culture, its most visceral parts are its music and its food."

Jim Leff is the host of the Web site www.chowhound.com. In sharing some of his favorite restaurants, he differentiates, "Foodies have favorite restaurants; chowhounds ask themselves what they're in the mood for."

● **Kabab Cafe**
25-12 Steinway St., Astoria (Queens)
(718) 728-9858
When I need cheering up, I go to Kabab Cafe. A caveat: Even though the chef here cooked for me for years before he became my friend, I still consider him a friend. You can get authentic Egyptian dishes here that you can't

even get in Egypt any more because they're too old-fashioned. And even though his cooking can be inconsistent, I'm willing to endure the lows for the highs.

● **Grange Hall**
50 Commerce St., Manhattan
(212) 924-5246
When I'm feeling celebratory and expansive, I like to go here. I like the food a lot, and I like the ambiance just as much. And the waiters are really funny and smart. It makes for better conversation.

● **Charles' Southern-Style Kitchen**
2839 Frederick Douglass Blvd., Harlem
(212) 926-4313
When I feel like eating fried chicken, I'll go to this restaurant. Soul food is one of my favorite things, and Charles Gabriel is unquestionably the best soul-food cook in the tri-state area. He has a huge cast-iron skillet with pieces of chicken bobbing up and down in the oil. Even the bulletproof glass cannot shield you from his warmth!

● **Bo**
59-16 Kissena Blvd., Flushing (Queens)
(718) 661-3775
This is a great restaurant, owned by the former pastry chef from Sign of the Dove. She decided to get back to her Korean roots and open up this little place. Her food is so homestyle, it's almost universally homestyle. When I eat her beef ribs, they taste Jewish because I'm Jewish. If I were Portuguese, they would taste Portuguese.

● **The Arepa Lady**, Northwest corner of Roosevelt Ave. and 79th St.,
Jackson Heights (Queens)
The best food I know of in all of New York is made by a tiny, ageless Colombian woman on the streets of Jackson Heights on weekends only after 10:30 P.M., and she is the sainted Arepa Lady. She grills corn cakes called *arepas*, and I've brought dozens of people there from all walks of life and as soon as they take a bite, they all smile the identical smile. They're so full of who she is—she just imbues them with so much attention and love. They're so full of feeling that it just moves you and inspires you. And it doesn't get better than that. [She's within walking distance of the E/F train's Roosevelt Avenue (74th Street) stop.] By the way, Jackson Heights is the best food neighborhood in the world. It's unequaled for authenticity, diversity, and quality.

Now, the standard food person's wisdom is that this kind of food is not as good as French food. But I think that attitude is really passing. People are now realizing that the categories are horizontal, not vertical. Food is food, feeling is feeling, and art is art. It's a post-Modernist view that sees the value in whatever is being done.

Critics' Favorite Restaurants:
PHILADELPHIA

SOME OF ELAINE TAIT'S FAVORITE RESTAURANTS IN PHILADELPHIA

Elaine Tait, restaurant critic for *The Philadelphia Inquirer*, joined the paper in 1963, and told us of plans to retire in 1998.

● **Brasserie Perrier**
1619 Walnut St.
(215) 568-3000
I've only been to Brasserie Perrier for the two meals for its review, but I really liked it a lot. It was imaginative, and I like that occasionally.

● **The Fountain**
The Four Seasons Hotel
One Logan Square
(215) 963-1500
We go to the Four Seasons all the time. I love the food at The Fountain. Marty Hananan is the chef, and Jean-Marie Lacroix is the executive chef, and has trained a bunch of executive chefs and lets them all be their own person, yet his control is there and he's there for guidance. If I could afford to eat there more often, I would.

● **Monte Carlo Living Room**
150 South St.
(215) 925-2220
I love seafood. Just plain, wonderful seafood. We were just sitting around at Monte Carlo Living Room the other day, and I was working on a story about dried figs. They made pork with a sweet and sour fig sauce, and I thought, "Oh my God—this is it!" It was kind of country cooking.

● **Lee How Fook**
219 N. 11th St. (Chinatown)
(215) 925-7266
Just about every restaurant in Philadelphia has something that I really love, although it may not be the entire menu. In Chinatown, Lee How Fook has wonderful salt-baked squid and Cantonese fried oysters.

● **Dilullo Centro**
1407 Locust St.
(215) 546-2000
I love wonderful, real thin homemade pastas. At Dilullo Centro they have a woman from Italy who makes some fabulous pastas. The pappardelle are great; hers are really silky and nice.

I like anything that's fresh and not tortured. Some restaurants are very popular where the food is pretty tortured, and I don't understand it. I'm a great believer in simplicity. I don't like the degustation menus, where you taste a little of this and a little of that. I want a beautifully orchestrated meal that has a first course that leads into a second course, that leads into a third, where flavors build. That's hard to do in a restaurant today because every course is a heavy-hitter in a lot of places. Not many do it well, except maybe The Four Seasons, where you can get a light first course.

SOME OF PENELOPE CORCORAN'S FAVORITE RESTAURANTS IN PHOENIX

Penelope Corcoran is the restaurant critic at *The Arizona Republic*.

"If I were going to have three favorite restaurants in town, these are the restaurants. They answer nearly all my needs. All three are devoted to the best ingredients they can obtain, and a simple, uncomplicated style of presenting those ingredients so that you can enjoy the goodness of those ingredients. And they have the details down: each has a compelling atmosphere, exceptional service at whatever level they're trying to perform, and killer food. It's hard to convince people in New York that we have good restaurants here, but we really do. And these are three of them."

● **Pizzeria Bianco**
623 E. Adams St.
(602) 258-8300

I find it interesting that of all the restaurants in Phoenix—considering that we've got more than our share of James Beard Best Chefs of the Southwest—the restaurant ranked highest for food among *Zagat* surveyors is Pizzeria Bianco. I adore this place. I go there when I'm not working. They've relocated to a little historic building, which we don't have a lot of here. Phoenix is a very new city that didn't value the past. So, we don't have our quaint little places. We have a lot of new structures, we have a lot of restaurants in strip malls, and we have a lot of hotel restaurants.

Chris Bianco, who's from New York, found this little machine shop with brick walls and a brick structure, and made it into this destination spot in downtown Phoenix. He makes about six signature pizzas in a wood-fired oven he imported from Italy. This is a town where you can't find good tomatoes, but he finds really, really good ones all year-round. His bread is wonderful. He makes and smokes his own mozzarella. It's not just that he makes it all himself—it's excellent.

He has servers and bussers who remember that you're a person who boxes up the last three slices of your pizza to take home, or that you always order Pellegrino, or that you're going to have a single espresso after dinner. It's a rare combination. Plus, the chef, who is modest to a fault, is in his restaurant. He's not giving lessons, he's not out on cruise—he's in his restaurant making pizza. I admire that. [5 forks]

● **Rancho Pinot Grill**
6208 N. Scottsdale Rd.
(602) 468-9463
It's owned and operated by a husband-and-wife team who have worked in California and traveled all over. It's more of a comfortable, fine-dining restaurant. The decor is charming. Chrysa Kaufman is the chef, and her husband is Tom. She's another person who doesn't seek publicity. She's in the kitchen, they work really hard, and they're emphatic about ingredients and details. The service is attentive, unobtrusive, and comfortable. When you dine at this restaurant, it feels like you're in somebody's living room, in a good sense. It's decorated with what I call "cowboy kitsch"—cool old rodeo posters, old photos of women at a rodeo. They did it in a great way. It's a limited menu; they're not trying to do too much. She considers herself a glorified home cook, and I like people who see themselves more as craftsmen than as celebrity chefs. [5 forks]

● **T. Cook's at Royal Palm**
5200 E. Camelback Rd.
(602) 808-0766
It's a historic, small resort that was recently purchased and renovated. It's the amalgamation of details that makes it special: excellent service, knowledgeable servers who make recommendations and back them up with reasons, a gorgeous room that is quintessentially Arizona. All the food works on the plate. There's nothing that's there by chance. There's nothing that's gratuitous. It's there for the texture, the flavor, the color, and it all works as a unit. [5 forks]

I got a big, long message from a gentleman from New York on my voice mail, who was looking for a restaurant. I feel like the concierge to the city sometimes! But I called him back and left a message recommending three restaurants: **Rancho Pinot Bistro**, **Mary Elaine's at the Phoenician** [5 forks], and **T. Cook's**. They went to Rancho Pinot Grill, and he left me a message saying they loved it, and thought it was excellent.

THE ARIZONA REPUBLIC'S FORK SYSTEM, according to Penelope Corcoran	
Five forks:	"Wow!"
Four forks:	"Very Good."
Three forks:	"Good."
Two forks:	"So-so."
One fork:	"Ugh."

"It may sound hokey or rinky-dink, but the idea is to capture the emotional response to the three criteria of food, service, and atmosphere. So it's entirely possible that I could be totally wowed by an Indian restaurant, or a Shanghainese dim sum place, or a Mexican restaurant, or a fine-dining restaurant—which is kind of the freedom of the rating system, that it's not so set in stone as to what things mean. So a little mom-and-pop Mexican restaurant, where the food is fabulous, could have four forks for food, two or three forks for service, with the atmosphere receiving only one fork."

(http://www.arizonarepublic.com/depts/dining/)

Critics' Favorite Restaurants: RALEIGH-DURHAM

SOME OF GREG COX'S FAVORITE RESTAURANTS IN RALEIGH-DURHAM

Greg Cox is the restaurant critic for *The Raleigh News and Observer*.

"I'd like to think I know something about the food I write about because I've made a real effort to educate myself over the years. Still, I take what in Zen would be called a 'beginner mind' approach, in that whatever the restaurant's terms are in presenting itself, those are the terms I take it on. So the range of things I like is pretty wide. I've been asked whether, to paraphrase Will Rogers, I never met a restaurant I didn't like. In a way, that's close to the truth, though I'd rather say that I've rarely met a restaurant I couldn't understand someone liking. What I try to do is to describe the whole dining experience well enough to bring that someone and that restaurant together."

● **Magnolia Grill**
1002 Ninth St., Durham
(919) 286-3609
If you asked just about anybody in the Triangle who knows about food, they'd probably say Ben Barker's Magnolia Grill is the best restaurant. And I have to agree. It's wonderful. He serves New American food, sometimes with a bit of a Southern touch. He takes the barbecue I knew as a kid, and turns it into smoked pork tenderloin served with sweet potato chips and a bourbon-cider *jus* that any good North Carolina barbecue-maker would be proud of as a barbecue sauce.

● **Nana's**

2514 University Dr., Durham

(919) 493-8545

Scott Howell had been Ben Barker's *sous chef* at one point. I look to Ben Barker and Scott Howell for my first chance to see some of the things that I read are going on in New York. They're both very creative, but Scott has more of a Mediterranean-Italian touch.

● **Fins**

Greystone Village

7713-39 Lead Mine Rd., Raleigh

(919) 847-4119

William D'Auvray is the chef of this Pacific Rim fusion restaurant. He grew up in the Philippines and later got classic training. He does wonderful dishes like slate-roasted salmon with Japanese udon noodles, with a bit of a gingery palm sugar glaze. He leans toward seafood on more than half the menu. When I think of his place, I think of really clean flavors, Asian and sometimes tropical flavors, and good seafood.

● **Blue Nile**

2300 Chapel Hill Rd., Durham

(919) 490-0462

I love ethnic restaurants. We have one Ethiopian restaurant here, and I love it just because of their spunk, and the food is good. A husband-and-wife team run it, and there is such a spirit there. At the end of the night, they'll start playing Ethiopian music, and the staff dances traditional dances and invites everyone to join in! Sometimes they'll even serve their own honey wine.

● **Tacqueria Mi Pueblo**, 223 Wellons Village Shopping Center (South Miami Blvd. at Holloway St.), Durham

(919) 688-3461

There are one or two other tacquerias that do as good a

job with the food, but this restaurant serves the real thing, which until five years ago we did not have here. Their *tacos al pastor* are wonderful—with pork, pineapple, and onion, served on tortillas. And they serve *aguas frescas*—homemade sweet drinks made from various fruits—which I'm excited to see. You go in there, and it's another world. Plus, they make more of an effort than other places to make non-Hispanics feel welcome, and you'll find English translations on the menu.

A few **downtown Raleigh** favorites:

- **Second Empire**
330 Hillsborough St., Raleigh
(919) 829-3663
This is a beautifully renovated old Victorian house within a couple of blocks of the Capitol building, serving New American food, like roasted guinea hen breast and a really nice crabmeat and codfish *galette*, all beautifully presented.

- **Vertigo**
426 S. McDowell St., Raleigh
(919) 832-4477
I really like this little funky place because they were one of the first to have the guts to open in the area. They took over an old '50s style diner and kept the chrome bar stools, but the rest of the decor is a rotating exhibit of local artists. Their menu is very short, but it pretty much covers the world, from Chinese tea-smoked duck, to a Southwest dish, to a vegetarian dish. They've got a really good attitude.

- **WickedSmile**
511 W. Hargett St., Raleigh
(919) 828-2223
This restaurant makes me think of New York. They opened in an old warehouse and converted it into a restaurant, with edgy urban decor, with lots of metal and exposed brick. They're big on plate architecture, too.

(http://www.news-observer.com/go/restaurants/restaurants.html)

 **Critics' Favorite Restaurants: SAN FRANCISCO**

SOME OF PATRICIA UNTERMAN'S FAVORITE RESTAURANTS IN (AND AROUND) SAN FRANCISCO

Patricia Unterman is the chef-owner of the Hayes Street Grill in San Francisco. A restaurant reviewer for more than twenty years, she currently writes for *The San Francisco Examiner*.

• Hong Kong Flower Lounge
5322 Geary Blvd., San Francisco
(415) 668-8998
I like to go here with a group, and order ahead so we can be served banquet style. Don't miss the pei pa tofu—juicy, lightly curried tofu dumplings served with baby bok choy.

• Yank Sing
427 Battery St.
(415) 362-1640
or
Ton Kiang
5821 Geary Blvd.
(415) 387-8273
These are two of the best dim sum houses in San Francisco.

• L'Osteria del Forno
519 Columbus Ave.
(415) 982-1124
I like this little Italian place, and my kid likes it, too. They serve our favorite thin-crust pizza and one of the best cups of espresso in town at amazingly low prices.

• Kyo-ya
Sheraton Palace Hotel
2 New Montgomery St.,
(415) 392-8600
or
Hama-Ko
108-B Carl St.
(415) 753-6808
When I eat sushi, I want it to be really perfect—and I'm willing to spend anything for it. Kyo-ya has the potential for doing it the best. Or I'll call ahead to Hamoko, where I know the sushi chef, who gets his hands on really great fresh raw fish.

• Chez Panisse
1517 Shattuck, Berkeley, California
(510) 548-5525
It feels like my family restaurant, like my home restaurant. No other restaurant in the world possesses its purity and charm. I'd rather eat here than anywhere else in the world.

Unterman also mentions "the perfect taco" at **Pancho Villa Taqueria** [3017 16th St., 415-864-8840]: "It's a wonderful place." And she admits, "When you're in the mood for a hamburger, and it's prepared just right, it's a great dish. Do you know where I just had a great hamburger? **Moose's** [1652 Stockton St., 415-989-7800]."

(http://www.sfgate.com/eguide/food/reviews)

SOME OF CAROLINE BATES'S FAVORITE RESTAURANTS IN SAN FRANCISCO

Caroline Bates is the restaurant critic for *Gourmet* in California.

● **Slanted Door**
584 Valencia St.
(415) 861-8032
I really love the Slanted Door. All of chef-owner Charles Phan's food is so incredibly bright and exciting, and you feel like you're learning something. Eating out becomes an adventure.

● **Swan's Oyster Depot**
1517 Polk St.
(415) 673-1101
I love to go there. There's nothing better than that—just to sit at that counter and get some clam chowder that is so incredibly good. Nobody out here knows how to make clam chowder. And the quality of their oysters is so good. I love that!

● **Bizou**
598 Fourth St.
(415) 543-2222
or
Fringale
570 Fourth St.
(415) 543-0573
I love Bizou, and Fringale, next to it.

● **Ton Kiang**
5821 Geary Blvd.
(415) 387-8273
It's way up on Geary. It has wonderful dim sum. In fact, you could spend your whole life eating on Geary! There's every imaginable kind of restaurant there. It's a great eating street.

One of three Italian restaurants:
● **Antica Trattoria**
2400 Polk St.
(415) 928-5797
Laghi's
1801 Clement St.
(415) 386-6266
or
Palio d'Asti
640 Sacramento St.
(415) 395-9800

There are three Italian restaurants that I love. Antica Trattoria has very good northern Italian cuisine; I think he's from Bergamo. The chef at Laghi's is from Emilia-Romagna, and he's a Romagnan. His cooking is very specific to that area. It's a little place and very charming. I also like Palio d'Asti. That's Piedmont cooking, because that's where the owner comes from. Since I've been to those parts of Italy, I think that's perhaps why I respond to them. I can see where they're coming from and can taste what they're trying to do.

● **Eos**
901 Cole St.,
415-566-3063
Chef Arnold Wong is a very interesting cook who does Asian things. Eos has the most incredible wine list. They have a wine shop, and a wine bar next door, so it's exciting to go there for that.

Critics' Favorite Restaurants: SEATTLE

SOME OF TOM SIETSEMA'S FAVORITE RESTAURANTS IN (AND AROUND) SEATTLE

Tom Sietsema is the former restaurant critic for *The Seattle Post-Intelligencer*, and now reviews restaurants for *Washington Sidewalk*.

● **Cafe Nola**
101 Winslow Way, Bainbridge Island, WA
(206) 842-3822
I love it. It's my favorite. And it was so much fun to write about because it was indeed a discovery: these two sweet little sisters [Melinda Lucas and Mary Bugarin] in this tiny little shop, with extraordinary salads, beautiful soups, great breads, and sour cherry doughnuts. Mmmmm.... Boy, the food is good! And it's just such a wonderful thing to get on that ferry [from Seattle] and to walk through Maintown to eat at the restaurant.

● **Palace Kitchen**
2030 Fifth Ave.
(206) 448-2001
It's the best of Tom Douglas's three restaurants; he also has **Edda's** and **Dahlia Lounge**. The Palace Kitchen is always fun. I like the way it looks. He serves Northwestern-style tapas, and if that doesn't sound very appetizing, I should say he does a nice job with them. He has a big open kitchen that looks like the set from *The Cook, The Thief, His Wife, and Her Lover*, but not as gory.

- **Lampreia**
2400 First Ave.
(206) 443-3301

The chef is not friendly or outgoing, but he turns out beautiful food, simple and elegant. It's a beautiful dining room—a golden, glowing high-tech meets warm-colored walls dining room. He has a beautiful wine list and seeks out small farmers, so he's got great ingredients. Nobody does better things with seafood.

- **Marco's Supperclub**
2510 First Ave.
(206) 441-7801

It is sort of a "Cheers"-like bar. Very friendly, low ceilings. I think every place I like is warm-amber lit!

SOME OF NANCY LESON'S FAVORITE RESTAURANTS IN SEATTLE

Nancy Leson is the restaurant critic for *The Seattle Times* and serves as editor of the Seattle *Zagat Survey*.

- **Dahlia Lounge**
1904 Fourth Ave.
(206) 682-4142

I'm particularly fond of Tom Douglas's three restaurants, and Dahlia Lounge is my favorite. He's at the forefront of what a lot of chefs are doing here, dabbling internationally, a little heavy on the Asian, in a really attractive downtown setting. The restaurant was featured in *Sleepless in Seattle*. It's a really beautiful spot, and the food is very, very good. Seattle's bar scene has become huge again, and his restaurant **Palace Kitchen** [2030 Fifth Ave., 206-448-2001] has turned into a giant cocktail bar and noshery.

- **Campagne**
86 Pine St., Seattle
(206) 728-2800

This is probably the restaurant where I spend more of my own money than any other. It's a French-styled restaurant downtown in the Pike Place Market. What appeals to me so much about it is not so much the food, which is very, very good, but the extraordinary service. That's something you don't find very often in Seattle. They've spun off a less expensive restaurant called **Cafe Campagne** below it. Jim Drohman, who was former chef Tamara Murphy's *sous chef* for several years, took over the kitchen and is doing a terrific job—as well as if not better than she was. Jim has a real love for cheeses, and their cheese course is gorgeous.

- **Lampreia**
2400 First Ave. (Belltown)
(206) 443-3301

Lampreia is another one of my favorite restaurants that I feel gets absolutely not enough attention. Chef-owner Scott Carsberg is somewhat of an *enfant terrible*. He's a stylist and a perfectionist, and he uses the best of everything, which holds him in good stead. His contemporary Northwest menu is relatively small, and it changes a lot. His cheese course, which features Egg Farm Dairy cheeses, is the best in the city.

● **Marco's Supperclub**
2510 First Ave. (Belltown)
(206) 441-7801
This is a hip, eclectic restaurant and bar with a really nice, moderately priced menu that's a trip around the world, with specialties ranging from a fried sage appetizer to Jamaican jerk chicken. It's owned by a couple, Donna Moodie and Marco Rulff, who used to work at Topolobampo in Chicago and at Campagne and Serafina here. They also just opened **Lush Life** [2331 Second Ave., Seattle, 206-441-9842], which has an Italian bent, as an answer to the "What'll-we-do-now?" question that arises whenever Marco's is full.

● **Shanghai Garden**
524 6th Ave. S.
(206) 625-1689
I like Chinese food a lot, and Shanghai Garden is a restaurant in our small Chinatown here that I'm pretty nuts about. It's regional as opposed to a specific provincial style. The chef Hua-Te Su, is really interested in healthy Chinese food, but you'd never know it to eat it—only that the food tastes very different and clean and good. He makes hand-shaved noodles and other specialties.

SOME OF GREGORY ROBERTS'S FAVORITE RESTAURANTS IN (AND AROUND) SEATTLE

Gregory Roberts is the restaurant critic for *The Seattle Post-Intelligencer*.

"Seattle, for some reason, doesn't have knockout desserts—which a top restaurant really should have. The restaurants here tend to have good, but simple, desserts."

● **Campagne**
86 Pine St., Seattle
(206) 728-2800
Tamara Murphy was succeeded here by her *sous chef* [Jim Drohman], who continues to serve upscale country French cooking. It's a nice atmosphere, and it's got a wine list with personality. The service is highly capable and professional. (3 $\frac{1}{2}$ stars)

- **Third Floor Fish Cafe**

205 Lake St., Kirkland, Washington

(425) 822-3553

This is also quite an upscale restaurant. The dining room has banked seating, and every table has a great view of the water. There are some terrific fish dishes on the menu, which is a little more contemporary or cross-cultural. (3 ½ stars)

- **El Gaucho**

2505 First Ave., Seattle

(206) 728-1337

El Gaucho is a kick. It's a lot of fun! It's a very theatrical restaurant housed in a big open space, with a pianist and a lot of flaming dishes served at the table. It also has both a martini bar and a cigar bar. It's expensive, but it's not cutting-edge food: the menu ranges from venison to grilled fish. (3 stars)

- **Roy St. Bistro**

174 Roy St., Seattle

(206) 284-9093

This restaurant would be perfect on a day like today, which happens to be gray and drizzling. They serve comfort food like pot pies and stews in a low-key atmosphere. While the food isn't scintillating, I've certainly enjoyed it, and I look forward to going back. (2 ½ stars)

- **Raga Cuisine of India**

555 108th Ave. NE, Bellevue, Washington

(425) 450-0336

It's got some really good Indian dishes. (2 ½ stars)

SOME OF PHYLLIS RICHMAN'S FAVORITE RESTAURANTS IN WASHINGTON, DC

Phyllis Richman is the restaurant critic for *The Washington Post*.

Richman told us, "Every fall, I prepare a dining guide to my fifty favorite restaurants in Washington, DC. And it's really hard to narrow it down to fifty. So I don't want to give you a list of my five favorites because while it might be today's list, it might not be tomorrow's.

"I love casual food because I spend so much of my time eating formally. And I love light, fresh things. I love sushi because it's kind of an antidote to a lot of the other heavy eating I have to do. A great sandwich. A bowl of good soup. Otherwise, when I'm eating normally in restaurants and choosing, I love food across the board. What I choose depends on what I've been eating, and what the weather is," she says.

- Okay, we counter, "You're lying in bed with a cold, in cold weather, and we'll bring you anything you want from anywhere in the DC area." Richman laughs. "Yeah, that's what I did yesterday," she chuckles. "I had a sandwich and soup from the **Bread Line** [1751 Pennsylvania Ave. NW; 202-822-8900], which is currently the place where, if I'm not going out to eat, I stop to get something to eat at my desk. A friend of mine runs it, but that's not why I do that; it's because it's carry-out food that's of enormously high quality. And I get cravings for a really great sandwich—a turkey sandwich made on freshly baked country bread, and the turkey's well-seasoned and just roasted and carved off the bone before it's been refrigerated, with homemade mayonnaise and arugula. It's a great place! I just had a $3 bowl of saffron seafood chowder, and it was as good as you would find at **Kinkead's**, which makes incomparable soups. The **Bread Line** also has the best bread in town and really good high-quality sandwich fillings. But it's silly to mention one restaurant that I like. That's just the one I crave these days."

- Richman's favorite indulgence? She says she doesn't have a sweet tooth. "Potato chips. I like salty, crunchy things. Or I'll ask them to put some turkey skin on my turkey sandwich at the **Bread Line**. For breakfast, I'll go to **Sholl's Colonial Cafeteria** [1990 K St. NW, downtown Washington, DC, (202) 296-3065], where they make their own biscuits and doughnuts. It's a very plain, simple cafeteria. Sometimes in the summer they'll have all the corn-on-the-cob you can eat for 75 cents!"

- What about when she's craving sushi? "**Sushi-Ko** [2307 Wisconsin Ave. NW, 202-333-4187]," says Richman. "It's sort of our little Nobu. He [chef Kazuhiro Okochi] is very creative with raw fish dishes and knows what he's doing."

- "For another casual and quick but wonderful meal, I'll go to the bar at **Kinkead's** [2000 Pennsylvania Ave. NW, 202-296-7700]. They have some amazing soups and stews."

- "When my daughter comes into town and we want a good, long talk and a really nice meal, we'll just walk down the alley to **Obelisk** [2029 P St., NW, 202-872-1180]. It's an Italian restaurant with a very small fixed-price menu, and it's very simple, pure, excellent food."

- "Or sometimes we'll go for a nice long walk over Key Bridge and get a bowl of soup at **Pho 75** [1711 Wilson Blvd., Arlington, VA, 703-525-

7355]. It was the first of the Vietnamese soup restaurants. It's very simple and plain, and filled with Vietnamese families. And it's a quick $5 meal that's very satisfying."

(http://www.washingtonpost.com/wp-srv/style/restaurants)

SOME OF TOM SIETSEMA'S FAVORITE RESTAURANTS IN WASHINGTON, DC

Tom Sietsema is the restaurant reviewer for *Washington Sidewalk*.

● **Cafe Atlantico**
405 8th St. NW
(202) 393-0812
[3 stars from *Washington Sidewalk*]
I love this place. It is an upscale Latin American restaurant on three levels that is bright and colorful, and there is always something really exciting on the menu. I was served a martini glass filled with chilled puree of potato with just the slightest whisper of vanilla. It sounds dreadful, and in someone else's hands it might have been. But it was one of the more intriguing things I've had in a long time.

● **Taberna del Alabardero**
1776 I St. NW
(202) 429-2200
[3 stars from *Washington Sidewalk*]
It's an old world Spanish place, quite expensive, with classical Spanish food and wonderful formal, but friendly, service. I recently spent three weeks in Spain, and it just reminded me of being on vacation.

● **Rupperts**
1017 7th St. NW
(202) 783-0699
[3 ¹/₂ stars from *Washington Sidewalk*]
I think he's a very forward-thinking chef. He doesn't write his menu for the next day until 11 P.M. the night before when he talks to his suppliers. He has a whole host of small purveyors of greens and mushrooms and small game birds that he calls on. They are not "healthniks," but aside from dessert they use no butter or cream in any of their dishes. And they have an extraordinary wine list. They take food very seriously, but they have fun doing it—and that comes across on the plate.

● **Pesce**
2016 P St. NW
(202) 466-3474
[3 stars from *Washington Sidewalk*]
It's owned by Jean-Louis Palladin and Roberto Donna. I love it because
while it's not the most comfortable dining room, they really pay attention
to wine and good fish. They treat it well and present it in interesting combinations.

● **1789**
1226 36th St. NW
(202) 965-1789
[3 stars from *Washington Sidewalk*]
It's in a Federal-style Georgetown home. And the chef there has turned out
some really marvelous food. It's kind of a Republican crowd, but it's fun.

● **Cashion's Eat Place**
1819 Columbia Rd. NW
(202) 797-1819
[3 stars from *Washington Sidewalk*]
Chef Ann Cashion is a really soulful cook. Her food is served in a sepia-toned
dining room filled with old black-and-white photographs. And her pastry
chef Ann Amernick used to be at the White House, and turns out beautiful
desserts. Her caramels, and anything she does with lemon, are extraordinary.

(http://washington.sidewalk.com)

B

An Internet Guide to Restaurant Review Resources

ARIZONA

Phoenix

The Arizona Republic/Phoenix Gazette
(http://www.azcentral.com/depts/dining/)
Browse reviews by Penelope Corcoran by name, cuisine, price, area, or special features. Links to "Taste the Town" (Penelope's favorites), "Restaurant Reviews," "Cheap Eats," and "Dining Forum." "These are my picks, pure and simple," Corcoran insists. "Not *The Arizona Republic*'s, not the consensus of some anonymous group of survey takers, not another critic's."

Phoenix magazine
(http://www.azfamily.com/ott/dining/index.html)
Dining editor Nikki Buchanan's "Eat Beat" appears monthly in *Phoenix* magazine. Search database of Valley restaurants by cuisine, location, name or price.

Phoenix New Times
(http://www.phoenixnewtimes.com)
Under "Cafe" you'll find new and recent reviews by critic Howard Seftel, plus a database of Valley restaurants receiving favorable reviews searchable by cuisine, area, price, and keyword.

Tucson

The Arizona Daily Star
(http://dinnerat8.azstarnet.com)
Reviews by critic Kim Westerman of Tucson restaurants, and features such as "Perfect Settings" and "Tucson's Top Tables," which touts among the city's best Café Poca Cosa, Janos, Le Rendez-Vous, and The Ventana Room.

ARKANSAS

Little Rock Arkansas Democrat Gazette
(http://www.ardemgaz.com)
Search Weekend Section for full-text restaurant reviews by cuisine, rating, or keyword, or browse a list of recommended restaurants. Read reviews of Little Rock's seven four-star restaurants, which are Alouette's, Brave New Restaurant, Capers, Cassinelli 1700, Hamilton House, Spaule, and Star of India.

CALIFORNIA

Statewide

KGO and KABC Radio
(http://www.ronn.com/foodwine.html)
Radio host Ronn Owens shares his restaurant recommendations in Northern and Southern California (such as Hawthorne Lane and Jardiniere in San Francisco, and The Grill in Los Angeles), and provides links to other food and wine-related Web sites.

Los Angeles

FoodPlex
(http://www.gigaplex.com/food/index.htm)
Restaurant reviews by critic Merrill Shindler.

Los Angeles magazine
(http://www.lamag.com/rstrev.htm)
Browse current reviews by Jonathan Gold.

The Los Angeles Times
(http://www.calendarlive.com/LA_Times/Art_and
Entertainment/Dining_Out/)
Search by reviews by critic S. Irene Virbila by name or area, or browse by cuisine, price or special features.

L.A. Weekly
(http://www.laweekly.com/restaurants)
Search reviews of Los Angeles restaurants by locale, cuisine, or restaurant name. Also, find recent features and reviews by Jonathan Gold in archives.

Orange County

Orange County Register
(http://www.ocregister.com/letseat/reviews)
Browse recent reviews by Elizabeth Evans. Restaurant listings (with links to maps and restaurant Web sites) are searchable by cuisine.

Sacramento

The Sacramento Bee
(http://www.sacbee.com/leisure/goingout/diningout/finedining/finediningindex.html)
Bee restaurant critic Mike Dunne reviews area restaurants (and shares his philosophy about doing so), searchable by type of cuisine. Don't miss his reviews of area standouts like Alexander's Meritage, Biba, Habanero Cava Latina The Kitchen, Paragary's Bar and Oven, and Slocum House.

San Diego

San Diego Sidewalk
(http://sandiego.sidewalk.com/restaurants)
Searchable database of restaurant reviews by critic Robin Kleven of San Diego standouts like Anthony's Star of the Sea, Azzura Point, The Belgian Lion, Grant Grill, Marine Room, Mille Fleurs, and Rancho Valencia Resort.

The San Diego Union-Tribune
(http://www.uniontrib.com/entertainment/dining/)
Searchable database by location, restaurant name, or food type. Links to critics' favorites (such as The Brasserie in Mira Mesa, Marius in Coronado, Pizzeria Via Italia in Clairemont, and Sushi Ota in Pacific Beach) and recent reviews by critics Maria Hunt and Leslie James.

San Francisco Bay Area

The San Francisco Chronicle and The San Francisco Examiner
(http://www.sfgate.com/eguide/food/reviews)
Restaurant reviews from the *Chronicle*'s Michael Bauer and Robin Davis and the *Examiner*'s Bill Citara. Search by date or keyword. Links to Top 100 area restaurants and best bargain restaurants. To find Patricia Unterman's *Examiner* reviews, search via her byline.

San Francisco Sidewalk
(http://sanfrancisco.sidewalk.com/restaurants)
Search more than 1,500 restaurant reviews by Sidewalk critics Meesha Halm and Sharon Silva.

San Francisco Weekly
(http://www.sfweekly.com/current/food.html)
Search database of 200 restaurant reviews by critic Naomi Wise by location, cuisine, price, and keyword.

San Jose

San Jose Mercury News
(http://www.sjmercury.com/justgo/diningbest.htm)

Reviews by Deborah Byrd, and Sheila Himmel, and recommendations in Santa Cruz, East Bay, San Francisco, Peninsula, and South Bay.

Santa Rosa

The Santa Rosa Press Democrat
(http://www.pressdemo.com/goingout/dine/dine.html)
Search restaurant reviews by Jeff Cox by location, cuisine, or name. Use the "Quick Browse" feature to search by ambiance, service, or wine list.

Wine Country (Napa/Sonoma)

Epicurious - Napa & Sonoma
(http://food.epicurious.com/e_eating/e03_restguide/napa/intro.html)
Under "Eating," and then "Restaurants," you'll find The Essential Restaurant Guide, which lists reviews by Karen MacNeil of 10 Napa & Sonoma standouts including The French Laundry, John Ash & Co., Mustards, and Tra Vigne.

COLORADO

Aspen

Epicurious - Aspen
(http://food.epicurious.com/e_eating/e03_restguide/aspen/intro.html)
Read reviews by Janet O'Grady of standouts like Ajax Tavern, Cache Cache, Campo de Fiori, Caribou Club, Carnevale, Kenichi/Takah Sushi, The Little Nell, Pinons, Renaissance/R Bistro, and Woody Creek Tavern.

Boulder

The Boulder Daily Camera
(http://www.bouldernews.com/inside boulder/downtown/dining/index.html)
Browse recent reviews of Boulder restaurants by category.

Denver

The Denver Post
(http://www.denverpost.com/movie/food.htm)
Search reviews of recommended restaurants, including La Coupole, Palace Arms, and Q's Restaurant.

Denver Sidewalk
(http://denver.sidewalk.com/restaurants)
Search Bill St. John's restaurant reviews, including his Top 10 picks among everything from "Brewpubs" to "Offbeat Eateries" to "With the Kids," not to mention the "Top 5 Tough Reservations," which include restaurants like Aubergine, Jax Fish House, and Papillon.

CONNECTICUT

The Hartford Courant
(http://interact.courant.com/taste/queries/index.idc)
Search online collection of Connecticut restaurant reviews from *Northeast* magazine reviewer Bill Daley. Search by restaurant name, cuisine, town, or number of stars.

DISTRICT OF COLUMBIA

The Washingtonian
(http://www.washingtonian.com/dining)
Reviews by Thomas Head and *Washingtonian* staff searchable by name, location, rating, price, or cuisine. Features include "100 Very Best Restaurants" (which spotlights four-star Galileo, Inn at Little Washington, and Vidalia) as well as "Best Bargain Restaurants."

The Washington Post
(http://search.washingtonpost.com/wp-srv/searches/restrant.htm)
Searchable database of more than 250 Phyllis Richman reviews and more than fifty Eve Zibart "Courses" columns by restaurant name, neighborhood, price range, or cuisine. Links to Richman's "Top 50 Restaurants" list.

Washington Sidewalk
(http://washington.sidewalk.com/restaurants)
Reviews by critic Tom Sietsema and *Sidewalk* staff are searchable by name, neighborhood, cuisine, price, rating, or special options.

FLORIDA

Miami

City Link Online–South Florida
(http://www.clo-sfl.com/culture)
Under "Eats," you'll find the current week's review, as well as an alphabetical listing of past reviews and a searchable database by location and cuisine of South Florida restaurants.

The Miami Herald
(http://www.herald.com/justgo/diningbest.htm)
Features latest week's review, plus links to editor's picks and what's cooking at South Florida restaurants.

South Florida magazine
(http://www.sfl.com)
To access recent reviews by critic Bob Hosmon, search "Metro Diner."

The Sun Sentinel
(http://www.sun-sentinel.com/showtime/restaurant)

Reviews by *The Sun-Sentinel* restaurant critic who uses the pseudonym of M.L. Warren to maintain his (or her!) anonymity. Search hundreds of reviews of South Florida standouts by city, cuisine or price range, including Bex, Boulevard Grille Royal Palm Plaza, and Chef Reto of Boca Raton, and Two Chefs of South Miami.

Orlando

The Orlando Sentinel
(http://www.orlandosentinel.com/entertainment/dining)
Search critic Scott Joseph's reviews, including Orlando standouts like Del Frisco's, La Coquina, Victoria & Albert's, and Yachtman's Steakhouse. Includes link to Orlando DigitalCity's searchable database of restaurants (http://orlando.digitalcity.com/entertainment/dining/main.htm).

Tampa Bay/St. Petersburg/Sarasota

The St. Petersburg Times
(http://www.sptimes.com/tampabaycom/diversions/taste/index2.htm)
Reviews by Chris Sherman and other *Times* staffers. Search by cuisine, including "New American" picks like The Blue Heron, Mise en Place, and Next City Grill.

Tampa Bay Online/The Tampa Tribune
(http://tampabayonline.net/feature/dining.htm)
Search reviews by *Tampa Tribune* restaurant critics.

The Palm Beach Post
(http://www.gopbi.com/aroundtown/restfeature.html)
Search more than 1,500 restaurants in Palm Beach, Martin, and St. Lucie county.

GEORGIA

The Atlanta Journal-Constitution
(http://www.accessatlanta.com/life/restaurants/archive_reviews.html)
Reviews and dining advice from John Kessler and the staff of *The Atlanta Journal-Constitution*. Search under "Recent Reviews," "Good 'n' Cheap," "Just Opened," or "Hungry with Kids." Links to dining notes, as well as such features as one on the local boom in French restaurants like Brasserie Le Coze, Ciboulette, Frog & Peach Bistro, Gauguin, Le Saint Amour, Provence, Riviera, and Soleil.

***Atlanta* magazine**
(http://atlantamag.atlanta.com/atld.html)
Search reviews by critic Christiane Lauterbach. Plus, see how *Atlanta*'s best restaurant choices (e.g. The Dining Room in The Ritz-Carlton, Buckhead) stack up against readers' picks (e.g. Pano's & Paul's), by category.

Creative Loafing
(http://www.creativeloafing.com/newsstand/current/eats.htm)
Browse an alphabetical list of dozens of bite-sized reviews by Cliff Bostock, Elliot Mackle, and Shelly Skiles Sawyer, or search reviews by restaurant type.

HAWAII

Honolulu.com
(http://www.honolulu.com/dining/nav.html)
Search dining resources in the Honolulu area.

The Honolulu Star-Bulletin
(http://starbulletin.com/doit/restaurants.html)
Browse reviews of Honolulu area restaurants by Nadine Kam, "The Weekly Eater."

ILLINOIS

Chicago magazine
(http://www.chicagomag.com/text/dining/cover.htm)
Browse recent reviews by Dennis Ray Wheaton and Chicago staff, as well as feature stories on a wide range of dining topics, including "Best New Restaurants" and "Great Dining."

Chicago New City Net
(http://www.newcityChicago.com/listings/food.html)
Search new and archived restaurant reviews. "Best of Chicago" picks include everything from the city's best brunch (House of Blues's Sunday gospel brunch) to its "best transgender Mexican restaurant" (Lolita's).

The Chicago Sun-Times
(http://www.suntimes.com/index.bruno.html)
An alphabetical listing of recent reviews by Chicago Sun-Times critic Pat Bruno, with star ratings.

The Chicago Tribune
(http://www.metromix.com/restaurants)
Search restaurant reviews by William Rice and critic Phil Vettel by cuisine, location, style, price, or name. Features include "Tablehopping" (openings, closings, and restaurant news). The Chicago Tribune also has an alphabetical restaurant review archive on America Online (keyword=Tribune).

INDIANA

The Indianapolis Star
(http://www.circlecity.com/roundtown/dining/)
Search recent restaurant reviews by restaurant and art critic (and professor of

painting at the Herron School of Art) Steve Mannheimer, whose Top Restaurants include Essential Edibles, Mikado, Sangiovese, and Sullivan's Restaurant.

IOWA

The Des Moines Register
(http://www.dmregister.com/dgdb/dining/index.html)
Search restaurant reviews by W.E. Moranville by name, location, or cuisine, or browse recent reviews.

KANSAS

The Wichita Eagle
(http://www.wichitaeagle.com/leisure/food/restaurants/index.htm)
Browse current and recent bi-weekly restaurant reviews by Lori Linenberger.

KENTUCKY

The Courier Journal
(http://www.louisvillescene.com/dining/diningreviews.html)
Browse Susan Reigler's reviews (featuring star ratings based on food, mood, and value) of such Louisville standouts as the English Grill at the Brown Hotel, Lilly's, and the Oakroom at the Seelbach Hotel by name or date.

LOUISIANA

New Orleans.com
(http://www.neworleans.com/foodfest/critics.html)
Search Tom Fitsmorris's reviews of more than 400 New Orleans restaurants by name, cuisine, or location.

The New Orleans Times-Picayune
(http://www.nolalive.com/tastes/guide. html)
Search restaurant listings by name and cuisine, as well as features like "Neighborhood Joints" and "Cream of the Crop Restaurants" (such as Bayona, Brennan's, Emeril's, Grill Room, La Provence, and Mike's on the Avenue).

MARYLAND

The Baltimore Sun
(http://www.sunspot.net/our_town/restaurants)
Search an alphabetical listing of restaurant reviews.

Baltimore magazine
(http://www.baltimoremag.com/wte/eats.html)
Cynthia Glover reviews restaurants in Baltimore City, Baltimore County, and Outside Baltimore.

MASSACHUSETTS

Boston

The Boston Globe
(http://www.boston.com/globe/calendar/dining/)
Searchable archives of recent restaurant reviews by critic Alison Arnett.

Boston magazine
(http://www.bostonmagazine.com/restaurants)
Read recent Corby Kummer's restaurant reviews and features, plus search Lisa Amand's database of "150 Places to Dine."

The Boston Phoenix
(http://www.bostonphoenix.com)
Search the *Phoenix*'s "Dining Out" and "On the Cheap" archives of restaurant reviews by critics Robert Nadeau and Rob McKeown.

Boston Sidewalk
(http://boston.sidewalk.com/restaurants)
Searchable reviews by Patricia Harris, David Lyon, and Mat Schaffer, under the direction of Alexandra Hall. Features include a weekly "Big Review," and "Cuisine Course," "In the Neighborhood," "Night Out," and "Reviewers' Notebook."

Worcester

The Worcester Telegram and Gazette
(http://www.telegram.com/arts/dine_review.html)
William Young and staff reviews of local standouts like four-star winners Agresti's, The Castle, Le Bearn Restaurant Français, and Thymes Square on Hudson.

MICHIGAN

Crain's Detroit Business
(http://www.crainsdetroit.com/detmonth.html)
Browse "The Best Restaurants in Detroit" by name, community, or cuisine.

The Detroit Free Press
(http://www.freep.com/fun/food/reviews/index.htm)
Reviews by Patty LaNoue Stearns, John Tanasychuk and *Free Press* staff are summarized geographically, with links to full-length reviews and maps.

The Detroit News

(http://www.detnews.com/showtime/rest/reviews.htm)

Browse recent Jane Rayburn reviews, with accompanying star ratings, of area standouts like Five Lakes Grill, Pi's Thai Cuisines, and Tribute.

MINNESOTA

City Pages

(http://www.citypages.com/restaurants)

Featuring "Eaters' Digest" reviews by Dara Moskowitz.

Just Go/The Twin Cities Entertainment Guide

(http://www.justgo.com/twincities)

The "Dining" section lets you browse recent and archived (since 1995) restaurant reviews by Kathie Jenkins of *The St. Paul Pioneer Press*, alphabetized by type of restaurant and cuisine. Link to Rick Nelson's "Eating Around."

The Minneapolis Star Tribune

(http://www.startribune.com/freetime/dining)

"Dining Out" features Jeremy Iggers's 25 Favorites, which includes such local standouts as Bayport American Cookery, D'Amico Cucina, and Goodfellow's, and the *Star Tribune's* "Special Occasion" restaurants like Dakota Bar & Grill (outdoor dining), Loring Cafe (romantic), and Table of Contents (haute cuisine). Review database by name, cuisine, price, location, alcohol, or smoking preference.

Minneapolis/St. Paul magazine

(http://www.wcco.com/bestof/restaurants)

Read reviews of the Twin Cities' Top 10 restaurants, according to readers: 1) Kincaid's, 2) St. Paul Grill, 3) Palomino, 4) Goodfellow's, 5) D'Amico Cucina, 6) Murray's, 7) Lake Elmo Inn, 8) Ruth's Chris Steak House, 9) Manny's Steakhouse and Table of Contents, and 10) Buca di Beppo.

Twin Cities Sidewalk

(http://twincities.sidewalk.com/restaurants)

Searchable database of reviews of more than 1,100 restaurants in Minneapolis and St. Paul by lead reviewer Sylvia Paine and other *Sidewalk* staff, including standouts like D'Amico Cucina and Goodfellow's, the only area restaurants to earn *Sidewalk's* four-star rating.

MISSOURI

St. Louis

The St. Louis Post-Dispatch

(http://www.stlnet.com/postnet/getout/dining.nsf)

Search dining guide by city, area, food, or price, or alphabetically by restaurant.

NEVADA

The Las Vegas Sun
(http://www.lasvegassun.com)
Search for restaurant reviews by food and travel editor Muriel Stevens.

NEW JERSEY

The Bergen Record
(http://www.bergen.com/index/dineout.htm)
Food editor Patricia Mack and *Record* staff review New Jersey restaurants.

The Newark Star Ledger
(http://www.nj.com/restaurants)
Search more than 3,000 New Jersey restaurants by county, town, cuisine, price, or name. Also check out critic Rosie Saferstein's "Food Bytes."

NEW MEXICO

Santa Fe Online
(http://www.sfol.com/sfol/calendar/thedining.html)
Browse the "Dining Guide" provided by *THE* magazine by restaurant name. Starred reviews of restaurants (such as Josie's Casa de Comida, The Pink Adobe, The Shed, and Tia Sophia's) indicate "a special, unique place—possibly a local legend."

NEW YORK

New York City

Crain's New York Business
(http://www.crainsny.com/cgi-bin/crains/pick)
Search Bob Lape's reviews by keyword or parameters (e.g., name, cuisine, location, or stars).

Forbes New York City Dining Directory
(http://www.forbes.com/tool/toolbox/restaurant/index.asp)
Forbes Editor-in-chief Steve Forbes shares his ratings of New York City restaurants (in his traffic-light system, green means go; yellow, consider; and red, stop). Searchable by cuisine and neighborhood. Among *Forbes*'s neighborhood (Fifth Avenue at 12th Street) favorites: Blue Water Grill, Gotham Bar & Grill, Mesa Grill, and Union Square Cafe.

New York magazine
(http://www.newyorkmag.com/critics/)
Browse recent *New York* magazine reviews by "The Insatiable Critic" Gael Greene, or Hal Rubenstein.

The New York Daily News
(http://restaurant.mostnewyork.com)
Search 2,000 restaurant reviews, among them Daniel Young's of *The Daily News*. Search by cuisine, location, features, or price. Also includes listings of new establishments by neighborhood.

The New York Observer
(http://www.observer.com)
Moira Hodgson's recent reviews are available under "Arts & Entertainment" as well as on America Online (keyword = NYObserver).

New York Sidewalk
(http://newyork.sidewalk.com/restaurants)
Sidewalk's "Fast Restaurant Finder" lets you search by cuisine or name. You'll also find listings of "Good for Kids," "Good Value," and "New and Romantic" restaurants.

The New York Times
(http://www.nytimes.com)
Current week's restaurant reviews are available in "News by Category—Style." Requires user ID and password (free). *The New York Times* has a far more easily searchable database of restaurant reviews on America Online (keyword=Times).

The Village Voice
(http://www.villagevoice.com/restaurants/)
"*Voice* Choices City Eats" is a database of restaurants reviewed and recommended by *Voice* critics. Search by location, cuisine, price, or special service (open late, wheelchair accessible, outdoor dining, etc.). Also featured: "Down the Hatch," a random review from *Voice* critic Robert Sietsema for adventurous types.

WCBS Radio
(http://www.newsradio88.com/style/dining/welcome.html)
Bob Lape's "Dining Diary Archives."

Long Island

Newsday
(http://www.newsday.com/features/dineguid/dining.htm)
Browse critic Peter Gianotti's Long Island and Queens restaurant reviews by name, location, and star rating, including four-star standouts like Benny's (Westbury), La Pace (Glen Cove), Mirabelle (St. James), Navona (Great Neck), Panama Hattie's (Huntington Station), Starr Boggs' (Westhampton Beach), and Stresa (Manhasset).

Rochester

The Rochester Democrat and Chronicle
(http://www.rochesterdandc.com/community/living/)

Under "Food and Entertainment," you can browse tips for sampling the local cuisine.

NORTH CAROLINA

Charlotte

The Charlotte Observer
(http://www.charlotte.com/justgo/dining)
Browse recent restaurant reviews by "Dining Out" columnist Helen Schwab.

Raleigh-Durham

The News & Observer
(http://www.news-observer.com/go/restaurants/restaurants.html)
Reviews by critic Greg Cox organized by neighborhood, both inside and outside the Triangle.

OHIO

Akron

The Beacon Journal
(http://www.ohio.com/bj/fun/rest)
Browse restaurant index by name or cuisine type, or search database of recent reviews.

Cincinnati

The Cincinnati Enquirer and *The Cincinnati Post*
(http://gocinci.net/freetime/dining/archive.html)
Browse reviews of more than 125 Cincinnati restaurants, including standouts like The Precinct, or check out Polly Campbell's "Nibbles" column.

Cleveland

Cleveland Plain Dealer
(http://www.cleveland.com/ultrafolder/food/)
Search an alphabetic listing of reviews of more than 100 restaurants in the greater Cleveland area, or link to "Dine-O-Rama," a searchable guide to more than 600 local restaurants.

Columbus

The Columbus Dispatch
(http://www.cd.columbus.oh.us/news/grumpygourmet)
Search reviews by Doral Chenoweth ("The Grumpy Gourmet"), as well as

features like a twice-yearly round-up of his Top 10 fine and casual dining restaurants (which include Handke's Cuisine, L'Antibes, and The Refectory among the former).

Dayton

The Dayton Daily News
(http://www.activedayton.com/entertainment/dining/dining.htm)
Browse reviews by restaurant critic Ann Heller.

OKLAHOMA

Tulsa World
(http://www.tulsaworld.com)
Browse restaurant reviews by Suzanne Holloway in the "Entertainment" section under "Dining."

OREGON

Epicurious - Portland
(http://food.epicurious.com/e_eating/e03_restguide/portland/intro.html)
Read reviews by Robert Sullivan of local standouts like Genoa, The Heathman Hotel Bar, and Zefiro.

The Portland Oregonian
(http://www.oregonian.com/diner)
Search a database of more than 180 notable restaurants reviewed by critic David Sarasohn in "Diner," *The Oregonian*'s restaurant guide, by cuisine or location. Also features recent reviews from *The Oregonian*'s "A&E" Section.

PENNSYLVANIA

Philadelphia

The Philadelphia Daily News and **The Philadelphia Inquirer**
(http://www.phillylife.com/goingout/restaurants/rover.asp)
Features "Restaurant Rover," a searchable database of 2000 Philadelphia restaurants, including reviews by *Philadelphia Inquirer* and *Daily News* critics, such as Elaine Tait. Also features a "Talk Show Forum" on restaurants, where readers can share tips on places to eat in the Philadelphia area.

Philadelphia magazine
More than 800 restaurant listings are searchable via America Online (keyword=Philadelphia).

Pittsburgh

The Pittsburgh Post-Gazette
(http://www.post-gazette.com/dining/diningguide.asp)
Features the "Dining with Woodene Merriman Dining Guide," covering more
than 800 restaurants, searchable by name, location, or cuisine.

RHODE ISLAND

The Providence Journal-Bulletin
(http://www.projo.com/horizons/postcard/eatpg4.htm)
Under "Entertainment," search "Dining Out" for reviews from the past few years
listed alphabetically by restaurant. You'll also find features by food editor Donna
Lee on the city's hip restaurants like Al Forno.

SOUTH CAROLINA

The Charleston Post and Courier
(http://www.charleston.net/entertain/dining.html)
Search Jane Kronsberg reviews by cuisine, name, location, or price range, or
her top-rated choices (such as Peninsula Grill and Restaurant Million in
Charleston, and Woodlands Resort in Summerville).

TENNESSEE

Memphis

The Memphis Commercial Appeal
(http://www.gomemphis.com/capages/playbook/dining)
Browse recent restaurant reviews by critic Fredric Koeppel, including top
Memphis picks like Aubergine, Chez Philippe, Erling Jensen, La Tourelle, and
Restaurant Raji.

Nashville

The Tennessean
(http://www.onnashville.com/restaurants/restaurants.html)
Search reviews by critic Thayer Wine by name, location, cuisine, or price of
Nashville restaurants like Apples in the Field, Cafe 123, Capitol Grille, Mere
Bulles, and Pinnacle.

TEXAS

Statewide

Texas Monthly
(http://www.texasmonthly.com/food/)

Reviews by Patricia Sharpe and *Texas Monthly* staff covering restaurants in Austin, Dallas, Houston, and San Antonio. Features on such topics as the rise of the "Übersteakhouse, represented in Texas mainly by Pappas Brothers (Houston), Del Frisco's Double Eagle (Dallas and Fort Worth), Chamberlain's (Addison), the Steakhouse at the San Luis Hotel (Galveston), and Sullivan's (Austin)."

Austin

The Austin American-Statesman
(http://www.austin360.com/enter/eats/eatstop.htm)
Browse restaurant review archives, or check out "Dining with Dale (Rice)."

Dallas/Fort Worth

D magazine
(http://www.dmagazine.com/cgi-win/search.exe)
Search Mary Brown Malouf and Nancy Nichols' Dining Out database by category, price, or county.

The Dallas Observer
(http://www.dallasobserver.com/dining/index.html)
Search restaurant reviews by Mark Stuertz by cuisine, area, price, or keyword.

The Dallas Morning News
(http://www.dallasnews.com/index/dining-reviews-nf.htm)
Search Dotty Griffith and *Morning News* staff reviews by cuisine or date.

The Fort Worth Star-Telegram
(http://www.star-traveler.com/startime/justgo_dining.html)
Search reviews by *Star-Telegram*'s Beverly Bundy.

Houston

The Houston Chronicle
(http://www.chron.com/dining)
Browse reviews by Kathy Mosbacher, Alan Truex, and *Chronicle* staff by cuisine, category (restaurants and cafes, drive-through gourmet, etc.), brief reviews, or star ratings.

Houston Sidewalk
(http://houston.sidewalk.com/restaurants)
Search reviews by James Beard Award-winning critic Alison Cook, which include summary "Cheat Sheets," by neighborhood, cuisine, price range, star rating, or special options.

Sally's Place/My Table: A Critic's Guide to Dining in Houston
(http://www.bpe.com/food/dining/nam/houston.html)
Teresa Byrne-Dodge shares capsule reviews of twenty leading Houston restaurants, including Anthony's, Goode Co. Barbecue, Kim Son, and Ruggles Grill.

San Antonio

The San Antonio Express-News
(http://www.express-news.com/dine)
Browse restaurant features by editor Karen Haram and reviews by critic Ron Bechtol, which are searchable by name, category, or location, including San Antonio hits like Bistro Time, Chez Ardid, Crumpets, and L'Etoile.

VIRGINIA

The Virginian-Pilot
(http://www.pilotonline.com/restaurants/index.html)
Browse critics' picks for the best of Hampton Roads dining, or search the database of reviews by city, cuisine, or name.

The Roanoke Times
(http://www.roanoke.com/roatimes/restrevu/rindex.html)
Search reviews by Dolores Kostelni and JoAnne Anderson covering Downtown Roanoke, Roanoke Valley, and outlying areas.

WASHINGTON

Seattle

Seattle.com
(http://www.seattle.com/dining/dining.html)
Provides such dining links as *The Seattle Times* and *Seattle Weekly* restaurant reviews, *Gourmet* restaurant survey, and *Zagat Survey* results.

Seattle magazine
(http://www.seattlemag.com/eat.html)
Reviews by Providence Cicero, who shares her favorites (including downtown spots like Axis, Blowfish Asian Cafe, El Gaucho, Obachine, Roy's, and Theoz).

Seattle Sidewalk
(http://seattle.sidewalk.com/restaurants)
Reviews by Kathleen Flinn and other *Sidewalk* critics. Searchable by neighborhood, cuisine, price, star ratings, or special options, or "*Sidewalk* Choice" restaurants like four-star Campagne and Rover's and three-and-a-half stars Relais, Virazon, and Wild Ginger.

The Seattle Times
(http://www.seattletimes.com/datebook)
More than 1,600 reviews by critics John Hinterberger and Nancy Leson are searchable by location, price range, rating, or cuisine type. Features include "Hinterberger's Top 10 Restaurants of the Year" (Saleh al Lago, Kaspar's Wine

Bar, Szmania's, Theoz, Sazerac, ObaChine, El Gaucho, Blowfish Asian Cafe, Cassis, and Asian Wok & Grill).

WISCONSIN

The Milwaukee Journal-Sentinel
(http://www.jsonline.com/letsgo/dining)
Search the *Journal Sentinel's* "Culinary Compass." Features include "Dining with Dennis Getto" (current week's restaurant review, with links to previous reviews).

NATIONWIDE

AAA Five-Diamond Awards
(http://www.opus1.com/emol/dining/5diamond.html)
This site lists the forty United States restaurants that received AAA's five-diamond award in 1998, from Chicago's Ambria to Nashville's Wild Boar, not to mention the site's host, Tucson's Tack Room.

Chowhound
(http://www.chowhound.com)
Jim Leff's passionate site inspires optimism about the potential of the online medium for sharing information with other restaurant-lovers! This site is dominated by real chowhounds (experts at sniffing out great restaurants of any type), mostly in New York but increasingly nationally. There is also an impressive number of professional restaurant critics paying visits to share tips (including Eric Asimov, Jonathan Gold, and Irene Sax). The message boards are great fun to browse, and the site provides links to other soulful sites like "An astronomy grad student's Denver ethnic restaurant guide."

CuisineNet Menus Online
(http://www.menusonline.com)
Access menus (and highlights of reviews from publications ranging from *American Way* to *The New York Times*) of selected restaurants in Atlanta, Boston, Chicago, Dallas, Houston, Kansas City, Long Island (New York), Los Angeles, Miami/South Florida, New Orleans, New York City, Philadelphia, San Diego, San Francisco, Seattle, Washington, DC, and other cities.

Digital City Dining Guide
(http://dining.digitalcity.com/dining)
Access restaurant reviews in cities nationwide, including Atlanta, Dallas/Fort Worth, Denver, Los Angeles (reviews by Gayot Publications), Minneapolis/St. Paul, New York City (reviews by *Passport to New York*), Philadelphia, San Diego, San Francisco, and Washington, DC.

Epicurious' Eating Index

(http://food.epicurious.com/e_eating/e01_index/frm/e01index_page.
html#rest)
Browse articles and reviews by *Gourmet* critics David Rosengarten (New
York) and Caroline Bates (California), and roadfood scholars Jane and
Michael Stern (United States). Also, find *Bon Appetit*'s regional restaurant
reviews.

Epicurious' Essential Restaurant Guide

(http://food.epicurious.com/e_eating/e03_restguide/guide.html)
Browse reviews by "insiders" of restaurants in Aspen, Chicago, London, Los
Angeles, Napa and Sonoma, New Orleans, New York, Portland, and San
Francisco.

Midwest Living magazine

(http://midwestliving.com/goodbets/states.shtml)
Browse for restaurant recommendations in Illinois, Indiana, Iowa, Kansas,
Michigan, Minnesota, Missouri, Nebraska, North Dakota, Ohio, South
Dakota, and Wisconsin.

Playboy's "The 25 Best Restaurants in America"

(http://www.playboy.com/magazine/current/english/critics.html)
The magazine polled leading chefs, critics, and food writers to come up with its
1998 list. Read reviews of 1) Restaurant Daniel (New York City), 2) The French
Laundry (Napa), 3) Jean-Georges (New York City), 4) Charlie Trotter's
(Chicago), 5) Patina (Los Angeles), 6) The Inn at Little Washington
(Washington, Virginia), 7) Frontera Grill/Topolobampo (Chicago), 8) Nobu
(New York City), 9) Chez Panisse (Berkeley, California), 10) Le Bernardin (New
York City), and fifteen others.

WCBS Radio

(http://newsradio88.com/style/foodwine/welcome.html)
Browse radio host Anthony Dias Blue's archives of restaurant features and
reviews.

Zagat Survey

(http://cgi.pathfinder.com/cgi-bin/zagat/homepage)
Access *Zagat* ratings of restaurants in Atlanta, Atlantic City, Baltimore,
Boston, Chicago, Cincinnati, Cleveland, Columbus, Dallas/Fort Worth,
Denver, Detroit, Fort Lauderdale, Honolulu, Houston, Kansas City, Las Vegas,
Los Angeles, Miami, Minneapolis/St. Paul, New Orleans, New York City,
Orange County (California), Orlando, Palm Beach, Philadelphia,
Phoenix/Scottsdale, Portland (Oregon), Salt Lake City, San Diego, San
Francisco, Santa Fe, Seattle, St. Louis, Tampa Bay/Sarasota (Florida), Tucson,
Washington, DC, and other cities.

WORLDWIDE

CitySearch

(http://www.citysearch.com)

Reviews of restaurants in Austin; Los Angeles; Nashville; New York City; Portland, Oregon; Raleigh, Durham, Chapel Hill, and Cary, North Carolina; Salt Lake City and Park City, Utah; San Francisco; Washington, DC; Melbourne and Sydney, Australia; and Toronto, Canada.

Fodor's

(http://www.fodors.com/ri.cgi)

Searchable database of reviews of restaurants around in the world, in cities including Acapulco, Amsterdam, Anchorage, Athens, Atlanta, Auckland, Baltimore, Bangkok, Barbados, Barcelona, Bergen, Berlin, Bermuda, Bombay, Boston, British Virgin Islands, Brussels, Budapest, Buenos Aires, Calcutta, Cancun, Cape Town, Caracas, Chicago, Cleveland, Copenhagen, Dallas-Fort Worth, Delhi, Denver, Dublin, Edinburgh, Florence, Geneva, Havana, Helsinki, Hong Kong, Istanbul, Jamaica, Jerusalem, Johannesburg, Kyoto, Las Vegas, Lima, Lisbon, London, Los Angeles, Madrid, Maui, Melbourne, Memphis, Mexico City, Miami, Milan, Montreal, Moscow, Munich, Nashville, New Orleans, New York City, Oahu, Orlando (Disney World), Oslo, Paris, Philadelphia, Phoenix, Portland, Prague, Puerto Rico, Rio de Janeiro, Rome, San Diego, San Francisco, San Jose, Santa Fe, Santiago, Seattle, Singapore, Stockholm, Sydney, Tokyo, Toronto, United States Virgin Islands, Vancouver, Venice, Vienna, Washington, DC, Zurich, and others.

The International Herald-Tribune

(http://www.iht.com/iht/dine/index.html)

Restaurant reviews and dining features by Paris-based critic Patricia Wells. In "The World's Top Tables," she profiles her top picks from Tokyo to Luxembourg, and provides tips on dining in different parts of the world.

Sally's Place

(http://www.bpe.com/food/dining/index.html)

Search restaurant reviews by local critics in Atlanta, Austin, Big Sur, Boston, Buffalo, Chicago, Charleston, Hawaiian Islands, Houston, Lake Tahoe, Las Vegas, Los Angeles, Marin County (California), Maui, Miami, Napa Valley, New Mexico, New Orleans, New York City, Palo Alto, Philadelphia, Phoenix, Portland, San Diego, San Francisco, San Jose, Seattle, Sonoma County, St. Louis, and Washington, DC. Outside the United States: Florence, Hong Kong, Jerusalem, London, Mexico City, Montreal, Paris, Rome, Tel Aviv, Toronto, Vancouver, and Venice.

Tokyo Food Page

(http://www.twics.com/~robbs/tf-rest.html)

Search more than 600 Tokyo-area restaurants by cuisine or neighborhood.

The Toronto Star CitySearch
(http://www.starcitysearch.com/Toronto/Eat_and_Drink/Restaurants)
Browse recent reviews, or search archives of restaurant reviews by cuisine, price, location, or special features.

The Wine Spectator
(http://www.winespectator.com/Wine/Spectator/rest/)
Nearly 2,000 reviews of restaurants worldwide of special interest to wine-lovers. Search by name, city, or country.

Biographies of Those Interviewed

Alison Arnett is the restaurant critic for *The Boston Globe*, a position she has held for 5 1/2 years. In addition to writing a weekly review, she writes a weekly column on restaurant news, dining issues, and profiles of chefs and others in the restaurant world. A longtime journalist, Arnett previously was the assistant managing editor for ten years for the Sunday *Globe*, overseeing staff and production for ten sections, such as arts, book review, and travel, and several specialty magazines.

Caroline Bates, a native New Englander, has been a *Gourmet* staff writer and editor since 1959, writing the monthly column on California restaurants since 1974. She has also written hundreds of articles on such food arcana as the history of forks and the Rhode Island jonnycake wars. Her numerous food-oriented travel articles, photographed by her husband, Ken Bates, have covered subjects as diverse as edible Hawaiian seaweeds and Italy's Piedmont. She is the co-author with Ken Bates of *Baja California*, and the author of *Recipes from Around the World*, compiled from her articles and recipes for *Faces*, an anthropological magazine for children.

Michael Batterberry, with his wife, Ariane, has founded two national food magazines: *Food & Wine*, one of the country's leading consumer publications, and *Food Arts*, for top food and beverage professionals. The couple has co-authored more than eighteen books on food, entertaining, art, and social history. They have lectured extensively around the country on food and drink in America, and are included in the Who's Who of Food and Beverage in America.

Rick Bayless is the chef-owner of Frontera Grill and Topolobampo in Chicago. In 1991 he was named Best Chef: Midwest, and in 1995 he received Outstanding Chef awards from the International Association of Culinary Professionals and the James Beard Foundation. He is the award-winning co-author with his wife, Deanne, of two books, *Authentic Mexican Cooking* and *Rick Bayless's Mexican Kitchen*, with Jean Marie Brownson. Bayless also chairs the Chefs Collaborative 2000.

Karen Berk has been the co-editor of the Los Angeles *Zagat Survey* since 1986. With partner Jean Brady, she founded and operates The Seasonal Table, an avocational cooking school, in Santa Monica, California. She served as the food editor of *California Cooking: A Cookbook by the Art Museum Council of the Los Angeles County Museum of Art*, and was a contributing editor of *The Los Angeles Food Guide*.

Grant Blank is currently finishing a Ph.D. in Sociology at the University of Chicago, working on a dissertation on the social organization and cultural consequences of reviews which includes a chapter on the construction, history, and culture of restaurant reviews. He is the author of two books, *New Technology in Sociology* and *Desktop Data Analysis*.

Daniel Boulud is the chef-owner of Restaurant Daniel at the Surrey Hotel in New York City, which was awarded four stars from the *New York Times* and Cafe Boulud, and a partner in Payard Patisserie and Bistro in New York City. In 1992 he was named the Best Chef: New York, and in 1994 he received the Outstanding Chef Award from the James Beard Foundation. A member of the Who's Who of Food and Beverage in America, he is also is the author of *Cooking with Daniel Boulud*.

Terrance Brennan is the chef-owner of Picholine in New York City. An alumnus of Le Cirque, The Polo Lounge, and Prix Fixe, in 1995 he was named one of the Best New Chefs in America by *Food & Wine* magazine, and *Condé Nast Traveler* magazine's Readers Poll voted Picholine the Best Restaurant in New York City. Picholine was awarded three stars from *The New York Times* in 1996. In 1997, Brennan was nominated for the Best Chef: New York Award by the James Beard Foundation.

Alison Cook is the restaurant critic for *Houston Sidewalk*. She won the James Beard Award for Restaurant Criticism in 1995, when she was with the *Houston Press*. Cook is a frequent contributor to a number of national magazines, and is the food writer for *Condé Nast House & Garden*. A native of Vermont, she earned a B.A. from Rice University and began reviewing restaurants for the *Houston Business Journal*. She later served as restaurant critic and senior editor for *Houston City* magazine and went on to fill the same posts at *Texas Monthly*. Cook lives on the banks of Brays Bayou in

Houston, where she cultivates an ancient fig tree and two varieties of limes.

Penelope Corcoran has been the restaurant critic for *The Arizona Republic* since 1992, and began her career as a restaurant critic for *New Times* in 1990. The third daughter of two college professors, she grew up in Brockport, New York, where her youthful food influences included extensive United States travel, a semester of boarding school in Rome, and 1,512 meals away from home during nine summers of camp. A 1977 graduate of Smith College, she holds an M.B.A. from Syracuse University and an M.F.A. in creative writing from Arizona State University. She was the first recipient of the James Beard Foundation Journalism Award for Restaurant Criticism in 1994.

Greg Cox is *The Raleigh News & Observer*'s restaurant critic. He was born in El Paso, and grew up in North Carolina on a diet of Southern fried chicken (the real thing, cooked up in a big, black cast iron skillet), fried okra, and the best biscuits on the planet. He has cooked, catered, waited tables, and dined in Europe, Canada, Mexico, and much of the United States. Though not a graduate of a professional culinary institute (he graduated from Duke in 1977), he has studied and worked in many of the world's cuisines for more than two decades.

Bill Daley is a staff reporter and restaurant reviewer for *The Hartford Courant* and *Northeast* magazine. A graduate of Manhattanville College, he holds a master's degree in journalism from Columbia University.

George Germon and **Johanne Killeen** are the chefs and co-owners of Al Forno and Provincia in Providence, Rhode Island. Al Forno was named one of the Distinguished Restaurants of North America by *Food & Wine* magazine. In 1993, they were named Best Chefs of the Northeast by the James Beard Foundation and in 1998, they were nominated Outstanding Chefs of the Year. They are the co-authors of *Cucina Simpatica*.

Cynthia Glover spent fifteen years as a freelance corporate marketing writer before deciding to spend some time pursuing her passion for all things culinary. In 1994, she became chief restaurant reviewer for *Baltimore* magazine, and was appointed food and wine editor in 1997. She has contributed to numerous publications as a freelance writer, and is a member of the International Association of Culinary Professionals.

Jonathan Gold writes "Counter Intelligence," a long-running restaurant column exploring Los Angeles's ethnic neighborhoods, for *L.A. Weekly*. He also serves as the restaurant critic for *Los Angeles* magazine and is a contributing editor for *Details*, where he writes about culture. He was for several years a columnist for *The Los Angeles Times*, and has written for *Spin*, *Vanity Fair*, *Rolling Stone*, *Travel & Leisure*, and *Saveur*.

Joyce Goldstein was the chef-owner of San Francisco's Square One restaurant, which won numerous awards for food, wine, and service since its founding in 1984. The restaurant closed in 1996. Goldstein is the author of many cookbooks, including *Back to Square One*, *Old World Food in a New World Kitchen*, *The Mediterranean Kitchen*, and *Kitchen Conversations*. She was named the Best Chef: California in 1993 by the James Beard Foundation. In addition she is currently consulting around the country with various restaurant clients.

Gael Greene has been cited as perhaps the most-imitated restaurant critic in American history. Greene has been "The Insatiable Critic" at *New York* magazine for thirty years, after having started her journalism career as a reporter for *The New York Post*. She is the author of several books, including *Bite* and *Blue Skies, No Candy*. In 1992, she received the James Beard Foundation's Humanitarian of the Year Award for her work in founding City Meals-on-Wheels.

Dotty Griffith reviews restaurants for *The Dallas Morning News*, and was the food editor at the paper for seventeen years.

Gordon Hamersley is the chef-owner Hamersley's Bistro in Boston, Massachusetts. His restaurant has been awarded four stars by *The Boston Globe*. Hamersley was named one of America's Best Chefs by *Food & Wine* and was named the Best Chef: Northeast by the James Beard Foundation in 1995. He is an alumnus of Boston University.

Bob Hosmon has been writing about food and wine for twenty years. Currently, he writes a weekly wine column that is based at *The Ft. Lauderdale Sun-Sentinel* and is internationally syndicated by the Knight-Ridder-Tribune New Service. He is also a senior editor for *The Wine News* magazine, a restaurant critic for *Miami Metro* magazine, and a guest host on the Television Food Network (TVFN). In his other life, Dr. Hosmon is a dean in the School of Communication at the University of Miami.

Kathie Jenkins cut her teeth on food and restaurant reporting at *The Los Angeles Times*, where she learned to say what she means. She moved back to Minnesota in 1995 to become the restaurant critic for the *St. Paul Pioneer Press*, and was later promoted to editor of both the Wednesday Food and Friday Eat sections.

Hubert Keller is the chef-owner of Fleur de Lys in San Francisco. The restaurant holds four stars from *The San Francisco Chronicle* as well as one of the top food ratings in San Francisco according to the 1998 *Zagat Survey*. He is also the author of *The Cuisine of Hubert Keller*. In 1997, he was named the Best Chef: California by the James Beard Foundation, after having been nominated for the award several years in a row.

Bob Kinkead is the chef-owner of Kinkead's in Washington, DC, which he opened in October 1993. He received a James Beard Award as the Best American Chef: Mid-Atlantic in 1995. Previously, he was a chef and partner in 21 Federal in Washington, DC, and in Nantucket, Massachusetts. Before that, he was the chef at the Harvest Restaurant in Cambridge, Massachusetts. He is a self-trained chef who began his career as a teenager working summers in restaurants on Cape Cod.

Corby Kummer is the restaurant critic for *Boston* and *Departures* magazines, and senior editor of *The Atlantic Monthly*. He is also the author of *The Joy of Coffee*. Kummer holds a degree in English from Yale University.

Gray Kunz is the executive chef of Lespinasse at New York City's St. Regis Hotel, where he earned a four-star rating from *The New York Times*. Kunz spent five years working with Fredy Girardet in Switzerland, and was later executive chef of the Hong Kong Regent's restaurant Plume and of the Peninsula Hotel in New York City. In 1995, he was named the Best Chef: New York City by the James Beard Foundation.

Jean-Luc Le Dû is the sommelier of Restaurant Daniel in New York City. He came to the United States in 1984 to pursue his interest in rock and roll by writing articles for a French music magazine. Since his "wine epiphany" upon tasting a 1964 Cheval Blanc in 1989, he has taught himself about wine while working as a waiter and then as a captain at Bouley. He joined Daniel as a captain before being named sommelier in 1996. He won first prize for the northeastern U.S. in the 1997 SOPEXA Sommelier Competition, in which he placed third nationally.

Nancy Leson is the restaurant critic for *The Seattle Times*. She also edits the Seattle *Zagat Survey*.

Sirio Maccioni is the owner and manager of Le Cirque 2000 in New York City, which holds a four-star rating from *The New York Times*. Born in Tuscany, Maccioni underwent restaurant and hotel training in Paris and Hamburg, and apprenticeships in Montecatini and Paris. In New York City, following a stint at Delmonico, he became *maitre d'* at The Colony before opening Le Cirque in 1974, which the James Beard Foundation named the Restaurant of the Year in 1995.

Elliott Mackle was the dining critic for *The Atlanta Journal* and *The Atlanta Constitution* for ten years. He has reviewed restaurants for *Creative Loafing*, and began appearing on WCNN Radio and WXIA–TV as dining commentator. He earned a Ph.D. in American studies from Emory University, and an M.A. from the University of Miami.

John Mariani is the restaurant critic for *Esquire* magazine; co-creator of *Passport to New York Restaurants*; and the author of a number of books on food and wine, including *America Eats Out*, *The Dictionary of American Food and Drink*, *The Four Seasons: A History of America's Premier Restaurant*, and *Vincent's Cookbook*, co-authored with Vincent Guerithault. Mariani is a winner of the Barbi-Colombini Journalism Prize for outstanding wine writing, and in 1985 he was named to the Who's Who of Food and Beverage in America.

Max McCalman joined Picholine restaurant in New York City in 1994 as its *maitre d'* and evolved into the position as its *maître fromager*. He was previously the general manager at The Water Club in Manhattan, and has also held management positions in other hotels and restaurants. From 1992 to 1994, he took a leave of absence from the restaurant business to be the primary parent and caregiver to his first child, Scarlett.

Richard Melman is the president of Lettuce Entertain You Enterprises, Inc., in Chicago, through which he has created more than twenty-five different restaurant concepts, from his first R.J. Grunts in 1971 to Corner Bakery, Ed Debevic's, and Maggiano's, to four-star restaurants Ambria and Everest. He has described himself as "part artist and part businessman."

Danny Meyer is the owner of Union Square Cafe and Gramercy Tavern in New York City, and is in the midst of opening two more restaurants: Eleven Madison Park and Tabla. An active leader in the fight against hunger, Meyer serves on the boards of Share Our Strength and City Harvest. He and his restaurants have earned an unprecedented five James Beard Awards, including: Outstanding Restaurant of the Year, Humanitarian of the Year, Who's Who of Food & Beverage in America, Outstanding Service, and Best Restaurant Graphic Design. He co-authored the *Union Square Cafe Cookbook* with chef Michael Romano in 1994.

Mark Miller is the chef-owner of Red Sage in Washington, DC, and the Coyote Cafe in Santa Fe, New Mexico among other distinguished restaurants. He is an alumnus of Chez Panisse. In 1984, he was inducted into the Who's Who of Food and Beverage in America; he has also been named Best Chef of the Southwest by the James Beard Foundation. He is the author of several cookbooks including *Coyote Cafe*, and has produced the Great Chili Poster.

Bradley Ogden is the chef-owner of several restaurants in the San Francisco Bay area, including the Lark Creek Inn in Larkspur and One Market restaurant in San Francisco. He is the author of *Bradley Ogden's Breakfast, Lunch and*

Dinner. In 1984, he was inducted into the Who's Who of Food and Beverage in America, and in 1993 he was named the Best Chef of California by the James Beard Foundation.

Tim Page has been the chief classical music critic for *The Washington Post* since 1995 and was awarded the Pulitzer Prize for Distinguished Criticism in 1997. He is the author and/or editor of eight books, including *The Glenn Gould Reader, William Kapell, Selected Letters of Virgil Thomson, The Diaries of Dawn Powell*, and a collection of criticism, *Music from the Road: View and Reviews 1978–1992*. He is presently at work on the first biography of writer Dawn Powell.

Charlie Palmer is the chef-owner of several restaurants including Aureole, The Lenox Room, and Alva in New York City, and an investor in the Egg Farm Dairy in Peekskill, New York. Aureole holds top food ratings in the New York City *Zagat Survey* and was named one of the Top 25 Restaurants in America by *Food & Wine*. He is the author of *Great American Food*. In 1997, he was named the Best Chef of New York by the James Beard Foundation.

Mark Peel is the chef and co-owner, with his wife, Nancy Silverton, of Campanile in Los Angeles. An alumnus of Chez Panisse and the opening chef of Spago, Peel is the co-author of *Mark Peel & Nancy Silverton at Home: Two Chefs Cook for Family & Friends* and *The Food of Campanile*. He has been nominated several times for the Best Chef of California Award by the James Beard Foundation.

Len Pickell is the president of the James Beard Foundation in New York and heads Pickell Associates, a wine consulting company which develops wine lists and provides staff training. He also teaches wine classes at The New School in Manhattan. He holds an MBA from Temple University.

Ruth Reichl is the restaurant critic at *The New York Times*. Previously, she was restaurant reviewer and food editor at *The Los Angeles Times* and a chef-owner of The Swallow, a cooperative restaurant in Berkeley, California. She is the author of *Mmmmm: A Feastiary* and *Tender at the Bone: Growing Up at the Table*, and won the James Beard Foundation Journalism Award for Restaurant Criticism in 1996 and 1998. Reichl studied sociology at the University of Michigan, where she also earned a graduate degree in art history. She first reviewed restaurants for *New West* magazine in San Francisco before being tapped by *The Los Angeles Times* and then, as of 1994, *The New York Times*.

William Rice is a food and wine columnist for *The Chicago Tribune* who is equally comfortable appraising food ranging from barbecue to *haute cuisine*, to wine and spirits. Rice earned a B.A. in history at the University of Virginia and an M.S. with honors at Columbia University's Graduate School of

Journalism, as well as a certificate with honors from Le Cordon Bleu in Paris. He joined *The Washington Post* as executive food editor in 1972, and was named editor-in-chief of *Food & Wine* in 1980. In 1984, he was one of fifty people named to the original Who's Who in Cooking in America. He was also named Chevalier of the French government's Ordre du Merite Agricole.

Phyllis Richman is the restaurant critic for *The Washington Post*. For more than two decades, she has held that position as well as food editor, syndicated columnist, and author of restaurant guidebooks under her own name and for *Gault-Millau*. She is a member of Who's Who in of Food and Beverage in America, the James Beard Awards Committee, and the Julia Child Cookbooks Awards Committee. Richman recently completed her first gastronomic crime novel, *The Butter Did It*.

Gregory Roberts is the restaurant critic for *The Seattle Post-Intelligencer*. After spending the first eighteen years of his journalism career in news and feature writing and editing, he was named the restaurant critic for *The New Orleans Times-Picayune* in 1994. In 1996, he and his wife and children moved to Seattle when he assumed the same position at the *Post-Intelligencer*.

David Rosengarten is the New York restaurant critic for *Gourmet*, the nightly co-anchor of "In Food Today" on the Television Food Network (TVFN), and the host of "Taste," a daily TVFN cooking show devoted to teaching the principles of good taste in food and wine. He is the co-author of *The Dean & DeLuca Cookbook* (Random House, 1996) and *Red Wine with Fish: The New Art of Matching Wine with Food* (Simon & Schuster, 1989). He holds a doctorate in dramatic literature from Cornell University.

Anne Rosenzweig is the chef-owner of Arcadia and The Lobster Club in New York City. Her pioneering efforts in American cuisine led her to be tapped as a member of the White House's "Kitchen Cabinet" of American chefs. Rosenzweig was inducted into the Who's Who of Food and Beverage in America in 1987 and has been nominated several times for the Best Chef of New York Award by the James Beard Foundation. She is the author of *The Arcadia Seasonal Mural Cookbook*.

Chris Schlesinger is the chef-owner of the East Coast Grill in Cambridge, Massachusetts. In 1996 he was named the Best Chef of the Northeast by the James Beard Foundation. He is the co-author of several books with John Willoughby, including the James Beard Award-winning *The Thrill of the Grill*; *Big Flavors of the Hot Sun*; *Salsas, Sambals, Chutneys, and Chows Chows*; *Lettuce in Your Kitchen*; and *License to Grill*, and regular contributor to *The New York Times*.

Arthur Schwartz is a cookbook author, cooking teacher, and host of "Food Talk with Arthur Schwartz," a daily program heard on WOR Radio, New

York City's #1 talk station. He is the former restaurant critic at *The New York Daily News*. All three of his cookbooks were nominated for national awards: *Cooking in a Small Kitchen, What to Cook When You Think There's Nothing in the House to Eat*, and *Soup Suppers*. He is currently working on a book tentatively titled *Naples at Table: A Cook's Tour of Campania*.

David Shaw is the media critic for *The Los Angeles Times* and has won a number of awards for journalism, including the Pulitzer Prize for Distinguished Criticism in 1991. He is the author of *The Pleasure Police: How Bluenose Busybodies and Lily-Livered Alarmists are Taking All the Fun Out of Life* (Doubleday, 1996). He has also written for many magazines, including *Cosmopolitan, Esquire, GQ, Rolling Stone*, and *Smithsonian*.

Merrill Shindler is the editor of the Los Angeles *Zagat Survey*, restaurant critic for the Santa Monica *Evening Outlook*, and host of KTZN's top-rated weekly restaurant and travel show, "Dining Out with Merrill Shindler." Beginning in the early 1970s as the restaurant critic for the *San Francisco Bay Guardian*, he has also written about cuisine as a restaurant critic for *San Francisco* magazine and *The Los Angeles Herald Examiner*.

Robert Sietsema has worked as a photographer, editor, rock musician, real-estate analyst, and restaurant critic over the last two decades. Currently, he writes two columns for *The Village Voice*, "Counter Culture" and "Chow Choices." He also contributes to *Food & Wine, Salon Internet, Request*, and since 1990 has edited the country's first foodzine, *Down the Hatch*. He lives in Greenwich Village with his wife, Gretchen, and daughter, Tracy.

Tom Sietsema is *Washington Sidewalk's* restaurant producer and food critic. Before joining Microsoft and the national *Sidewalk* team in 1996, he was food critic for *The Seattle Post-Intelligencer* (1994–1996), restaurant reviewer and food writer at *The San Francisco Chronicle* (1990–1994), food editor at *The Milwaukee Journal* (1988–1990) and a member of the "Food" section staff of *The Washington Post* (1983–1988). He is a graduate of Georgetown University. His idea of a good workout: "aerobic chewing."

Nancy Silverton is the chef and co-owner, with her husband, Mark Peel, of Campanile and La Brea Bakery in Los Angeles. She was the first recipient of the Pastry Chef of the Year Award from the James Beard Foundation in 1991. Silverton is the author of *Breads from La Brea Bakery* and the co-author of *Mark Peel & Nancy Silverton at Home: Two Chefs Cook for Family & Friends* and *The Food of Campanile*.

André Soltner is the former chef-owner of Lutèce in New York City where he established a reputation as one of the premier chefs in America over more than 30 years. He currently teaches at the French Culinary Institute in New

York City. In 1986 he was inducted into the Who's Who of Food and Beverage in America, and in 1993 he was honored with a Lifetime Achievement Award by the James Beard Foundation. He co-authored *The Lutèce Cookbook* with Seymour Britchky.

Bill St. John is the restaurant producer for *Denver Sidewalk*. He is the author of *Bill St. John's Rocky Mountain Restaurants*, a collection of his dining reviews for the *Rocky Mountain News* where he was a reporter for 14 years. He has also reviewed restaurants for KCNC-TV Channel 4, Denver's CBS affiliate, and has been the editor for *Zagat Survey's Rocky Mountain Restaurants* since 1992. He is a member of the National Board of the American Institute of Wine & Food, and holds Master's degrees in economics and philosophy and a Ph.D. in theology from the University of Chicago.

Patty LaNoue Stearns is a feature writer and former food columnist and restaurant critic for *The Detroit Free Press*. Previously managing editor of *Detroit Monthly*, she has been writing for the *Free Press* since 1991. She studied English and journalism at the University of Detroit, and culinary arts at Le Cordon Bleu in Paris. Stearns left the restaurant critic beat in February 1998 after her blood pressure and weight started soaring; she is now happily cooking fine meals again in her own kitchen and watching the numbers fall.

Jane and Michael Stern have spent the last 20 years writing about many aspects of Americana, from bad taste to good food. In 1992, they won the James Beard Award for Lifetime Achievement and were inducted into the Who's Who of Food and Beverage in America.

Muriel Stevens has been the restaurant critic for *The Las Vegas Sun* since 1975. She also edits the *Las Vegas* Zagat Survey and the restaurant section of *The Unofficial Guide to Las Vegas*. She has also hosted "The Muriel Stevens Radio Show" since 1968.

Larry Stone is the sommelier at Rubicon in San Francisco. He previously held the same position at Charlie Trotter's in Chicago when the restaurant won its James Beard Award for Outstanding Wine Service. He received Bachelor and Master of Arts degrees in comparative literature from the University of Washington. As a Fulbright Scholar during his doctoral program, he studied in Tuebingen, Germany, and spent several years abroad in programs at the Universities of Vienna, Madrid, and Montpellier.

Elaine Tait is the restaurant critic for *The Philadelphia Inquirer*. Having begun her career at the paper in 1963, she is, perhaps, the country's longest-tenured restaurant critic. She also wrote a nationally syndicated food column. She is the author of a best-selling Philadelphia restaurant guide and the *In a Hurry Cookbook*, a collection of recipes from her column. Tait was a finalist in the J.C. Penney Awards, and won the Vesta Award for outstanding food pages.

Allan Temko, the architecture critic for *The San Francisco Chronicle*, was awarded the Pulitzer Prize for Distinguished Criticism in 1990. His books include *No Way to Build a Ballpark and Other Irreverent Essays on Architecture* (Chronicle Books, 1993) and *Notre Dame of Paris* (W.W. Norton & Co., 1996). He lives in Berkeley, "around the corner from Chez Panisse."

Jeremiah Tower is the chef-owner of a number of restaurants in the San Francisco Bay area including Stars. An alumnus of Chez Panisse, Tower was inducted into the Who's Who of Food and Beverage in America in 1993. He was named the Best Chef of California by the James Beard Foundation in 1993, and the Outstanding Chef Award in 1996. He is also the author of *Jeremiah Tower's New American Classics*. Tower holds a degree in architecture from Harvard.

Patricia Unterman is the chef-owner of the Hayes Street Grill in San Francisco, which was founded in 1979. She has been a restaurant reviewer for more than twenty years and is currently restaurant critic and food columnist for *The San Francisco Examiner*. Her food column runs bi-weekly in the *Examiner Magazine*; her restaurant reviews run bi-weekly in the "Weekend" section. Unterman's *Food Lovers' Guide to San Francisco* (Chronicle Books, 1997) is currently in its second edition.

Norman Van Aken is the chef-owner of Norman's in Coral Gables, Florida. He moved to Hawaii in 1970 and to Key West in 1973, where he developed a passion for vibrant Asian and Caribbean flavors. In 1996, he received the Robert Mondavi Award for Excellence. In 1997, he was named the Best Chef of Southeast by the James Beard Foundation. He is also the author of the books *Feast of Sunlight* and *Norman's New World Cuisine*.

S. Irene Virbila has been the restaurant critic for *The Los Angeles Times* since 1994. She won the James Beard Award for newspaper restaurant criticism in 1996. A contributor to numerous magazines, including *California*, *Food & Wine*, and *New West*, she is the author of two *Cooks Marketplace* guides to San Francisco and Los Angeles. Virbila was a chef-owner of the Swallow, a cooperative restaurant in Berkeley, California, and previously earned a degree in textiles from the University of California at Berkeley.

David Waltuck is the chef-owner of Chanterelle in New York City, which earned a four-star rating from *The New York Times*. He graduated from City College (New York) with a degree in marine biology, and briefly attended The Culinary Institute of America. He went on to La Petite Ferme, where he spent

two years as lunch chef. He opened Chanterelle with his wife, Karen, at the age of twenty-four.

Karen Waltuck is the co-owner of Chanterelle in New York City. She studied anthropology at Boston University and graduated in 1975. She spent the following year traveling throughout Central and South America touring archeology sites. She has also worked as a fashion coordinator and buyer for an East Side boutique. She opened Chanterelle with her husband, David, in 1979.

Alice Waters is the chef-owner of Chez Panisse in Berkeley, California, which she founded in 1971. Waters earned a degree in French Cultural Studies from the University of California at Berkeley in 1967. She then trained at the Montessori School in London and followed that with a seminal year in France. She is the author and co-author of several books, most recently the encyclopedic *Chez Panisse Vegetables*. She has also received numerous awards, which include being awarded the Best Chef in America and Best Restaurant in America honors from the James Beard Foundation in 1992. In 1997, the Foundation named her its Humanitarian of the Year.

Dennis Ray Wheaton has been the chief dining critic for *Chicago* magazine since 1989. At the University of Texas, he won a fellowship to spend his junior year traveling around the world, studying and living with families in Japan, India, Poland, and France. Following graduate study in cellular biology, Wheaton worked as a quality control biologist, bookstore manager, and photographer before returning to graduate school to study sociology at the University of Chicago, where he completed his PhD in 1987. While teaching at the University of Chicago and Northwestern, he began writing about food for *The Journal of Gastronomy*, published by the American Institute of Wine & Food. He has also written for *Food & Wine* magazine, and he contributes articles to *The New York Times* "Travel" section.

Index

Goldstein, Joyce, 135, 136–137, 151, 154–155, 168, 178–179, 225, 330
Gotham Bar & Grill, 38, 159, 283
Gourmet magazine, xiv, 7, 32, 42, 47, 50, 63, 83, 132
  restaurant survey by, 130
Gramercy Tavern, 95, 106, 120, 147, 156, 195
Greene, Gael, 4, 10, 11, 19, 25, 35–39, 41, 47–48, 56, 70–71, 82, 88, 124, 126–127, 128, 130, 134, 138, 141–142, 143, 145, 155, 168, 196, 229, 315, 330
  favorite restaurants of, 283–284
Griffith, Dotty, 320, 330
  favorite restaurants of, 262–263
Guide to San Francisco Restaurants (Bloomfield), 13

Hamersley, Gordon, 108, 144, 150, 158, 159, 199, 203, 206, 330
Hamersley's Bistro, 108, 144, 159, 254, 256
Hao muk, 78
Hard Rock Cafe, 21
Hartford, critics' favorites in, 267–268
Haute cuisine, 16
Hawaii, restaurant review resources in, 311
Hayes Street Grill, 33, 35, 294
Health-food movement, 4
Hines, Duncan, 7
Hosmon, Bob, 309, 330
  favorite restaurants of, 277–279
Hospitality, providing, 110–111
Houston, critics' favorites in, 268–270
Houston Sidewalk, 76, 137

Illinois, restaurant review resources in, 311
Indiana, restaurant review resources in, 311–312
Indian cuisine, 65, 77, 145
Ingredients
  importance of, 224–225
  quality of, 101–102
Inn at Little Washington, 95

International Association of Culinary Professionals, 228
Internet
  reviews on, 27
  guide to restaurant review resources on, 305–325
Iowa, restaurant review resources in, 312

James Beard Awards, 18, 95, 97, 137, 180–183
James Beard Foundation, 17, 132, 180–181, 227, 231
Japanese cuisine, 76, 80
Jean Georges, 19, 92–93, 95, 247, 282, 285
Jean-Louis, 89, 97
Jenkins, Kathie, 314, 330
  favorite restaurants of, 279–281
Jojo, 21
Judson Grill, xv, 41

Kabob Village, 91, 266–267
Kamman, Madeleine, xvii
Kansas, restaurant review resources in, 312
Keller, Hubert, 116, 119–120, 131–132, 180, 182–183, 193, 206–207, 330–331
Kelson, Carla, 42, 258
Kentucky, restaurant review resources in, 312
Killeen, Johanne, 57, 102, 105, 130, 131, 147–149, 150, 152, 199–200, 202, 206, 254, 329
Kinkead, Bob, 123, 129–130, 143–144, 178, 331
Kinkead's, 129, 301
Kitchens, testing, 74
Kummer, Corby, 85, 107, 131, 313, 331
  favorite restaurants of, 255–256
Kunz, Gray, 95, 100–101, 109–113, 114–115, 152, 228, 331
Kuruma Zushi, 237

L.A. Weekly, 30, 61, 167
La Colombe d'Or, 137–138
La Côte d'Or, 96
La Coupole, 125
Lagasse, Emeril, 3, 19, 245
La Goulue, 159
Lape, Bob, 315, 316
La Pyramide, 95
Lark, The, 91

Las Vegas, critics' favorites in, 270–272
Le Bec-Fin, 169, 243
Le Bernardin, 21, 56, 92–93, 243, 283
Le Cirque, 13
Le Cirque 2000, 19, 38, 81, 82, 92–93, 106, 118, 159, 207–208, 243
Le Dû, Jean-Luc, 214–218, 331
Leff, Jim, 322
  favorite restaurants of, 287–288
Le Français, 163, 237, 257, 258
Legal Sea Foods, 144, 255
Le Guide Culinaire, 6
Le Pavillon, 7, 9, 12
Leson, Nancy, 321, 331
  favorite restaurants of, 298–299
Lespinasse, 92–93, 95, 100–101, 114
L'Etoile, 106
Lettuce Entertain You Enterprises, 95, 107, 234, 242
Limoncello, 83
Lobster Club, 128, 225
Los Angeles
  critics' favorites in, 244–245, 272–277
  as a restaurant town, 242
Los Angeles magazine, 61
Los Angeles Times, 28, 33, 34, 57, 87, 150, 168
Louisiana, restaurant review resources in, 312
Louis XV, 108–109
Luger, Peter, 248, 249, 286
Luongo, Pino, 126, 138
Lutèce, 119, 134, 205–206

Maccioni, Sirio, 13, 38, 41, 79, 81, 89, 105, 106–107, 118, 152, 156, 207–208, 243, 331
Mackle, Elliott, 311, 331–332
  favorite restaurants of, 251–252
Maitre d', xv
Malaysian food, 72
Mariani, John, 14, 21, 44, 66–68, 70, 83–85, 127, 182, 193, 194, 196, 202, 227–228, 332
  favorite restaurants of, 241–244
Maryland, restaurant review

resources in, 312–313
Maslin, Janet, 172–173, 201
Massachusetts, restaurant review resources in, 313
Matsuhisa, Nobu, 196
McCalman, Max, 219–221, 332
Media
  influence of, 131–133
  preferences of, 76
Melman, Richard, 56, 66, 95, 107, 118, 234–236, 332
Menus
  French, 116
  seasonal, 105
Mexican cuisine, 99–100
Meyer, Danny, 46–147, 95, 106, 108, 110–111, 120, 156–157, 194, 204, 332
Miami, critics' favorites in, 277–279
Michael's, 145, 275
Michaels, Lorne, 104
Michelin Guide, 6, 7, 180
Michelin system, 86, 96
Michigan, restaurant review resources in, 313–314
Microsoft *Sidewalk*, 26
Middle Eastern cuisine, 90
Millau, Christian, 10, 16
Miller, Bryan, 21, 61, 75, 124, 129, 133, 146, 147, 157
Miller, Mark, 3, 136, 153–154, 170, 193, 197, 227, 233, 234, 237–238, 239, 332
Milliken, Mary Sue, 3, 19
Minneapolis/St. Paul, critics' favorites in, 279–281
Minnesota, restaurant review resources in, 314
Missouri, restaurant review resources in, 314
Mobil Travel Guide, 9
Moroccan cuisine, 83
Murphy, Tamara, 298, 299
Music, role of, 117

Napa, 153, 271
Nation's Restaurant News, 47
Neighborhood publications, 63
Nevada, restaurant review resources in, 315
New England Culinary Institute, 232
New Jersey, restaurant review resources in, 315
Newman, Paul, 20

128–129, 146, 147, 153,
158, 196–197, 225, 334

Salmon, smoked, 235
Salsas, 234
San Francisco
  critics' favorites in,
    244–245, 294–297
  as a restaurant town, 242
San Francisco Chronicle, 14, 33,
  35, 125
San Francisco Examiner, 33,
  73, 131
Saveur magazine, 18
Sawtelle district, 76
Schlesinger, Chris, xiv, 17,
  81, 86, 97, 159, 171, 180,
  239, 334–335
Schwartz, Arthur, 29–30, 39,
  57, 63, 71, 74, 75, 77,
  113, 115, 138, 165, 195,
  197–198, 229, 233,
  334–335
  favorite restaurants of,
    285–286
Seattle, critics' favorites in,
  245–246, 297–300
Seattle Post-Intelligencer, 55,
  163
Self magazine, 20
Senses, educating, 231, 236
Service
  as an aspect of excellence,
    95, 96
  excellence in, 106–108
  failures in, 113–115
  importance of, 119
Shanghai style restaurants, 66
Shaw, David, 187–188, 335
Sheraton, Mimi, 16, 21, 61,
  125, 128–129, 157
Shindler, Merrill, 3, 32–33,
  45, 55, 70, 76, 79, 80–81,
  179, 244, 306, 335
  favorite restaurants of,
    275–276
Shire, Lydia, 243, 255
Sidewalk, 194
Sietsema, Robert, 30–31, 48,
  77–78, 87, 316, 335
  favorite restaurants of,
    286–287
Sietsema, Tom, 27, 29, 41,
  64, 65, 86, 138, 163, 195,
  201–202, 309, 335
  favorite restaurants of,
    297–298, 302–303
Silverton, Nancy, 108, 130,
  134, 136, 145, 248, 273,
  274, 335

Smith & Wollensky, 21, 82
Sokolov, Raymond, 21, 76
Soltner, André, 55, 64, 106,
  119, 134, 154, 158–159,
  180, 205–206, 237,
  335–336
Soulé, Henri, 9
South Carolina, restaurant
  review resources in, 319
Spago, 21, 40, 45, 248–249,
  271–272, 274, 275, 277
Special requests, customer,
  200, 202
Spices, blending of, 65
Splichal, Joachim, 19, 242
Square One, 135, 168, 225
St. John, Bill, 308, 336
  favorite restaurants of,
    264–265
Staff, hiring, 107–108
Starless reviews, 87–89
Star rating system, 54, 71,
  85–86, 96, 97
  alternative, 89–91
  chefs and restaurateurs on,
    156–158
  interpreting, 158–159
Stars, 107, 125, 132, 195, 242
Stearns, Patty LaNoue, 42,
  50, 68–69, 89–91, 313,
  336
  favorite restaurants of,
    265–267
Stern, Jane, 4, 14, 32, 323,
  336
Stern, Michael, 4, 14, 32,
  323, 336
  favorite restaurants of,
    249–251
Stevens, Muriel, 315, 336
  favorite restaurants of,
    270–272
Stone, Larry, 209–213, 336
Success
  defined, 120–121
  understanding, 134–135
Sunset magazine, 7
Sushi bars, 237
Susser, Allen, 19, 234, 278

T. Cook's at Royal Palm,
  176, 291
Tait, Elaine, 44, 51, 64–65,
  69–70, 75, 98, 126, 127,
  140–141, 149, 151–152,
  168–169, 177, 194, 201,
  203, 204–205, 208, 318,
  336–337
  favorite restaurants of,
    289–290

Tang, Tommy, 19
Tavern on the Green, 143
Television Food Network, 3,
  18, 42
Temko, Allan, 14, 188–189,
  337
Tennessee, restaurant review
  resources in, 319
Texas, restaurant review
  resources in, 319–321
Thai restaurants, 65
Time Out magazine, 47, 56,
  63
Tipping, 204–205
Tommy Tang's, 19
Too Hot Tamales, 3
Topolobampo, 19, 100, 106,
  258–259
Tower, Jeremiah, 33, 97, 100,
  107, 117, 125, 131,
  132–133, 134, 150, 151,
  154, 176, 179–180, 193,
  337
Trader Vic's, 13
Tribute, 91, 266
Trillin, Calvin, 4, 12
Trotter, Charlie, 237, 242
21 Federal, 130, 143–144
Two Two Two, 63

Union Square Café, 95, 106,
  120, 156, 157, 195, 285
United States, dining out in,
  233–234
Unterman, Patricia, 15, 33,
  34–35, 50, 58–59, 73–74,
  85–86, 127, 133,
  136–137, 139–140, 147,
  168, 177, 307, 337
  favorite restaurants of,
    294–295

Van Aken, Norman, 82, 99,
  100, 120, 121, 130,
  135–136, 150, 153, 155,
  157, 163, 198–199, 236,
  278, 337
Vergnes, Jean, 13
Vettel, Phil, 49, 91, 257, 311
Video cameras, in dining
  rooms, 109
Vietnamese cuisine, 79
Village Voice, 30, 77
Virbila, S. Irene, 33, 39–40,
  43–44, 46–47, 49, 57, 64,
  68, 69, 87, 127, 134,
  136, 137, 168, 244, 306,
  337
  favorite restaurants of,
    276–277

Virginia, restaurant review
  resources in, 321
Vongerichten, Jean-Georges,
  19, 20, 95, 247, 282, 285

Waitstaff, 112–113
Waltuck, David, 107, 124,
  159, 337–338
Waltuck, Karen, 107, 124,
  125, 338
Washington state, restaurant
  review resources in,
  321–322
Washington, DC
  critics' favorites in, 300–303
  as a restaurant town, 243
Washingtonian magazine, 44,
  86
Washington Post, 2, 27, 32, 57,
  86, 88, 126
Washington Sidewalk, 27, 64,
  86, 195
Water Club, The, 16
Waters, Alice, 12, 13, 33, 95,
  96, 97, 100, 101, 103,
  129, 136, 153, 223, 224,
  226, 231–232, 234, 338
Weil, Andrew, 20
West African cuisine, 79
Wheaton, Dennis Ray,
  31–32, 38, 39, 40, 42, 48,
  49–50, 51, 56–57, 66, 71,
  75, 80, 86, 97, 112, 127,
  132, 138, 162–163, 165,
  167, 229, 237, 311, 338
  favorite restaurants of,
    258–260
White, Jasper, 243, 255
Wine, 302
  Jean-Luc Le Dû on,
    214–218
  Larry Stone on, 209–213
Wine Spectator, 84, 142
Wine tasting, 81
Winfrey, Oprah, 20
Wisconsin, restaurant review
  resources in, 322
WOR Radio, 29, 57
WQXR Radio, 47, 63

Yard, Sherry, 274

Zagat, Nina, 16
Zagat, Tim, 16, 176–177
Zagat Survey, 3, 15, 16, 17,
  27, 132, 194
  role of, 176–180
Zuni Cafe, 106, 244

Other Books by Andrew Dornenburg and Karen Page

Becoming a Chef: With Recipes and Reflections from America's Leading Chefs
(Wiley; $29.95 paperback; 320 pages; ISBN 0-471-28571-4)

Winner of the 1996 James Beard Book Award for Best Writing on Food. Essential reading for anyone who loves food, *Becoming a Chef* is an entertaining and informative insider's guide to the chef's profession, providing the first behind-the-scenes look into some of the most celebrated restaurant kitchens across America.

"One of the top 20 books of 1995 recommended as holiday gifts."
—*Gourmet*

"One of the top 5 Editors' Choice cookbooks of 1995."
—*The San Francisco Chronicle*

"You'll love *Becoming a Chef!*"
—Matt Lauer on NBC's *Today* show

"Offers excellent advice and wisdom."
—JeanMarie Brownson, *The Chicago Tribune*

"Its insight into the philosophy of chefdom today is invaluable."
—Alison Arnett, *The Boston Globe*

Culinary Artistry
(Wiley; $29.95 paperback; 426 pages; ISBN 0-471-28785-7)

For anyone who believes in the potential for artistry in the realm of food, *Culinary Artistry* is a must-read. This is the first book to examine the creative process of culinary composition as it explores the intersection of food, imagination and taste. Through interviews with more than 30 of America's leading chefs—including Rick Bayless, Daniel Boulud, Gray Kunz, Jean-Louis Palladin, Jeremiah Tower and Alice Waters—the authors reveal what defines "culinary artists," how and where they find their inspiration, and how they translate that vision to the plate.

"In *Culinary Artistry*...Dornenburg and Page provide food and flavor pairings as a kind of steppingstone for the recipe-dependent cook....Their hope is that once you know the scales, you will be able to compose a symphony."
—Molly O'Neill, *The New York Times Magazine*

"Andrew Dornenburg and Karen Page go where no culinary writers have gone before, exploring what inspires great chefs to create new flavor combinations, dishes and menus."
—*International Cookbook Review*

"A major achievement."
—Patrick O'Connell, The Inn at Little Washington (Virginia)